'*Mary in the Qur'an* is a splendid example of comparative theology at its best: clear and straightforward, dutifully attentive to history and to textual evidence, respectful of both communities' distinctive sensitivities, yet constructive in its conclusions. It is wonderfully collegial, as Tatari and von Stosch show us how comparative theological work can be the fruits of open and respectful conversation between scholars of two traditions. As a result, we all learn better the depth and beauty of Mary as a singular figure in tradition and piety, and thus a grace for believers even today.'

FRANCIS X. CLOONEY
SJ, Parkman Professor of Divinity, Harvard University

'*Mary in the Qur'an* offers a groundbreaking example of how to engage in comparative theology in a reciprocal way. Through their mutual interrogation and creative collaboration, Muna Tatari and Klaus von Stosch succeed in shedding significant new light on the role and meaning of the figure of Mary in both the Muslim and the Christian traditions.'

CATHERINE CORNILLE
Professor of Comparative Theology, Boston College

في ذكرى

مارك لينز

INTERFAITH SERIES

Series Editor
Joshua Ralston

Mary in the Qur'an

Friend of God, Virgin, Mother

Muna Tatari
Klaus von Stosch

Translated by Peter Lewis

GINGKO

First English edition published in 2021 by
Gingko
4 Molasses Row
London SW11 3UX

First published in the German by Verlag Herder GmbH in 2021

Jacket image: Detail of miniature from the *Compendium of Chronicles* by Rashid al-Din. Shows the Annunciation to Mary. Copyright © The University of Edinburgh.

A CIP catalogue record for this book is available from the British Library.

ISBN 978-1-909942-62-2
e-ISBN 978-1-909942-63-9

Typeset in Times by MacGuru Ltd
Printed in the United Kingdom

www.gingko.org.uk
@GingkoLibrary

Contents

Note on Transcription ix
Introduction 1

I. MARY IN THE CHRISTIAN TRADITION 5

1. Mary in the Bible 7
a) Mary in the Corpus Paulinum and the Gospel of Mark 7
b) Mary in the Gospel of Matthew 11
c) Mary in the Gospel of Luke 15
d) Mary in the Gospel of John 26
e) Summary 34

2. Mary in Patristics 37
a) The Protevangelium of James 37
b) Mary as the New Eve 42
c) Mary as the archetype of the Church 45
d) Mary's purity and lack of sin 47
e) Virginity and labour pains 49

3. Dogmatic Precepts of Mariology 53
a) Perpetual virginity 53
b) Mary as the new human being freed from original sin 69
c) Other dogmatic precepts 74

4. Mary in the Political Theology of Late Antiquity 82
a) The political situation during the emergence of the Qur'an 82
b) The religious propaganda of Heraclius 90
c) Mary as military commander 93

d) Jewish apocalyptic counter-images 100

II. MARY IN THE QUR'AN 105

1. The Surah *Maryam* 107
a) Zechariah and John the Baptist (1–15) 107
b) Mary's withdrawal and the proclamation of Jesus's birth (16–21) 121
c) Pregnancy and birth (22–26) 132
d) Mary's conflicts and Jesus as the bringer of peace 142
e) Mary as the mother of Jesus and as a prophet? 149
f) Summary 158

2. The Surah *Āl 'Imrān* 159
a) On the genealogy of Mary 161
b) Mary's birth and childhood – the connection with Zechariah 165
c) The first Annunciation scene 176
d) The second Annunciation scene 186
e) Other verses from the Medinan period prior to the confrontation with Byzantium 192
f) Summary 199

3. The Surah *al-Mā'ida* 202
a) Criticism of the political Mariology of Byzantium 202
b) Criticism of the imperial downplaying of Mary's humanity 205
c) On the significance of Mary's eating 210
d) Limits and opportunities of the presentation of Mary in the Surah *al-Mā'ida* 218

III. MARY IN THE CONTEXT OF ISLAMIC SYSTEMATIC THEOLOGY 221

1. The Qur'anic Mary as an Impulse for Prophetology 223
a) The portrayal of Mary as an impulse for Islamic prophetology 224
b) On the meaning of vulnerability in the relationship with God 226
c) Was Mary a prophet? 229

2. The Qur'anic Mary as a Stimulus to a Traditional Understanding of God's Actions 239
a) Distinctions in the perception of miracles in classical scholastic theology 239
b) On the crisis of the classical perception of the concept of miracles in the modern period and its consequences for the distinctions drawn by classical theology 243
c) A reappraisal of our understanding of miracles through the Qur'anic Mary 247
d) Mary and Muhammad 251

3. Mary as a Figure of Emancipation 254
a) The story of Mary in the Qur'an as a stimulus for greater gender equality 254
b) Mary as a boundary breaker 257
c) Mary as a stumbling-block and an incitement to subversion 261

4. Mary as an Aesthetic Role Model 265
a) An invitation to visibly reserve something for God alone 266
b) An invitation to a culture of disruption and renunciation 268

5. In Dialogue with Christianity 273
a) Obstacles to dialogue 273
b) Between appropriation and syncretism 275
c) A warning against projecting 279

IV. IMPLICATIONS FOR COMPARATIVE THEOLOGY 283

1. Christian Perspectives 285
a) Intensification: freedom through devotion 285
b) Recovery: Mary as a prophet and as a protagonist of anti-imperial theology 286
c) Reinterpretation: Mary as a transgressor of boundaries 287
d) Appropriation: from a Christian mascot to a typological figure binding together religions 289
e) Rectification: rehabilitation of a Mariology based on prerogatives 291
f) Reaffirmation: Mary's lowliness as a pointer to God's kenosis 295

2. Islamic Perspectives 298
a) Intensification: on the beauty and the political significance of Mary 298
b) Recovery: Muhammad's special connection with Mary 299
c) Reinterpretation: on the dialectical interconnectedness of 'Yes' and 'No' before God – clarity in the process 301
d) Appropriation: Mary and God's unqualified gift of grace 305
e) Rectification: Mary as a warning to exercise care in passing theological judgement on others 306
f) Reaffirmation: radicalism and the Golden Mean 308

Bibliography 313
Index 331

Note on Transcription

This book uses the DIN standard for transcription of Arabic. This is largely similar to the widely used ALA-LC standard, with the following main variant characters:

DIN	ALA-LC
ǧ	j
ḫ	kh
ḏ	dh
š	sh
ġ	gh

The German letter 'ß' has been retained in names; it is pronounced and alphabetised as 'ss'.

Introduction

Mary is the only woman who is mentioned by name in the Qur'an. After Moses, Abraham, and Noah, Mary is also the person most frequently named in the Qur'an; in other words, her name appears more frequently than those of either Muhammad or Jesus. And in general, the manner in which she is portrayed in the Qur'an is one of great respect and reverence.[1] The history of Islam is also replete with examples of Mary being seen in a positive light. And to the present day, Christians and Muslims alike hold this figure in high regard.[2] As a result, you might think that Mary would be an obvious choice as a bridging figure promoting dialogue between Christians and Muslims.[3]

Unfortunately, however, the figure of Mary has also been repeatedly embroiled in conflicts between the two religions. Time and again, she has become a lightning rod for expressions of mutual mistrust and lack of understanding between Christians and Muslims.[4] Mary has even been turned into a protagonist for imperialist policies and something like a goddess of war. If one were to view the veneration of Mary from a purely historical standpoint, one would find a roughly equal number of positive signs of fellowship between Christians and Muslims and tokens of alienation and enmity. Equally, one would encounter touching and fascinating tales alongside absurdity and ugliness.

The aim of our book, however, is not to go in search of such historical traces;

1 Cf. Geagea, *Mary of the Koran*, 113.

2 Cf. Horn, 'Intersections', 121.

3 Indeed, from the very outset she was regarded as just such a bridge by Eastern Christians, whereas Byzantine Christians preferred to emphasise the contrasts between the Qur'anic and the biblical images of Mary (cf. George-Tvrtković, *Christians, Muslims, and Mary*, 33 f.). While the latter position was also dominant in the Latin West, William of Tripoli and Nicholas of Cusa are prominent examples of Latin voices which, even in the Middle Ages, drew attention to Mary's role as a bridge-building figure between Islam and Christianity (cf. ibid., 69 f.).

4 Cf. Smith and Haddad, 'The Virgin Mary in Islamic tradition and commentary', 85.

its purpose, rather, is a theological one. Following all the rules of the art of exegesis, we will attempt to reconstruct the evidence about Mary in the Qur'an and use this to make normative deductions regarding the Islamic faith. At the same time, the intention of this work is to bring the belief in Mary as practised in the Catholic Church into conversation with the evidence from the Qur'an and to show how both sides can learn from one another to their mutual benefit.

In a methodological sense we are breaking new ground with this book in three ways. To begin with, we are presenting what is in all likelihood the first work about Mary jointly written by a Muslim theologian and a Christian theologian. We really have written the whole book together and take joint responsibility for it in its entirety. Only in the final part does each of us draw her/his separate conclusions, whereby our different confessional perspectives lead us to summarise our findings in our own particular ways. Apart from this, we authored the book jointly – even in those places where we struggle to get to the truth on an exegetical, historical and systematic level.

A second innovation of this book in comparison with previous works is that, in undertaking our exegesis of the Qur'an, we have worked in a consistently diachronic fashion while at the same time adopting a holistic approach toward the surahs. This means on the one hand that, in the case of every verse of the Qur'an that mentions Mary, we investigate how the verse functions within the literary context of the surah in question. On the other hand, we attempt to organise the verses of the Qur'an chronologically and to contextualise them historically. We learned this form of Qur'anic exegesis from Angelika Neuwirth, and in writing this book we were assisted by Zishan Ghaffar, whose work has been shaped by Professor Neuwirth's philological approach and who has since become a valued academic colleague of ours at Paderborn.

The third distinctive feature of our exegetical *modus operandi* resides in the fact that we attempt to deal with each of the verses of the Qur'an in a comprehensively intertextual fashion.[5] A great deal of preparatory work has already been achieved in the field of Islamic Studies in this regard. However, because no extensive work has yet been carried out on intertextual relations precisely in the Syriac tradition, we were able to make some exciting discoveries of our own in this realm. However, we did not just undertake a thorough study of the Syriac Church Fathers, we also systematically investigated the veneration of Mary in

5 On the significance of intertextual work for modern Islamic systematic theology, cf. also Abboud, *Mary in the Qur'an. A literary reading*, 4, 6; Ali, 'Destabilizing gender, reproducing maternity', 92, f. 5.

Greek patristics and were thus able to place the texts from the Qur'an in their patristic context within Late Antiquity. We are greatly indebted to Nestor Kavvadas for his invaluable help with this historical research. Without his energetic assistance, we would never have attained the historical precision that we aspired to reach in this book.

Throughout, we compare the results generated by the three innovative steps mentioned with the findings of classical Islamic exegesis, so that the exegetical outcome has the broadest possible basis. In this, we were grateful for the assistance of the Muslim members of our work group, who ensured that we were constantly alert not only to classical approaches but also the great variety of interpretational methods offered by modern Islamic theology in our exegetical endeavours. We would especially like to thank Nasrin Bani Assadi, Ahmed Husic, Muhammad Legenhausen, Vahid Mahdavi Mehr, Abdul Rahman Mustafa and Nadia Saad. They have all rendered a great service to this book and helped give the Muslim tradition a very vivid and diverse profile in the work. In addition, Ahmed Husic ensured that the transcriptions from Arabic were consistent, while Elizaveta Dorogova was responsible for proofreading the text.[6]

As a background for our intertextual work, in the first part of this book we start by providing an outline of the belief in Mary within the Christian tradition; this begins by considering the biblical evidence[7] before raising the question of how this phenomenon manifested itself among the Syriac Church Fathers. After a brief look at the dogmatic cornerstones of the belief in Mary in the Catholic Church and how these evolved during the history of ecclesiastical dogma, we finally explore the particular question of the veneration of Mary in Byzantium around the time when the Qur'an came into being.[8]

The second part, which forms the core of our book, comprises an exegesis of the Qur'an, the guiding principles of which we have just laid out. If one compares our approach with classical exegesis, the latter is primarily concerned with confirming the faith, and motifs of apologia become repeatedly evident in it. Yet

---

6 In addition, the complete manuscript was given a final proofreading by Hamideh Mohagheghi and Lukas Wiesenhütter. Julian Heise was responsible for preparing the index. We would like to thank all of them most sincerely.

7 Our thanks are due here to our colleagues and experts on the NewTestament, Hans-Ulrich Weidemann and Christian Blumenthal, both of whom provided numerous helpful suggestions for the part of our book which covers the Bible.

8 Our colleagues Martha Himmelfarb, James Howard-Johnston and Johannes Pahlitzsch gave us a number of extremely helpful hints in this regard, and we are most grateful to them for taking the time to come to Paderborn. With his iconographical expertise, Lars Rickelt was also of great assistance to us.

the work of classical exegesis was naturally also interested in reconstructing historical events and connections. It operated on a very high level, especially in philological terms, and should not be ignored in any modern treatment of the subject. Methodologically, however, this classical approach does not always make a clear enough distinction between what can be reconstructed through historical–critical analysis and a historical account based on faith. The beginnings of a historical–critical exegesis of the Qur'an here will supplement the rich fund of classical Qur'anic exegesis and reveal levels of profundity that have hitherto largely remained undiscovered.

Our efforts in the third part are directed at sounding out the evidence within the Qur'an regarding Mary from the standpoint of Islamic systematic theology. In the process, we incorporate findings from Islamic literature and works from the field of Islamic Studies, in an attempt to underscore the contemporary relevance of Mary from a Muslim perspective.

In the fourth and final part, we summarise from a Christian and Muslim viewpoint respectively the results of our foregoing endeavour. To do so, we use the methodology of comparative theology; as a general rule, this has also been our guiding principle throughout the book.[9]

We would like to thank the University of Paderborn, which granted us both a sabbatical in the winter semester of 2019–2020 and also provided us with the means and the opportunity to invite four internationally renowned guest academics to participate in our working group. By thus providing research arrangements specially tailored to our needs, the university furnished us with the perfect conditions and impetus to write this book. Our thanks are also due to the Deutsche Forschungsgesellschaft and the Federal Ministry for Education and Research, whose funding of a total of five research assistant posts enabled us to get on top of the great mass of material that we had to deal with in this book.[10] This special support framework has, we believe, enabled us to present a number of genuinely exciting findings, which we are now delighted to share with interested readers.

Muna Tatari and Klaus von Stosch
Paderborn, October 2020

9 For an introduction to this methodology, cf. Klaus von Stosch, *Komparative Theologie als Wegweiser in der Welt der Religionen*, Paderborn and elsewhere 2012 (Beiträge zur Komparativen Theologie; 6).

10 Special mention should be made here of Elizaveta Dorogova, who in addition to proofreading the text raised many pertinent content-related queries.

I

MARY IN THE CHRISTIAN TRADITION

In beginning this book with an overview of how Mary is portrayed in the Christian tradition, our intention from the very start is to use this as a stepping-off point from which to engage with the Muslim tradition and with the Qur'an in particular. Because the literature of Mariology is so extensive, our objective within the scope of this comparative study cannot be to develop our own mariological thesis. Instead, this work is all about reviewing the current state of research on Mariology within Catholicism and presenting it in such a way that it can enter into a meaningful dialogue with the Qur'an. Accordingly, in the following study we aim to present an especially thorough synopsis of the various strands of tradition that were picked up and expanded or commented upon by the proclaimer of the Qur'an.[1] However, because we must in addition constantly reckon with the possibility of a negative intertextuality that can manifest itself among other things in the omission of certain aspects of tradition, we must also include within our overview those elements of tradition which, at least at first sight, are of no concern to the proclaimer of the Qur'an.

---

1 From an Islamic perspective, the Qur'an is the direct word of God, meaning that God is the proclaimer of the Qur'an. Because this viewpoint is not so easy to process for non-Muslims, we have chosen to use a neutral formulation here, which does justice to the different religious identities of both 'authors'. This formulation enables the non-Muslim commentator to also regard Muhammad or his community as the proclaimer(s) of the Qur'an. The term *proclaimer* alludes to the fact that the Qur'an is meant to be read out or proclaimed from the Arabic so from its very origins was first and foremost an oral text.

For the biblical tradition, this means that we will concentrate above all on the story of the Annunciation and birth of Jesus presented in the Gospel of Luke, since this is clearly the focus of attention in the Qur'an. We will, however, also take other biblical traditions into consideration, especially the gospels of Matthew and John insofar as they are significant for understanding the Qur'an. We will also make at least passing reference to other possible biblical points of contact for Mariology, albeit without being in a position to examine them exhaustively in the context of our study.

Where patristics are concerned, we will focus our attention primarily on the Syriac Church Fathers, since they are in all likelihood the people with whom the proclaimer of the Qur'an principally took issue. As regards the dogmatic tradition, we will first and foremost treat those articles of faith concerning Mary that were in widespread circulation around the time that the Qur'an was compiled and which were also discussed by the proclaimer of the Qur'an. The primary tenet of faith in question here is that of Mary's perpetual virginity. By contrast, less attention will be given to the doctrine of Mary as the Mother of God, as promulgated by the Council of Ephesus in 431. Likewise, the doctrine of the Immaculate Conception of Mary, which was only formulated as Catholic dogma in 1854, and the Assumption of Mary into heaven (first defined in 1950), will only be treated in the form in which they already existed and were the subject of discussion at the time when the Qur'an came into being.

Our study as a whole is structured in such a way that the progression through the Bible, the Church Fathers and faith tradition should help create an initial approach to the figure of Mary via the concept of monotheism and through her role as witness to Jesus Christ. She should therefore appear as the paradigm of a faithful believer, who is able to exert a charismatic appeal beyond the Christian tradition while at the same time being portrayed without compromise in her special connection with her son. Thus, even in the manner in which the Christian tradition elaborates her character, we may readily understand how the Qur'an comes to acknowledge Mary in such a strikingly positive way.

1

Mary in the Bible

It is customary in historical–critical analysis of holy scriptures to present the contents of the sacred text in question in the chronological order in which they were created. For this reason, we will begin the Muslim section of our study by considering the Surah *Maryam*, and by the same token we will now commence this section on the Bible by looking at the oldest parts of the New Testament: the letters of Paul and the earliest of the gospels.

a) Mary in the Corpus Paulinum and the Gospel of Mark

In the entire Corpus Paulinum – that is, the collected letters of the apostle and his followers – Mary appears on just one occasion, namely in the Letter to the Galatians. At a theologically significant point in this important letter, Paul stresses that Jesus was 'born of a woman' (Galatians 4:4). It is noteworthy that the corresponding Greek formulation begins with the same word as the following characterisation of Jesus as 'born under the law' (each phrase being introduced with *genomenon*). It therefore seems fair to assume that both formulations belong together and are intended to emphasise that Jesus was born to a Jewish woman. The verse that follows makes it clear that this birth to a Jewish woman takes place so that we might be redeemed under the law and adopted into sonship. For Paul, the actual act of a woman giving birth and her belonging to the Jewish race evidently form a pretext for speculating on the Christian message of salvation. An integral part of the doctrine of justification, which is enunciated for the first time in the Letter to the Galatians, is the fact that the son of God genuinely enters into the *conditio humana* – joining the human race quite 'normally' by being born to a woman from God's chosen people, the Israelites.[1] Here, therefore, Mariology is completely at

1 Cf. Adrian Wypadlo, '"Geworden aus einer Frau" (Gal. 4:4). Ein mariologischer Splitter bei Paulus?' In: Weidemann (ed.), *'Der Name der Jungfrau war Maria'*, 361.

the service of Christology. Paul is at pains to emphasise that Jesus truly was a person, and Jesus's birth to a woman provides Paul with a striking proof of this fact. Mary is the guarantor here of Jesus's genuine humanity, while at the same time forming a link between the ministry of Jesus and the people of Israel.

Likewise the Gospel of Mark (hereafter abbreviated as Mk) has very little to say on the subject of Mary. As in the letters of Paul, Mk is largely uninterested in Mary.[2] But unlike in Paul, Mary is accorded a somewhat negative role in Mk. So much is evident from her very first appearance in the book. It is Jesus's mother, supported by his brothers, who calls him away from the crowd of followers surrounding him (Mk 3:31f.). Jesus brusquely dismisses her: 'Who are my mother and my brothers? Then he looked at those seated in a circle around him and said: "Here are my mother and my brothers! Whoever does God's will is my brother and sister and mother"' (Mk 3:33–35). In order to understand this uncouth response in the context of the narrative of Mk, we need to relate to Jesus's family another incident also recounted by Mk. For Mk 3:21 tells of how 'his associates' (Greek: *hoi par'autou*) – some translations render this as 'his kinsmen' – reached the conclusion that Jesus had lost his mind. The verse does not specify whether his mother is included in this catch-all term too. Indeed, it may merely mean the inhabitants of his own village, and possibly his neighbours who were not part of his family. However, the narrative context strongly suggests that this term does actually denote Jesus's mother and brothers, which would explain why he rebuffs them so fiercely shortly after.

However, regardless of how one interprets Mk 3:21,[3] the pericope Mk 3:31–35 alone provides sufficient evidence of a real quarrel between Jesus and his family. Quite clearly, there was an estrangement between Jesus and his mother, at least for a time. Immediately before our pericope here, Jesus states that anyone who blasphemes against the Holy Spirit will never be forgiven (Mk 3:29). Indeed, it is the Holy Spirit which, in Mark, descends upon Jesus (Mk 1:10), sends him out into the wilderness (Mk 1:12), and enables him to drive out the demons. In contrast, the scribes accuse Jesus of being possessed by an impure spirit (Mk 3:30). Their opposition poses an existential threat to Jesus and his ministry, and spurs him to issue this uncompromising rebuttal. In Mk 3:31, the family of Jesus

2 Cf. Mußner, *Maria, die Mutter Jesu im Neuen Testament*, 23.

3 Rainer Kampling highlights the fact that this passage was even occasionally used in patristics for the purpose of anti-Jewish polemics, by seeing Mary as a paradigm of the Jewish faith, with the result that the passage was then interpreted as anti-Marian. Cf. Kampling, '... die Jüdin, aus deren Fleische der geboren wurde ...', 18. Yet Kampling is insistent that by no means all Jewish Christians agitated against the virginity of Mary.

effectively side with his adversaries when they summon him away from his group of followers. At this point, Jesus relativises the binding power the family exerts over him and emphasises that his true brothers and sisters and his true mother are those who are working with him to establish the Kingdom of God. If one considers how vehemently Jesus argues at this point with the Jewish elites of his age, it is all too understandable that his mother and family should intervene in an attempt to mediate.

If they are indeed the people described in the phrase 'his kinsmen' in Mk 3:21, then the principal reason for their intervention would be the fact that their son has gathered so many followers around him 'that he and his disciples were not even able to eat' (Mk 3:20). The problem here is therefore no longer a political dispute with the Jewish elites but rather a lack of common sense. Here, too, it cannot be wrong to want to bring a young man to his senses. And so we learn from these passages that Mary keeps a close eye on her son and intervenes when he places himself and his family in danger or when his preaching has politically dangerous consequences. All in all, we can perhaps say that Mary appears to struggle to accept Jesus's calling and to regard him as anything more than her son. She has found it impossible to fall into line with his great sense of mission and was simply wishing to bring him to his senses. If one stops to consider the powers and authority to which Jesus laid claim right from his first public proclamation of his mission, it is easy to understand his mother's reaction. Our first impression of Mary is therefore of someone who has doubts about Jesus's authority and vocation and is in conflict with him.

Comparing Mk 3:31–35 with the corresponding passages in the other synoptic gospels, it is apparent that the Gospels of Luke (hereafter abbreviated as Lk) and Matthew (Mt) pick up on this theme of conflict but at the same time divest it of its drama. Although Lk 8:19–21 does not seek to deny that the conflict with Mary took place – which speaks strongly to its historical veracity – like Mt 12:46–50, it removes it from the context of the 'Beelzebub argument' with the scribes.[4] Thus, while Jesus's mother and brothers in Mark's account (Mk 3:22) still align themselves with the scribes, who assume that Jesus has been possessed by an evil spirit, in Luke's gospel Jesus's family's lack of faith is linked to the passage concerning the storm on the Sea of Galilee and the disciples' absence of faith and thereby relativised.[5] The family of Jesus therefore exhibits behaviour that is

4 Cf. Hagemann and Pulsfort, *Maria*, 38.

5 Mt occupies an intermediate position here. Unlike in Lk, the text from Mark is not abridged by Mt and stripped of its key point. Nor does Mt draw any parallels with the disciples' lack of

akin to that of the followers of Jesus and which no longer contains the germ of any conflict.

By contrast, the Gospel of Mark (Mk 3:31–35) clearly testifies to a temporary estrangement between Jesus and his mother, which is furthermore not resolved within this gospel.[6] The focal point here is the statement that Jesus's true family is the community of believers. The critical attitude of those who felt closest to Jesus reappears in Mk 6:1–6a, but with no mention of his mother. Even so, here too Jesus complains about the lack of respect shown to him by his relatives (Mk 6:4 'A prophet without honour…among his relatives…'). A comparison with the parallel texts from the other synoptic gospels (Mt 13:53–58 and Lk 4:16–30) shows that only Lk tries to exempt Mary from criticism. Accordingly, Lk 4:23f. only speaks about a prophet being without honour in his own hometown, not the rejection by his family attested in Mk 6:4 and Mt 13:56.

The synoptic gospels thus exhibit a gradation of criticism of Jesus's family. Especially the criticism voiced in Mk has to be regarded as nothing short of a polemic against the family. Nonetheless, we must be careful not to read too much into this regarding the historical relationship between Jesus and Mary. For the polemic in Mk against the relatives of Jesus may possibly be directed at the notion of a caliphate of sorts, which may have existed among the original Christian community in Jerusalem.[7] Precisely against the background of the debate within Islam on the question of whether the true disciples of Muhammad were to be found among his followers or his relatives, it is extremely interesting to note that similar conflicts appear to have existed within the early Christian community in Jerusalem, and that the brothers of Jesus, in particular James, evidently laid claim to leadership. Yet in exactly the same way as Sunni Islam eventually decided the conflict in the Muslim community in favour of the companions and friends of the Prophet, so too in Christianity the view prevailed that authenticity of a person's

---

faith. But the decontextualisation from the Beelzebub controversy also occurs in Mt 12:46–50. However, as a transition to Jesus's parables, the new context is not as manifestly apologetic as Luke's version.

6 Cf. Becker, *Maria*, 89: *Auch interessiert das Leben der Maria weder vor noch nach Jesu öffentlichem Wirken. Nur die zweimaligen episodischen Kontaktaufnahmen in Galiläa (Mk 3:31 ff.; 6:1 ff.) erscheinen berichtenswert. ... Sie zielen auf ein besseres Verstehen des Weges Jesu, der abseits der Familie und Heimat wirkt.* ('Nor is Mary's life either before or after Jesus's public ministry of interest [to Mark]. Only the two episodic meetings between them in Galilee are deemed worthy of mention…the aim of these is to gain a better understanding of the path taken by Jesus, who conducts his ministry away from his family and homeland.')

7 Cf. Schweizer, *Das Evangelium nach Markus*, 43. On the idea of a caliphate in the original Jerusalem Christian community, cf. also Dassmann, *Kirchengeschichte I*, 60.

discipleship was not linked to how closely they were related to Jesus. Jesus's harsh utterances in Mk may well have to do with this outcome.

Nevertheless, interpreting the criticism of Jesus's family in the context of the controversy concerning a caliphate in the early Christian community in Jerusalem does not mean that actual conflicts described here have no basis in historical fact. For if there had been no recollections within early Christian communities of these kinds of conflicts between Jesus and his family, it would surely have been difficult for Mk to derive an argument against Jesus's relatives' claim to leadership from these conflicts. And the clear attempt in the corresponding passages in Lk to take Mary out of the firing line indicates that the Marcan version of events most definitely had the potential to be an effective irritant to the growing Marian belief in the early church. We should not lose sight of this irritant factor, even though it is not treated in the Qur'an.

b) Mary in the Gospel of Matthew

In the previous section, we touched upon some references to Mary influenced by Mk that are also addressed in Mt. We want now to focus all our attention on the opening of Mt, because this section of the gospel is particularly important for the way in which the Qur'an handles the narratives surrounding Mary.

To start with here, it is worth mentioning Jesus's family tree as revealed by the gospel (Mt 1:1–7). The purpose of the family tree is clearly to present the story of Jesus Christ as the fulfilment of the Old Covenant.[8] According to Mt 1:17 the genealogy is divided into three parts, which link Jesus with the Patriarchs, the monarchical period and the resurgence following the Babylonian Exile. Abraham and David appear as key figures, who accordingly are specifically named in Mt 1:1 as forebears of Jesus. The first part of the family tree (Mt 1:2–6) names fourteen generations from Abraham to David, the second part (Mt 1:7–11) the same number from Solomon to Josiah and the third part another fourteen generations from Jeconiah to Jesus.[9] It is striking that, unlike all the other individuals named, Joseph is not described as the person who begets the next generation (Jesus) but is merely presented as the husband of Mary, who is then in her turn introduced

---

8 Cf. Hagemann and Pulsfort, *Maria*, 28.

9 It is often pointed out in the secondary literature that, if one carefully tallies up all the names, one does not always arrive at the figure of fourteen generations that the biblical text maintains it is listing. Consequently the current authors took it upon themselves to tally up the names, several times; we can report that we did not encounter the alleged problem, and that each of us did indeed arrive at the final figure of fourteen generations.

into the genealogy as 'the mother of Jesus who is called the Messiah' (Mt 1:16). Mary is therefore implicitly given her own role in the family tree, even though the genealogy actually runs via Joseph, who as the adoptive father was the legal guarantor of Jesus's descent from the line of David.

Comparing Mt 1:1–17 with the family tree from Lk 3:23–38, which appears in Lk after the account of the baptism of Jesus, one notable difference is that the family tree in Lk goes back to Adam. In a typically Lk-like manner, this expands the rather Judeo-Christian perspective of Mt to give it a more universal flavour. Abraham and David appear in Lk, as does Noah, though no particular emphasis is placed on these figures.[10] In both Mt and Lk the genealogies are of the linear family tree type, which in antiquity, and doubtless also here, had a legitimising function. Moreover, the two family trees differ significantly from one another; their marked dissimilarity points to the fact that they were not intended to reflect historical reality but instead are theological constructions.[11]

In Mt 1:1–17, the intention is to show Jesus as a genuine Jew and descendant of David.[12] 'He is the son of Abraham and the royal Messiah and as such is the bearer of all of Israel's messianic hopes in accordance with God's plan.'[13] 'Jesus is the son of David, that is he has been sent by God to Israel as his Anointed One, and at the same time as the son of Abraham, because God also wishes, through him, to speak to the entire world of Gentiles.'[14] In other words, the family tree introduces Jesus as a human, historical figure, while at the same time acknowledging the special role he plays for Israel.

Another remarkable feature of the family tree in Mt is that it includes four women in the genealogy, and while they do not replace their respective husbands, they are still individually mentioned by name. All four of them appear as non-Jews – a covert indication that the Messiah of Israel also brings salvation for the

---

10 Cf. Luz, *Das Evangelium nach Matthäus*, 129.

11 Even Jesus's grandfathers are different in Lk and Mt (Luz, *Das Evangelium nach Matthäus*, 131). The Church Fathers explained these discrepancies by claiming that '...the one evangelist was referring to the natural father, whereas the other was referring to the legal father' (Luz, *Das Evangelium nach Matthäus*, 137). These discrepancies became an important polemical argument used by the emperor Julian the Apostate, especially since the name of Jesus's grandfather was not known (cf. Luz, *Das Evangelium nach Matthäus*, 138). It is interesting to note that the preacher of the Qur'an does not place himself within this polemical tradition, but instead develops his own genealogical ideas, which likewise have a particular theological purpose, as we shall see.

12 Cf. Luz, *Das Evangelium nach Matthäus*, 130.

13 Ibid., 132.

14 Ibid., 139.

Gentiles.[15] In addition, all four play a somewhat dubious role in the Bible. Tamar disguises herself as a courtesan and seduces and blackmails her father-in-law (Genesis 38:15–19), Rahab is a prostitute known all over town (Joshua 2:1), while Ruth tricks her kinsman Boaz into intimate sexual contact with her, and Bathsheba aids and abets King David in committing adultery (2 Samuel 11).[16] Yet however scandalous their behaviour, all four are strong female figures who exude a positive force. These are women who, precisely by virtue of being mothers, 'have been enrolled into service by God in fulfillment of his plan of salvation.'[17] To some extent, therefore, they all point to Mary, who after all herself is first presented as an adulteress and who has to struggle to earn herself respect.

In Mt, the family tree of Jesus is followed by an account of his birth, although Mary only plays a subsidiary role in this (Mt 1:18–25). It is simply mentioned that Mary was found to be pregnant 'through the Holy Spirit' (Mt 1:18). This is the first attestation in the Bible that when Mary conceived Jesus, she had not yet engaged in any intimate physical contact with her husband-to-be Joseph. However, this fact is not interpreted by the gospel in, say, a mariological sense, but merely acts as a springboard in the narrative to highlight Joseph's role. For from verse 19 onwards, all attention is focused on Joseph and the question of how he reacts to his fiancée's pregnancy.[18]

Joseph's initial reaction is to decide to separate from Mary (Mt 1:19). Traditionally, most Protestant exegetes proceeded from the assumption that Joseph 'suspected his wife of adultery and therefore wanted to be rid of her.'[19] By contrast, in traditional Catholic exegesis, there is a tendency to interpret this passage rather as an expression of Joseph's awed reluctance to even touch the sanctified Mary.[20] However, this latter interpretation does not easily square with the pronouncement of the angel in Mt 1:20, who first has to win Joseph around to the idea of acknowledging the exceptional nature of Jesus's conception through the Holy Spirit. Accordingly, in more recent times, as a general rule even Catholic exegesis has tended to give precedence to the classical Protestant reading of this

15 Cf. Luz, *Das Evangelium nach Matthäus*, 135.

16 Cf. Beinert, *Maria*, 31.

17 Müller and Sattler, 'Mariologie', 165.

18 It is repeatedly noted in the exegetical literature that Mt is clearly much more interested in Joseph than in Mary. Cf. for example Konradt, *Das Evangelium nach Matthäus*, 34.

19 Luz, *Das Evangelium nach Matthäus*, 146 and the footnote, which observes that in Deut 22:23 f. it is stipulated that the penalty for a person who is pledged to be married committing adultery is to be stoned to death, although this custom had fallen into desuetude by the time of Jesus.

20 Cf. ibid., 147.

passage. For instance, the renowned German Catholic exegete Michael Theobald has written: 'When he (Joseph) notices that she is pregnant, he suspects her of adultery and wants to "dismiss" her, but because he is "righteous" (i.e. he has no wish to expose his wife to scandal by instituting very public divorce proceedings, but instead to be indulgent and lenient towards her) to do so surreptitiously without making any great fuss.'[21] To put it rather bluntly, one might even say: precisely *because* Joseph is a 'righteous man', and as such lives his life entirely in accordance with the Torah (Jewish law), he is *duty bound* to dismiss a woman who has committed adultery and has hence become a permanent source of impurity for him (thereby jeopardising his relationship with God). For on the literary level of Mt, according to the so-called 'sexual immorality clause' mentioned in Mt 5:32, in the case of adultery on the part of a wife Jesus's strict proscription against divorce is rendered null and void. And seen in historical terms too, even in pre-rabbinical Judaism, forms of textual exegesis existed according to which extramarital sexual intercourse on the part of a married woman effectively defiled her for her husband and made any further sexual relations between the married couple impossible.[22] As a result, it is highly probable that it was precisely Joseph's observance of the Torah which prevented him from behaving in any other way towards Mary. Accordingly – again on the literary level of the gospel – it is only the intervention of an unnamed angel that can persuade him to keep Mary by his side. We are not given any more details on the circumstances of Jesus's birth.

We likewise search in vain for a more extensive appreciation of Mary in the episodes that follow: the adoration of the Magi (Mt 2:1–12), the Flight to Egypt (Mt 2:13–15), the slaughter of the innocents on Bethlehem (Mt 2:16–18), and the return from Egypt (Mt 2:19–23). All that is said is that the Magi find Jesus with his mother Mary (Mt 2:11) and that Joseph is told by the angel that he should take Mary with him on the flight to Egypt and when he returns to Israel (Mt 2:13, 2:20). In Mt, Mary appears entirely as the mother of the Messiah. She derives 'respect exclusively from her *child*',[23] and does not develop an independent profile. Yet at the same time, some indications are nonetheless given of what a difficult situation Mary's pregnancy and giving birth to Jesus places Mary in – a theme that would later come to be expanded upon by the proclaimer of the Qur'an.

21 Theobald, 'Siehe, die Jungfrau wird empfangen', 28.

22 Cf. Vahrenhorst, 'Ihr sollt überhaupt nicht schwören', 407–409.

23 Hagemann and Pulsfort, *Maria*, 37.

c) Mary in the Gospel of Luke

We have already seen in our exposition of Mark's Gospel that of all the books of the Bible, the Gospel of Luke has most to say about Mary. This scripture is also the main source for the veneration of the Virgin Mary within Christianity, which commences very shortly after its writing. Interestingly, it is also the text with which the proclaimer of the Qur'an engages most intensively. The most prominent episode in this treatment is the story of the proclamation of Jesus's coming and of his birth; accordingly, these are the passages from Lk that we will focus on here too.

After a short preface, Lk begins his gospel with the announcement of the birth of John the Baptist (Lk 1:5–25), from which he immediately proceeds to portray the birth of Jesus (Lk 1:26–38).[24] Genealogically it is almost certainly the case that Lk himself creates the link between the scene with Mary and the preceding scene where the Angel Gabriel appears to the priest Zechariah and proclaims the birth of John the Baptist.[25] Lk's intention in doing so is not only to highlight the fact that the announcement to Zechariah is overtrumped by the same angel foretelling the birth of Jesus to Mary, but also to point out the clear parallels between the two scenes: 'Both Zechariah and Mary are called upon by name by the angel who visits them and are told: "Do not be afraid!"; both raise an objection to the "birth proclamations", which the angel allays in each instance; both receive a sign from the angel – Zechariah is dumbstruck, while Mary is told of the pregnancy of her aged relative Elizabeth.'[26] At the same time, not the slightest criticism is evident in the portrayal of the temple and the priesthood in the announcement to Zechariah. The Jewish milieu and the details of Jewish ceremonies are described with great care and without any discernible anti-Jewish agenda.[27] Evidently Lk is greatly concerned to locate the story of Jesus firmly within a Jewish setting. It is important to note this here, since an anti-Jewish interpretation of the relationship between Zechariah and Mary quickly came to play an influential role in patristics.

We will come to investigate this history of reception in greater depth presently. At this juncture we are solely concerned with the mariologically relevant verses in the announcement of the forthcoming birth of Jesus. The Annunciation scene exhibits clear parallels with Old Testament narratives and can be read in

24 On the breakdown of Lk 1 f. used here, cf. Bovon, *Das Evangelium nach Lukas*, 46 f.
25 Cf. Theobald, 'Siehe, die Jungfrau wird empfangen', 46.
26 Theobald, 'Siehe, die Jungfrau wird empfangen', 37 f.; on this and other parallels, cf. Müller, *Mehr als ein Prophet*, 109 f.
27 Cf. Bovon, *Das Evangelium nach Lukas*, 50.

conjunction with, say, Judges 6:11–24.[28] In formal terms, the passage here is, like Mt 1:18–25, a narrative exposition in the manner of the Haggadah[29] or 'tales of fulfillment, which pick up on Isaiah's "birth proclamation" in Isaiah 7:13 (in the Septuagint [LXX] version) and set the narrative scene with regard to the messianic significance of Jesus's birth.'[30] The verses in Lk form part of a genre of birth announcements, which in antiquity were a favoured method of conveying the idea 'that figures of legend, but also certain historical personages, were destined by God for greatness even prior to their birth.'[31]

As with Zechariah, in the announcement scene involving Mary, Gabriel appears as an angel sent by the Lord (he introduces himself in Lk 1:19, and again in Lk 1:26). While in biblical terms, the angel of the Lord can also be interpreted as a manifestation of God,[32] in both of these passages the angel acts solely as a messenger. In the Hebrew Bible – with the exception of the Book of Daniel – angels actually have no names.[33] The fact that the name of Gabriel is given here may well have to do with the fact that a meeting between a young woman and an angel who remained anonymous might evoke sexual connotations,[34] especially because angels in the New Testament are customarily depicted as good-looking young men.[35] Gabriel was regarded here as especially trustworthy[36] and in addition was commonly associated with God's military might;[37] both of these factors place a question mark over any thoughts of a romantic encounter right from the outset. Likewise, the emphasis on Mary's virginity and the mention of her betrothal to Joseph effectively preclude any misplaced interpretation of the encounter with the angel (cf. Lk 1:27).

---

28 Cf. Menke, *Fleisch geworden aus Maria*, 29 f.

29 Cf. Theobald, 'Siehe, die Jungfrau wird empfangen', 29.

30 Ibid., 20. LXX is the standard abbreviation used for the Greek Bible translation, the Septuagint.

31 Ibid., 24.

32 Cf. von Stosch, 'Eine urchristliche Engelchristologie im Koran?', 69–91. The angel's role in Lk 2:9, when he radiates the glory of the Lord, is therefore different to that in the Annunciation scene (cf. Bovon, *Das Evangelium nach Lukas*, 124). Lk 2:13 then immediately proceeds to talk in terms of a whole host of angels (cf. Michalak, 'The Angel Gabriel in the Lukan Infancy Narrative', 208). This may be an allusion to the ideas of Zealotry (cf. Michalak, 'The Angel Gabriel in the Lukan Infancy Narrative', 211).

33 Cf. Michalak, 'The Angel Gabriel in the Lukan Infancy Narrative', 204.

34 Cf. ibid., 215.

35 One need only think of the angel at Jesus's tomb or those which accompany him on his Ascension, all of which are depicted as young men (Mk 16:5; Lk 24:4; Acts 1:10). And of course the heavenly host in Lk 2:13 are also male.

36 Cf. Michalak, 'The Angel Gabriel in the Lukan Infancy Narrative', 217.

37 Cf. ibid., 211.

At this point, Mary is introduced as *parthénos*, which in Hellenistic Greek has the meaning *virgin*,[38] but which also hints at her youthfulness. Presumably we are to think of her as having just passed the age of sexual maturity, in other words around 12 years old. 'However, she is already legally bound to Joseph by a marriage contract, even though she is not yet living with him. According to the customs of the time, this only happened after the wedding, in other words generally a year after the marriage contract was signed.'[39] We will presently treat the topic of Mary's virginity in a separate section (see below, 53 ff.); our prime concern for the time being is to continue with the narration.

Gabriel greets Mary in Lk 1:28 as 'highly favoured', thus making it clear right from the very beginning that she had been chosen by God in advance, in other words prior to any consent on her part.[40] Mary does not earn the encounter with the angel through her grace and virtuousness, but instead is endowed with God's grace for no reason. Even the consoling words 'The Lord is with you' in the same verse are offered without Mary having done anything to deserve them. These words of encouragement in turn pick up on a pledge made in the Old Testament (Zephaniah 3:14), which is directed at the 'daughter of Zion' and assures her that the Lord is with her. 'In receiving this greeting, Mary appears as the daughter of Zion in person.'[41]

Like Zechariah, Mary's first response is one of shock (Lk 1:19 and 12) and to ask herself what this salutation might signify. Yet while the shock causes Zechariah to be beset by fear, it prompts reflectiveness in Mary. This fact illuminates an important character trait of Mary in Lk. For this trait reveals itself once more following the birth of Jesus. While the angels and the shepherds vent their feelings in the form of loud praise, 'Mary is conspicuous as the one who keeps her counsel and reflects silently on what has taken place.'[42] In her interpretation, Andrea Ackermann scrutinises the verse under discussion here (Lk 2:19), and focuses especially on the word that is used to describe the emotion that Mary feels in her heart, commonly rendered in English as 'pondered' and in the Koine Greek of the New Testament as *symballousa*: 'Therefore, the term *nachdenken* [German for 'to ponder, contemplate'] chosen by the EÜ [*Einheitsübersetzung*, the 'standard

38 Cf. Bovon, *Das Evangelium nach Lukas*, 72; Theobald, 'Siehe, die Jungfrau wird empfangen', 59.

39 Kremer, *Lukasevangelium*, 27.

40 Weidemann, 'Embedding the Virgin', 113, with reference to Wolter, Lk, 25.

41 Ratzinger, 'Et incarnatus est de Spiritu Sancto ex Maria Virgine …' In: H. U. von Balthasar, *Maria*, 71–84, 77.

42 Kremer, *Lukasevangelium*, 38 with reference to Lk 2:19.

translation' of the German ecumenical version of the Bible] is a highly apposite translation of *symballousa* in Lk 2:19 (also in the extended sense of *nachdenken* as "to grapple with"). If we also take into consideration here Acts 17:18, it is even conceivable that this grappling with the news imparted by the shepherds might have occurred somewhat in the manner practised by philosophers, namely entirely inwardly and contemplatively.'[43] Of course, we cannot be certain that Lk really intended to depict Mary's attitude here as one of philosophical contemplation. At any rate, though, it is plain that Mary does not obey blindly but rather attempts to understand what is about to happen to her. She takes a reflective, inquisitive approach, seeking to know exactly what will happen, and so quite fearlessly challenges the angel to go into greater detail. Lk 2:51 subsequently pinpoints this character trait a little more precisely. Just like her husband, Mary cannot understand the 12-year-old Jesus's debates with the elders in the temple courts in Jerusalem, but she nonetheless retains ('treasures') his words and deeds in her heart. In other words, she doe not merely seek to understand things on an intellectual level, but also to gain an existential grasp of what is going on with her son, and to patiently assimilate this insight into her life. This trait of Mary's of patiently enduring things that we as yet cannot comprehend, while at the same time tenaciously querying points that we are complicit in accepting unquestioningly, is clearly presented to us by Lk as a model to emulate.

Let us return, however, to Mary's dialogue with the angel. Gabriel's explanation begins by reiterating that Mary has found grace with God (Lk 1:30). There then follows the proclamation of the Virgin Birth and an initial Christological clarification of significance of the impending event: 'He will be great and will be called the Son of the Most High. The Lord God will give him the throne of his father David, and he will reign over Jacob's descendants forever; his kingdom will never end' (Lk 1:32 f.). John the Baptist was also described as great in the sight of the Lord (Lk 1:15) – once again, we note the parallels between the announcements made to Zechariah and to Mary. But the title 'the Son of the Most High' in Lk 1:32 is genuinely Christological and only appears here. Like the designation of Jesus as the Son of God in Lk 1:45, the title refers to his role as a ruler.[44] In being dubbed the Son of God, Jesus is given an official title 'of the kind that the Kings of Israel carried from the day of their enthronement onwards (cf. Psalms 2:7) and as befits him as the occupant of "the throne of David".'[45] Of course, these imperial

43 Ackermann, '... und Maria dachte darüber nach', 255.

44 Cf. Bovon, *Das Evangelium nach Lukas*, 65.

45 Kremer, *Lukasevangelium*, 28.

associations are reinterpreted in the context of the gospel of Luke. Even so, it is intriguing to note that precisely the angel who in any case is already associated with God's military might now uses a complex of metaphors that stand within the tradition of the Davidian royal Messiah.[46] In particular, Lk 1:33 evokes imperial associations and generates a Christology with political implications, which ultimately holds out the promise of a perpetual reign. Thus we see that even in Lk, the ground is laid for a political interpretation of Christology and Mariology, whose reception in Late Antiquity will be discussed later.

Mary is neither cowed nor impressed when confronted by this momentous piece of news. In her previously described critically contemplative frame of mind, she enquires how she can possibly have a child without having intimate physical contact with a man (Lk 1:34). What she wants are precise answers to her questions, not to be overwhelmed by the pure majesty of God.

In literary terms, Mary's enquiry in Lk 1:34 obliges the angel to provide a fuller explanation: 'The sequence of narrative elements *Objection by the human being/Explanation that rebuts the objection/Signalling of acceptance* (cf. also Luke 1:18–20) is part of a formula of divine vocation already evident in the Old Testament,'[47] which is now also applied to Mary here. Once more, there is a parallel here to Zechariah (Lk 1:18). With regard to this parallel, it is interesting that not only the exegesis of the Church Fathers, but also the modern exegetical tradition takes a more positive view of Mary's questioning than it does of Zechariah's.

Thus, according to François Bovon, Mary's further questioning in Lk 1:34 is, unlike in Zechariah, 'an expression of an enquiring faith and therefore legitimate.'[48] He goes on to explain: 'Depending on a person's inward intention, the same sentences and the same actions can become declarations of faith or of the lack of it, or good or evil deeds.'[49] Even so, claims Bovon, Zechariah is ultimately rehabilitated by singing the Benedictus, in being aligned with Mary through the act of incantation.[50] But this rehabilitation is of course conveyed in Christological terms, with the result that Zechariah's questioning is still primarily downgraded in comparison with that of Mary. This hierarchical arrangement is something that subsequently also becomes a point of interest for the proclaimer of the Qur'an.

Yet however one tries to define the relationship to Zechariah here, one thing at least is clear, namely that in the eyes of Lk, Mary perfectly legitimately demands

---

46 Cf. Bovon, *Das Evangelium nach Lukas*, 75.

47 Theobald, 'Siehe, die Jungfrau wird empfangen', 42, f. 79.

48 Bovon, *Das Evangelium nach Lukas*, 75.

49 Ibid., 76.

50 Ibid., 99.

more from Gabriel before she is prepared to believe him. In response, the angel refers to the Holy Spirit that will come upon her (Lk 1:35a) and will sanctify her child (Lk 1:35b). First and foremost, however, in citing Elizabeth's pregnancy, he provides Mary with a tangible example of God's power that is designed to instil confidence into her (Lk 1:36), and reminds her that nothing is impossible for God (Lk 1:37). On a narrative level, it may well primarily be the specificity of the reference to Elizabeth that serves to convince Mary. For this too is a completely unprecedented occurrence, and the dramaturgical role of the extensive narration of the birth announcement to Zechariah now becomes clear. It is Zechariah and Elizabeth who really bring home to Mary the historical power of God in practical terms and so enable her to place her trust in the angel. Thus, it is only when Mary comes to place herself within the history of Israel and relates this to her own contemporary experience that she can trust the angel's pronouncements and give her assent to the birth of Jesus Christ. Generally speaking, it is the case throughout Lk that Mary is shown to be firmly embedded within the customs of Israel. Together with Joseph, she ensures that, in line with Jewish tradition, Jesus is circumcised soon after his birth (Lk 2:21) and presented to the Lord (Lk 2:23). In doing so, they fulfil everything that is required by the Torah (Lk 2:39). Every year, they celebrate Passover (Pesach) with their son Jesus (Lk 2:41) and see themselves as part of the Temple community. Consequently, there can be no doubt that Mary practised her faith – based on the promises that God gave to Israel and on the Torah – as a devout Jew.

The other elements in the angel's reply help promote a theological reading of the scene rather than explain Mary's ultimate consent. According to Lk too, it is the Holy Spirit that facilitates Mary's pregnancy and sanctifies her son or his birth.[51] And it is the immeasurable power of God which enables this incredible event with Mary to occur – an explanation which in all likelihood represents a Lukan pre-emptive defence against critics who were sceptical of Mary's virginity.[52]

Ultimately, therefore, it is the religion of Israel in whose light Mary is able to place trust in the message delivered by the angel. In Lk 1:38 she utters her

51 Menke makes great play of the idea that the syntax of Lk 1:35b suggests that 'the attribute 'holy' refers to the act of being born and not to the 'Son of God … : *"So the Holy One to be born will be called the Son of God"*' (Menke, *Fleisch geworden aus Maria*, 36). Menke's intention here is clearly to develop an argument for the virginity of Mary during the birth of Christ. On the interpretation of the theologoumenon of the perpetual virginity of Mary which underpins this notion, cf. our exposition below, 53 ff.).

52 Cf. Kremer, *Lukasevangelium*, 29.

famous words consenting to the birth of Jesus: 'I am the Lord's servant[...] May your word to me be fulfilled.' In the Latin tradition of Christianity, following the corresponding formulation in the Vulgate (the Latin translation of the Bible), this pronouncement is commonly referred to as Mary's *fiat*.[53] In the eyes of Lk, her consent is the prerequisite for God, through her son, to show his all-embracing care by taking human form. So, however blessed she may be from the outset, and notwithstanding the fact that she can only be filled with the spirit of God through being thus chosen, it ultimately requires her freely given consent, because the God of Israel and the God of Jesus Christ has no desire to enter this story other than with this human agreement. For Lk, it is precisely in her accordance with the will of God that Mary the chosen one becomes God's handmaiden, with the result that references to her as the handmaid of the Lord (Greek *doule kyriou*) become her key defining characteristic (Lk 1:38).

If we shift our attention from this narration in Lk to the ensuing scene describing the meeting between Mary and Elizabeth (Lk 1:39–56), it quickly becomes apparent that this encounter is meant to symbolise the mutual dependency of Israel and the Church. In Elizabeth, Mary encounters precisely the sign that supports her faith and which has enabled her to give her *fiat*. Conversely, it is the case that Elizabeth is imbued with the Holy Spirit through her meeting with Mary and her unborn child – 'the Virgin Mary, who is already filled with the Holy Spirit and overshadowed by the power of the Most High, therefore "transmits" the spirit, so to speak, to her relative and her unborn child.'[54] In response to being touched by the power of God through the agency of Mary, Elizabeth utters the following words, which are of enduring importance for the Christian tradition: 'Blessed are you among women, and blessed is the child you will bear!' (Lk 1:42). Up to the present day, these words are repeated in one of the most important prayers of the Church, the Ave Maria. And as we shall presently see, they also find an echo in the Qur'an.

What is surely the most significant section of the meeting between Elizabeth and Mary is the Magnificat, which Mary intones as a hymn of praise as part of this scene (Lk 1:46–55). The Magnificat has become a permanent feature of the daily evening prayer service (Vespers) in the Roman Catholic Church. The Magnificat is a hymn inspired by the song of praise offered up by Hannah before the birth of the Prophet Samuel, and which also has points of contact with numerous other

53 *Fiat* is the Latin for 'Let it be'.
54 Weidemann, 'Embedding the Virgin', 115.

Old Testament passages.[55] We will refrain from giving a line-by-line interpretation of the text here, since it is not taken up in detail by the Qur'an. Instead, we will confine ourselves to three short observations:

The Magnificat shows Mary to be a prophetess. Even though she is not explicitly identified as such by Lk, the rhetoric employed here has distinct prophetic connotations.[56] In the process, Lk devises a combination of 'inspiration by the Spirit, prophecy and sexual abstinence'[57] that is peculiar to his gospel. This is explained in the narrative around the figure of Mary and lays the foundation for the prophetic oratory of the Magnificat.

The Magnificat is 'one of the texts of the New Testament with the most pronouncedly political and freedom-oriented content. It encourages us to take its words at face value and fight against oppression and thereby take seriously the message proclaimed by the Lord of History [i.e. Jesus Christ]'[58] In this way Mary has become a key figure in liberation theology and more recent political theological schools of thought, and her Magnificat has been used repeatedly to legitimise a theology that is critical of established power and anti-imperialist in tone. However, these political implications can also, of course, be misappropriated, as for example when Mary is used by rulers and other figures in power to legitimise their claims to sovereignty. The promise that God will 'bring down rulers from their thrones and lift up the humble' (Lk 1:52) can also be abused by those who have attained positions of power from humble beginnings and now seek to justify their own imperialist actions. Lk surely did not have such a theology in mind, though this is precisely what the proclaimer of the Qur'an found there in Late Antiquity; the absence of any comment on the Magnificat becomes understandable against this background.

A third point regarding the Magnificat should also be mentioned: the text makes Mary into a mouthpiece of the poor.[59] Jesus's lowly birth in a manger and the offering of doves in the Temple – a typical sacrificial offering by poor people – are fully consonant with this interpretation.[60] Despite the fact that Christian tradition quickly spiritualised this poverty, construing it as 'that poverty before

---

55 Cf. Menke, *Fleisch geworden aus Maria*, 39.

56 Cf. Weidemann, 'Embedding the Virgin', 115, with reference to N. Clayton Croy and Alice E. Connor, 'Mantic Mary? The virgin mother as prophet in Luke 1:26–56 and the early church.' In: *JSNT* 34 (2012) 254–276, here 271.

57 Weidemann, 'Embedding the Virgin', 115 f.

58 Bovon, *Das Evangelium nach Lukas*, 94.

59 Cf. Hagemann and Pulsfort, *Maria*, 52.

60 Ibid., 61.

God which anticipates salvation as coming solely from God',[61] Lk unequivocally means real poverty here. The redemptive presence of God's essential Word can therefore actually be found within the humility of the servant figure. Accordingly, this very real and enduring poverty also represents a critical corrective to the possibility of the aforementioned imperialist misappropriation of the political theology of Lk.

One final observation: the proclamation in the Magnificat to the effect that all generations will henceforth call Mary blessed (Lk 1:48b) only makes sense if there were 'already signs of adoration of the Virgin Mary'[62] at the time when Lk was written. As a result, it is reasonable to conclude that the veneration of Mary in Lk is not an isolated instance, but rather an expression of an emerging Christian history of piety at the end of the first century, which first becomes apparent in Lk.[63]

The encounter between Elizabeth and Mary is followed in Lk 1:57–80 by an account of the birth of John the Baptist; this passage also forms the framework for the singing of the Benedictus by Zechariah (Lk 1:68–79). Lk here expressly refers to a prophetic utterance by Zechariah (Lk 1:67), which leads him to give voice to a prayer incantation which even today forms the core of the morning prayer service (Matins) in the Catholic Church. Like the Magnificat, this song is not picked up by the Qur'an either. Also, because it contains no significant clues regarding the figure of Mary, it needs no further discussion here.

Let us turn instead to the story of Jesus's birth (Lk 2:1–40), a Christmas tale familiar to everyone brought up in the Christian faith. Given the lack of any detailed engagement with this story in the Qur'an, and also because the verses in question have little relevance for Mariology, just a few remarks will suffice here.

The Christmas story likewise amply confirms the lowliness, poverty and simplicity of Mary and her child. The fact that Mary is forced to wrap her child up in rags and lay it in a manger because there is no room for them at the inn (Lk 2:7) is an eloquent image of the poverty and simplicity of the Holy Family that still resonates today. While the Emperor Augustus orders that a census be conducted (Lk 2:1) to raise taxes to support the 'ruinously expensive military machine

61 Ibid., 53.

62 Mußner, *Maria*, 49.

63 The blessing bestowed on Mary by an anonymous woman in Lk 11:27 is likewise a feature that is peculiar to Luke, and which he would surely not have included had this kind of veneration of Mary not already been commonplace by the time he was writing his gospel; cf. Mußner, *Maria*, 51. Mußner puts forward a convincing argument as to why Lk 11:28 raises no objection to this interpretation (cf. ibid., 53 f.).

which safeguards the Pax Augusta and imperial power,'[64] nothing of the messianic splendour we might expect attaches to Mary and Joseph. Instead, they are 'poor, helpless, weak and even looking for shelter,'[65] and as such are living testimony to an inhospitable world viewed 'from the perspective of a socially marginalised minority'.[66]

It is stated on no fewer than three occasions that Jesus was born in a manger (Lk 2:7,12,16), though the Greek word leaves it open as to whether this was located in a stable, a cave or simply in the open air.[67] However, this fact not only underlines the poverty of the Holy Family but also and most importantly 'the lack of power of this son of David, in marked contrast to the powerful Caesar Augustus and popular conceptions of the Messiah.'[68] In other words, the Christmas story testifies not only to the poverty and simplicity of Mary and her son but also to their powerlessness. Rather than show Augustus's political theology being confronted, say, by a rival claim to power, the sheer powerlessness of the heavenly child instead serves to expose it in all its cynicism and propensity to violence. At the same time, by referring to Joseph and Mary's obedience regarding the census, Luke also directs his polemics at Zealot movements. Luke is therefore not playing one political theology off against another. 'The Gospel is a criticism of both the ruling ideology and of zealotry.'[69] We will see presently to how great an extent this anti-imperialist tendency in theology, which takes a highly critical stance towards any utilisation by human pretensions to power, also characterises the Qur'an's image of Mary.

And yet this renunciation of worldly power does not mean renouncing the majesty of God, which is clearly attested by the presence of the host of angels in the Christmas story and which underlines God's heavenly claim to power. Thus, in Lk, grandeur and lowliness are not mutually exclusive but mutually dependent.[70]

64 Appel, 'Wen erwarten wir?', 648. Bovon also underlines how the census story establishes a clear antithesis between the Roman Emperor, a figure known to all and sundry, and the hidden Messiah (Bovon, *Das Evangelium nach Lukas*, 126). Similarly, the proclamation of the gospel by the angel is paralleled by the proclamation of the census by imperial messengers, and both the Emperor Augustus and Jesus are described as 'saviours' (Lk 2,10 f.; cf. Kremer, *Lukasevangelium*, 37). The census shores up the emperor's claim to power, because it forms the basis of a poll tax and military conscription (Bovon, *Das Evangelium nach Lukas*, 118).

65 Appel, 'Wen erwarten wir?', 648.

66 Schreiber, *Weihnachtspolitik*, 68.

67 Cf. Bovon, *Das Evangelium nach Lukas*, 127.

68 Kremer, *Lukasevangelium*, 36.

69 Bovon, *Das Evangelium nach Lukas*, 117 f.

70 Cf. ibid., 130: *Typisch für Lukas ist das Ineinander von Herrlichkeit und Niedrigkeit. Engelscharen begleiten eine ärmliche Geburt.* ('Typical of Luke is the intertwining of magnificence and baseness. Hosts of angels accompany a lowly birth.')

It is precisely the lowliness of being born in a manger that radiates splendour and enthrals the shepherds and others. And similarly, in Christian popular observance there is nothing more glorious even for children than the festival of Christmas, though this is undergoing an entirely new experience of debasement and profanity by being so weighted down with consumerist desires. The splendour, magic and grace of God are encountered, so to speak, *sub contrario* in everyday life or at least only in figures that work on a symbolic level. 'God's majesty cannot exist without the heavenly court. It has neither disappeared nor is it restricted to the Temple. It radiates in the here and now with extraordinary vividness.'[71] This is an idea that we will encounter again in the Qur'an's portrayal of Mary.

Immediately following the Christmas story, it becomes clear in Lk that the specific interlinking between the majesty and the lowliness of God, to which Mary too bears witness through her life, will entail suffering for her. Thus, Simeon says to Mary that Jesus will be a sign 'that will be spoken against' (Lk 2:34), and with regard to Mary's fate he points out: 'And a sword will pierce your own soul too' (Lk 2:35). Together with John 19:25f., this remark of Simeon to Mary established an image of Mary in the Christian tradition as a 'Mother of Sorrows' (*mater dolorosa*).[72] Even though Lk does not give a description of Mary beneath the Cross, he nevertheless helps to lay the foundations of this important character trait within the Christian veneration of Mary. Mary, the contemplative questioner, who takes on responsibility by giving her *fiat*, and who from a Christian viewpoint is the figure who makes possible the incarnate form of God's care for humankind, is also ultimately prepared to testify to God's solicitude by means of love and hence to take on all the pain that results from humanity's rejection of this love. At this point we may concur with the view voiced by Joseph Ratzinger: 'An inherent part of Mary's journey is the experience of being rejected (Mk 3:31–35; John 2:4); in being "given away" to another disciple by Jesus on the Cross, Mary undergoes the same rejection that Jesus himself was forced to suffer at the Mount of Olives and on the Cross.'[73]

In Lk, Mary appears like Abraham as the archetype of the faithful believer. 'Her faith is an active faith in two senses: she understands and she experiences what she believes.'[74] And like Abraham, she is also prepared to endure all the

71 Bovon, *Das Evangelium nach Lukas*, 124.

72 Cf. Kremer, *Lukasevangelium*, 42; Hagemann and Pulsfort, *Maria*, 63.

73 Ratzinger, 'Erwägungen zur Stellung von Mariologie und Marienfrömmigkeit im Ganzen von Glaube und Theologie.' In: H. U. von Balthasar, *Maria*, 14–30, here 28.

74 Bovon, *Das Evangelium nach Lukas*, 132.

existential consequences of her faith. In doing so she trusts in a historically powerful God, who makes good on promises however unreasonable they may appear.[75]

Considering Luke's two works (the Gospel and Acts) as a whole, it is noteworthy that, according to Acts 1:14, Mary, the mother of Jesus, joins together in prayer in Jerusalem with the apostles, Jesus's brothers and the women. Consequently, she must have been present at the events of Pentecost. Mentioning Mary at this point 'demonstrates the significance that Luke accords to her from an ecclesiological standpoint.'[76] According to Lk, then, Mary finds faith in Jesus Christ and her faith is of paradigmatic importance. This volte-face on her part explains why, over time, Mary increasingly comes to be regarded within Church doctrine as the primal image of the Church and the archetype of the believer.

d) Mary in the Gospel of John

The Gospel of John (hereafter abbreviated to Jn) contains no account of the birth of Jesus; as a result there can be no discussion of Mary in this context. Even so, there is one verse in the prologue to Jn which is the source of much controversy regarding Mary's virginity. At first sight this verse appears to rule out the Virgin Birth. Thus, Jn 1:12f. states: 'Yet to all who did receive him, to those who believed in his name, he gave the right to become children of God – children born not of blood, nor of the will of the flesh or a husband's will, but born of God.' The wording 'not born… of a husband's will' is reminiscent of the formulation describing the Virgin Birth in Mt and Lk, and in consequence the application of this statement to all believers might appear to represent an implicit criticism of any biological understanding of the Virgin Birth. However, verse 13 not only rejects birth as a result of a husband's will but also birth through blood and the will of the flesh. In all likelihood, the reference to 'blood' here means the menstrual blood of a woman: Hellenistic and early Jewish thinkers held that it was precisely this blood that was the key substance in procreation.[77] According to this line of thought, it was not only the father's semen but also the mother's menstrual blood which gave rise to human life. When John states that believers were born neither of the husband's will (or flesh) nor of the woman's blood, he is pointing out that being a child of God has nothing to do with the biological birth process or natural

75 Franz Mußner essentially identifies two common elements in the faith of Mary and that of Abraham: '1. The faith of both figures is a belief in the God of miracles. 2. Both believe that the Utopian-sounding pledges which each of them make will be fulfilled' (Mußner, *Maria*, 65).

76 Hagemann and Pulsfort, *Maria*, 69.

77 Cf. Theobald, *Das Evangelium des Johannes*, 125.

descent. The background to this statement was most likely a dispute with contemporary Jewish Christianity, which wanted to tie being a child of God to belonging to the nation of Israel.[78] In other words, the verse actually has nothing to do with the theme of the Virgin Birth.

The situation is different if one follows a reading of the verse that was current among several Church Fathers in the Latin West and which is found in some manuscripts. This proceeds from the assumption that verse 13 was not framed in the plural but rather speaks in the singular about a person who is not born of blood or of the will of the flesh or the husband's will. In this version, the verse would refer to Jesus Christ and would be evidence of Jesus's exceptional birth. Yet if that were so, then this verse from Jn, unlike the Synoptic Gospels, would not be positing a virgin birth from the material disposition of Mary but instead proposing a birth entirely devoid of human agency. Thus, although the verse might ostensibly attest a virgin birth, it can also easily be misconstrued as docetism. In other words, one might well be tempted to ask whether Jesus's real human nature was actually being substantiated here or whether his human form was nothing but an illusion.

In text-critical terms, it appears that the Codex Veronensis, the Toledo Lectionary and some Syriac manuscripts contain a singular reading of this verse – Tertullian, Irenaeus and other early Christian authors also read it in this way. However, not a single Greek manuscript contains the singular form, meaning that this is a phenomenon that is exclusive to the Latin Church.[79] This is noteworthy insofar as the New Testament was originally written in Greek, and Greek was the language of the imperial church in the first few centuries CE. This divergent reading in the West can easily be explained by presuming that, as early as the second century the need arose to identify references to the Virgin Birth in Jn as well. On the other hand it is hard to imagine, once belief in Mary's virginity had become so firmly established, quite how the plural reading managed to insinuate itself into the text and become generally accepted.[80] In line with this, biblical exegesis has unanimously rejected the singular reading,[81] and does not see Jn 1:13 as presenting an

78 Cf. ibid.

79 Cf. Wikenhauser, *Das Evangelium nach Johannes*, 46 f.

80 Cf. Theobald, *Das Evangelium des Johannes*, 125.

81 In addition to Theobald and Wikenhauser, cf. also Gnilka, *Johannesevangelium*, 15, Schnackenburg, *Das Johannesevangelium*, 239, together with all the other commentaries regarding this question that were available to us, which we have attempted to comprehensively review. Against this exegetical consensus, Menke ('Fleisch geworden aus Maria', 49, with reference to the work of Hofrichter, 'Nicht aus Blut, sondern monogen aus Gott geboren'), argues that all the Church Fathers of the second century are unanimous in adopting the (only subsequently attested) singular reading. However, even the most cursory reading of the

argument either for or against Mary's virginity. Quite simply, either John had no interest in this question, or he had no wish to engage with the tradition of Mary's virginity.

Another verse in Jn also hints at this reluctance. In Jn 6:42, 'the Jews'[82] grumble about Jesus because, they claim, he is the person 'whose father and mother we know' – an obvious allusion to the conflicts between Jesus and his family as recounted in the synoptic gospels, which we discussed above. The evangelist seems, 'on the basis of the "Jewish" argument not to want to undermine the idea of Jesus's *earthly* provenance from *human* parents… in other words he either does not know about the concept of Mary giving birth through the Holy Spirit without any involvement by Joseph, or does not wish to know about it.'[83] What is important for his theology is that Jesus's provenance from human parents is not a counterargument against his (Jesus's) ultimately divine origins. 'While, in the eyes of the "Jews", Jesus's birth to human parents excludes any possibility that he might originate from God, the believer takes a deeper view and recognises precisely in this Jesus – the son of human parents – the Son of Man descended from heaven.'[84]

---

patristic passages in question (for the specific references, see Hofrichter, 'Nicht aus Blut…', 20–29) shows that most of the Greek references which supposedly corroborate the singular reading are not correct. Thus – at variance with what Menke and Hofrichter claim – Justin Martyr does not include any quotations from Jn 1:13, but instead his own quite independent formulations of similar thoughts. The same is true of Ignatius – one of the other six or seven witnesses for the singular reading adduced by Menke and Hofrichter; their citing of Hippolytus of Rome in support of their argument is equally untenable. According to our own researches, the only Church Fathers to actually attest the singular reading are Tertullian and Irenaeus, a fact that is well known in research and which has been amply acknowledged in the relevant commentary literature. Since, in the case of Irenaeus's *Adversus Haereses,* we only have the Latin translation of the Greek original (along with a few Greek fragments, though these do not include the quotations from Jn 1:13 that are at issue here) and cannot assume that this translation is always accurate, there do not appear to be any valid grounds for presuming that a singular reading of Jn 1:13 also existed in the Greek original in the second century. We are most grateful to Nestor Kavvadas for supplying this information. Moreover, Schnackenburg has pointed out that the plural reading does not suit the purposes of the Valentinians; consequently, Tertullian's (and Menke's!) contention that the plural reading is attributable to the Valentinians (and hence to a heretical influence on Christianity!) cannot be correct, and indirectly indicates that the plural form must in fact have been the original reading, since this was evidently the one that Tertullian encountered (Schnackenburg, *Das Johannesevangelium*, 240).

82 When John refers to 'the Jews' he is using it as a typological categorisation of Jesus's adversaries. As such, then, one must tread very warily when drawing conclusions from his terminology about the attitude of the Jewish community to Jesus.

83 Theobald, *Das Evangelium nach Johannes*, 370.

84 Ibid., 371 (italicised in the original).

Clearly, then, where the New Testament is concerned, it is perfectly possible to devise an advanced Christology with a clear belief in incarnation without having to embrace the idea of Jesus's Virgin Birth. Accordingly, in Jn even one of the disciples can quite unselfconsciously address Jesus as the son of Joseph (Jn 1:45) and so likewise call into question the Virgin Birth.

Yet John's lack of interest in Mary's virginity does not mean that he has no general interest in Mary as a person. Certainly, Mary is not mentioned by name in Jn and only appears twice. Yet both these passages are really telling and mark two decisive points in the life of Jesus: the start of his public ministry and his crucifixion. As noted, Mary is not named on these occasions, but appears as the mother of Jesus; in consequence, we will refer to her in the following analysis in the same way.

In Jn, the wedding at Cana marks the first occasion on which Jesus reveals his glory through an external sign (Jn 2:11). The mother of Jesus plays a key role in this, without ever becoming active herself in any way.[85] The first mention of her is a very terse reference to the fact that she was present at the wedding (Jn 2:1). Moreover, she keeps a close watch on the proceedings, so that she is well aware when the wine runs out. Whereupon she immediately turns to Jesus and relates the problem to him: 'They have no more wine' (Jn 2:3). The sentence does not contain any direct call to action.[86] The mother of Jesus does not know what Jesus should do and does not offer any advice. Yet she clearly expects and trusts in the fact that he can help, and so she brings the predicament of the married couple – who face considerable embarrassment at the wine running out – to the attention of Jesus. In doing so, she appears like a supplicant, as someone interceding with Jesus on behalf of others, whose distressing situation she has taken to heart.[87] In the process, she takes a back seat and trusts in her son to make things right, even though he has not done anything remarkable hitherto and in spite of the fact that there is no objective reason why she should turn to him for help.

Jesus's reaction to this request is one of curt dismissal, delivered in a remarkably harsh tone of voice: 'Why are you involving me, woman?' he snaps at her (Jn 2:4). Even to a contemporary audience, this mode of address would seem to

85 Although Jesus's miracle at the wedding at Cana is not featured in the Qur'an, interestingly it does appear repeatedly in Muslim commentary literature (cf. Ashkar, *Mary in the Syriac Christian tradition and Islam*, 179).

86 Cf. Theobald, *Das Evangelium nach Johannes*, 332.

87 The Christian tradition later invokes such texts when it calls upon Mary in intercessory prayers; this tradition can be traced back to the third or fourth centuries (cf. Beinert, *Maria*, 96).

require some explanation. And for a Jew in antiquity, a dismissive remark such as this directed at one's own mother would have been even more offensive. At this point, we see a reflection of the same internal family conflicts that characterised Jesus's relationship with his mother in Mk also. Evidently, the mother of Jesus found dealing with him difficult, and clearly Jesus too – like many an adolescent son – felt a strong need to put some distance between himself and his mother.

However, the Greek text also admits of another interpretation. Literally, Jesus asks: 'What is between you and me, woman?' This is not necessarily to be taken as insulting. It may also simply indicate that Jesus, who is right at the start of his public ministry, is pointing out that his mother must also now see him as an independent person and that she will need to revise her view of the relationship between them. Only the things that are between them and which define their relationship should be up for discussion. In other words, the gist of the question might also be whether the mother of Jesus really regards this concern of other people as a matter that belongs within the personal relationship between herself and Jesus. The rest of the story indicates that this is indeed the case, and the upshot of this is that the mother of Jesus appears as an advocate for people in need. But to begin with, Jesus does not accept his mother's request and tells her that his hour has not yet come. The wedding, which in the Bible is invariably symbolic of the union between God and man, has not yet become the wedding at which Jesus's majesty will be revealed. The union between God and man which is made visible in his person on the Cross has not yet arrived and so he cannot yet make this wedding his celebration.

Even so, the mother of Jesus trusts in him and insists upon taking him to task. She does not take the slightest offence at the brusque rebuttal by her son, but remains true to her role as advocate. She does not come up with any ideas of her own about how to solve the problem but instead keeps focusing all her attention on Jesus.[88] Thus, Jn has her saying to the servants at the wedding: 'Do whatever he tells you' (Jn 2:5). Thus she points at Jesus, she places her trust in him, she does not absolve him of his duty, and she continues to pester him with the admittedly very worldly yet at this moment existentially important concern of the married couple. In this way she indirectly forces him to act, and so catalyses the first outward sign of his divinity and the start of his trajectory as a miracle worker.

---

88 Cf. Kästle, 'Die Mutter Jesu im Johannesevangelium', 305: *Alleinige Aufgabe der Mutter ist es hier, den Wundertäter auf die eingetretene Mangelsituation hinzuweisen und somit ein Handeln Jesu 'in Gang zu setzen'*. ('The sole task of the mother here is to make the miracle-worker aware of the shortage that has occurred and thereby to "set in motion" action on Jesus's part.')

The mother of Jesus does not appear while the actual miracle is being enacted. Even at the conclusion we do not learn what she thinks about it. For all that is stated is that the disciples believed in him (Jn 2:11). It remains a moot point whether the mother of Jesus is not mentioned here because she believed in Jesus even before the miracle took place or because she still cannot be counted among the believers. It may simply be the case that she is someone who trusts in her son without yet comprehending what is so special about him and what role he might play. And indeed, thereafter she plays no further role in the whole of Jesus's public ministry. All that is clear (from Jn 2:12) is that she remains by his side. Evidently, she is simply present and refers to him. Consequently, the mariological message from Jn 2 might simply be that we humans get to interact with Jesus through Mary and that we should turn to her when we are incapable of recounting our distress to Jesus or God on our own. Admittedly, this role of Mary is not explicitly mentioned in the text. Yet her actions at the wedding at Cana do strongly suggest it. She clearly stands ready as an advocate and helper, but not as a teacher or saviour. She is simply there as a pointer to her son. But she is also the one who prompts him to act in the first place. Without her intervention – another interpretation that could be placed on the story – Jesus would not have become active and embarked on the series of miracles he performed. It is she who impatiently urges him to act and so stimulates the start of his mission. As such, therefore, she is not only the mother who brings Jesus into the world and makes his ministry possible – a supposition that Jn naturally implies. More importantly, she is also the person who reminds the grown-up Jesus of his mission and connects us to it.

Briefly foreshadowing the Qur'an, it is noticeable that the Mary depicted there also focuses entirely on Jesus and trusts him right from the outset, even before he has had a chance to achieve anything. In the Qur'an too, Jesus embarks on his public ministry because Mary turns to him. Likewise, the Qur'an picks up on the idea of the dependence of Jesus's mother on her son. However, she no longer appears as an advocate for others, but instead asks him to help her. Mary's existential crisis is thereby brought more sharply into focus, and she becomes more of a person with whom we can identify when we find ourselves in distress and in need of help. Jesus appears here as an aid sent by God, while Mary points to him but does not herself step into a role as mediator. Thus, on the one hand the Qur'an reduces Mary's significance in the relationship between God and humankind. On the other hand, though, it does erase any trace of a conflict between Jesus and his mother, and it does mention her by name. Indeed, the first draft of the *Maryam* surah actually inverts the relationship, since although the surah carries the name of Mary and Mary plays a prominent part in it, Jesus's name vanishes and he only appears as the son of Mary. Clearly, then, Mary is upgraded here, albeit without altering the Christocentricity of her figure. For even in Surah *Maryam*, Mary is solely focused on her son. However, we are pre-empting the part of this book on the Qur'an and so should swiftly return to Jn.

Let us look at the ending of Jn. The other scene in this gospel in which the mother of Jesus plays a role marks the end of his journey. Jesus is nailed up on the Cross (Jn 19:23) and the Roman legionaries are casting lots for his clothes (Jn 19:24). At this point, in other words shortly before Jesus breathes his last, and following the logic of Jn just before his final hour has come and he is glorified, his mother appears once more – again without being called by her proper name, but even so as the first to be identified in the group of people standing beneath the Cross (Jn 19:25). This time she does not speak. She is simply present – together with two other women called Mary and with the unnamed disciple 'whom Jesus loved' (Jn 19:26). The mother of Jesus is now declared by her son to also be the mother of this favourite disciple, and hence appears as the mother of the nascent Christian Church (Jn 19:27). Yet, thereupon, it is the mother of Jesus who is taken under the wing of the disciple. Here, the mother of Jesus is, so to speak, taken under the Church's protection, but in the process imparts to it a centre and sense of direction.[89] If we consider what this centre and direction that Mary can give to the Church might consist of, it strikes us anew that she puts herself entirely at the disposal of God's might, whose benevolence has manifested itself through the person of Jesus Christ. 'In this scene, Mary is wholly at the disposal of others. She stays silent and inactive. There is not the slightest indication either of her love for her son, or of her pain as a mother, or of her quiet faith, or of her role as an advocate.'[90] She remains someone who is completely self-effacing and who facilitates God's work through her existence as the handmaiden of the Lord. The brutality of the destructive power of the Cross is mirrored by the mother of Jesus effacing her own existence in favour of the One self-offering God.

89 Cf. Hans Urs von Balthasar, 'Maria in der kirchlichen Lehre und Frömmigkeit.' In: Joseph Ratzinger, *Maria*, 87–111, here p. 97: *Maria wird von ihrem Sohn in die Obhut eines der Apostel und so in die apostolische Kirche hinein verfügt. Er schenkt damit der Kirche jene Mitte oder Spitze, die in unnachahmlicher und doch immer anzustrebender Weise den Glauben der neuen Gemeinschaft verkörpert: das makellose, uneingeschränkte Jawort zum ganzen Heilsplan Gottes für die Welt*. ('In being assigned to the care of one of the apostles by her son, Mary is effectively incorporated into the Apostolic Church. In the process, Jesus lends the Church that focus or point which embodies the faith of the new Christian communion, in a form that is inimitable yet towards which we should constantly strive: namely, unimpeachable, unequivocal assent to God's entire plan of salvation for the world.')

90 Becker, *Maria*, 208.

It is remarkable that this decisive role played by the mother of Jesus, which is of such unparalleled importance in Christian devotional practice and which finds expression in countless Pietà scenes, has only come down to us in the Gospel of Jn. Only in Jn is the mother of Jesus mentioned at this stage, just before his death, and above all it is only in Jn that we find the women 'in the immediate vicinity of the Cross.'[91] And only in Jn is the mother of Jesus depicted among these women, in other words only in this gospel is she present at the moment when Jesus is dying.[92] She endures his fate alongside him – silent, devoted and helpless. While the brothers of Jesus are viewed very critically in Jn (cf. Jn 7:5), with regard to his mother a whole series of valuable theological stimuli are generated, which we should keep at the back of our minds when examining the treatment of Mary in the Qur'an. Looking at Jn as a whole, it is noteworthy that the mother of Jesus is present both at the commencement of Jesus's public ministry and miracle-working (Jn 2:11) and at the Cross, where his work is 'completed' (Jn 19:30). In other words, she stands at the beginning (*arché*) and at the end (*télos*) of the ministry of the Word made Flesh.

And so we have reached the end of our brief conspectus of biblical references to Mary. Before we come to evaluate these in the round once more, we should mention in passing here why we have not dealt specifically with the Book of Revelation (hereafter abbreviated as Rev). The woman who appears in Rev 12 was interpreted as Mary as the fourth century by Epiphanius, the Bishop of Salamis, and thereafter in the commentaries written by Bishop Promasius and the theologian Oecumenicus in the sixth century. However, in the early church there are only a few such references,[93] and these are scarcely verifiable with regard to any bearing they might have on the contemporary emergence of the Qur'an. Even so, the content of Rev 12:6 might be of interest for a dialogue with the Qur'an, if the unnamed woman who is described as crying out loud in her labour pains, and who after giving birth flees into the desert, where she is provided with sustenance by God, really is to be identified with Mary. If this were indeed the case – a point disputed by many scholars – then this simply would be a reprise of the episode of the Flight to Egypt as described in Mt 2:13–15, and only a very indirect connection could be made to Q 19. We will presently see that the corresponding formulations in the Qur'an are better explained in a different way. Let us therefore in conclusion

91 Kästle, 'Die Mutter Jesu im Johannesevangelium', 316.

92 Cf. ibid., 317.

93 Cf. Konrad Huber, 'Wer ist diese Frau? Biblische Texte, die nachträglich auf Maria hin gelesen werden.' In: *BiKi* 68 (2013) 203–207, here 204.

attempt to summarise the image of Mary as presented in the Bible. After this diachronic consideration of the various theological elements, we should at least by way of experiment attempt to synthesise these elements and come up with an initial overview of the figure of Mary. In doing so, we will follow the chronology of events and try to combine the different New Testament theological sketches into a synchronic overall picture, in order that we may gain an initial theological foothold on the figure of Mary.

e) Summary

According to the evidence of the New Testament, as a young girl of perhaps twelve, Mary learns from an angel that she will become pregnant through the power of the Holy Spirit. Anyone who tries to picture this scene will immediately realise the great distress this incident must cause Mary. After all, who nowadays would take a young girl seriously who attributed her pregnancy at such a tender age to supernatural powers? And even though belief in God was undoubtedly more widespread in the ancient world than it is today, we should not imagine the reaction of those around Mary to have been any more comprehending than we are today when we confront this story head-on without the filter of faith. Thus, to begin with, the supposed Virgin Birth puts Mary in a very difficult situation. Initially, even her partner turns against her, and we too can scarcely understand her.

Nonetheless, she has an angel of God on her side. For us modern individuals, it is by no means easy to envision such a phenomenon. Our first thought is to regard angels as apparitions and so imagine that Mary must have been insane. But in biblical and Qur'anic thought, the angel is a highly reliable image of God's benevolent presence. So, in the face of the scepticism she encounters all around her, Mary can place her trust in this caring power of God and accept her challenging assignment. In turn, thanks to the angel's acting as an intermediary, Mary's fiancé Joseph comes round to supporting her. One might actually imagine that it shouldn't have first required an angel's mediation for a person's own partner to start trusting them. Perhaps one might even go so far as to say that a relationship in which a man first has to be persuaded by a supernatural agency to believe his partner when she confides her innermost secrets to him doesn't have much of a future. Yet we surely ought not take the relationship between Mary and Joseph to be the model of a romantic love life. And although Joseph is ultimately brought back into line through divine intervention, during the most significant crises in her life, Mary repeatedly finds herself alone – without the support of either her husband or her family.

This solitary and courageous young woman comes from a poor, entirely insignificant family and lives her life far distant from any important political events. Her lowliness, poverty and simplicity makes her quite literally a handmaiden and a servant. Yet for all her lowly status, by virtue of her faith and through being chosen by God, she participates in something truly momentous. Even so, this greatness, this glory does not negate her lowliness but instead is locked into a dialectical relationship with it. Therefore, it is precisely in her lowliness and poverty that she is God's servant, who draws attention to his might and grandeur while at the same time qualifying it.

Through the angel's agency, Mary is taken into service by God. She does not simply passively allow this to happen to her, however, but instead chooses to dig deeper, to reflect on her destiny and enquire exactly what will become of her. Fearlessly, she poses her questions, though she is also able to retain the words and deeds she encounters silently and reflectively in her heart and in this way to gradually find existential answers to her questions. At any rate, she wants practical answers to her questions, not simply to be overwhelmed by God's sheer might. But she is also patient and at the decisive moment she comes to trust God implicitly – albeit still without comprehending everything. She risks putting all her eggs in one basket. She gives her *fiat* long before she can even foresee how she will set about organising support from those closest to her or how she will manage her life with her new child.

It is impressive how forthrightly and unreservedly she allows herself to be taken into service. We have seen how she gains the courage to give her assent by considering the history of Israel and placing her own contemporary experience in this context. She can trust the voice of the angel and agree to give birth to Jesus Christ because she finds within her experience traces of the historically powerful God to whose existence the scriptures of Israel bear witness. It is therefore ultimately the courage and trust in the historical might of God which Mary possesses as a Jew that enable her to give her *fiat*. And concrete signs such as Elizabeth's pregnancy confirm her in her decision. She believes in God as the Lord of History and is not prepared to release him from his responsibility. Rather than identify the events of this world with God's will and so invest them with benevolent religious significance, she uses the history of Israel to remind God of his pledges and promises. Because God has done great things for Israel and has given her a sign that she will experience such things in her life too, she demands on a large scale that a societal order be instituted in which the lowly shall be raised up and God's all-embracing justice enacted. Instead of affirming the political legitimacy of the existing order, she prophetically sketches out the vision of a new world order shaped by God. Once embarked on this path of faith, she is ready to read everyday signs as confirmation and to place her trust in God even when her understanding is stretched to its very limits.

Equipped with this faith, Mary willingly accompanies Jesus on his public ministry, during which she attempts to moderate his radicalism and to encourage him to follow certain basic practical commonsense rules. For perfectly understandable reasons, she gets into conflict with him and is forced to watch him grow apart from her. All the same, she endures this distance between them and stays faithful to the God of Israel by remaining at her son's side and drawing people's attention to him. Her whole existence therefore increasingly becomes a pointer towards Jesus. She points to him and trusts in him, she holds him to his obligations, and irritates him by alerting him to the suffering of those around her. In this way, she becomes visible as a sign pointing towards Jesus.

Mary, the contemplative questioner, who takes on responsibility in her *fiat* and who from a Christian point of view facilitates God's benevolent approach to humankind, is also ultimately ready to attest to God's solicitude through love, and consequently to take on all the pain that results from humankind's rejection of that love. At the end, she brings succour to the crucified Christ and becomes his disciple. As such, she becomes someone who increasingly effaces herself and who through her existence as the handmaid of the Lord facilitates God's work. The brutality of the destructive power of the Cross finds its counterpart in her renunciation of herself in favour of a loving God. It is precisely in this active passivity, this glorious lowliness and this potent powerlessness that Mary bears witness to the Christian faith.

2

Mary in Patristics

The way in which the figure of Mary is treated in patristics is far too multi-faceted and complex for us to even begin to cover it in detail here. As a result, to an even greater extent than in the preceding chapter on the Bible, in the following pages our focus should be on looking for clues relating to the way in which the figure of Mary is presented in the Qur'an. Accordingly, in the expositions that follow, alongside the Protevangelium of James, we will concentrate exclusively on the works of the Syriac Church Fathers. For recent research has demonstrated ever more clearly that the Qur'an was primarily in dialogue with this element of the Christian tradition.[1] The principal figures of interest here are Ephrem the Syrian (306–373) and Jacob of Serugh (451–521), since it was they who exerted a decisive influence on the liturgy of the Syriac Church in Late Antiquity. There is also much evidence to suggest that they are the theologians who are discussed at the greatest length in the Qur'an.

a) The Protevangelium of James

The so-called Protevangelium of James (henceforth abbreviated to ProtEvJam) – which is actually far more a partial biography of Mary up to the birth of Christ than it is a 'gospel' – was in all probability written in the second half of the second century and forms part of the so-called Christian Apocrypha. In other words, this text is not one of the scriptures that became canonical or was officially approved by the Church; instead it is an expression of popular Christian piety. However, in contrast to other apocryphal texts, the ProtEvJam was never regarded as heretical

1 Cf. Griffith, 'The poetics of scriptural reasoning', Chap. 4; Madigan, *The Qur'ân's self-image*, 198.

by the major Christian churches in antiquity, but was respected as a testament to popular devotion. Likewise, the ProtEvJam came to exercise a strong influence on the further development of the cult of Mary and Mariology.[2] It was especially popular in the Eastern Churches and was even used in services on specific occasions: Not only hymns and church iconography but also liturgical feasts like that of Saints Joachim and Anne or the Presentation of Mary in the Temple, which were subsequently adopted by the Western Church too, are based on the ProtEvJam. The ProtEvJam was translated from an early date into all the languages of ancient Christianity – Latin, Syriac, Coptic, Armenian, and Georgian – and in light of this we can be certain that it was widespread in the region where the Qur'an came into being.[3] In terms of content, it is the first text to evince a clear special interest in Mary. It is a hagiographic portrayal of the life of Mary from her birth up to the birth of Christ.[4] The text maps out what is for the period a very appealing narrative theology, which is specifically aimed at fleshing out all the instances of vagueness which appear in Lk. As its central message, it develops the doctrine of the perpetual virginity of Mary.

The text generates the following narrative line: Joachim, who is expressly depicted as a very rich, upstanding and devout man (ProtEvJam 1) and his wife Anne pray desperately for a child (ProtEvJam 2). Finally an angel of the Lord appears, who promises that Anne will bear a child, and in gratitude Anne pledges to dedicate the child to the Temple – regardless of whether it turns out to be a girl or a boy (ProtEvJam 4). Without having lain with her husband Joachim again, she is delivered of a girl, to whom she gives the name Mary (ProtEvJam 5).

When Mary is three years old, Anne puts her in the care of a priest, who greets

2 Cf. Greshake, *Maria-Ecclesia*, 195; on the Coptic tradition cf. Horn, 'Mary between Bible and Qur'an', 513–529.

3 In the post-Qur'anic period, translations of the ProtEvJam then swiftly followed into Arabic, Ethiopian (Ge'ez), and Old Church Slavonic (cf. Toepel, *Das Protevangelium des Jakobus*, 16–31 and 272 ff.).

4 It is no coincidence that the ProtEvJam comes from around the same period in which the Martyrdom of Polycarp of Smyrna – in other words the very first instance of a liturgical veneration of a saint in Christendom – and also the apocryphal Acts of Peter (Actus Vercellensis) were written. The ProtEvJam appears to be precisely the hagiographic text that the veneration of Mary that was evolving at that time called for, even though this tendency did not immediately take on tangible shape in the form of a liturgical celebration. Moreover, this also holds good *mutatis mutandis* for the Acts of Peter. Incidentally, the fact that the ProtEvJam ends with the birth of Christ and not with the death of Mary fits in well with the liturgical development of her adoration which then ensued. For the first liturgical feast of Marian devotion evolved – most likely from the fourth century on – in connection with Christmas (and not with her Dormition).

her by blessing her (ProtEvJam 7:2); 'and all the house of Israel loved her' (ProtEvJam 7:3). Mary remains in the Temple until the age of twelve, when following a council of priests under the High Priest Zacharias, who commands that all the widowers of the people should assemble, 'and let each of them bring a rod, and to whomsoever the Lord shall show a sign, his wife shall she be!' (ProtEvJam 8:3), '...and behold, a dove came out of the rod and flew upon Joseph's head' (ProtEvJam 9:1), thus clearly indicating that Mary should be taken into the care of Joseph, who is already very advanced in years and has grown-up children (ProtEvJam 9:2). He is expected to receive Mary 'as a virgin' and to 'watch over' her (ProtEvJam 13).

After another council of priests, a number of virgins are chosen by lot to make a veil for the Temple of the Lord: '...and the true purple and the scarlet fell to the lot of Mary' (ProtEvJam 10:2). Having thus been involved in the project, she becomes active as a seamstress. One day, while drawing water from a well, Mary hears a voice saying: 'Hail, you who have received grace; the Lord is with you; blessed are you among women!' (ProtEvJam 11:1). Mary cannot understand where this voice is coming from and is afraid. Only then does an angel of the Lord appear to her and announce the impending birth of Jesus (ProtEvJam 11:3), and she answers him by giving the *fiat* from Lk 1:38. Yet at this point the Holy Spirit is missing; it is only identified by name as the cause of the Virgin Birth in ProtEvJam 19:1.

When Joseph returns from a journey he has had to undertake for his work and finds that Mary is pregnant, he questions her moral integrity and heaps accusations on her (ProtEvJam 13) that are only dispelled when the angel of the Lord appears to him in a dream. The priest in the Temple is similarly sceptical (ProtEvJam 15:2), but because both Mary and Joseph survive the 'ordeal of the (poisoned) water of the Lord' (cf. Numbers 5:11–31) and the ensuing banishment to the desert, the priest is ultimately convinced of Mary's virginity (ProtEvJam 16).

To help Mary with her confinement in a cave near Bethlehem, Joseph specially engages the services of a Hebrew midwife, who is instantly struck by the miracle of Mary's virginity. An acquaintance of the midwife by the name of Salome, however, is only prepared to believe after convincing herself by putting her fingers into Mary's vagina to test whether her hymen is still intact (ProtEvJam 19:3) – a scene that is completely analogous, even in its choice of words, to that of 'doubting Thomas' in Jn 20:25. Later, Mary lays the child in a manger in an ox-stall in order to conceal him from Herod's persecution (ProtEvJam 22:2). Once again, the mother and child are saved thanks to the help of the angel of the Lord (ProtEvJam 22:3). The book ends with the murder of Zacharias, who is replaced as High Priest by Simeon (ProtEvJam 24). For the author of the Protevangelium, this innocently spilt blood in the vestibule of the Temple seems to mark the decisive turning-point in the story of salvation, with Mary being seen allegorically as the rightful heiress of the priestly cult and the new Temple.[5]

As already noted, the ProtEvJam, which was originally known as 'The Birth of Mary – Revelation of James' or the 'Genesis Marias', develops for the first time in the history of Christian literature a special mariological interest. In the process, it eclipses the Christological nucleus of the treatment of Mary in the New Testament. This is why Protestant commentators often criticise this text for being the first instance where Mariology displaces Christology.[6] However, because the ProtEvJam is not a gospel but a partial biography of Mary, which is specifically intended to promote the veneration of Mary as a saint, this criticism is somewhat one-sided. Moreover, the Christological orientation is preserved through the fact that the book ends with the birth of Jesus Christ and not the death of Mary. In addition, the theme of saintliness in the book remains tied to 'inward asceticism and abstention from anything ritually unclean and from all sexual activity.'[7] Mary's transformation in the ProtEvJam seems to mirror exactly the lifestyle of Christian ascetics of the second century. At that stage, there was still no such thing as organised monasticism, meaning that people who pursued an ascetic lifestyle lived within the community – often within the parental home – and so played a part in determining its devotional practices and ideals.[8] Ultimately the purpose of the book is to socially upgrade the family of Jesus. Joachim and Anne are presented as distinguished representatives of Israel, and Joseph as a prosperous carpenter and builder. All traces of poverty and birth in a stable have been expunged. By contrast, in antiquity being born in a cave was a favourite motif in accounts of the birth of divine children.[9]

5 Cf. Ghaffar, *Der Koran in seinem religions- und weltgeschichtlichen Kontext*, 32 f.

6 Cf. Becker, *Mutter Jesu und erwählte Jungfrau*, 274.

7 Becker, *Mutter Jesu und erwählte Jungfrau*, 275.

8 Cf. Goehring, *Ascetics, society and the desert*, 20 and 24; Bumazhnov, 'Some further observations concerning the early history of the term ΜΟΝΑΧΟΣ (monk)', 21–26; cf. also Pevarello, *The Sentences of Sextus and the Origins of Christian Asceticism*, esp. 209 f.

9 According to Hesiod, even the father of the gods Zeus was taken by his mother Gaia (= Earth) to a cave immediately after his birth and hidden there (Hesiod, *Theogony*, 453–491). Hermes likewise was born in a cave. And finally Eileithyia, the 'midwife goddess' who assisted mothers in labour, was also associated with caves, at least where her cult was concerned (Pausanias 1, 18, 5). In addition, caves played a central role in the Roman cult of Mithras, which was especially prevalent in the Near East during the imperial period; cf. also the discussion among scholars regarding whether Mithras might have been born in a cave (or just 'out of the rock'), reported in Alvar, *Romanising Oriental Gods*, 409, f. 73 (cf. also ibid., 410 f., on whether 25 December was Mithras's birthday).

In the literature of Late Antiquity, a book about Mary dating from the fifth century at the latest has come down to us, which portrays the whole of her life from her birth to her death.[10] This book was most probably a compilation of excerpts from the Protevangelium of James, the Infancy Gospel of Thomas and the Dormitio Mariae,[11] with the Infancy Gospel of Thomas only being added sometime during the sixth century.[12] The creation of the Dormitio Mariae has a great deal to do with the fact that a central aspect of the veneration of saints consisted in celebrating the death date of the individual in question as a day of remembrance. The relevant information for this event was missing in the Mary tradition, and accordingly this gap was filled by the apocryphal legends of her 'Dormition' or 'Assumption' (*transitus*). Over time this first gave rise, in the Eastern churches, to a Feast of the Dormition of Mary, and subsequently in the West to the Feast of the Assumption of Mary.[13]

It is intriguing to note at this point that the Qur'an ignores this tradition; in so doing, it insists upon linking Mariology to Christology and sets its face against any treatment of Mariology in isolation. However, we do not want to pre-empt our study of the Qur'an here. Besides, for all its lack of interest in the death of Mary, the image of her presented in the Qur'an is unequivocally engaged in dialogue with the apocryphal literature of Christianity.

The fact that not just the death of Mary but also her entire life became the focus of ever greater attention also has to do with the anthropological shift that occurred in Late Antiquity, which helped to 'highlight Mary's position as an individual to such an extent that she became detached from her former purely soteriological field of reference.'[14] Even though talk of an anthropological shift can be more readily substantiated with reference to the soteriological developments in the Latin Church, it also holds good for the Eastern Churches too if one relates it to the ever greater emphasis on male and female saints that became evident during this period.[15] Increasingly therefore, a special interest in other saintly figures comes to mirror the newly developed special interest in Mary apparent in the ProtEvJam. It is only in the context of the Council of Ephesus, in other words from the fifth century onwards, that Mariology begins to evolve into a systematic

10 Cf. Horn, 'Syriac and Arabic perspectives', 270–272.
11 Cf. ibid., 272, footnote 8.
12 Cf. ibid., 278.
13 Eggemann, *Die 'ekklesiologische Wende' in der Mariologie des II. Vatikanums*, 12.
14 Ibid., 8.
15 Cf. the groundbreaking essay by Brown, 'The rise and function of the Holy Man in late antiquity', 80–101. Cf. also the more recent study by Doerfler, 'The Holy Man in the Courts of Rome', 192–211.

theological 'treatise' distinct from Christology and to take on an anthropologically and prophetologically revealing life of its own.[16] As the writings of the Syriac Church Fathers also document, in this doctrine Mary takes centre stage in all her virginity and purity. At the same time, she appears typologically as a new Eve, and hence as an archetype of successful humanity per se. We will therefore subsume the depiction of Mary by the Syriac Church Fathers under these guiding principles as we consider first her characterisation as as the new Eve (b) and hence as the primal image of the Church (c), before proceeding to investigate her purity and lack of sin (d), and her virginity (e).

b) Mary as the New Eve

The veneration of Mary as the new Eve begins even in the Protevangelium of James,[17] though this motif is subsequently expanded upon by such early Christian writers as Justin Martyr, and later Irenaeus of Lyons and finally Jerome in the West and Gregory of Nyssa in the East.[18] This interpretative tradition lives on in Catholic theology to the present day. Gisbert Greshake, for example, talks about Mary as the new Eve: 'In the same way that Christ through his life and death made good the misdeeds of Adam, so Mary rehabilitated the misdeeds of Eve through her obedience.'[19] This Adam–Christ typology, which was first posited by Paul, is thus supplemented with an Eve–Mary typology – with all the ramifications that this entails, even for the doctrine of salvation (soteriology).

Consonant with our aim of discussing the Qur'anic tradition where it impinges on Mary, we will concentrate in the following on how the Syriac Church Fathers enlarge upon the parallels between Eve and Mary. In the Christian tradition, there are two different ways of understanding the Eve–Mary typology. The first, more dynamic construction proceeds from the assumption that although Mary is affected to begin with by the consequences of the fall of man and therefore suffers from original sin, she later frees herself from its grip by giving birth to Jesus. In this line of thought, which represents the mainstream of the Syriac tradition, the typical Christocentricity of the biblical viewpoint is preserved. This is the construction that is clearly preferred by Ephrem the Syrian and Jacob of Serugh. The second,

16 At the time when the ProtEvJam was written, no dogmatic treatise on Mariology yet existed. Similarly, we only find treatise-like sermons on this subject from the fifth century CE onwards. Accordingly, it is only meaningful to talk in terms of Mariology after this period.

17 Cf. Müller and Sattler, 'Mariologie', 166.

18 Cf. Gerwing, 'Mariologie', 414; Müller and Sattler, 'Mariologie', 168.

19 Greshake, *Maria-Ecclesia*, 139.

more static reading conceives of Mary as the new Eve, who is spared all along from the consequences of the fall.[20] This understanding is nowhere to be found among the earliest Church Fathers, nor have we been able to verify that it appears anywhere in Syriac literature. In the final analysis, both viewpoints led to a blossoming of Marian veneration and to a more intense dedication to the figure of Mary.

Ephrem the Syrian writes about Eve and Mary that 'one is the cause of our death, the other (the cause) of our life.'[21] In his view, it is ultimately Mary's *fiat* that overcomes the dominion of death and makes new life possible.[22] Just as Eve was the mother of the old life, he claims, so Mary is the mother of the new life.[23] She is, he maintains, the good eye, through which people once more find their way back to faith in God.[24]

Jacob of Serugh picks up this idea and formulates its even more pointedly: 'Through her [i.e. Mary] remission is granted to all those burdened with debt... Through her, the barred route to paradise is opened up once more, the snake is put to flight, and people gain free access to God.'[25] Michael Schmaus has taken such passages as a reason to claim that Jacob believed that Mary had 'redeemed and destroyed the promissory note of her mother Eve.'[26] Jacob (according to Schmaus) was firmly convinced that, through her, the curse of sin had been overcome.[27]

Of course, we are also never in any doubt in Jacob's work that Mary's role in freeing us from sin always remains constantly bound to God's actions through Jesus Christ. Nonetheless, Jacob's formulations are sometimes ambiguous. At least from our modern perspective, the impression can arise of Mary radiating some kind of '"redemptive" power right back to the very beginnings of humankind and throughout the entire history of salvation.'[28] In accordance with this, some Syriac hymns from Late Antiquity maintain that Mary leads us back to Eden[29] and expunges all traces of the serpent.[30]

---

20 Cf. Brock, 'Introduction'. In: Jacob of Serugh, *On the mother of God*, 1–14, here p. 9.
21 Ephraem der Syrer, *Hymnen de ecclesia*, 35,1.
22 Cf. Ashkar, *Mary in the Syriac Christian tradition and Islam*, 94: 'Ephraem clarifies that life and death entered humanity through the fiat of Mary and through the seduction of Eve, respectively.'
23 Cf. ibid., 72.
24 Cf. ibid., 71.
25 Jakob von Sarug, 'Gedicht über die selige Jungfrau und Gottesmutter Maria', 245.
26 Schmaus, *Mariologie*, 291.
27 Jakob von Sarug, 'Gedicht über die selige Jungfrau und Gottesmutter Maria', 229.
28 Grass, *Traktat über Mariologie*, 30.
29 Cf. Ps-Ephraem der Syrer, 'Marienhymnen', 27, 30.
30 Cf. ibid., 28,2.

Hence, from a Christian viewpoint this gives rise to 'the danger of somehow levelling off Christ's incomparability with the figure of Mary, and of an increasing tendency to equate their two roles within the story of salvation.'[31] Such equating of Mariology and Christology is not borne out in the Bible.[32] As a result of this, it is interesting to note the repeated attempts that are made in the Western–Latin tradition to manipulate the biblical text in order to justify its raising of the profile of Mariology. Thus, in the majority of Vulgate manuscripts of Genesis 3:15d, the masculine 'ipse' is changed into the feminine 'ipsa', meaning that it is now the woman Eve herself who crushes the serpent's head.[33] So, in the typological interpretation of this passage of scripture, it is no longer Christ who overcomes the power of the serpent but Mary. The Reformation period raised a new awareness in this regard, the upshot of which was that Jesus – in contrast to the Marian piety of the Catholic tradition – was once again given full credit as the person who alone has the power to conquer evil and hence to crush the head of the serpent; this reading became universal in modern biblical exegesis, even on the Catholic side.[34]

In this passage, Jacob of Serugh – in common with the Syriac translation of the Bible – retains the original wording. In his writings also, it is Christ alone who crushes the serpent's head.[35] However, it is Mary who, through her *fiat*, first enables Jesus Christ to undertake his act of redemption. Therefore, when Jacob ascribes greater powers to Mary that many modern Christians are prepared to concede, this is not because he has lost sight, say, of the essential Christocentricity of every Christian theology. But he does take every opportunity to explore the potential for human involvement in Christ's redemptive actions on the basis of the figure of Mary. He too is adamant that all salvation comes from God alone, who became man in Jesus Christ. Yet this self-affirmation requires human assent if it is to resonate with people. And for Jacob, such resonance is realised in exemplary form by Mary's *fiat*. Only when mediated through this Christocentric train of thought can he write that we are are fulfilled in Mary and that our resurrection is imparted to us through her.[36] And he is also able to say that Mary has given us a

31 Eisele, 'Krieg und Frieden', 190.

32 Cf. ibid., 192.

33 Cf. ibid., 193.

34 Cf. ibid., 194.

35 Cf. Jacob of Serugh, *On the mother of God: Homily III*, 82: 'through me the reproach of Eve is removed from womanhood. The babe who is in me will crush the head of the great serpent.'

36 Cf. ibid. I, 33: 'By that former the fall, by the latter resurrection for all our race; sin by Eve but righteousness from within Mary.'

sweet fruit full of life, so that through her we might be able to dwell with the Lord for all eternity.[37] He addresses Mary in prayer and thanks her: 'You have settled Eve's account.'[38] And so – mediated through Christ – she enters an original state of righteousness and becomes like Adam before his fall from grace.[39] Through her *fiat*, the repercussions of the fall of man are finally healed.[40]

It is interesting how Jacob takes the demeanour of Mary that is depicted in Lk as an opportunity to expound his own thoughts. Thus, he too acknowledges the tough critical questions that we have also entertained in our enquiries and finally comes to see Mary as a typological counterpart to Eve. Where Eve, he claims, simply accepted the advice of the serpent without comment, Mary assiduously questioned how the events that were foretold might come to pass. In doing so, Jacob believes, she demonstrates not only her shrewdness but also her distance from Eve.[41] Solely as a result of her questioning, he maintains, does the truth about God's salvation become intelligible reality in the first place.[42] While Eve, then, unquestioningly succumbs to temptation, Mary poses a whole series of questions in the Annunciation scene[43] and in the process becomes the epitome of faith.

c) Mary as the archetype of the Church

In ancient Christianity, the stylisation of Mary as the epitome of faith and the anti-Eve quickly led to her also being seen as the archetype of the Church. In this regard, scholarly literature speaks in terms of a merging of the parallels between Eve and Mary and those between Eve and the Church.[44] This development began as early as the time of the Syriac Church Fathers, though it only became a standard component of Mariology in the post-Qur'anic period. In the West, Ambrose was probably the first person to describe Mary as the archetype of the Church. 'What he meant by this was that Mary is the epitome, the embodiment and the

37 Cf. ibid., 40: 'She gave us a sweet fruit, full of life, that we might eat from it and live forever with God.'
38 Ibid. I, 19.
39 Ibid., I, 36. Strictly speaking, Jacob states that Mary resembled Adam before he fell from grace. At this point, therefore, Jacob could also be read in the sense of the aforementioned static Mariology, though this would not fairly reflect his work as a whole.
40 Cf. Söll, *Mariologie*, 103.
41 Cf. Jacob of Serugh's homilies on the nativity. First Homily, v. 220–226.
42 Cf. ibid., v. 360: 'without request not even the truth is able to demonstrate itself.'
43 Cf. Brock, 'Introduction', 4.
44 Cf. Gerwing, 'Mariologie', 414.

ideal form of the Church.'[45] Augustine of Hippo also corroborated this tradition.[46] By contrast, in the Greek East, this identification of Mary with the Church – which throughout the entire body of Marian literature produced in this period only appears once, in a sermon whose author and date are uncertain – had not become established by Late Antiquity.[47]

For Ephrem the Syrian, it is precisely the typological parallelising of Eve and Mary that induces him to identify Mary typologically with the Church and to see prophecy fulfilled in both.[48] The typological identification of Mary with the Church works, he claims, on two levels – for one thing, Mary is understood as the mother of Christ, but then she is also the daughter of Christ inasmuch as her second birth in baptism is made possible through him.[49] In any event, everything is simultaneous in the sanctified age of God, meaning that Ephrem does not simply experience these apparent paradoxes as negative but also extols them as a manifestation of the majesty of God that surpasses all human understanding.[50] In his *Hymn on the Nativity of Christ in the Flesh*, Ephrem writes: 'Blessed are you, O Church, for lo! Over you – Isaiah also exults in his prophecy – Lo a Virgin shall conceive and bear – a Son whose name is a powerful symbol! O interpretation

45 Schmaus, *Mariologie*, 294.

46 Cf. Laato, Eve, Rebecca, and Mary as prophetical images of the church.

47 Greshake, *Maria-Ecclesia*, 357, following Henri de Lubac, comes to a different conclusion here. He points to a strict identification of the Church with Mary, which is to be found in a sermon (CPG 5248) attributed to Cyril of Alexandria (cf. Greshake, *Maria-Ecclesia*, 154). However, as Greshake himself notes, this sermon could be a pseudepigraphon, i.e. a work that is not by Cyril but by a later, unknown author. The question of authenticity remains unclear. Münch-Labacher, 'Cyrill von Alexandrien', 176, regards the sermon as 'probably inauthentic'; other commentators, however – among them Wessel, *Cyril of Alexandria and the Nestorian controversy*, 224 f. – proceed from the assumption that it is genuine; cf. ibid., 'Nestorius, Mary and Controversy in Cyril of Alexandria's Homily IV.' (De Maria deipara in Nestorium, CPG 5248). In: *Annuarium Historiae Conciliorum* 31 (1999) 1–49. Yet regardless of whether it is authentic or not, this sermon must have been written in the fifth century, since it would otherwise be hard to explain how it could have found its way into the Acts of the Council of Ephesus. However, this finding alone cannot alter the bigger picture: although, as de Lubac points out, the Greek Church Fathers repeatedly associated Mary and the Church with the same biblical symbols (Jacob's Ladder, the Ark of the Covenant, the Temple etc.), it seems they were at pains not to identify them directly with one another. Even so, the fact that such an identification was not yet commonplace at the time does not mean that the Greek Church Fathers had any fundamental objection to the typological identification of Mary with the Church.

48 Cf. Murray, 'Mary, the second Eve in the early Syriac fathers', 380.

49 Brock, 'St. Ephrem on Christ as light in Mary and in the Jordan', 141.

50 Cf. ibid.

(of the symbol) revealed in the Church!'[51] A similar identification of the Church with Mary as a virgin is also found in Jacob of Serugh when he writes: 'When she posed this question, the wise Virgin was the mouthpiece of the Church, and listened to the explanation for the whole of creation.'[52] Yet in spite of these isolated instances, the typological identification of Mary with the Church was not nearly as widespread in the Syriac Church as her image as the new Eve at the time when the Qur'an came into existence. Among the Eastern Church Fathers, talk of Mary as the archetype of the Temple or as the new Ark of the Covenant was on the whole more important than her identification as the archetype of the Church, even though the two ideas are of course connected.

d) Mary's purity and lack of sin

Right from the beginning, the central linchpin of the veneration of Mary was the idea that, through her freely given and courageous decision to trust the Angel Gabriel and to assent to conceiving her son, Mary set in motion the entire process by which God became man. As a result, the Syriac Church Fathers repeatedly stress the enabling role played by Mary at this very earliest stage of the act of Incarnation.[53] Generally speaking, therefore, a dialectical relationship of grace and freedom evolves with regard to Mary. Thus, on the one hand the Syriac Church Fathers point out Mary's great advantages, presenting her in all her beauty, humility and purity.[54] Mary is characterised by this beauty and purity right from her mother's womb.[55] It was precisely Mary's beauty that prompted God to choose her as the mother of his son.[56] For, according to Jacob of Serugh, no human soul was more magnificent and sacred than hers,[57] and no woman was so completely pure as she was.[58] To quote Jacob verbatim: 'It would be easier to picture the radiance and the heat of the sun than to give an account of the splendour of Mary.'[59]

51 Ephrem the Syrian, *Hymnen de nativitate*, 117 (= Hymnus 25, Strophe 5).

52 Jakob von Sarug, 'Gedicht über die selige Jungfrau und Gottesmutter Maria', 244.

53 Brock thus highlights the 'emphasis one finds, throughout Syriac literature, that the Annunciation, and Mary's role there, is the crucial starting point for the events of the Incarnation: in other words, the view is taken that, without Mary, the Incarnation would not have taken place' (Brock, 'Introduction', 3).

54 Cf. Jacob of Serugh, *On the mother of God: Homily I*, 21–24.

55 Cf. Grass, *Traktat über Mariologie*, 26.

56 Cf. Jacob of Serugh, *On the mother of God: Homily I*, 33.

57 Cf. ibid. I, 23.

58 Cf. Jakob von Sarug, 'Gedicht über die selige Jungfrau und Gottesmutter Maria', 234.

59 Ibid., 230.

Jacob even goes so far as to justify Mary's selection on the grounds of her beauty, which existed prior to her being chosen. However, in the usage of the Syriac Church Fathers, the concept of 'beauty' meant first and foremost also being inwardly beautiful and virtuous.[60] His argument runs thus: God would surely have chosen another woman if she had pleased him more.[61] At points such as this, one sometimes gets the impression that Mary might even have further merits that lie beyond the grace of God. But time and again, Jacob returns to the elective power of God, which enabled this special nature of Mary to exist in the first place. So, on the one hand Mary only becomes beautiful through exercising her free will and is also praised on this account.[62] On the other hand, however, her beauty and purity are gifts that have been endowed upon her from the very outset by God's grace.

Ephrem the Syrian in particular makes clear the extent to which Mary's purity first requires the agency of Jesus Christ. Ephrem has been wrongly cited as the first Syriac Church Father to teach the doctrine of Mary's immaculate conception.[63] Certainly, just like Jacob he emphasises how beautiful and pure Mary is from the start.[64] But at the same time, Ephrem also expounds the idea that Jesus Christ is the only person wholly without sin,[65] and stresses that Mary is first baptised in Christ and also that this baptism is essential in order to preserve her purity. In his writings, Mary emerges as the first individual to be absolved of sin through baptism, and Ephrem sees this baptism as residing in her conception of Jesus.[66] In other words, Mary is born anew from her son, and cleansed of sin through him. In similar fashion, Jacob of Serugh also proceeds from the assumption that Mary is freed from sin, including original sin, from the moment she conceives Jesus,

60 In the light of such quotations, Grass, *Traktat über Mariologie*, 27, draws attention to disconcertingly erotic features of Mary's beauty. However, these jarring elements only arise as a result of rather one-dimensional translations, which render the Syriac adjective meaning 'good' and/or 'beautiful' (and related words from the same ambiguous root) simply as 'beautiful' – which immediately puts the reader in mind of outward beauty.

61 Cf. Jacob of Serugh, *On the mother of God: Homily I*, 26: 'If another had pleased more than her, He would have chosen that one, for the Lord does not respect persons since He is just and right.'

62 Cf. Jacob of Serugh, *On the Blessed Virgin and Mother of God Mary*, 235.

63 Cf. Ashkar, *Mary in the Syriac Christian tradition and Islam*, 73, with reference to Hilda Graef, *Mary: A History of Doctrine and Devotion*, New York 1963, 57.

64 Cf. Ashkar, *Mary in the Syriac Christian tradition and Islam*, 73 in connection with the Nisibene Hymns (27,8).

65 Cf. Beck, 'Die Mariologie der echten Schriften Ephräms', 27.

66 Cf. ibid., 32.

though for Jacob this is a necessary prerequisite for the conception of Jesus that the Holy Spirit effects prior to the event.[67]

For all their mariological enthusiasm, therefore, the Mariology of Ephrem and Jacob remains emphatically Christocentric. And notwithstanding all her advantages, Mary does still require cleansing.[68] At the same time, though, she is so pure by virtue of her connection with Christ that she can become the model for all human life *per se*. Yet it is not merely her status as a role model for human existence that the Syriac Church Fathers consider important, but also her virginity.

e) Virginity and labour pains

With the idea of Mary's virginity before the birth of Jesus, the Syriac Church Fathers are operating entirely within the general mainstream of the Christian literature of Late Antiquity. Even within the logic of Lk, we have had cause to note how insistently the evangelist bears witness to Mary's virginity. In the same way that Elizabeth falls pregnant as an old woman, thereby entirely confounding the natural order of things, in Lk so too is the business of Jesus's conception an exceptional act of God within human history.[69] For the Syrian Philoxenus of Mabbug (450–523), the churchman who played the key role in spreading the doctrine of

67 Cf. Krüger, 'Die Frage der Erbsündigkeit der Gottesmutter im Schrifttume des Jakob von Serugh', 196. The idea of Mary's being free from original sin in the sense of later Catholic dogma could only be surmised on the basis of mistranslations of Jacob (cf. Puthuparampil, *Mariological thought of Mar Jacob of Serugh*, 84).

68 Cf. Jacob of Serugh, *On the mother of God: Homily I*, 35: 'He purified the Mother by the Holy Spirit while dwelling in her, that He might take from her a pure body without sin.'

69 Cf. Ashkar, *Mary in the Syriac Christian tradition and Islam*, 80. With particular reference to the narrative structure of Lk 1–2, Wolter explains that it it impossible to determine the precise verse or verses in which the narrator of the Gospel of Luke presumes that Jesus has been conceived (cf. Wolter, *Theologie und Ethos im frühen Christentum*, 336). Wolter also highlights this chronological ambivalence in the narrative structure in his commentary on Luke's gospel: *Die Skizzierung des zeitgeschichtlichen Hintergrunds in V. 1–3 (4) hat also keine andere Funktion, als ein plausibles Szenario für Marias Reise nach Bethlehem aufzubauen. An einer Übereinstimmung mit der realen Enzyklopädie der Leser, die bereits in V. 4 arg strapaziert worden war, hat Lukas keinerlei Interesse. Dies wird auch daran erkennbar, dass er auf den* census *als den eigentlichen Grund für die Reise im Folgenden mit keinem Wort mehr eingeht.* ('The sole reason for sketching in the historical background in verses 1–3 (4) is to construct a plausible scenario for Mary's journey to Bethlehem. Luke does not have the slightest interest in matching his story to the real historical knowledge of his readers, whose credulity has already been severely strained in verse 4. This is also apparent from the fact that, in his ensuing account, no further mention is made of the census as the real reason for the journey') (Wolter, *Das Lukas-Evangelium*, 124). As a result, this extraordinary intervention by God in human history is characterised on a narrative level by an element of indeterminacy.

miaphysitism throughout the Near East, it is clear that the Virgin Birth is a sign of Christ's divinity[70] – and this position remains paradigmatic for the Syriac Church. Jacob of Serugh also contends that Mary's virginity points in this same direction.[71] The only contentious issue was the question of whether this concept can also be applied to Mary during and after the birth of Jesus.

The background to the question of Mary's virginity during the birth of Jesus is the idea that women's labour pains are to be seen collectively as a consequence of the fall from grace. Genesis 3:16 expressly hints at this interpretation of labour pains being the result of original sin, and if Mary is regarded as the new Eve (see above, 'Mary as the New Eve'), it was a short step from there to conclude that her parturition must have been free of labour pains – at the same time, this was frequently regarded as a necessary concomitant to her preservation of virginity during the birth. And yet, no evidence of this theological interpretation can be identified in the works of the early Syriac Church Fathers; nor is there any mention of a connection between (absent) labour pains and (the preservation of) virginity during parturition. The only detail that was of importance to Ephrem the Syrian was that Mary suffered no harm as a result of giving birth.[72]

It is repeatedly claimed of Jacob of Serugh that he denied the existence of labour pains in the case of Mary. Indeed, Jacob's sermons portray the devil boasting that he has hitherto, ever since the time of Eve, seen to it that every woman invariably suffered labour pains,[73] and complaining about the fact that he can do nothing to harm Mary and her newborn infant.[74] It is not a great leap from quotations like this to the verdict of the secondary literature, namely that the writings that are attributed to Jacob of Serugh offer contradictory statements about whether Mary suffered labour pains or not.[75] Yet the words in the relevant passages that are frequently translated by the term '(labour) pains' are primarily to be assigned to the semantic field 'lesion/wound/injury', with the result that Jacob's denial of such 'pains' on Mary's part simply means – just as it does in the work of Ephrem – that she did not suffer any lasting harm from giving birth. Thus, what

70 Cf. Philoxenus of Mabbug, *Tractatus tres de trinitate et incarnatione*, 24.

71 Cf. Puthuparampil, *Mariological thought of Mar Jacob of Serugh*, 176.

72 Fiores, 'Maria in der Geschichte von Theologie und Frömmigkeit', 129 f. A corresponding assertion is made in Pseudo-Ephrem the Syrian, *Hymns on Mary*, 27,5 f. Brock, 'Mary in Syriac tradition', 184, cites further examples of this belief, which was clearly widespread.

73 Cf. Jacob of Serugh's homilies on the nativity. Second Homily, v. 188.

74 Cf. ibid., v. 197–200.

75 Cf. Krüger, 'Die Frage der Erbsündigkeit der Gottesmutter im Schrifttume des Jakob von Serugh', 203.

are unequivocally authentic texts by Jacob state clearly that, although the birth of Jesus passed off without any injury occurring to the intact body of the Virgin, he nonetheless emerged from her womb while she was in labour.[76] Evidently, the labour or pains mentioned here are meant to act as signs that Jesus Christ was a real human being; as such, they are significant in balancing out Jacob's miaphysitic Christology – i.e., his focus on Christ's divine nature.[77]

In common with Ephrem, therefore, Jacob also appears to represent the position that Mary – much to Satan's chagrin – remains unharmed by the birth, despite the fact that she had to endure the customary labour pains. Thus, Ephrem speaks of the intactness of the seal of virginity,[78] or of the silent seal and a doorway curtain.[79] And Jacob too refers to Mary as a sealed letter, 'within which the secrets and the profundities of the son are concealed.'[80] So, in describing her virginity, repeated use is made of the metaphor of the seal, which Mary embodies as the guardian of God's word.[81] The frequent use of this metaphor by the Syriac Church Fathers is of course striking in view of the prominent treatment of this term in the Qur'an. On a symbolic level, the decisive feature here is Mary's inviolacy and integrity, which through this very intactness points to the divinity of Jesus Christ's conception.

By comparison, the motif of the labour pains was only secondary and was evaluated in various different ways. The Syriac Church Fathers were in agreement that Mary's virginity did not just pertain to her life before the birth of Jesus but was a permanent part of her nature.[82] In Jacob von Serugh's writings, for example, the ideal of perpetual virginity is extolled time and again precisely because there were at that time a number of opponents of the notion of perpetual virginity within the Syriac Church. These opponents may have come from an eastern Syrian, anti-miaphysitic movement that was very strong at the time, which forbade deacons from remaining unmarried and sought to marginalise or even abolish monasticism (which was then increasingly under the influence of miaphysitism throughout

76 Cf. Jakob von Serug, *Die Kirche und die Forschung*, 18.

77 Likewise Krüger, 'Die Frage der Erbsündigkeit', 202 f., quotes Jacob in such a way that he is seen to attest to the idea of Jesus emerging from Mary's womb amid labour pains.

78 Cf. Ephrem the Syrian, *Hymnen de nativitate*, 12,2.

79 Cf. ibid., 12,5.

80 Jakob von Sarug, 'Gedicht über die selige Jungfrau und Gottesmutter Maria', 244; cf. Puthuparampil, *Mariological thought of Mar Jacob of Serugh*, 195–207.

81 Cf. Jacob of Serugh, *On the mother of God: Homily II*, 44. The metaphor of the seal also appears when Jesus is called upon to seal the law as the subject of prophesies (Jacob of Serugh's homilies on the nativity. Third Homily, v. 163), or when, in light of the Virgin Birth, God is called upon to set the seal on the law (Jacob of Serugh, *Select Festal Homilies*, 134).

82 Cf. Brock, 'Mary in Syriac tradition', 185.

Syria).[83] So, when Jacob repeatedly argues for Mary's virginity even after the birth of Jesus and in a long homily[84] refutes the counterarguments that were then in circulation, his aim was in all likelihood to lobby for a common viewpoint on this question within Syria and to indirectly adopt a particular position in a topical debate concerning ecclesiastical politics. In any event, Mary was seen as a role model for a celibate lifestyle[85] and so was well placed to become a guarantor of the connection between occupancy of a church office and celibacy.

One final detail should be mentioned here, however fleetingly, since it will be of significance presently for our study of Mary's role in the Qur'an. For Jacob of Serugh and many other Syriac Church Fathers it is important that Mary is aurally receptive and that the truth of Jesus Christ is imparted to her through her ear.[86] Just as Eve let herself be seduced into sin by the serpent whispering into her ear, so the rebirth of humanity in Mary is also made possible through the ear. But this only brings us back to the typological interpretation of Mary as the new Eve, which we have already dealt with above.

At this point it should be noted again for one final time why, despite their insistence upon the perpetual virginity of Mary and her characterisation as the new Eve, the overwhelming majority of the Syriac Church Fathers still tended to accept her labour pains as given. For this can only be plausibly explained by surmising that the Syriac tradition had already taken on board the biblically well attested role of Mary as a Mother of Sorrows (*mater dolorosa*). Of course, the primary point at issue here was the grief experienced by Mary on the death of Jesus.[87] But having accepted these sorrows, it is perfectly natural and reasonable to acknowledge her labour pains as well and see these as an integral part of Mary's journey through life.

83 Gerö, *Barsauma of Nisibis and Persian Christianity in the fifth century*, especially 46 ff. and 95; Kavvadas, 'Das ostsyrische Mönchtum im Spannungsfeld der großen Kirchenspaltung der nachchalkedonischen Zeit'.

84 Cf. Puthuparampil, *Mariological thought of Mar Jacob of Serugh*, 381 ff. ('Homily on the Perpetual Virginity of Mary').

85 Cf. Weedman, *Mary's Fertility As the Model of the Ascetical Life in Ephrem the Syrian's Hymns of the Nativity*, especially 172–181.

86 Cf. Jacob of Serugh, *On the mother of God: Homily I*, 30.

87 Cf. ibid. V, 90.

3

Dogmatic Precepts of Mariology

In this third chapter, too, we are not attempting to give a comprehensive account of all the dogmatic precepts of Mariology, but rather to process those facts that are of relevance for conducting a dialogue with the proclaimer of the Qur'an. Catholic tradition recognises a total of four so-called Marian dogmas. In the Catholic Church, the term 'dogma' denotes an article of faith which constitutes part of the binding creed of the church. Only one of the Marian dogmas is clearly treated and discussed the Qur'an. In consequence, we intend to begin with this dogma and to devote most of our discussion in this chapter to it. In doing so, we will also draw direct connections to the reflections of the Syriac Church Fathers that we outlined above.

a) Perpetual virginity

Let us first briefly recap the findings from the Bible. The concept of virginity is not mentioned in most of the texts of the New Testament.[1] No pointers to this doctrine are to be found in either the Corpus Paulinum or any of the other letters within

1 Cf. Theobald, 'Siehe, die Jungfrau wird empfangen', 95: *Die literarische Basis der Vorstellung der Empfängnis/Erzeugung Jesu aus göttlichem Geist im Neuen Testament ist ausgesprochen schmal. Paulus (samt Deutero- und Tritopaulinen), das Markus- und Johannesevangelium, der Hebräerbrief, das Corpus Catholicum und die Johannesoffenbarung kennen sie nicht, was bedeutet, dass der christliche Glaube in weiten Teilen der frühen Kirche* ohne sie *auskam, ohne deswegen defizient zu sein* ('The literary basis of the idea of Jesus's conception/generation from a divine spirit in the New Testament is extremely narrow. There is no mention of it in the Corpus Paulinum (including the Deutero- and the Trito-Pauline letters), in Mark or John's gospels, in the Letter to the Hebrews, the Catholic Letters or the Book of Revelation, which means that the Christian faith of the early Church managed to a large extent without this doctrine *without* thereby being in any way deficient').

the New Testament. Furthermore, two of the four gospels contain no references whatsoever to it. It is only in evidence in the gospels of Matthew and Luke. Yet even those gospels only attest to Mary's virginity prior to the birth of Jesus. The question of Mary's perpetual virginity appears to have been of no consequence to these two gospels either. Only in Lk do we come across some hints that could be construed as pointing in this direction.

We have already explained above that Lk introduces Mary as a virgin in his gospel (Lk 1:27). It also becomes clear from Mary's inquiry in Lk 1:34 that, within the literary construction of Lk, she has not yet had any intimate physical congress. The statement to this effect that Mary makes, namely that 'she knows not a man', is framed in the present tense; so, as far as the evidence of the text is concerned, interpreting this statement as signifying a perpetual state of virginity is by no means out of the question.[2] However, for Lk this matter is clearly of no importance.[3] Thus, later in the gospel Lk talks quite openly of Jesus's 'mother and brothers' (Lk 8:19–21) and regards Mary as Joseph's wife (Lk 2). If he had been concerned to characterise Mary as a perpetual virgin, he would surely have provided relevant clarification at these points.

However, generally speaking it remains a moot point whether Jesus really did have actual siblings. Certainly, from a philological standpoint, the traditional Catholic interpretation – that the frequently mentioned siblings of Jesus were merely cousins – is virtually out of the question.[4] Yet the old interpretation of the Eastern tradition, which regards the oft-cited siblings of Jesus[5] in the New Testament as children of a former marriage of Joseph, remains perfectly feasible. Also, the description of Jesus as the first-born does not necessarily suggest the existence of siblings: the term is used in this context to indicate 'a preferential relationship with God, rather than in relation to younger siblings.'[6]

The author of the 'gospel of Luke', whom we do not actually know by name

---

2 Some Church Fathers, like Gregory of Nyssa and Augustine, 'concluded that Mary gave her vow never to have carnal knowledge of a man under the pressure of the ideal of virginity… vows of this kind are anachronistic in the early church but not in the reform movements of Judaism' (Bovon, *Das Evangelium nach Lukas*, 76). Taking his starting point from Lk 1:34, Menke has ascertained the following: 'Mary knows – perhaps not on the conscious level of an explicit decision, but certainly in the depths of her heart – that she ought to remain a virgin' (Menke, *Fleisch geworden aus Maria*, 34).

3 Cf. Bovon, *Das Evangelium nach Lukas*, 73.

4 Cf. Schweizer, *Das Evangelium nach Markus*, 65. Moreover Mk 3:23 and Mk 6:3 also refer explicitly to 'sisters' of Jesus.

5 Luke also quite unselfconsciously adopts this tradition (cf. Lk 8:19 f. and Acts 1:14).

6 Bovon, *Das Evangelium nach Lukas*,121.

but whom for the sake of simplicity we shall refer to henceforth as *Luke*, therefore fully allows for the interpretation of a perpetual virginity on Mary's part. But it is not so much her sexual purity that is important to him but instead the ascetic attitude that is in evidence when Mary is taken by the Holy Spirit in a manner that is far removed from any intimate physical congress. At this point in the story, Luke is the only evangelist who draws an unequivocal connection between possession by a spirit and sexual abstinence. This is evident from the fact that Luke clearly depicts Mary as single not only before Jesus is born but also before the Pentecost event. She is therefore the only figure in his narrative who is embraced twice by the Holy Spirit.[7] Hans-Ulrich Weidemann of the University of Siegen, an authority on the New Testament, therefore states: 'In any event, Luke portrays Mary as *single*, which evidently 'qualifies' her to be visited a second time by the Holy Spirit. To put it bluntly, Luke therefore places the mother of Jesus at the beginning of his gospel as a *virgin* who has been affected by the Spirit and speaks prophetically – and at the outset of the Acts of the Apostles as a *single* person filled with the Spirit and speaking in tongues, in other words, as a woman who has been widowed or is living apart from her husband.'[8]

In his analyses, Weidemann comprehensively demonstrates that other narrative figures in Lk also show evidence of this combination of sexual asceticism and prophetic spirit-possession[9] and that these figures had definite parallels in Judaism of the period. Thus, in both rabbinical Judaism and in the writings of Philo of Alexandria, we find the idea 'that since being called to serve by God, Moses permanently abstained from sexual intercourse, to the detriment of his wife Zipporah.'[10] Luke's theology thus clearly operates within the context of a Jewish 'inspiration asceticism,'[11] which saw sexual abstinence as a key prerequisite for receiving prophetic inspiration – as indeed Philo and Flavius Josephus also did in their writings – and focused all its attention on this aspect.[12] Hence, Luke has no interest in stating whether Mary was a perpetual virgin, but is instead intent on making it clear that she is filled with God's spirit when she brings Jesus into the world and continues to bear witness to him after his death. As such, then, availing

7 Cf. Weidemann, 'Embedding the Virgin', 167.

8 Ibid., 117 f.

9 Cf. ibid., 150: 'Luke shows a clear interest in Jewish (and God-fearing) narrator figures, who either at times or as a general rule do not evince any sexuality.'

10 Ibid., 119.

11 Ibid., 120.

12 Cf. ibid., 121. Philo regards virginity as an 'allegory of the ecstatic union of the soul with God' (Bovon, *Das Evangelium nach Lukas*, 66).

himself of a typical Jewish narrative motif of the time, he places her firmly within a prophetic context.

Matthew does not make any similar link between virginity and prophetic inspiration. Accordingly, in his gospel there is even less evidence of any idea of the perpetual virginity of Mary. The only reason why he does not expressly rule out any possibility of it is 'because it was totally alien to him.'[13] On the other hand, like Lk, Mt sets great store by Mary's virginity prior to the birth of Jesus (Mt 1:25). For both evangelists, Jesus emanates entirely from God's spirit, and can therefore only be conceived by a virgin. Naturally, this motif of being conceived by a Holy Spirit has its antecedents in Hellenistic Judaism.[14] But if one is to understand this insistence upon Mary's biological virginity correctly, it is most important to first cast an eye over the theory of procreation that was widely accepted in antiquity.

In the Hellenistic period, theories of procreation that were influenced by the work of Aristotle were widespread. Aristotle's concept of so-called 'hylemorphism' posits that every being (or natural body) also possesses, alongside its primary matter, a form that lends it shape, and which constitutes its essential nature. Following on from this, Aristotle's theory of procreation holds that the man's semen contains within it an active force and vigour that imparts this shape and form to every being, 'while the menstrual blood of the female, by contrast, contains the purely passive matter…; which requires forming for life to emerge in the first place.'[15] To quote Aristotle verbatim: 'The body is therefore a female principle, whereas the soul is a male one. For the soul is the essence of a material body.'[16] Aristotle sees the creative male principle as being inherent within the spirit (*pneuma*).

Thus, for the Aristotelian theory of procreation, replacing the male sperm cell with the Holy Spirit did not represent a disruptive interference on the level of the actual material, biological measurable links. According to his theory, from a biological viewpoint it was the case when every human life came into being that a form of spiritual matter guided the emergence of the individual. Thanks to its 'pneumatic' constitution, this spirit is conceived of in such a way in the work of Aristotle as to make it – from a modern standpoint – indescribable by conventional scientific means. Customarily, this spiritual principle is only transmitted through the father, and finds its material correlate in the male semen. However,

---

13 Luz, *Das Evangelium nach Matthäus*, 153.

14 Cf. Theobald, 'Siehe, die Jungfrau wird empfangen', 83.

15 Ibid., 84.

16 Aristoteles, *De generatione animalium*, ed. by Hendrik J. Drossaart Lulofs, Oxford 1965, 738b 26–28.

this biologically quantifiable substance has no causal effect; instead, it is the creative spirit deriving from the man which constitutes the form-giving principle that manifests itself as the soul of the new human being.

The female ovum was only discovered in the nineteenth century.[17] Consequently, the interweaving of the female–material principle and the form-giving male principle cannot convey any biological sense compatible with our modern conceptual categories. The aim of the assertion of Mary's virginity in the Bible is simply that Jesus the human being receives his human form solely and exclusively from the divine spirit. The point of the declaration is not – from an Aristotelian standpoint – that Joseph's (in any event, irrelevant) seed is supplanted by a seed that has been created by God. Rather, it is the case that it is not Joseph's spirit that forms Jesus and enables his existence, but only the spirit of God. 'This human comes from God!'[18] This is the statement that Mt and Lk wish to impress upon us in their gospels. And John testifies to the same theological assertion in his talk of the pre-existence of the Word, which in his conceptual world renders all mention of Jesus's Virgin Birth superfluous. In other words: 'In narrative terms, the object of both the Virgin birth and the pre-existence of the Messiah is to bear witness to the divine origin of the Son.'[19]

The great difference between the account of Jesus's origin given in the Bible

17 For the sake of completeness here we should at least mention that as early as the second century, in opposition to Aristotle, Galen of Pergamon took the view that there was also a female 'seed'. However, it was Aristotle's views that continued to shape the ideas that are expressed in the Bible. The Qur'an also harks back to his worldview.

18 For this very reason, Jesus's genealogy in Lk is also traced back to Adam (Lk 3:38), who according to Luke also comes directly from God, like Jesus. And just like Jesus, Adam is the son of God: *Gerade diese Bezeichnung Adams gebietet eine deutliche Zurückhaltung gegenüber der Interpretation, dass mit dem Sohnestitel im Zusammenhang mit der jungfräulichen Empfängnis vom Verfasser des Lukasevangeliums etwa eine göttliche Wesensbestimmung Jesu vorgenommen worden wäre.* ('The very fact that Adam is described in these terms calls for decided caution regarding the interpretation that the creator of the Gospel of Luke was using the title of son in conjunction with the Virgin Birth to indicate, for instance, that Jesus is defined by his divine nature.') (Woyke, 'Mit Jesus ist es vor Gott wie mit Adam' (Sure 3,59), 140). See also Wolter, *Lukasevangelium*, 177: *Lukas benutzt die Gottessohnschaft Adams als Modell, um den Bedeutungsrahmen für das Verständnis der Gottessohnschaft Jesu abzustecken* ('Luke uses Adam's status as a son of God as a model to define the framework of meaning for understanding the nature of Jesus' role as the son of God'). Consequently, one may confidently state that the proclaimer of the Qur'an adopts his idea of the son of God and the associated concept of Mary's virginity from Lk. The fact that Jesus is not called the son of God in the Qur'an, therefore, does not have to do with Luke's use of this title. On the relationship between Lk and the Qur'an as a whole, cf. the highly illuminating essay by Woyke, 'Mit Jesus ist es vor Gott wie mit Adam' (Surah 3,59).

19 Bovon, *Das Evangelium nach Lukas*, 69; cf. Kremer, *Lukasevangelium*, 29.

and all the various pagan origin myths that exist is that it refrains from offering any form of narrative elaboration regarding the act of conception.[20] 'The fact of the divine conception stands front and centre; the way in which this actually comes about remains a secret and indeed should remain so.'[21] The single, solitary thing that matters to the biblical testimony is that Jesus's existence 'originates from the spirit of God.'[22]

Aristotle's concept of hylemorphism not only helped shape the theories of procreation that were current in the Hellenistic environment in which the New Testament emerged, it also continued to play a decisive role in the further elaboration of the Catholic doctrine of the virginity of Mary. Indeed, its influence is still apparent in medieval scholasticism. One should therefore be somewhat wary of talking in terms of a biological fact at this point, since this would amount to applying modern categories to a context which obeys a quite different form of logic. For in the mindset of the Ancient Greek theory of procreation, it is not a question of God having altered the material nature of Joseph's sperm cell by interfering with the laws of nature, with the result that Jesus came into existence from the female ovum of Mary and the sperm cell of the Holy Spirit, created from nothingness. This would represent the worst kind of mythologising.

Instead it is the case that the person Jesus, as the essential word of God, was only made possible through God's spirit. It is God alone who, according to the testimony of the Bible, lends this human being his divine form and his authority. In Aristotelian-influenced ways of thinking, it is therefore crucial that this individual does not owe his shape and form to the 'spirit' inherent within the seed of Joseph and instead is born of the Virgin Mary. In modern parlance, one would have to find other metaphors to express the complete provenance of the figure of Jesus from the power of God. When the Church continues to maintain that Jesus was born of the Virgin Mary, even going so far as to turn this into a dogma since the Council of Nicaea in 325, this does not represent the adoption of a particular natural-philosophical theory as part of Church doctrine, but rather the uptake of a tradition within the framework of a mutable theory of procreation. And this tradition lends especially powerful expression to the idea of Jesus's provenance from God.

---

20 Cf. Kremer, *Lukasevangelium*, 29: *Von mitunter als Parallele herangezogenen Mythen unterscheidet sich der biblische Bericht vor allem durch das Fehlen jeglicher Schilderung der geistgewirkten Lebensentstehung* ('The account in the Bible differs from the creation myths that are sometimes cited as parallels primarily in the total absence in the former of any type of depiction of the spirit world's agency in the emergence of life').

21 Dibelius, 'Jungfrauensohn und Krippenkind', 20.

22 Theobald, 'Siehe, die Jungfrau wird empfangen', 44.

This interpretation is also largely unchallenged in contemporary Catholic dogma. According to the theologian Wolfgang Beinert, it signifies nothing other than the entry of the Word into history, the transformation from transcendence to immanence – ideas which find symbolic expression in the image of the Virgin Birth.[23] Having said this, it is extremely important from a conservative point of view that talk of 'symbolic expression' is not taken to mean that the Virgin Birth does not denote a metaphysical reality. For this reason, Georg Söll quite rightly insists that, in the secular sphere too, a symbol 'can only possess symbolic power if it exists.'[24] Talk of the Virgin Birth cannot therefore be seen as purely figurative language, but must express a state of affairs that exists in reality. All that modern dogmatic theology does, in accordance with biblical testimony, is to insist that these very real circumstances cannot be reduced to a biological question, because the incarnation of God is a matter of theology or metaphysics, not of biology or gynaecology.

The work of Karl Rahner has provided great clarity on this question. He has written: 'The incarnation of the Son of God is, in all its actuality, the absolutely incalculable, free mystery of divine grace; it therefore does not originate from below, but uniquely and exclusively from above.'[25] It is this provenance from above that talk of the Virgin Birth is meant to convey. Quite simply, the act of making God into a man is not something that is within the power of human beings. This provenance cannot be brought about, in formal causal terms, by the semen of a man or the 'spirit' inherent within that seed. But this then also means that God's incarnation, precisely because it is not achievable from below, cannot be construed as an ethical demand upon us. In Rahner's view, recognising this relieves us of superhuman efforts and help us to examine and weigh up excessive claims. In its theological interpretation, what the Virgin Birth tells us about Jesus is that he does not emanate 'from below, from the internal workings of this world, nor yet from the noblest and most sacred form of human love, but exclusively from above.'[26] 'From on high, God's unpredictable mercy dawns and shines down upon us: the procreation of the Son who… is the pure effect of an act of free will performed from above by eternal God.'[27]

Gisbert Greshake takes up this discussion and correctly points out that Mary's virginity thereby hints at the innovative and irreducible nature of the Incarnation.

23 Cf. Beinert, 'Die mariologischen Dogmen', 323 f.

24 Söll, *Mariologie*, 246.

25 Rahner, *Maria*, 546.

26 Ibid., 546.

27 Ibid., 547.

'The actual scope of the statement of faith concerning the Virgin conception of Jesus ought to consist of recognising that Jesus represents the beginning of something new and unique – a "new Adam" who owes his existence solely to the initiative of God, not to a man.'[28] This locates Greshake's observations as being very much in the same vein as the line of interpretation described above, which sees the Virgin Birth as a sign that Jesus in his human form derives entirely from God. Rahner is at pains to stress how misguided it would be to reduce what is meant by this to a biological occurrence.[29]

Yet even if it is not one's intention to reduce or demean belief in the virginity of Mary to a biological event, one is still entitled to ask whether this biological occurrence does not nonetheless form a necessary part of belief in Mary's virginity. How exactly does a belief in the metaphysical reality of God's incarnation relate to the biological virginity of Mary? Is the biological event an indispensable part of the Christian belief in the Incarnation and the Virgin Birth? Karl-Heinz Menke is clearly of the view that metaphysics and biology are inseparable here. He states: 'The virgin birth is an expression of the fact that the human Jesus, whose personality, under the conditions of space and time, is that of the Son with the Holy Trinity, cannot derive from creatural origins (i.e. from the potentialities of the creature). Whereas the Resurrection…is an act of God *mediated* through the love of the human Jesus, God's impartation of *himself* (the incarnation of the pre-existing Son) is an exclusive and innovatory act of the creator; because this is not mediated through the joining together of a sperm cell and an ovum, it is literally 'im-mediate', i.e. a direct act of God. In its uniqueness, this act can only be compared to the act of creation at the beginning of time (*creatio ex nihilo*)…The only way in which it differs from the original act of creation is that Jesus is created into an already existing world – that is, from the material disposition of Mary!'[30]

Where the first sentence of the above statement is concerned, one would in all good conscience have to agree with Menke. The incarnation of God naturally surpasses the potentialities of the human creature. Indeed, this goes right to the heart of all discussion about Mary's virginity. And of course, God acts from above, as we have seen in our analysis of Karl Rahner's viewpoint. In his next sentence, though, Menke develops a theory of God's agency in the world which appears to try and resolve the 'how' of Mary's virginity on a biological level, and in so doing departs from the classical thought framework of Christian belief in the virginity

28 Greshake, *Maria-Ecclesia*, 227.
29 Cf. Rahner, *Maria*, 531.
30 Menke, *Fleisch geworden aus Maria*, 127.

of Mary. And unfortunately this only makes much of what he has to say very unclear. Instead of locating God's actions on the level of formal causality and seeing God's intervention as a force that lends form and shape, thus enabling the incarnation of God from the womb of the Virgin Mary, Menke suggests a radically innovative creative act from the material disposition of Mary, while not exactly making it clear to the reader what that might be. Leaving aside any idea that Jesus was created as a clone of Mary – which would indeed be biologically impossible, given his gender – then Menke can really only mean that God through his intervention replaces Joseph's seed and causes a freshly created sperm cell to fuse with Mary's ovum. Yet this surely amounts to mythological thinking and would not do justice to the Christian belief in incarnation (and therefore cannot really be what Menke is driving at). Bearing in mind the thought framework of Aristotelian ontology and theory of procreation outlined above, the Virgin Birth is precisely not about replacing a biological component with a divine one, but rather about making clear that procreation as a whole is exclusively an act of God. The biological question of whether a male sperm was also involved in the procreation of Jesus is completely irrelevant to the metaphysical situation. In line with this, Michael Schmaus quite correctly points out: 'In particular, the notion that an earthly father stood in the way of a heavenly one can only arise in the realms of pagan mythologies and theories of divinity that speak of father and mother deities. In these, a god customarily lies with a mortal woman in the way a man normally would.'[31] Menke surely cannot have meant all that. But what exactly does he mean when he talks about a new creation from the material disposition of Mary? Frankly, we have no idea. Evidently, fear of a purely symbolic interpretation of Mary's virginity prompted more conservatively minded members of the theological fraternity to find formulations that were designed to exclude this purely symbolic explanation and corroborate the reality of her virginity. But because faith can never be corroborated without symbolic forms of expression and the Christian faith tradition, especially when dealing with the Virgin Birth, has always employed arguments

31 Schmaus, *Mariologie*, 154. Schmaus therefore identifies the following bases of Mary's virginity: first and foremost he sees it as a 'pointer to the grace-filled nature of salvation. Man is not capable of liberating himself from his forlorn state by his own efforts. Redemption is not the result of male entrepreneurial spirit and drive' (ibid., 155). Secondly, he sees in the Virgin Birth a sign of the novelty of a life guided by salvation, which is entirely a 'heavenly gift' and not a 'human achievement' (ibid., 157). Finally Schmaus claims Mary's virginity is 'an indication of the uniqueness of the Messiah who is conceived and born in such a manner' (ibid., 157). None of these bases allow us to determine Mary's virginity as a simple biological fact.

that transcend our rational, scientific mindset, all attempts to underpin the event with a biological factuality only end up distorting the Christian faith. Instead, we should be quite relaxed about constantly reminding ourselves that the Virgin Birth has faith at its core: it was not Joseph's semen or the 'spirit' inherent within it, but the spirit of God that allowed Mary to bring the God made flesh into the world.[32] In theological terms, nothing more can be said on this score, and indeed nothing more need be said to safeguard the core of faith. And so we do not even need to venture into the realm of biological or gynaecological concerns.[33]

However, this also means that it would be wholly misguided to link Mary's virginity to some kind of transcendental–logical inevitability and hence to assume that divine incarnation is only possible in circumstances where the essential word of God is delivered by a virgin.[34] Accordingly, Karl Rahner emphasises that the hypostatic union could of course only 'make a fleshly reality into that of the Logos, which comes about through the act of woman *and man*.'[35] Likewise, Karl Barth does not identify any inevitable connection between incarnation and virginity. 'The Virgin Birth cannot therefore be 'postulated' a priori 'with absolute necessity.'[36] Rather, Barth maintains, it should simply help people to better understand the mystery of God's incarnation. [37] Yet if Mary's virginity is primarily intended to be an aid to comprehending the mystery of the incarnation, in other words if it is exclusively there to enable people to better understand that God himself really did set a new beginning with the birth of Jesus, one is tempted to ask how one might reformulate this statement of faith in the present day so as to preserve this function. For even though this article of faith does continue to perform this role for many Christians, for many others it is very hard to grasp.

---

32 Similarly, according to Barth, the decisive message regarding the Virgin Birth is 'that God commences with himself here' (Barth, *Kirchliche Dogmatik I/2*, 194), in other words that it is God 'who instigates a new action within history at this point' (Riesenhuber, *Maria im theologischen Verständnis von Karl Barth und Karl Rahner*, 47).

33 If it is Menke's intention to preclude the possibility that 'God retrospectively communicates his will to an individual who has been conceived by Joseph and born of Mary, in an adoptionistic sense,' then one can only agree with him (Menke, *Fleisch geworden aus Maria*, 127). However, on its own the assumption that God uses Joseph's seed to facilitate Mary's giving birth does not necessarily lead to adoptionism, so long as we hold fast to the idea that it is God's Holy Spirit alone which enables the person of Jesus to come into the world.

34 Cf. Greshake, *Maria-Ecclesia*, 234.

35 Karl Rahner, 'Dogmatische Bemerkungen zur Jungfrauengeburt.' In: ibid., *Sämtliche Werke*, vol. 22/1b, Freiburg – Basel – Wien 2013, 734–765, here p. 750.

36 Riesenhuber 43 with reference to Karl Barth, *Dogmatik im Grundriss*, Stuttgart 1947, 131.

37 Cf. Barth, *Credo*, 63: 'The miracle of the Virgin Birth does not have ontic but rather noetic meaning. It signifies what is taking place here.'

At this juncture we should remind ourselves of the symbolic function of Mary's virginity and search for ways of enabling it to speak to us anew in our current age. We will come back to considering this task in the final part of the book.

Thus far, we have concentrated almost exclusively on Mary's virginity prior to the birth of Jesus and remarked that this is the only article of faith that is clearly attested in the Bible. However, we have also noted that, even in Luke, a connection was drawn between the idea of prophetic inspiration and sexual abstinence. We would now like to pursue this line of enquiry in order to gain an understanding of the Church's belief in the perpetual virginity of Mary. This belief, which was strongly in evidence both among the Church Fathers and in the testimonies of early Christian popular religiosity, was also the subject of discussion and analysis by the Second Council of Constantinople in 533, as expressed in its edict that the Word 'was incarnate of the holy and glorious mother of God and ever-virgin Mary' (second capitula of the council DH 427; cf. also DH 422).[38] This belief has two dimensions, which can be described as Mary's virginity during and after the birth of Jesus. Let us begin by considering Mary's virginity after the birth, since this is easier to understand. In truth, this is tantamount to stating that even after the birth of Jesus, Mary continued to have no intimate physical congress.

We have already seen that the idea of a perpetual virginity of Mary accords well with the ascetic ideals of Luke, and as such can readily find attestation in the biblical tradition. In Luke, as we have observed, Mary is 'one of several narrative figures who in quite different ways either occasionally or permanently follow an ascetic lifestyle.'[39] Sexual abstinence for Luke is one of the keys to getting really close to the spirit of God and letting oneself be possessed by that spirit. In Church tradition, ideas of this kind together with Jesus's talk of people 'living like eunuchs for the sake of the kingdom of heaven' (Mt 19:12) soon gave rise to the concept of a life spent in permanent sexual abstinence, for which Mary was then held up as a prime example. The Church Fathers made similarly strenuous efforts to find firm points of reference for the perpetual virginity of Mary in the Bible too.

For instance, Gregory of Nyssa and Augustine of Hippo therefore interpret Lk 1:34 as evidence that Mary had already decided to lead a life of celibacy and for that reason initially found it impossible to accept the message imparted by the angel.[40] While, as far as the biblical text is concerned, this notion strikes us as possible though not very likely, we find ourselves able to relate more readily

38 For a more extensive discussion of this point, cf. Söll, *Mariologie*, 108.

39 Weidemann, 'Embedding the Virgin', 108.

40 Cf. Schmaus, *Mariologie*, 126.

to Michael Schmaus's contention that Mary only resolves later to live her life as a virgin, for the sake of Christ.[41] For him and other Catholic theologians who study the faith tradition, it is axiomatic that 'the instant when Christ is conceived is also the moment when the Christian concept of virginity is born' (Guardini).[42] Behind this interpretation, which goes beyond what is actually stated in scripture, is the idea that Mary is intent upon devoting her life entirely to her son and hence does not want to have any more children.[43] Or to put it another way: 'Opting for God, in the way that Mary has done, evokes the response of a love that is entirely personal both qualitatively and temporally, and whose outward sign is the virgin's constant dedication of her life.'[44] In other words, in this interpretation Mary feels herself so firmly ensconced within God's special care, which becomes a tangible reality for her through the birth of Jesus Christ, that she wishes to devote herself entirely to this love.

At the same time, however, it is important to Schmaus that Mary's sexual abstinence does nothing to change her personal affection for Joseph.[45] Once again, it seems obvious that the focus here is on the idea of purity and inviolability. This aspect is also evident in the patristic tradition. Since Origen at the latest, this tradition stressed Mary's sanctity, purity and virginity.[46] To quote Origen directly: 'And

41 Cf. ibid., 128.
42 Ibid., 128.
43 For the present authors, both of whom are the parents of several children, the line of argument which holds that unconditional and undivided love for one child makes it more difficult to extend the same degree of complete love to another child is only comprehensible to a very limited extent. Nonetheless, because this logic is widespread in the Catholic tradition whenever the ideal of virginity comes up for discussion, we reproduce it here without further comment.
44 Beinert, 'Die mariologischen Dogmen', 328.
45 Cf. Schmaus, *Mariologie*, 159: *Es sei nochmals daran erinnert, dass Marias Haltung personaler Zuwendung zu Joseph durch ihre Jungfräulichkeit nicht aufgehoben, sondern, von dem naturhaften Trieb befreit, auf höherer Ebene bleibt.* ('We need to remind ourselves once more that Mary's personal affection for Joseph is not annulled by her virginity but instead, once divested of its natural impulses, continues to survive on a higher plane.') Of course, such an interpretation is susceptible to the charge that its is informed by body hostility. Thus, while Schmaus's reminder to all Christians 'not to lose themselves in the physical aspects of marriage' is perfectly understandable, from an ideological–critical standpoint it is nevertheless dubious. For in the cold light of day, the danger of 'getting lost in the physical aspects of marriage' is in all likelihood not that great. Our impression here, rather, is that, without insight into the dimension of mutual personal affection, which certainly goes well beyond the physical dimension of marriage, no marital coexistence can succeed anyway. Cf. our reflections on marriage in Klaus von Stosch and Ann-Christin Baumann (eds.), *Ehe in Islam und Christentum*, Paderborn 2016 (Beiträge zur Komparativen Theologie; 19), 15–30, 85–103.
46 Cf. Menke, *Fleisch geworden aus Maria*, 79.

I think it in harmony with reason that Jesus was the first fruit among men of the purity [which consists in] chastity, and Mary among women.'[47]

Sacred purity plus complete devotion to Jesus Christ through sexual asceticism is surely not something that would readily appeal to a modern individual as an ideal mode of existence. But at least we can try, even from a viewpoint that is far removed from religiosity, to identify some positive aspects within this ideal. For instance, it is interesting to note that, for women in antiquity, a life of celibacy was the only way to avoid being defined entirely in terms of a man.[48] And even people who are perfectly happy within relationships would concede that doing without a steady partner while at the same time practising sexual abstinence has the potential to free up time that can be devoted to other people.

On the other hand, something that is far more difficult to grasp is the fact that the Church tradition speaks not only in terms of virginity before and after the birth of Jesus, but also of virginity during the birth (*virginitas in partu*). To be sure, there is no direct evidence of virginity post-partum, and the concept is certainly open to ideological abuse, though it does fit well within the theological tradition of the Catholic Church. However, our first response to talk of virginity during birth is one of sheer bewilderment.

The first official enunciation of this doctrine is found at the Lateran Synod of 649, when it is expressly stated that Mary gave birth intact. This is the first occasion on which her virginity during parturition is formulated as a doctrine in its own right. As biblical evidence, Church tradition cites Lk 2:7, since this verse allegedly indicates that Mary was able to suckle her infant immediately after giving birth.[49] In this way, the entire birth process is imbued with something miraculous, though it takes a great deal of creativity to deduce this from the available biblical evidence. In the theological writings of several Church Fathers, the following motifs are elaborated upon to characterise virginity during birth: 'painless parturition, no opening of the birth canal, intactness of the hymen, the re-closing of the womb.'[50] Here, we finally enter realm of theological inventions. The idea of an intact hymen as proof of virginity is, according to the researches of Michael Rosenberg,

47 Origenes, Matthäus-Kommentar, Buch 10, Abschnitt 17, edited by Robert Girod, *Commentaire sur l'évangile selon Matthieu*, Paris 1970 (Sources chrétiennes 162), 216.

48 Cf. Beinert, *Maria*, 139.

49 Cf. Söll, *Mariologie*, 46.

50 Wolfgang Beinert, 'Die mariologischen Dogmen und ihre Entfaltung.' In: Heinrich Petri (eds.), *Handbuch der Marienkunde. vol. 1: Theologische Grundlegung – Geistliches Leben. Zweite, völlig neu bearbeitete Auflage*, Regensburg 1996, 267–363, here p. 316.

a construct of Late Antiquity;[51] his investigations further revealed that this motif started to appear in the works of Christian authors only around the middle of the fourth century.[52] Nonetheless, it is also implicit in the review of Mary's virginity presented in the ProtEvJam, as we discovered earlier. In light of this, it appears to have found its way into theological constructions somewhat earlier than Rosenberg claims. What is certainly true is that it has no point of reference in the Bible and that it contains an alarming potential for violence.[53]

Fortunately, neither the gynaecological details mentioned here nor any others were ever established as part of official Church doctrine, and they are therefore not binding as articles of faith even within a conservative understanding of the Catholic religion.[54] But one should not underestimate their shaping force at the time when the Qur'an was emerging. Even Jacob of Serugh defended the enduring virginal intactness of Mary against attacks by Eastern Syriac Christians.[55] And in the seventh century, Ildefonso of Toledo and others defended this doctrine in a pamphlet written to refute Jewish anti-Marian polemics.[56] We will presently see how the clash between Christianity and Judaism over Mary came to form an important backdrop to what the Qur'an had to say about Mary. For now, though, we will continue to examine Church doctrine regarding Mary.

As early as the 1950s, in academic theology that was still characterised by neo-scholasticism, an increasing number of voices made themselves heard which interpreted the motif of virginity during birth (hereafter abbreviated to *vip*, for '*virginitas in partu*') 'not literally as regards the birth process and its consequences, but in the sense that this parturition was precisely devoid of that natural prerequisite which, as a naturally occurring phenomenon, it ought to have had in the natural order of things, and for which the birth of a baby is normally the

51 Cf. Rosenberg, *Signs of virginity*, 13.

52 Cf. ibid., 14.

53 Cf. ibid., 16: 'I highlight the violence inherent in this kind of description of virginity testing.'

54 Cf. Beinert, 'Die mariologischen Dogmen und ihre Entfaltung', 317. Likewise Söll, *Mariologie*, 109, leaves us in no doubt on this score: 'None of those in the Church who bore witness to tradition wanted to engage with gynaecology.' This view is seconded by Gerhard Ludwig Müller: 'However, it is not the gynaecological details, which in each individual case were evaluated differently, which determine the content of this article of faith, but rather the true nature of Mary as a mother, seen from a faith perspective, is to be enunciated in such a way that its fundamental relation ('virginity') to the self-manifesting God is not negated, i.e., 'harmed' (Müller, *Maria – die Frau im Heilsplan Gottes*, 211).

55 Cf. Puthuparampil, *Mariological thought of Mar Jacob of Serugh*, 381 ff. ('Homily on the Perpetual Virginity of Mary').

56 Cf. Fiores, *Maria in der Geschichte von Theologie und Frömmigkeit*, 133 f.

unmistakable sign: namely, conception of a child from a man.'[57] According to this view, all that the *vip* signified was that the doctrine of virginity before birth was being applied to the birth process itself. Proponents of this reading argued that traditional interpretation contained 'a temporally and culturally conditioned over-estimation of the hymen, jeopardised real motherhood … and sought to deny the presence of pain, despite the fact that Mary was otherwise no stranger to pain.'[58] This, then, was a *de facto* refutation of any intrinsic significance of the doctrine of the *vip* in comparison with virginity before birth. However, this outright denial that the *vip* had any significance in its own right was unable to gain traction.

The interpretative suggestions that Karl Rahner put forward as a way of mediating in this debate were of greater consequence. Thus, in response to the tendency outlined above, he analysed the dogmatic precepts and determined that it was unclear quite how the *vip* should be understood. He established that the Church Fathers had construed it in various different ways. Accordingly, he maintained, the situation around the turn of the second to the third century was such that the majority of the Church Fathers had no conception of the *vip* as understood in biological terms (take Tertullian, for instance, who saw the opposite of the *vip* as a key component of the anti-docetic, true belief in the real birth of Jesus Christ), while from Clement of Alexandria onwards there were an ever-increasing number of Church Fathers who defended this doctrine.[59] Many Church Fathers considered it a mystery precisely how the virginity of Mary could have been preserved during the act of giving birth – in much the same way as the incarnation of God as a whole was a mystery to them.

Yet some of them (including Ephrem the Syrian, or perhaps actually the Pseudo-Ephrem) hankered after a more precise interpretation.[60]

Rahner tried to develop a middle position in this regard. On the one hand, he claimed, it was clear that virginity had nothing to do with the question of labour pains.[61] On the other hand, though, in view of her freedom from original sin, Mary's birth must already have been different to a normal birth. To quote Rahner's own words: 'She who, as someone free of concupiscence, completely (albeit in an infralapsarian way) integrates the passive events of her life into the basic make-up of the persona she has decided upon for herself, and who has the capacity to make what she passively experiences an expression of her active decision, does not register

57 Rahner, *Maria*, 654.
58 Ibid., 654.
59 Cf. ibid., 666.
60 Cf. ibid., 669.
61 Cf. ibid., 673.

the passive experience of the (active) birth in the same way as those people who invariably experience what happens to them in the world as a result of the forces of life as something alien and restrictive, which has taken command of them to the detriment of their freedom.'[62] What Rahner is driving at here is that the only way in which Mary's experience differs from that of other women is in her 'subjective, experiential side of giving birth.'[63] In saying this, Rahner proceeds from the trite insight that everyone is unique in the way she or he experiences things, thus making the basic contention of his argument incontestable. Yet in addition, as the point of reference for the doctrine of the *vip* he takes Mary's lack of sin – an aspect we will treat subsequently – relating it in the process to Genesis 3:16. For him, then, the difference between Mary's parturition and a normal birth resides not in the experience of pain but in the experience of passivity during the birth process.

We, however, are not sure whether passivity is an entirely fortunate term to use in this context. At the very least, during the pushing contractions alone, women have to be extremely active and summon up an incredible effort. It is certainly true that they are required to 'go along' with the birth process, and hence that this introduces an element of passivity into their activity. Their autonomy is unavoidably compromised here by being obliged to rely on external support. At this point, what happens during the birth process shows itself to be a positively paradigmatic illustration of what human freedom really means. We will have more to say presently about the relationship between grace and freedom that lies behind this process, in order to properly appreciate Mary's very special role. But in any event, we might conclude here that her specialness is not to be sought within the framework of gynaecology or biology but rather in the way she determines and enacts the parameters of her freedom. Accordingly, Karl-Heinz Menke has said: 'The "Yes" word uttered by the mother of Christ – which is untainted by sin and therefore 'immaculate' – has come to characterise not only the birth of our saviour but also Mary's parturition, and subsequently the rest of her life, and finally her death in the sense of a personal integration of everything that is natural.'[64] If this is taken to encapsulate the heart of the doctrine of the *vip*, then it represents nothing other than the application of the doctrine of Mary's purity and lack of sin to the birth process. By contrast, if one were to associate the *vip* with such phenomena as 'the integrity of the mother's hymen, with a trouble-free pregnancy and a confinement

62 Ibid., 675. In Christian theology, 'infralapsarian' denotes the fallibility of human beings which, given the fall from grace, is an intrinsic part of the human condition.

63 Ibid., 676.

64 Menke, *Fleisch geworden aus Maria*, 82.

devoid of all complications, one would be in serious danger of selling the Christological dogma short … the physiological processes that occur during pregnancy and childbirth, including the associated pains, all form part of the biological constitution of human beings. If the incarnation had taken place outside this frame, then something would also have been lacking in the act of redemption.'[65]

Gathering together all the elements of the perpetual virginity of Mary and summing up, it is all about demonstrating that Mary's entire life is geared to the conception of the Word and hence to her obedient receipt of grace.[66] It is above all this attitude to faith which has ensured that Mary 'has become a model of all Christian virginity'[67] In practical terms, this virginity means refraining from intimate physical congress, but it is interpreted by Mary as devotion to the incarnate God; and this devotion should constitute the core of every Christian's existence.[68] Only in this recognisable connection between sexual asceticism and attachment to God does virginity retain its symbolic function and become susceptible to theological interpretation.

b) Mary as the new human being freed from original sin

In clarifying the question of Mary's virginity during the birth process we have seen how closely the doctrine of Mary's virginity is bound up with that of her lack of sin, or more precisely with the doctrine of her freedom from original sin. At this point, we should remind ourselves of the stance of Church doctrine on this question in Late Antiquity.

We have already seen that the Syriac Church Fathers, while full of enthusiasm for the purity and sinlessness of Mary, at the same time had no knowledge of the doctrine of Mary's immaculate conception. Theologians like Ephrem the Syrian or Jacob of Serugh were adamant that Mary was only freed from all sin through

---

65 Beinert, 'Die mariologischen Dogmen', 326 f. Jacob of Serugh also regards Mary's labour pains as a necessary consequence of Christ's human form; as a result, he is adamant that anyone who denies these labour pains also denies Christ's human nature (cf. Jakob von Sarug, *Die Kirche und die Forschung*, 18).

66 Rahner, *Maria*, 547. (Translator's note: In the German, both 'conception' and 'receipt' are the same word, *Empfang*.)

67 Ibid., 548.

68 Virginity therefore demonstrates by example here 'an ability to practice abstinence, because one truly believes in practical terms and not just in abstract and cheap theory that everything which is not God's grace from above is second-rate in comparison and in the final analysis is of no consequence.' (Rahner, *Maria*, 548). Of course, this should be the attitude of every Christian, and refraining from taking a life partner is just one example of this.

her conception of Jesus and the connection with him. The decisive factor for them is less about the cleansing of original sin and much more about freedom from sinning. Prior to the Annunciation scene, Mary would anyway, like every other person, be burdened with original sin. In Late Antiquity, this doctrine was promulgated not only in the East but also in the Latin West. The reason for this in the West was the 'strongly held belief in the Augustinian tradition in the ubiquity of original sin and hence *everyone's* need of salvation.'[69] This same emphasis on the need of all people for redemption was also characteristic of the theological tradition of the Eastern Church, despite the fact that this tradition never accepted the doctrine of original sin in the Augustinian sense. In the West, too, Mary would not have represented an exception here, and as a result Thomas Aquinas too was an implacable opponent of the 'immaculists'.[70]

This situation only changed in any significant way for the following centuries thanks to the theological creativity of John Duns Scotus (1266–1308). As a solution to the aforementioned problem, he formulated the idea of Mary's anticipated redemption (*praeredemptio*) in view of the merits of Jesus Christ,[71] though of course 'anticipated' in this context is not to be understood in a temporal sense.[72] The only thing that is important is that Mary's immaculate conception is inherently made possible by God's incarnation in Jesus – and not vice versa. In formulating this idea, Duns Scotus provided a theoretical concept which allowed Mary's need for redemption to be coupled with her original purity and lack of sin. But why was this coupling so important, and what is the theological issue which connects the Catholic Church with talk of Mary's Immaculate Conception?

To gain a clearer insight here we first need, however briefly, to explain the possible implications of the doctrine of original sin.[73] In short, this teaching states that every person repeatedly becomes more distant from God by attempting through their own efforts to attain unconditional love. To expand briefly upon this idea: humans long to love and be loved. In a somewhat simplified and formalised way, one might even say that people want to say 'Yes' to those whom they love. But in actual fact we can only ever manage this in a limited sense. Time and again,

69 Müller and Sattler, 'Mariologie', 171 f.

70 Ibid., 172.

71 Cf. ibid., 172.

72 Ibid., 185.

73 For a more extensive treatment of the theology of original sin, cf. Klaus von Stosch, 'Streit um die Erbsünde?' In: Jürgen Werbick (ed.), *Sühne, Martyrium und Erlösung? Opfergedanke und Glaubensgewissheit in Judentum, Christentum und Islam*, Paderborn and elsewhere 2013, 81–96.

we are misunderstood, and over and over again we inadvertently create distance by choosing inappropriate signs to express our love. Our 'Yes' is never therefore pure affirmation, but always contains within it elements of 'No'. However, it is precisely in love that we are averse to acknowledging this painful fact. We think we understand ourselves and expect that the object of our love will recognise us and understand us for what we are. We are all too keen to ignore the 'No' implicit in the 'Yes'. At the same time, we imagine that we are able to overcome the many minor problems of love through our own efforts. Indeed, we believe we can simply achieve a pure 'Yes' if we try hard enough.

On this matter, the Bible states that we desire to be like God (Genesis 3:5). We cannot manage to give the person we love a pure 'Yes'. If we try to bring it about through our own exertions, we tangle ourselves up in what Church tradition calls original sin. In view of the fact that we humans can never fully understand and accept one another, we run the risk that we will begin to mistrust any 'Yes' that is directed at us in history. For over the course of our lives, we increasingly notice that even the 'Yes' that we might first have encountered in the love shown to us by our parents does not express complete understanding or love, but instead, like all 'human, all-too human' striving and love, remains fragmentary and ambiguous. When faced with this primal anthropological experience, how can one possibly trust the 'Yes' of another person?

From the standpoint of the Christian faith, this problem is only exacerbated by the fact that, for the believer, everything depends upon ultimately saying 'Yes' to the love of God embodied in Jesus Christ, and integrating this 'Yes' into his or her life in all its fragmentation and forlornness. In the end – so the faithful Christian hopes – he or she will become one who only always says 'Yes' to God. But how can that be a rational hope, when such a 'Yes' is simply not humanly possible?

Mary's *fiat* comes into play at this juncture. In Catholic doctrine, this is regarded as a pure 'Yes' to Jesus Christ, in other words as a 'Yes' with no element of 'No'. It is precisely this 'Yes', this affirmation of hers, which integrates everything fragmentary and forlorn about her existence into Christ. This 'Yes' is made possible for Mary through her complete devotion to God. The doctrine of the Immaculate Conception maintains that she is once more supported in this devotion by the love of God, who from the very first moment of her existence has shaped her towards expressing this 'Yes'.

And so we return to the relationship between grace and freedom, which finds paradigmatic expression in the person of Mary. From a Catholic point of view, it is the case that every act of human free will is already premised upon the facilitating love of God. Man is part of God's plan, and so he shows him his love from the very outset. Provided man shows an interest in this plan of God's, he is free and can, little by little, signal his affirming 'Yes' to life.[74] But if man misunderstands or rejects God's plan, he is unfree and proceeds to mingle more and more elements of 'No' into his response to life. From a Catholic viewpoint it is an empirical fact that this is exactly what happens to almost all humans. Time and again, we lose our inner compass, time and again we are blinded to God's great 'Yes', and time and again we erode parts of the original purpose with which God endowed us. In this, Mary is the great counter-example. She succeeds in resoundingly affirming her purpose and God's 'Yes' to man, which from a Christian perspective is embodied in Jesus Christ. Yet this great counter-example does not reside in her meritorious nature, but in the fact that she has been chosen and shown grace by God. Of course, being chosen in this way does not render human consent redundant, and so Mary's *fiat* is an indispensable part of God's agency throughout history. It is the one part of his providential plan that God cannot replace through his own action and which at root remains beyond his control, because it is based upon the formal unconditionality of human freedom.[75] Even God can do nothing except employ love as a way of soliciting the consent of this self-determining freedom. In other words, God seeks to gain man's assent to him solely through soliciting, and Mary would be the example of a person who has opened herself up completely to this 'Yes' of God.

Our gratitude is therefore due to Mary, because she fulfilled her unique mission – just as every person has a unique mission or purpose. Of course, her mission is a special one, but her exemplary nature resides not in the uniqueness of her mission and hence not in her virginity as such either, but rather in the fact that she says 'Yes' to her mission without qualification – just as we ought to enthusiastically say 'Yes' to our particular mission.[76] Yet this 'ought' should not be subject to moralising, since it must always be about a responsive affirming 'Yes' that is called forth by God's love. In giving her *fiat*, Mary is the great affirmer here, who exemplifies to us humans how we are all meant to be. She shows us that a 'Yes' without ambiguity and dichotomy can exist provided it understands itself as relying entirely on God's own unconditional 'Yes'. To cite Karl-Heinz Menke: 'However, Mary's "Yes" was not characterised by this dichotomy. She said "Yes" without any ifs

---

74 For a more detailed explanation of this position, cf. Klaus von Stosch, 'Impulse für eine Theologie der Freiheit'. In: Klaus von Stosch et al. (eds.), *Streit um die Freiheit. Philosophische und theologische Perspektiven*, Paderborn 2019, 195–224.

75 On the unconditionality factor within freedom, based on the transcendental logical analysis of freedom, cf. Pröpper, *Theologische Anthropologie I*, 512–535.

76 Cf. Beinert, 'Die mariologischen Dogmen', 326.

or buts.'[77] For this reason, she is the new Eve and represents a new figure among God's chosen people.[78] The fact that Mary utters her 'Yes' in a world that is full of ambiguity makes her 'Yes' a 'Yes' that can only be spoken while suffering the wrongdoings of this world. 'As a person, Mary is the principle of all affirmation, all fecundity of obedience, and as such she is the mother with the sword in her heart, crying out in her birthing pains between heaven and earth.'[79]

Therefore, according to Catholic doctrine, in Mary we encounter a person who is formed exactly as God desired.[80] This doctrine also implies that Mary remained free of personal sin, even if no statement to this effect was ever formally enunciated. However, it might well be regarded as a conviction that consistently informs a whole series of documents of the Church's teaching authority (cf. DH 1573, 2800, 3908, 3915). If it is true that Mary and Jesus, despite the fierce conflicts between them that are chiefly attested in Mk, are to be thought of as being without sin, then this casts a very interesting light on the conflicts between the two of them that were evidently played out within the family. Clearly, adolescent children who have to go through a long phase of difficulties with their parents need have no concerns that they are thereby automatically distancing themselves from God. And beyond the parent–child situation: evidently Mary's alienation from Jesus, which she has to endure at least for a time, can itself become part of the pure 'Yes' that she speaks in affirmation of Jesus Christ. To be sure, this is not very easy to understand, yet it is enormously heartening for all those who find it difficult to affirm Jesus Christ and who take issue with many of the things that he introduced into the world. Only a consideration of the figure of Mary in the round, as she appears to us in the New Testament, can give us an insight into the great potential for hope that is contained within Catholic doctrine concerning this woman.

---

77 Menke, *Fleisch geworden aus Maria*, 141.

78 Cf. Ratzinger, *Erwägungen zur Stellung von Mariologie und Marienfrömmigkeit im Ganzen von Glaube und Theologie*, 24: *Maria ist in dem Augenblick ihres Ja Israel in Person, die Kirche in Person und als Person. Sie ist diese personale Konkretisierung der Kirche zweifellos dadurch, dass sie auf Grund ihres Fiat leibhaftig Mutter des Herrn wird.* ('In the instant she gives her assent, Mary is Israel in person, the Church in person and incarnate. Without a doubt, what makes her the personal embodiment of the Church is the fact that, as a result of her fiat, she becomes the mother of the Lord in the flesh.')

79 Hans Urs von Balthasar, 'Das Katholische an der Kirche.' In: Joseph Ratzinger, *Maria*, 142–159, here p. 158 f.

80 Cf. Beinert, 'Die mariologischen Dogmen', 337.

c) Other dogmatic precepts

Thus far, we have discussed two dogmas concerning Mary: her perpetual virginity and her immaculate conception. From a historical point of view, the latter dogma only dates from the modern period. At the time when the Qur'an came into being, on the other hand, the Marian dogma that was known was her designation as the Mother of God (Greek *Theotokos*, literally 'birthgiver of God'), which was confirmed at the Council of Ephesus in 431 and was already virtually omnipresent in the Eastern Church. Though the actual term was definitively attested for the first time as early as 332 in the works of Alexander of Alexandria,[81] it still does not appear in the writings of Ephrem the Syrian.[82] But following the Council, the title 'Mother of God' soon became an important part of the Syriac tradition too, establishing itself throughout all schools of thought, despite the fact that the Eastern Syriac (the so-called 'Nestorian') tradition was only prepared to accept the title provided it was (generally speaking) interpreted in the kind of way that Nestorius – whose doctrines were refuted at Ephesus – would have interpreted and accepted it himself. As a result, this title is no longer a bone of contention within the many Christological controversies that raged throughout the sixth and seventh centuries, becoming instead a self-evident part of Mariology in Late Antiquity.

In terms of its content, the title 'Mother of God' is an inevitable consequence of the development of Christological doctrine by the first ecumenical councils. If it is taken as read that Jesus Christ possesses a divine nature from the outset, it necessarily follows from this that his mother can be designated as the Mother of God in some way. This does not of course mean that she gave birth to the Triune God. Instead, it signifies that, in Jesus Christ, the essential word of God was inseparably connected to man through Mary. Talk of Mary as the Mother of God is therefore fully consistent with the rejection of an adoptionistic Christology – that is, a Christology which proceeds from the premiss that Jesus was only adopted as God's son either after his birth, or after his resurrection and other achievements in his lifetime. By contrast, the Christian doctrinal tradition works from the assumption that Jesus is the essential word of God from the moment of his conception in Mary's womb and that Mary through her *fiat* therefore makes possible the birth of this Word of God, and hence can be called the 'Mother of God'. This title is thus first and foremost a Christological title, or at least a title that has its basis in Christology and is primarily focused on it.

81 Cf. Gerwing, 'Mariologie', 417. The term may also occur in prayer texts from the third century.

82 Cf. Beck, 'Die Mariologie der echten Schriften Ephräms', 23.

All the same, from a history of religion perspective, the title does make it easier to associate the figure of Mary with pagan maternal deities, and in this same regard it is possible to demonstrate links between cults of Mary and such pagan cults.[83] But also, quite independently of the title of the Mother of God, a direct connection can be shown to exist between the worship of pagan fertility goddesses and Mariology.[84] However, more recent studies have called into question whether one can really go so far, as for instance Stephen Benko does,[85] as to trace talk of Mary as the Mother of God back to pagan origins.[86] In any event, though, there are certainly many instances from popular religious practice where the veneration of Mary supplanted the worship of local deities[87] – a phenomenon that can still be observed today in indigenous religions during inculturation processes conducted by the Catholic Church.[88] Thus, for example, when formulating the iconography and rituals to be used in the veneration of Mary, Christianity in Late Antiquity borrowed from the worship of goddesses such as Isis, or Dido the heavenly queen of Carthage, or the Syrian goddess Dea Syria in Hierapolis.[89]

Yet for all her affinity in history of religion terms to pre-Christian pagan cults, theologically there was never any question that Mary was to be regarded as a goddess. For this reason, it was quite common for her attribute as the Mother of God to be disengaged from its Christological context and viewed instead in an anthropological light. In the words of Karl Rahner, the title therefore indicates that 'the most perfect example of Christianity – in its receiving of God in completely tangible physicality – is divine motherhood, albeit only provided that this motherhood is not understood in a narrow sense simply as a biological occurrence, but rather as something that takes hold of the entire corporeal and spiritual being of the Blessed Virgin.'[90] According to this logic, it is the task of

83 Cf. Peter W. van der Horst, 'Sex, Birth, Purity and Asceticism in the Protoevangelium Jacobi.' In: Levine (ed.), *A Feminist Companion to Mariology*, 56–66, here p. 65.
84 Cf. Benko, *The Virgin Goddess*, 263.
85 Cf. ibid., 264: 'The motherhood of Mary, which is the basic principle of Mariology, came from the pagan "Magna Mater" and "Mother of Gods" designations of certain goddesses.'
86 Cf. McGuckin, 'The early cult of Mary and inter-religious contexts in the fifth-century church', 7–16; Brown, 'The cult of the saints', 1–22; Bradshaw, 'The search for the origins of Christian worship', 21 f., 213–221.
87 Cf. Benko, *The Virgin Goddess*, 264.
88 For example, on corresponding tendencies in the Andean vision of the cosmos, which has meant that sites of Marian worship now thrive at sites where the fertility goddess Pachamama was once venerated, cf. Klaus von Stosch, 'Apu Yaya Jesucristo – Suchbewegungen nach einer inkulturierten Christologie im andinen Kontext.' In: *Religionen unterwegs* 24 (2018) 5–10.17.
89 Cf. Ashkar, *Mary in the Syriac Christian tradition and Islam*, 30.
90 Rahner, *Maria*, 531.

every individual, indeed his or her entire *raison d'être*, to bring God's word of assent into the world. It is incumbent upon me too to speak God's assent to my fellow human beings and thereby enable them to experience God's unequivocal and unconditional love as a reality. To quote a famous line from the seventeenth-century German mystic poet Angelus Silesius: 'I must be Mary and give birth to God.'[91] Taking our cue from another mystic, Meister Eckhart, we can formulate this idea in a different way, that it is the spiritual duty of each and every person to bring the Redeemer into the world.[92]

This touches upon an important turning point in Mariology, which becomes apparent in the hermeneutics of dogma after the Second Vatican Council (1962–65) at the latest. Whereas in the Old Church, dogmas relating to Mary focused primarily on her prerogatives,[93] namely things that could only be said of Mary and which distinguished her from us commonplace individuals, Vatican II emphasised that Mary is the archetype of the Church and as such is the touchstone of what we all wish for ourselves.[94] Mary thus no longer appears as an unattainable special case but as a model for human life whom we may reasonably strive to emulate.

In accord with this, the Dogmatic Constitution on the Church known as *Lumen gentium*, one of the principal documents of the Second Vatican Council (hereafter abbreviated to LG), states that Mary is to be understood as a type of the Church 'in the order of faith, charity and perfect union with Christ' (LG 63). The intimate love which, in her capacity as the mother of Jesus, binds Mary to her son and also puts her in contact with God, hence becomes a form of intimacy that every Christian can strive to attain and through which he or she may be reunited with Mary: 'The Virgin in her own life lived an example of that maternal love, by which it behooves that all must be animated who cooperate in the apostolic mission of the Church for the regeneration of men' (LG 65). It is fascinating to see how the

---

91 (*Ich muss Maria sein und Gott aus mir gebären*) Angelus Silesius, quoted in Greshake, *Maria-Ecclesia*, 536.

92 Cf. Meister Eckhart, *Deutsche Predigten*, with 18 illustrations, trans. and ed. by Louise Gnädinger, Zurich 1999 (Manesse Bibliothek der Weltliteratur 2000), 115 f. (from the sermon 'Ave gratia plena', DW no. 22, Walshe no. 53): *Es ist Gott wertvoller, daß er geistigerweisegeboren werde von einer jeglichen Jungfrau oder von einer jeglichen guten Seele, denn daß er von Maria leiblich geboren wurde* ('It is more worth to God to be born spiritually of the individual virgin or good soul, than that he was physically born of Mary' Translation: Maurice O'C Walshe).

93 Cf. Eggemann, *Die 'ekklesiologische Wende' in der Mariologie des II. Vatikanums*, 4.

94 'The commonly held view is that, with Vatican II 'Mariology' underwent a sea-change. This saw the long period of Counter-Reformation Mariology focusing on the prerogatives of Mary supplanted by one which viewed Mary as the "archetype of the Church"' (Eggemann, *Die 'ekklesiologische Wende' in der Mariologie des II. Vatikanums*, 67).

motherly nature of Mary's love for her son becomes the model and the norm for the official agenda of the Church. Evidently, then, Mary is here being made to 'epitomise the Church's mission, a calling that all believers should heed.[95]

However, this paradigm shift, which saw Mariology move from its former emphasis on prerogatives and relocate to the realm of ecclesiology, was highly controversial and is open to very different interpretations, even from a contemporary standpoint. Ultimately, only a slim majority of Council fathers at Vatican II decided that Mariology should henceforth be treated in the context of ecclesiology rather than in the context of soteriology.[96] This represented a direct attack on the heart of the traditional prerogatives-focused Mariology, which ultimately always culminated in co-redemptive Mariology.[97] What exactly lies behind the idea of designating Mary as a co-redeemer, an image so completely rejected by Vatican II? And is there any way of giving this notion, which at first sight appears very odd, a more intelligible substance?

The idea of including Mariology within soteriology is one that appears in the Old Church. For instance, as early as Irenaeus it becomes clear that Mary herself has soteriological significance 'insofar as, through her religious obedience, she contributes to the execution of God's plan of salvation in the world: in contrast to Eve, who through her disobedience and lack of faith brought death into the world, Mary has become the "new matriarch" of a human race.'[98] It is therefore this Eve–Mary typology, which we treated at some length above, which prompted Church Fathers like Irenaeus to mistakenly designate Mary as a *causa salutis*, in other words as the cause of our salvation.[99] The correct core of this statement consists of the insight that God does not wish for our salvation to take place in any other way than through people's freely given assent. And so here the *fiat* of the Mother of God stands at the very beginning of the dramaturgy of the Christian redemption.

Naturally, though, we must not construe this connection as God making himself completely dependent upon Mary in his act of redemption. Of course we

---

95 Ibid., 68 with reference to LG 53.

96 Cf. LG 52–69, Greshake, *Maria-Ecclesia*, 183, Müller and Sattler, 'Mariologie', 175.

97 Cf. Eggemann, *Die 'ekklesiologische Wende' in der Mariologie des II. Vatikanums*, 6.

98 Greshake, *Maria-Ecclesia*, 140.

99 Cf. ibid.: *Ähnlich denkt Kyrill von Jerusalem: ,Da durch eine Jungfrau, die Eva, der Tod kam, sollte auch durch eine Jungfrau bzw. aus einer Jungfrau das Leben erscheinen. Während jene von einer Schlange betrogen wurde, sollte diese von Gabriel die frohe Botschaft erhalten.'* ('Cyril of Jerusalem takes a similar view: "Since death was brought into the world by a virgin, Eve, it is only fitting that life should appear through or from a virgin too. Whereas the former was deceived by a serpent, the latter was destined to receive the joyous message from the Angel Gabriel."') (Schmaus, *Mariologie*, 287)

can count on God finding other ways for us humans to attain salvation when an individual refuses to heed his call. But his aim in taking the individual, including Mary, into his service is that, through that person, his offer of salvation might become tangible reality. And a gap and a problem only exist if we refuse. Consequently, therefore, Mary can help – indeed, we too can help – in mediating salvation. All of us (parents, teachers, catechists) are 'also intermediaries, mediators of salvation or others.'[100] For God commends us, for example, when through our word our unconditional love becomes tangible reality for our children. In the same way God also solicits help from Mary. 'Everyone is a mediator to everyone else!'[101] Yet we perform that role to one another to extremely varying degrees. And according to the Catholic conviction, there is 'no-one among us humans who has played a more profound, all-embracing role, one that has determined the whole course of the history of salvation, than the Blessed Virgin and Mother of Our Lord.'[102]

This distinction of Mary forms the justified core of traditional prerogative-based Mariology. Whenever the Church confuses her sanctity with its own purity and sinlessness, it is easy to see that it is perfectly possible for there also to be illegitimate ways for the Church to identify with Mary all too readily. It is vital, in all anthropological negotiation of Mariological dogmas, to always keep in mind that the things we profess about her are ultimately what we hope for ourselves. At this point we should note an important difference that should also prevent us from simply allowing Mariology to be absorbed into ecclesiology. Mary is the paradigm of the redeemed person and exemplifies what the Church aspires to itself. If we believe that the Church is already just like Mary, then we fall prey to a dangerous ideology. This might lead us to designate Mary – in her role as a paradigm of the redeemed human and a paradigm of the way in which people might be drawn into participating in God's work of salvation – as also being a co-redeemer. Yet the only way we might justify such a designation theologically is if we were prepared to apply it as a matter of principle to all human beings. For this reason, it seems to us far more accurate to characterise Mary as the person in whom God's redemptive actions are made visible in a quite extraordinary way, and who exemplifies human participation in God's programme of salvation. To cite the words of Karl Rahner: 'Mary is the practical actualisation of the complete Christian. If Christianity in an ideal sense is the pure acceptance of the

100 Rahner, *Maria*, 563.
101 Ibid., 564.
102 Ibid., 564.

redemption of the eternal, three-in-one God made flesh in Jesus Christ, then Mary is the perfect Christian, the very epitome of the Christian person, because she received the eternal word of the Father in complete faith in the Holy Spirit and in her blessed womb – in other words with body and soul and with all the strength of her being.'[103] This unequivocally places Mary wholly on the responding side of humanity, or of the Church.[104]

It is intriguing to revisit the question of the relationship between grace and freedom, as exemplified by Mary. For feminist theology in particular has repeatedly criticised the passivity of the traditional image of Mary. It is therefore important to emphasise that Mary's aforementioned readiness to open herself entirely to God when he approaches her does not imply any lack of active involvement or free will on her part. Thus, Rahner has explicitly stated that Mary's act is an 'act of freedom'.[105] Nevertheless, it is axiomatic of this and every other act of freedom in Rahner's theology that God first of all enables it to take place 'through the efficacy of his grace, with the result that the history of people receiving God is, once again, actually the glorious history of God's grace. In this matter, too, God creates the prerequisite for his self-communication in grace, albeit in such a way that this prerequisite for God's appearance in the world really does become – like God himself as grace – a reality for man.'[106] In Mary, therefore, genuine human freedom and activity is facilitated, but this is only made possible and sustained through God's grace. Rahner speaks at this point about a direct proportionality of the relationship between divine action and human freedom. Because God wants to liberate humans to freedom, by this rationale people become more free the more they open themselves up to God's liberating acts of grace. The relationship between merit and grace, which we have already discussed in relation to the Church Fathers,

---

103 Ibid., 530.

104 Cf. Menke, *Fleisch geworden aus Maria*, 12: *Maria ist nicht neben Christus ‚Mit-Erlöserin', sondern das ‚immakulate Konzept' des erlösten Menschen.... Weil der Erlöser seine Menschwerdung im Sinne des Bundesgedankens an das Ja-Wort des Menschen bindet, durch den er eintritt in diese Welt, ist Maria der heilige Rest Israels, Urbild und Stellvertreterin aller Gläubigen.* ('Mary is not a co-redeemer alongside Christ, but instead the 'immaculate concept' of the redeemed person… Because the Saviour, in the sense of the covenant idea, links his incarnation as man with human assent, through which he gained entry to this world, Mary is the Holy Remnant of Israel, the archetype and the representative of all believers.') As should have become apparent above, the alternative opened up here strikes us as plausible only to a limited degree.

105 Rahner, *Maria*, 517.

106 Ibid..

would by this reckoning show itself to be proportional and explain why Jacob of Serugh, for instance, is able to praise Mary's virtues with such enthusiasm while in the same breath admitting that absolutely everything that she is is the result of God's actions and grace.[107]

Thus, according to Rahner, Mary, in complete accord with the thinking not only of the Second Vatican Council but also of an important strand of patristic theology, is every inch the exemplar of a human being. In her freedom, she is in dialogue with God and symbolises the frankness of this dialogue between free agents.[108] In both her life and her death, she is the model of human existence. Consequently, it seems obvious that we should also regard her perfection as a pattern for the way we ought to live our lives. Once one has grasped this connection, it comes as no surprise to learn that the fourth Marian dogma of the Catholic Church deals with Mary's perfection. It states that Mary was taken up in body and soul to heavenly glory; here too it professes something of Mary that we would all wish for ourselves. Particularly in the aftermath of the Second World War, with all its images of piles of bodies, which photographs and newsreels made ubiquitous and seared into the memories of survivors, it was of vital importance to the Catholic Church to hold up as an example the Christian belief that the whole human being is redeemed and perfected by God. Here too, therefore, Mary is once again the model and epitome of what awaits every believer. She clearly symbolises the very essence of Christian hope.

This also makes Mary an obvious expression of the sacramental nature of the Catholic faith.[109] Her life is sacramentally emblematic of what the Church should represent in this world and what people are destined for. It is precisely when she acknowledges that she is a lowly handmaid of the Lord that she becomes the antithesis of a world in which everything revolves around power and possessions.[110] But

107 Accordingly Rahner states that Mary was nothing but 'Purity, love, goodness, faithfulness, patience, mercy, and love of the cross, a person who was devoted to God alone, to such an extent – as the Church ventures to say – that this person "deserved" to become the mother of the Redeemer, even though this "merit" resides exclusively in the grace of God.' (Rahner, *Maria*, 554)

108 Cf. ibid., 541: 'Thus, there really does arise in this world history a formidable dialogue between the free God and the free human being … Seen from God's perspective, this dialogue as such is always open.'

109 Cf. Greshake, *Maria-Ecclesia*, 485: 'The involvement of all creatures in God's acts of salvation can only be sacramental action, that is an act whose authorization derives entirely from God's son and God's spirit, and which remains constantly reliant upon these and hence finds itself obliged to refer to them.'

110 Cf. ibid. At another point Greshake defines lowliness, poverty and virginity as the fundamental characteristics of Mary, and declares her to be the antithesis of the otherwise

unfortunately it was precisely this aspect of Mary's symbolic character that was thrown into serious crisis in Late Antiquity.

omnipresent lust for power, wealth and sex (ibid., 414). The fact that we have chosen to single out the aspect of sexuality here is because this triad was no longer regarded as a unit in Late Antiquity. While Mary's virginity continued to have a high profile in church proclamations as the antithesis to sexual desire, her lowliness and poverty did not unfortunately become key determinants of the Christian world.

4

Mary in the Political Theology of Late Antiquity

One might imagine that the analysis we have undertaken thus far has prepared the ground sufficiently well for a reading of the Qur'an. For we have not only provided an initial overview of the available evidence from the Bible and the writings of the Church Fathers, but also surveyed key aspects of the figure of Mary as represented in the dogma of the Catholic Church, both in Late Antiquity and today. However, as we shall see in this chapter, an extremely important factor that influenced the portrayal of Mary in the Qur'an, and which in our view has been almost entirely overlooked thus far, is still missing.[1] For in the seventh century, the proclaimer of the Qur'an was confronted with an image of Mary that had been pressed into service – to an extent that we would find shocking nowadays – to support the imperialist policies and military expansionism of the then Byzantine emperor Heraclius. Let us therefore first examine the political clashes that occurred during the period when the Qur'an came into being before going on to take a closer look at the way the figure of Mary was exploited in Byzantine imperial propaganda.

a) The political situation during the emergence of the Qur'an

The first decades of the seventh century were shaped geopolitically by the war conducted by the Byzantine emperor Heraclius (r. 610–641) against the Persians. Since the late third century, under the reign of the Eastern Iranian Sassanid dynasty the Persian Empire had evolved to become the second major power

1 The only exception that we know of is Ghaffar, *Der Koran in seinem religions und weltgeschichtlichen Kontext*, 27–56. However, he only hints at many of the points that need to be discussed in this regard.

of Late Antiquity alongside the Byzantine Empire. Heraclius had already been a general under Emperor Maurice (r. 582–602). Thereafter, during the troubled reign of the emperor Phocas, who overthrew Maurice in 602, Heraclius rose first to become a consul in 608 and then a usurper. In 610, he sailed with his fleet from Egypt to Constantinople and seized the throne, holding on to power until his death in 641. Historians commonly regard Heraclius as the last great ruler of Late Antiquity.[2]

In his conflict with the Persians, he initially found himself on the retreat. In 613, his forces suffered a crushing defeat at Antioch, which left the way open for the subsequent conquest of Jerusalem by the Persians in the following year. By 614, therefore, Jerusalem found itself no longer under Christian control for the first time in many centuries – a traumatic experience for Christendom in Late Antiquity. In particular, the loss of the relic of the True Cross was a topic of burning concern in Constantinople. Heraclius was not in a position to launch a counterattack until 621, so for the time being he was forced to confine his response to the field of propaganda.[3] As early as 615–616 the Persian Shah Chosroes II (r. 590–628) took the decision to liquidate the Byzantine Empire. Nor was this decision mere wishful thinking on his part: Chosroes's armies were able to seize and occupy for a long time not only Syro-Palestine, which played a key role in the trade and economy of the Byzantine Empire, but also Egypt, the breadbasket of Constantinople. This effectively placed half of all Byzantine territory, and moreover those regions which were by some distance the most economically significant, in Persian hands. What is more, this took place in a period when the Balkans and Greece, the European half of the Byzantine Empire, were completely destabilised as a result of repeated armed incursions by groups that were at times allied with Persia, such as the Avars, the Slavs and the Bulgars. And so, for the first time in the long history of conflict between the Persians and the Byzantines, the Persian plan to conquer Constantinople – and with it the entire Byzantine Empire – began to look perfectly feasible. Heraclius thus found himself fully occupied in fending off the Persian attacks.

Only in the spring of 622 – interestingly at almost exactly the same time as the Prophet Muhammad relocated from Mecca to Medina – did Heraclius launch

2 On this and the following, cf. Kaegi, *Heraclius*.

3 Cf. Howard-Johnston, 'Heraclius' Persian campaigns', 36: 'Almost the only type of aggressive action which Heraclius could take from 614 to 621 was the dissemination of propaganda. ... The sack of Jerusalem by Shahrvaraz's troops in 614 provided a rich seam of material, with plenty of gory details and shocking deeds.'

a major counteroffensive.[4] In 624, the year of Muhammad's first victory against the Meccans, Heraclius also managed to record his first military success against the Persians. The Emperor staked everything on this campaign, even going so far as to have his family by his side in camp.[5] Accordingly, he overwintered with his troops in Caucasian Albania (modern Azerbaijan), leaving Constantinople without the protection of his army for a protracted period. In the absence of the emperor, in 626 Constantinople duly found itself besieged, and almost taken, by the Persian general Shahrvaraz, but principally by Avar forces.[6] We will consider this dramatic incident in greater detail presently, but will concentrate for the moment on recounting the further course of historical events. In the very next year, 627, Heraclius managed to score a decisive victory over the Persians at Nineveh.[7] There followed in 628 his final triumph over Chosroes II, thanks to the treachery of a section of the Persian elite, who revolted and toppled the ruler in his imperial capital at Seleuceia–Ctesiphon.[8] However, the supreme Persian commander Shahrvaraz, the strategist behind Chosroes's earlier military successes, was initially disinclined to accept the peace treaty concluded with the Persian elites, so Heraclius was obliged to begin separate negotiations with him in 629. Only in the wake of a new treaty was the Byzantine East – i.e., Syria, Palestine and Egypt – formally regained and Heraclius was able to retake possession of Jerusalem on 21 March, 630, and bring back the relic of the True Cross.[9] Again, the coincidence of these events with the Prophet Muhammad's capture of Mecca is striking.

Having cast a brief eye over the conflicts between the great powers during the period of the Qur'an's gestation, let us turn our attention to the situation on the Arabian Peninsula. Since 320, the southern Arabian kings of Ḥimyar had looked favourably on Judaism, a fact recently attested by the discovery of several inscriptions. After 380, no more pagan inscriptions are found,[10] and up to 530 the only

4 Cf. ibid., 3.

5 Cf. ibid., 16.

6 We will discuss the siege of Constantinople in 626 in greater detail below ('The religious propaganda of Heraclius').

7 Cf. Howard-Johnston, 'Heraclius' Persian campaigns', 5.

8 Cf. ibid., 6.

9 Cf. ibid., 29.

10 Cf. Robin, 'Ḥimyar, Aksūm, and *Arabia Deserta* in Late Antiquity', 129. Of course – as Robin himself points put – one cannot infer from this disappearance of polytheism from grave inscriptions that no more polytheists existed in Southern Arabia henceforth. But its disappearance from the public sphere does make clear that its influence was waning markedly. In the following, we will reproduce – sometimes verbatim, but as a general rule abridged and slightly modified – some observations from Khorchide and von Stosch, *Der andere Prophet*, 55–60.

inscriptions in evidence are either Jewish or relate to the new faith of the 'God-fearing'[11] (clearly officially promoted by the royal house) – a form of monotheism inspired by Judaism, which in the Islamic tradition also goes by the name *Ḥanīfīya*. The southern Arabian kingdom of Ḥimyar is therefore of such great importance to us because it conquered large parts of central and western Arabia in the period from 420 to 445, including Mecca and Medina.[12] Around 500, it is likely that it controlled the whole of the Arabian Peninsula.[13] Over time, the ruler of Ḥimyar also appears to have converted to Judaism.

Shortly afterwards, however – most probably during the reign of Maʿdīkarib Yaʿfur (519–522) – the kingdom was taken over by the Ethiopian Christian kingdom of Aksūm.[14] The background to this event may possibly have been geo-political interests of the Byzantine Empire, which saw a Jewish kingdom of this kind as a potential sphere of influence of the Persians (who from time to time gave every impression of being sympathetic to Judaism) and therefore regarded it as a hostile power. The Byzantines thus appear to have prompted the Ethiopian Negus to take the action he did, in order to suppress Jewish and hence also Persian influence in the region.[15] Yet the very next king of Ḥimyar, Joseph, staged a revolt and brought southern Arabia back under Ḥimyaritic control. The Christians of the town of Nağrān offered fierce resistance, with the result that a massacre of Christians is believed to have taken place there in 523.[16]

This massacre triggered a response by the Ethiopians, and in 525 Joseph was murdered and the region brought back under Ethiopian control.[17] No sooner had they regained power than the Ethiopians set about Christianising the population and persecuting Jews.[18] However, the prince who was installed by Aksūm soon lost control over the Arabian heartland, after Abraha, the commander of his army in Arabia, turned against him and proclaimed himself king of Ḥimyar; Abraha is thought to have remained on the throne from 535 to 565.[19] We therefore have, from 535 onwards, a Christian kingdom in southern Arabia, which progressively expanded its influence. In an inscription dating from shortly after 552, Abraha

11 Cf. Robin, 'Ḥimyar, Aksūm, and *Arabia Deserta* in Late Antiquity', 129 f.
12 Cf. ibid., 138.
13 Cf. ibid., 145 f.
14 Cf. ibid., 146.
15 Cf. Berkey, *The formation of Islam*, 47.
16 Cf. Robin, 'Ḥimyar, Aksūm, and *Arabia Deserta* in Late Antiquity', 148; al-Azmeh, *The emergence of Islam in late antiquity*, 265.
17 Cf. Robin, 'Ḥimyar, Aksūm, and *Arabia Deserta* in Late Antiquity', 149.
18 Cf. ibid..
19 Cf. ibid., 150.

rejoices at the fact that Ḥimyaritic authority has now been restored throughout the whole of *Arabia Deserta*, including Medina. Under his rule, Christianity was the official religion, as several of his inscriptions indicate.[20] From relatively early on, he disengaged himself from Ethiopian Christianity, turning more towards Syrian or Arabian Christianity.

In exactly the same way as the rulers of Aksūm saw it as perfectly natural to use religion to legitimise their imperial ambitions and to ennoble their wars by embellishing them with Christian propaganda,[21] so King Abraha also developed an imperial theology. This doctrine, which is expressed in a stele inscription of 548, changed the formulaic invocation of the Holy Trinity (over and against the Ethiopian wording) so that it now spoke of God the Merciful (*Raḥmānān*), the Anointed (*msḥ-hw*) and the Holy Spirit (*rḥ qdś*).[22] What is significant about this is that it uses the Syriac or Arabic designation for the Messiah, and likewise the invocation of the Holy Spirit no longer follows the Old Ethiopian model but instead the Syriac/Arabian[23] one – just like the Qur'an.[24]

Mecca was in all likelihood also affected by Abraha's wars of conquest, though surely never subdued. At least according to Muslim tradition, the tribe of the Quresh who inhabited Mecca were known as the People of God because they defeated Abraha.[25] Similarly, in the surah of the Qur'an known as *al-Fil*/'The Elephant' (Q 105), we find an echo of Abraha's attempt to conquer the city. The backdrop to his bid to seize Mecca may perhaps have been his ambition to make the church at Sanaa, which was built at his behest, into the most important pilgrimage centre of the region and his accompanying desire to eradicate the competition

20 Cf. ibid., 153.

21 Cf. Ghaffar, *Der Koran in seinem religions- und weltgeschichtlichen Kontext*, 100, footnote 70. Thus, there are Ethiopian inscriptions that legitimise wars and imperialist claims on territory by using formulaic invocations of the Holy Trinity (with the Father and the Son given as *wld*, and the Holy Spirit as *mfs qds*).

22 Cf. ibid., 104.

23 These words for the Messiah and the Holy Spirit need not necessarily come from Syriac and so are not in themselves firm evidence of a direct Syrian influence on Abraha. From the very outset, they could just as easily have been Arabic words, or words used by Arab Christians or by Jews. The Syrian influence would then be more likely to consist in the early choice or possibly even loan coinage of both Arabic words and their establishment as theological terms. Thus, Abraha may simply have aligned himself with the religious language of Arabia (with, say, the Ethiopian word for spirit, *manfas*, simply replacing the Arabic – and Syriac – *rūḥ*, etc.).

24 The first mentions of being fortified by the Holy Spirit are found in Q 2:87; Q 2:253 and then once more in Q 5:110.

25 Cf. Robin, 'Ḥimyar, Aksūm, and *Arabia Deserta* in Late Antiquity', 152.

from Mecca.[26] We do not know this for certain, however. But in any event his influence clearly demonstrates how widespread Christianity had become on the Arabian Peninsula in the period immediately prior to the birth of Muhammad and how prevalent its miaphysitic strain must have been – whether in its West Syriac or its Ethiopian variant.

Most scholars assume that the Jewish presence on the Arabian Peninsula also remained firmly entrenched.[27] The Jews were presumably well integrated in their environment and had most likely arrived on the Arabian Peninsula after their expulsion from Palestine.[28] Perhaps they were also better organised and more widely distributed than the Christians. Ultimately, though, such thoughts are just as speculative as the assumption that, in spite of everything, Arabia had a predominantly polytheistic character.

All we know for sure is that Abraha's kingdom disintegrated under the rule of his sons sometime in the 570s,[29] and as a result the Eastern Roman (Byzantine) Empire lost its most important ally on the Arabian Peninsula. The area over which Abraha's kingdom had once held sway was overrun as early as 570 by the Persians and governed thereafter by the Iranian (Sassanid) Empire.[30] Not only the Jews but also the East Syriac Christians saw the Iranian Empire as a protecting force, and the widely held assumption is that under Persian influence, Christianity primarily in its East Syriac variant was of paramount importance; however, during the reign of Chosroes II, the West Syriac miaphysitic church, which in the meantime had scored some remarkable successes over the hitherto dominant East Syriacs in Persian Mesopotamia, came to be favoured by the Shah and his governing system.[31] The East Syriac Christians, whose heartland continued to be the area currently occupied by the modern state of Iraq, were also strongly represented not only in the ports of Yemen in the sixth and early seventh centuries, but also in Oman and in the region of present-day Qatar,[32] as well as on the islands of the Persian Gulf and doubtless also in al-Ḥira (south of Baghdad, on the fringes of the

26 Cf. Bell, *The origin of Islam*, 40.
27 Cf. Berkey, *The formation of Islam*, 46.
28 Cf. ibid., 42.
29 Cf. Robin, 'Ḥimyar', 152.
30 It has become the norm in more recent studies to refer to the polity ruled by the Sassanids as the 'Iranian Empire', thereby indicating that it did not consist solely of the Persian people.
31 Cf. Labourt, *Le christianisme dans l'empire perse sous la dynastie Sassanide*, 219–228; Frye, The political history of Iran under the Sasanians, 171 f.
32 On Oman cf. Ioan, *Muslime und Araber bei Iso'jahb III.*, 100 ff.; on Qatar: Kozah et al. (eds.), *The Syriac Writers of Qatar in the Seventh Century*.

Iranian Empire).[33] They therefore influenced not only the Persians but also their vassal state of the Lakhmids, which was situated in the northeast of the Arabian Peninsula.[34] We also know for sure that the East Syriac Christians already had a foothold at least in the city of Sanaa following the Persian occupation of southern Arabia.[35] As a result, Theresia Hainthaler concludes that they were 'without a doubt to be found in the cities and especially the ports of Yemen, though there is no evidence that they put down roots among the rural population.'[36] In consequence, any claim that there was an East Syriac influence on the Qur'an must remain in the realm of pure speculation.[37]

By contrast, the great influence of West Syriac theology can be identified at many points other than the clear sway it held over the kingdom of Ḥimyar. The similarly West Syriac-influenced Arab tribal grouping of the Ghassanids, who were ruled over by the Jafnids, inhabited the northwest of the Arabian Peninsula. Despite its miaphysitic orientation, the Jafnid royal house was initially a loyal ally of the Eastern Roman Empire against the Iranian Empire.[38]

Yet from the 570s onwards, and following the decline of Byzantine influence on the Arabian Peninsula, the Ghassanids came within the Persians' sphere of influence and were eventually completely overrun by them in 613–614.[39] During the conflict that arose between Muhammad and Byzantium in 629–630,[40] the Ghassanids again became important to Heraclius; in around 630 or shortly thereafter, they duly switched sides and became allies of Byzantium once more. James

---

33 Cf. Hainthaler, *Christliche Araber vor dem Islam*, 110, 134 f.

34 However, these Lakhmids were not Christians themselves. Even as late as the start of the sixth century, the Arab king of Hīra offered up a group of Christian nuns as human sacrifices (cf. Bell, *The origin of Islam*, 27).

35 This Eastern Syrian influence should not be overstated, if only for the fact that the Persians were thoroughly pragmatic in their dealings, supporting the miaphysite majority in Palestine and Syria, for example, and recognising it as the prevalent religion (cf. Frend, *The Rise of the Monophysite Movement*, 337).

36 Bell, *The Origin of Islam*, 134.

37 Cf. René Tardy, *Najrân. Chrétiens d'Arabie avant l'Islam*, Beirut 1999, 165 f., who sees 'Nestorianism' as a marginal phenomenon on the Arabian Peninsula and who also considers that 'Monophysitism' was influenced by Julianism (ibid., 172).

38 Cf. Fisher, *Between Empires*, 60 f.

39 Cf. Bell, *The origin of Islam*, 23.

40 Admittedly, there was no direct contact between the Byzantine Emperor and the Muslims. However, as early as 429, the first armed clash with Muslim forces does appear to have taken place east of the Dead Sea (at Mu'ta) , from which Heraclius's troops emerged victorious (Kaegi, *Heraclius*, 233). Therefore, it may well be the case that Byzantine theological ideas came more strongly into the purview of the Qur'an precisely during the later period of the Prophet's proclamation.

Howard-Johnston surmises that they only sided with the emperor after initially displaying some sympathy for Muhammad's movement.[41] Yet the evidence in the sources for this initial support of Muhammad's cause is very sparse indeed. The only incontrovertible fact is that the Ghassanids ultimately switched sides and supported Heraclius.

Even so, one cannot regard the Ghassanids as representatives of Byzantine Christianity. The close geopolitical alliance between the Jafnids and Byzantium had no influence on the popular church practices that from a very early stage had become widespread throughout their dominion,[42] and as we have already seen, the predominant strain of Christianity across the area they controlled was of a miaphysitic and anti-Chalcedonian nature. This influence is evident, for example, in the fact that it was the Jafnid king Ḥāriṯ who in 542 requested and secured the ordination of those three miaphysitic bishops who subsequently became the first to perform priestly and (most importantly) episcopal ordinations outside the jurisdiction of the official imperial church and its system of canon law and in so doing became the founders of a schismatic, separate 'miaphysitic episcopate'.[43] Although the Anti-Chalcedonians were only represented on the Arabian Peninsula by a weak ecclesiastical hierarchy, they appear to have been very popular among believers.[44]

Evidently, therefore, Arabs in the dominion of the Jafnids were, generally speaking, of a miaphysitic disposition, and it is perfectly possible that their influence may have extended as far as Medina.[45] Especially if one assumes that Abraha undertook successful missionary work in Medina, it is logical to suppose that West Syriac Christians came into contact with their co-religionists there. At the time when the Qur'an came into being, then, Byzantine Christianity was only present on the Arabian Peninsula to a limited extent.[46] By that stage, the Ḥimyaritic kingdom had been defeated, the Ghassanids (at least in religious-political terms)

41 Cf. Howard-Johnston, *Witnesses of a World Crisis*, 447 f.

42 Cf. Fisher, *Between Empires*, 63.

43 Cf. al-Azmeh, *The emergence of Islam in late antiquity*, 264; Menze, *Justinian and the making of the Syrian-Orthodox church*, especially 261 f.; Saint-Laurent, *Missionary stories and the formation of the Syriac churches*, especially 96–109; Wood, 'Christianity and the Arabs in the sixth century', 355–370.

44 On this and the following, cf. Hainthaler, *Christliche Araber vor dem Islam*, 67–80.

45 Cf. Bell, *The origin of Islam*, 22 f.

46 As the Greek versions of the martyrdom of Ḥāriṯ and the life of 'Gergentios' indicate, there were some points of contact at all events (though no further details of these can be found). These accounts make out that Christianity in Yemen and on the Arabian Peninusula was of the Chalcedonian–Byzantine kind (cf. Albrecht Berger, *Life and Works of Saint Gregentios, Archbishop of Taphar. Introduction, Critical Edition and Translation. With a contribution by G. Fiaccadori*, Berlin 2006).

were leaning towards the Miaphysites and at the time were also geopolitically opposed to Byzantium. Consequently, Byzantine Christianity seems only to have come to the attention of the Qur'an in the Late Medina period – at the same time as Heraclius finally triumphed over the Persians and Muhammad prevailed over the Meccans. The result of this was that a new constellation of opposing forces appeared on the horizon.

b) The religious propaganda of Heraclius

From the very outset, Heraclius tried to orchestrate his campaign against the Sassanids as a Holy War. This involved portraying his adversaries as fire worshippers and styling himself as the defender of Christendom – among other things, by exerting increasing pressure on the Jewish sectors of the populace. One can therefore imagine that the conflicts between Jews and Christians that are referred to in the Qur'an (e.g. in Q 2:113; 2:139 f.) as taking place precisely at this time were not just a regional phenomenon. In the summer of 624, when Heraclius's forces set foot on Persian soil for the first time, he exhorted his troops to fight as if inspired by the fear of God and to avenge the Persians' blasphemy.[47] He placed himself in the tradition of biblical land seizure under Joshua and expressly proclaimed a Holy War in 625. He classified death on the battlefield in this campaign as martyrdom – with the guarantee that all martyrs would gain direct entry into heaven.[48] The similarity between this war propaganda and the exactly contemporaneous verses of the Qur'an is striking.[49]

47 Cf. Howard-Johnston, 'Heraclius' Persian campaigns', 39.

48 Cf. ibid., 40.

49 'But it is unlikely to have been mere coincidence that Heraclius and Muhammad encouraged their troops with the prospect that those who were killed in action would earn the crown of martyrdom and gain direct entry to Paradise, in the same year. Heraclius first publicly announced the new doctrine (which had presumably been agreed earlier with the church authorities) in spring 624, as his army crossed the old frontier into Persia. Muhammad did likewise at the time of the Battle of Badr, which is conventionally dated to March 624' (Howard-Johnston, *Witnesses of a World Crisis*, 447). One key difference between the choice of words in the Qur'an and Heraclius's propaganda can be found in the fact that in the numerous instances where the word *šāhid* ('witness for God') appears in the Qur'an, the idea of an act of testimony that willingly embraces death is just one of several different meanings. By contrast, the English term *martyr* always carries an association of suffering and death; as a result, purely from a philological angle, one should be wary of drawing an equivalence between the Qur'an and Heraclius. Perhaps it might be fair to say that the Qur'an responds to the propaganda while at the same time keeping in mind a broader spectrum of meaning for the idea of 'testimony'.

At the same time, Heraclius's attitude amounted to a religious supercharging of his acts of aggression, a phenomenon that had never been encountered before in Byzantine history and which must have come as a shock to his contemporaries. The idea of martyrdom of those who were killed fighting against 'the ungodly' was a distinguishing feature of this campaign of Heraclius. However, it had almost no support in the Byzantine Church or its religious precepts: no fallen warrior was actually declared a martyr after the campaign, and also Heraclius's promise of an immediate 'admission to heaven' for the fallen was never confirmed by the Byzantine Church, its representative organs or its leading theologians. Thus, the whole idea of a 'Holy War' did not endure after Heraclius's reign, in the same way that it had no prehistory in Byzantium prior to Heraclius. This must have made it all the more conspicuous and impressive when Heraclius launched it.[50]

Heraclius therefore quite clearly gave all his wars this religious dimension. Repeatedly, prayers were offered up for God to lend his support to the Byzantine cause: the inscription *Deus adiuta Romanis* ('May God help the Romans'), for instance, was found on a coin that was minted in large numbers – a supplication that is taken up almost verbatim by Q 30:5. Taken as a whole, the Qur'anic verses Q 30:2–6 should surely be read as having a pro-Byzantine tenor.[51] This means that, at a time when Heraclius was using religious motifs for propaganda purposes while still in a relatively weak position militarily, the proclaimer of the Qur'an took a relaxed view of these developments; indeed, at this stage, Muslims still saw themselves as spiritually on the side of the Byzantines.[52]

This situation changed at the latest when a power-political struggle broke out between Muhammad's movement and the revitalised Byzantine Empire in 629–630. Even before this date, Heraclius's religious propaganda had attempted to paint his wars as eschatological events leading to the return of the Messiah. On

50 Cf. above all Tesei, 'Heraclius's war propaganda and the Qur'ān's promise of reward for dying in battle', 227–229. Tesei shows that the only prior instance of the concept of martyrdom promoted in Heraclius's propaganda is to be found in Armenian sources, and that it therefore has a specifically Armenian history. The thesis that has been put forward by some scholars, which sees Heraclius's concept of martyrdom as the expression of a tradition of Holy War in Byzantium that prefigures the Crusades, now seems outmoded. Cf. Regan, First Crusader; a recap of more recent research in this field is given in: Kolia-Dermitzaki, '"Holy War" in Byzantium Twenty Years Later', 121–132.

51 For a detailed justification and classification of this finding, cf. Ghaffar, *Der Koran in seinem religions- und weltgeschichtlichen Kontext*, 167–186.

52 This original connection between the proclaimer of the Qur'an and Heraclius is also reflected in the fact that Heraclius is highly praised in early Islamic literature, among others things for his knowledge of the Qur'an. Cf. El-Cheikh, *Byzantium viewed by the Arabs*, 39–54, especially 41; cf. ibid., 'Muhammad and Heraclius', especially 12 ff.

the basis of his victory and his subsequent repatriation of the relic of the True Cross, Heraclius was able in all seriousness to style himself as an eschatological figure. But even as early as the 620s we find statements adulating the emperor which could from a monotheistic standpoint be seen as thoroughly objectionable. Thus, it continued to be customary in Byzantine imperial ceremony of this period – which basically remained much like the reformed imperial ceremony under Diocletian, itself undoubtedly influenced by Persian practice – to venerate the emperor or other religious dignitaries by performing an act of proskynesis (prostrating oneself with outstretched arms and kissing the ground).[53]

Under Heraclius, adulation of the emperor also took on a religious dimension. It was he who introduced the title of Basileus for himself, presented himself as a Davidian figure[54] and drew comparisons between himself and Constantine the Great, though he stopped short of declaring the holder of the emperorship a God.[55] It is interesting to note that in the 620s Miaphysite Christians, evidently in response to Heraclius's propaganda, tried to present Chosroes II as the new Constantine.[56] The concept of adoration (proskynesis/*sağda*), which in the Qur'an is reserved exclusively for God, was applied by various warring Christian factions to their respective leaders; both philologically and generally speaking, this term was not the preserve of God in either Greek or Syrian Christianity. With regard to

53 Cf. for instance the report of the *Chronicon Paschale* on the ceremony at which Emperor Heraclius elevated his son, also called Heraclius, to co-emperor: Der neue [Mit]kaiser προσεκυνήθη ὑπὸ τῶνσυγκλητικῶν (*Chronicon Paschale*, edited by L. Dindorf (Corpus scriptorum historiae Byzantinae), Bonn 1832, 703); cf. also the testimonies of Procopius of Caesarea in the sixth century: *De bellis 4.9.12*, edited by J. Haury and G. Wirth, 2 vols., Leipzig 1962–3; however, the honour of proskynesis was also accorded to persons such as the wife of a Germanic 'king', cf. ibid., 7.1.39. On proskynesis performed before a revered leading monk and before simple priests, cf. Cyril of Scythopolis, Vita Cyriaci, 224 and Procopius of Caesarea, *De bellis 3.8.21*. In any event, it is clear that this kind of proskynesis was not considered objectionable within Christianity. For even within the Greek Old Testament, the Septuagint, the verb *proskynein* is used – as it is in early Christian texts too – in the sense of a deep bow and as such is not related to God (cf. for example Genesis 23:7: Αβρααμ προσεκύνησεν τῷ λαῷ τῆς γῆς, τοῖς υἱοῖς Χετ; the Syriac Peshitta at this point has sgd ('to bow down'); cf. also 1 Chronicles 21:21 [proskynesis before David]). The verb *proskynein* (along with its derivatives) was primarily used and understood in the sense of 'to make a low bow', and by no means exclusively in the sense of 'worshipping'(in the way that one may only worship God); the verb λατρεύειν (Noun: λα-τρεία) was used for the kind of veneration that was due only to God. Cf. Maraval, *Lieux saints et pèlerinages d'Orient*, 145 ff.

54 Cf. also Goar, *Euchologion sive rituale Graecorum*, 726 f.

55 Cf. Dagron, *Empereur et prêtre*, 78.

56 On the legend of the christening of Chosroes II, a product of pious wishful thinking on the part of the Syrians, cf. Schilling, *Die Anbetung der Magier und die Taufe der Sassaniden*, 185–190.

such a practice, it is perfectly understandable that the Qur'anic community might well have gained the impression that the leading secular and religious figures of the day were being venerated in a God-like way, and this most likely constituted the historical background to the reproachful reference to this custom in verse 9:30 f. of the Qur'an. For our context, the most important point here is that images of Mary were also venerated by means of proskynesis – and even by the ruler, what is more.[57]

A key role for the significance of Mary in the context of this questionable political theology of Byzantine propaganda was played by the interpretation of the successful resistance the Byzantines mounted against the siege of Constantinople in 626. This siege, which represented an existential threat to Byzantium, was undertaken primarily by the Avars, Slavs, Bulgars and other groups on the one hand, and on the other by the Persian army, and comprised both a land encirclement and a seaborne blockade.[58] At this time, the Empire of the Avars, which had its heartland in present-day Hungary, was able, together with its Slavic and Bulgarian allies, to exert military control over the Balkans and Greece, in other words most of the European territories of the Byzantine Empire.[59] Now, in concert with the Iranian Empire, it was the Avars' ambition to exploit the absence of the emperor and his army and seize control of Constantinople. We shall now examine this siege in greater detail and analyse how Mary came to be promoted as the city's saviour.

c) Mary as military commander

The exploitation of the figure of Mary for imperial purposes by Emperor Heraclius is actually quite a surprising development when one recalls how strongly Mary, both in the Bible and later in the works of the Syriac Church Fathers, was characterised by her humility and poverty.[60] For Ephrem the Syrian, Mary was the Mother of Weakness, who turned the *status quo* on its head.[61] Yet having said this, even in the

---

57 Cf. Theophylaktos Simokattes, *Historiae 5.15.10*, edited by C. de Boor, Leipzig 1887. This text is of interest for the theme of Mariology in that it contains an account of Shah Chosroes II venerating the icons of the Mother of God.

58 Cf. Hurbanič, *The Avar Siege of Constantinople in 626*, 1.

59 Cf. ibid., 112.

60 Cf. Ashkar, *Mary in the Syriac Christian tradition and Islam*, 78.

61 Cf. Ephrem, *Hymnen de Nativitate*, 11,7: 'The womb of Your Mother turned the world upside-down. The maker of the universe entered as a rich man and left as a beggar. The mighty came in and emerged as the lowly.'

Old Church, Mary was unfortunately not immune to being implicated in imperial fantasies. Thus, for example, in a fifth-century sermon usually attributed to Cyril of Alexandria it is stated quite unequivocally that secular kings only rule through the grace of Mary.[62] And especially for an emperor like Heraclius, who only came to power through toppling his predecessor from the throne, it comes as little surprise that the latent potential for violence in biblical texts that talked about the liberation of the poor now found itself exploited by the politics of imperialism.

Likewise, the role of Mary hinted at in the Gospel of John as an advocate is extremely prevalent among the Syriac Church Fathers and represents at least a possible connection point for her exploitation in wartime. Over time, Mary's role increasingly developed into that of an intercessor with God;[63] in this capacity she could be called upon directly and asked to help people and intercede on their behalf.[64] While Ephrem never refers to Mary directly as an intercessor, his writings do present her as a power that can make Christ present for the hungry and the needy.[65] And in the work of Jacob of Serugh at the latest, the figure Mary is unambiguously in use as an intercessor.[66]

Though we are still a long way here from any power-political or military context, this development does nonetheless signal a steadily growing significance of the figure of Mary for everyday life. When one considers that in the sixth century a well-attested tendency grew up during the conflict against the Persians to call upon saints for help in war,[67] the militarisation of Mary's role should come as no surprise either. And it was precisely her role as intercessor that was lighted upon in contemporary imperial theology and exploited so as to depict Mary as a potent mediator with God.[68] The reign of Justinian saw the beginning of a

62 Cf. Cyril of Alexandria, '4. Homily.' In: *Acta Conciliorum Oecumenicorum I.1/2*, edited by E. Schwartz, Berlin-Leipzig 1927, 102 f. Whether this sermon can be regarded as authentic is a matter of dispute. On the debate cf. footnote 47 on p. 65. For the most part, scholarly literature deems the oldest source in which Mary is laden with military motifs to be a sermon by Severian dating from around 400 (cf. George-Tvrtković, *Christians, Muslims, and Mary*, 25; Shoemaker, *Mary in Early Christian Faith and Devotion*, 177 f.).

63 Cf. Madey, *Marienlob aus dem Orient*, 115.

64 Cf. ibid., 102.

65 Cf. Horn, 'Ancient Syriac Sources on Mary's Role as Intercessor', 156.

66 Cf. ibid., 175.

67 On the corresponding role of Ephrem the Syrian and St. Jacob of Nisibis, cf. Peeters, 'La légende de saint Jacques de Nisibe', 295–304.

68 Cf. Cameron, 'The Theotokos in Sixth-Century Constantinople', 104: 'the Virgin of sixth-century Constantinople is before all else the most potent intercessor before God. What is most emphasised is her mediation; she stands between God and the suppliant, who looks to her for the assurance that his prayers will be answered.'

Imperial seal depicting (on the obverse) Heraclius and (on the reverse) the Mother of God with child, c. 610–613 (Dumbarton Oaks, BZS. 1958.106.523)[72]

systematic promotion of the veneration of Mary in the Byzantine Empire, a practice that his successors Justin II and Maurice developed still further, for instance by instituting a growing number of feast days and processions in Mary's honour.[69] By means of imperial propaganda, Mary became the authority that ensured the legitimacy of the imperial rule.[70] At the same time, she rose to become the protectress of Constantinople. From the reign of Justin II onwards, this new role of hers was reflected on the reverse side of seals: the Mother of God with the Christ child now appears instead of the hitherto customary figure of the goddess Victoria/Nike, and in her place guarantees imperial triumphs.[71]

Thus, the veneration of Mary was used by emperors from Justinian onwards to stabilise their grip on power and to exercise social control.[73] And from a somewhat earlier period, icons have been found in Rome portraying Mary as empress.[74] It is likely that such images also existed in Constantinople, since broadly similar artists worked in both imperial capitals, and iconography was developed in common.

69 Cf. ibid., 95. On the wide-ranging tendency towards liturgisation, cf. also Meier, 'Liturgisierung und Hypersakralisierung', 75–106.

70 Cf. Cameron, 'The Theotokos in Sixth-Century Constantinople', 97: 'It was, too, the Virgin herself who, in Corippus's imagination, carried the news of Justinian's death to the new emperor, and thus appeared in the iconographic guise of the divine figure who bestows the imperial insignia on the emperor. In all of this the role of imperial patronage does, I feel, need to be reiterated.'

71 Cf. Stepanova, 'Victoria-Nike on Early Byzantine Seals', 16.

72 We are indebted to Lars Rickelt for this reference. Dumbarton Oaks, *Research Library and Collection*, Washington, DC.

73 Cf. Cameron, 'The Theotokos in Sixth-Century Constantinople', 100 f.

74 Cf. Lidova, *The Earliest Images of Maria Regina in Rome*.

Presumably the only reason why no direct evidence of this has survived from Constantinople is because all images there were destroyed during the First and Second Iconoclasms.

The particular connection between Mary and Constantinople resulted from the fact that a number of relics relating to her were venerated there. Although no mortal remains of Mary were venerated, certain items of her clothing[75] were, and these helped greatly vivify the worship of Mary. As early as the end of the fifth century, churches dedicated to Mary were built at Blachernai and Chalkoprateia and furnished with suitable relics (probably veils and cloaks). She was also commonly depicted spreading out her cloak to protect the whole world as it was conceived at that time.[76] As a result, the Mother of God was actually omnipresent in both the physical city and in imperial theology well before the siege of Constantinople in 626 – which we will discuss at greater length presently – so that Constantinople was venerated as the city of the *Theotokos*.[77] The Mother of God's first saving of Constantinople took place in 619, when the city was besieged by the Avars.[78] At that time, the garment of Mary's that was housed in the church at Panagia Blachernai was brought out and used as a shield against the besieging forces, yet miraculously remained completely intact. It appeared to the city's inhabitants as though the Virgin had transferred her incorruptibility to her clothes.[79] Time and again throughout the history of Constantinople, it was this garment that proved to be the city's salvation.[80]

Henceforth, Mary was also called upon time and again in military matters, as well as to ward off diseases such as the plague. In any event, Mary's capacity to perform miracles was a decisive factor in her veneration. And talk of her as the Mother of God was also invoked in a major way in wartime, at least in popular religious observance and in imperial propaganda. If one were to speculate whether these forms of popular piety in Constantinople and the matching imperial theology were also known on the Arabian Peninsula, then the first basic fact to emerge is that the propaganda of the various Byzantine emperors would surely at least

75 Cf. Wenger, 'L'intercession de Marie en Orient', 55 f.

76 Cf. ibid., 75.

77 Cf. Wenger, 'Les interventions de Marie', 423 f.

78 Cf. ibid., 424.

79 Cf. ibid. The incorruptibility of the body and clothing of Mary is a topic that we shall return to later.

80 Cf. Wenger, 'Les interventions de Marie', 429. In 623 as well, it was this very garment that was considered to have played a decisive role in the victory over the Avars who besieged the city on that occasion too (cf. Hurbanič, *The Avar Siege of Constantinople in 626*, 324).

have engaged the interest of Syriac Christians.[81] It is certainly true that Emperor Heraclius had to fight hard to win the loyalty of Syriac Christians, and was not especially successful in his endeavours.[82] But quite clearly the Syrian region was heavily influenced by propaganda from Byzantium. The routes from the Byzantine Empire to Arabia took a long time to travel, so it is entirely possible that reactions only became apparent decades later. But of course a particular event might also have the power to evoke a much quicker response on the Arabian Peninsula.

One such momentous event may well have been the aforementioned siege of Constantinople in 626. Three contemporary sources have survived, all of which are in accord regarding the decisive role played by Mary in this military engagement: the sermon of Theodore Synkellos, the poem *Bellum avaricum* by the court poet Georgios Pisides (George of Pisidia) and the *Chronicon paschale*.[83] All these sources agree that the Byzantine capital was only saved by the intervention of the Virgin Mary.[84] For Georgios Pisides, it was Mary alone who defeated the Avars.[85] He saw Mary as the invincible Virgin *per se*.[86] In similar vein, Theodore Synkellos wrote that it was plain for all to see that the Virgin herself had carried the day, and furthermore had done so on her own. For the Byzantine fleet had been immediately put to flight by the enemy's superiority, and only Mary's intervention had

81 Even at the time of Jacob of Serugh and Severus of Antioch, Syrian Christians – despite the conflict between the miaphysite tendency and Chalcedonian Constantinople – remained fiercely loyal to the emperor, and pinned their hopes on the installation of a miaphysite emperor and the institution of a miaphysite imperial Church (cf. Papoutsakis, *Vicarious Kingship*, especially 191 ff.; Kavvadas, 'Severus of Antioch and changing miaphysite attitudes toward Byzantium', 124–137). Only when it became apparent in the second half of the sixth century that such an outlook was wholly unrealistic did the new leadership of the Syrian Miaphysite movement break with this tradition, and by the end of the sixth century matters had progressed so far that the Syrians of Edessa collaborated with the Persians against the emperor.

82 Heraclius's attempts to bring about a union with the Syrian churches clearly remained unsuccessful. Even the 'unions' that Heraclius was able to form with certain Armenian and Coptic bishops were undoubtedly the result of massive political pressure and did not outlive Heraclius (for the sources on these endeavours, cf. Booth, *Crisis of Empire*, 200–208; Booth, however, greatly overestimates the significance of certain local and purely temporary 'successes' at forming unions in Egypt).

83 Cf. Hurbanič, *The Avar Siege of Constantinople in 626*, 3.

84 Cf. ibid., 1, 248.

85 Cf. ibid., 249.

86 Cf. George of Pisidia, *Bellum Avaricum*, v. 1–9, 156, quoted in Hurbanič, *The Avar Siege of Constantinople in 626*, 249.

turned the tables.[87] It was she, Synkellos maintained, who had caused the enemy ship to sink right in front of her shrine.[88]

The historical background to such stories may have been a storm or some other natural occurrence, which played a decisive role in a sea battle directly off Blachernai. Whatever the case, this incident helped strengthen a popular belief that only a supernatural intervention could explain the outcome of the battle, especially in light of the absence of the emperor and his army.[89] But some observers claimed that Mary had acted directly to inspire the Byzantine defenders.[90] Theodore Synkellos for one was in no doubt that Mary had single-handedly decided the battle in favour of Constantinople – namely through her 'strength and power'.[91] In his view, the Khagan (emperor) of the Avars had been forced to learn the bitter lesson that there was no power on earth that could withstand the Virgin.[92] We will presently see how the proclaimer of the Qur'an responded directly to this military triumphalism. Certainly it was quite understandable from a Byzantine perspective, and also explicable given the dire existential threat facing the city. Yet this mood of triumphalism does appear to have been systematically promoted by the royal court. Theologically speaking, it was beyond objectionable and served to turn Mary into a figurehead of imperialism.

During the siege of Constantinople in 626, the Patriarch Sergios also ordered images of the Virgin to be painted on the city's Western Gate, so that she might be able to confront the enemy in person. Here, then, was at least one instance of official church collusion in the imperial exploitation of Mary. But given that it was the Patriarch of Constantinople who was involved, we may fairly assume that he had particularly close ties to the emperor. In the account of the court theologian, the general feeling in the city was that Mary had personally driven back the Avar attack,[93] and Constantinople was now seen as the new Jerusalem. Theodore Synkellos called Mary a protectress and commander.[94] A new introduction was added

87 Theodore claimed 'that the Virgin herself fought the battle and won a mighty victory because those who fought at sea on our ships had to flee due to a single attack of multitudes of enemies' (quoted in Hurbanič, *The Avar Siege of Constantinople in 626*, 217).

88 Cf. Hurbanič, *The Avar Siege of Constantinople in 626*, 256.

89 Cf. ibid., 247.

90 Cf. ibid., 217.

91 Ibid., 218; cf. also Cameron, 'The Theotokos in Sixth-Century Constantinople', 79 f.

92 Cf. Theodore Synkellos, 313.9–10, quoted in Hurbanič, *The Avar Siege of Constantinople in 626*, 248 f.

93 Cf. George-Tvrtković, *Christians, Muslims, and Mary*, 25.

94 Cf. Theodore Synkellos, 313.19, quoted in Hurbanič, *The Avar Siege of Constantinople in 626*, 248: 'Constantinople was a God-protected city, but Mary was its protector and "the leading warrior".'

to the famous fifth-century *Hymnus Akathistos*. It referred to the siege of Constantinople, and its effect was to firmly entrench in the public consciousness the idea of Mary's invincibility[95] – or at least, this is the impression we get from imperial propaganda. After the battle, as a mark of gratitude the Patriarch organised a great procession to Mary's shrine.[96] This provided the impetus for annual liturgical festivals, all of which commemorated the invincible Mary.[97]

Mary's role as protectress of the Byzantine Empire – A. M. Cameron even refers to her as a warrior goddess – was therefore a major topic in the 620s.[98] And Mary's cloak and veil became the outwardly visible symbols of the protection by the Virgin enjoyed by the imperial power.[99] Naturally, Heraclius also personally exploited this opportunity, interpreting his own victory over Chosroes II as a divine intervention occasioned by Chosroes blaspheming against Christ and his mother. As early as 610, Heraclius had attached an image of Mary to the masts of his ships as part of his war propaganda during his confrontation with his predecessor Phocas.[100] Other than this, however, there is little substantiated information to suggest that Heraclius also deployed images of Mary in his war propaganda. We do know, though, that generals of the Christian army of Egypt carried medallions of Mary with them,[101] which leads us to conclude that visual depictions of this imperial dimension of Mary were also familiar in the period when the Qur'an came into being.

Yet it was always evident that this form of imperialist Mariology was generated by the court in Byzantium and was not so readily transferable to the Syriac Christians with whom the proclaimer of the Qur'an had contact for most of the time.[102] For as Miaphysites, many Syriac Christians took a sceptical view of imperial theology and

95 Cf. Wenger, 'Les interventions de Marie', 424.

96 Cf. Hurbanič, *The Avar Siege of Constantinople in 626*, 269 f.

97 Cf. ibid., 285. From 626 on, a prayer to this effect was always repeated in the liturgy on the Saturday before the fifth Sunday of Lent (Beinert, *Maria*, 98).

98 'By the time of the victories of Heraclius the efficacy of the Theotokos as a warrior goddess was clear to everyone' (Cameron, 'The Theotokos in Sixth-Century Constantinople', 97, with reference to George of Pisidia, *Bell. Avar.* 1–9, p. 96 note 2).

99 Cf. ibid., 104.

100 Cf. Hurbanič, *The Avar Siege of Constantinople in 626*, 252, 321.

101 Cf. Horn, 'Intersections', 148.

102 Up to the sixth century, Syrian Christians continued to have strong links to Byzantium and came up with similar theological figures to explain military successes. Thus, it was assumed that the city of Nisibis would prevail against the Persian invaders thanks to the special protection it received from the national saint Ephraim von Nisibis (or from his teacher, St. Jacob of Nisibis). Likewise in Edessa, the capital of Syrian Christianity, protection from the Persians was based on a promise supposedly given by Jesus Christ to a legendary ancient ruler of the city named Abgar. In neither location was the figure of Mary involved.

from the second half of the sixth century onwards increasingly opted to refrain from engaging in politics, both generally and in their religious thinking. Among other things, this was a response to their disillusion with imperial ecclesiastical policies. Even so, there was one conflict concerning Mary that may well have had an impact on Syriac Christians on the Arabian Peninsula as well. This controversy arose from the defensive reaction by the Jewish community to imperial Mariology. At the same time, this is proof positive of the fact that imperial Mariology could have productive religious consequences even among the emperor's adversaries.

d) Jewish apocalyptic counter-images

We have already remarked how, in the conflict between the Sassanids and the Byzantines, the Jews tended to side with the Persians. On the one hand, this was due to Emperor Heraclius's propagandising for the conversion of Jews to Christianity as part of his efforts to forge a stronger union throughout the empire. There is evidence that forced conversions took place, at least at a local level,[103] in response to which Jews from the Eastern provinces emigrated to what was then Persian Mesopotamia. On the other hand, the capture of Jerusalem by Persian forces and the lifting of the ban (at least for a while, in 614–615) on Jewish settlement in Palestine raised hopes on the Jewish side.[104] In particular, the removal of the True Cross awakened messianic hopes,[105] among Palestinian Jews in any event, and may well, in the light of the involvement of the Jerusalem authorities in the wider Byzantine–Persian conflict, have resonated on the Arabian Peninsula too.

Telling evidence of the apocalyptic leanings among the Jewish community during the period when the Qur'an originated comes from the *Sefer Zerubbabel* ('Apocalypse of Zerubbabel'), which was written in Palestine sometime between 604 and 630.For the authors of this work, the wars between the Byzantines and the Persians were 'eschatological events, which would culminate in the appearance of

103 In the period immediately following Heraclius's decisive victory against the Persians, plans were drawn up – and possibly implemented – to forcibly convert Jews (for the sources on Heraclius's attitude to Judaism, cf. Cameron, 'Blaming the Jews'; Bonfil, 'Continuity and discontinuity', 78–84). In addition, there are a number of – unreliable – reports from this time of forced conversions of Jews in Jerusalem/Palestine, Northern Arabia and Egypt, plus one reliable account of forced conversion of the Jewish population of Carthage; the evidence for this comes from a letter thought to have been written by Maximos Confessor (cf. Starr, 'St. Maximos and the forced baptism at Carthage in 632', 195; cf. Devréesse, 'La fin inédite d'une lettre de saint Maxime', 35).

104 Cf. Howard-Johnston, *Witnesses of a World Crisis*, 441.

105 Cf. Hurbanič, *The Avar Siege of Constantinople in 626*, 84 f.

the Messiah.'[106] Whereas the Church Fathers had repeatedly argued that Christianity's superiority over Judaism was evident in the fact that Jerusalem had become a Christian city, from a Jewish point of view the changed circumstances now provided an opportunity to prove the contrary. In the process, Jewish commentators put an eschatological spin on the political events of the war, introducing not just a Jewish Messiah figure, but also a Jewish mother of the Messiah. Clearly, the imperial propagandising for a militarily triumphant Virgin provided the stimulus for creating a Jewish counter-image here. The figure of a mother of the Messiah seems to have been so charismatic from a Jewish perspective too that in Late Antiquity certain powers in Jerusalem began to lobby for a Jewish equivalent to counter the Virgin Mary.[107]

As regards the subject matter of the *Sefer Zerubbabel,* Zerubbabel was a prince of the house of David and governor of Judah, who oversaw the rebuilding of the Temple in Jerusalem during the sixth century BCE after the destruction of the First Temple by the Babylonians and who was supposedly carried off by a great wind to the city of Nineveh, which in the story is thought to stand for Rome or Constantinople.[108] The tale involves a number of Messiah figures: the first of these is the Davidic Messiah, Menahem, who is victorious in his final battle. His mother, who is married to Nathan and hence belongs to the house of David, is called Hephzibah. It is this Messiah who leads the people of Israel back to Jerusalem after the final victory.[109]

Hephzibah, the mother of this Davidic Messiah, triumphs over two kings at the end of the book with the aid of her retinue, and she guards the Eastern Gate of Jerusalem when the first Ephraimitic Messiah is killed, thereby saving a number of Jews.[110] Hephzibah is quite evidently being presented here as a counter-figure to the Virgin Mary in contemporary Byzantine culture.[111] She appears as a warrior[112] and is entirely lacking in the attributes traditionally associated with female role

106 Himmelfarb, *Sefer Zerubbabel*, 67.

107 'From the point of view of a late ancient Jew living in close proximity to Christians, a mother for the messiah might have seemed a very enviable figure.' Accordingly, all efforts were made 'to beat Christians in the messiah competition' (Himmelfarb, *The mother of the Messiah*, 378 f.).

108 For a concise summary of the Apocalypse of Zerubbabel, cf. Schäfer, *Weibliche Gottesbilder im Judentum und Christentum*, 273 f.

109 Cf. Himmelfarb, *Sefer Zerubbabel*, 79.

110 Cf. ibid., 69.

111 Cf. ibid.

112 Cf. Himmelfarb, 'The mother of the Messiah', 383. 'Her primary activity is warfare, about as masculine a pursuit as possible' (Himmelfarb, 'The mother of the Messiah', 385).

models.[113] Thus, while Hephzibah inherits the warlike aspect of Mary, in the *Sefer Zerubbabel* Mary's beauty is transferred to the magnificent stone statue of the mother of the Antichrist,[114] in other words to the mother of Armilus, who in the story stands for the Roman Empire and whose father is the Devil.[115] The stone statue is of enchanting beauty, yet it kills all those who do not prostrate themselves before it.[116]

It is therefore easy to see how this story can be seen as a Jewish reaction to imperialist religious policies. There are indications that, in the course of his forced conversions, Heraclius demanded that Jews pray to images of Mary. In response to this, the *Sefer Zerubbabel* contends that such images are lifeless, and accuses imperialist policies of killing anyone who refuses to submit to them. At the same time, while conceding that the images of Mary are beautiful, the story associates them with the Devil and the Antichrist.[117] One particularly striking element is the martial might of Hephzibah, who is quite clearly being built up as a counter-image to that of Mary as a military commander. Unlike the Byzantine Mary, whose ultimate purpose is to legitimise the power of the emperor, Hephzibah provides hope for the emergence of a new David, who will build the Third Temple and so usher in the Messianic Age.[118]

Zishan Ghaffar, who was the first to recognise the hermeneutic potential of the *Sefer Zerubbabel* with regard to exegesis of the Qur'an, identifies in the third Messiah of the book, the Messiah ben Joseph, an 'alternative to the Christian images of Zechariah and John the Baptist,'[119] inasmuch as he restores the cult of sacrifices and, following his murder, is raised from the dead by a Messiah from the line of David.[120] We will pick up on this idea again in our interpretive analyses of the Qur'an. The only point that needs stressing here is that the political Mariology of imperial theology in Late Antiquity definitely evoked a response in Jewish thought, and as a result it should come as no surprise that the proclaimer of the

113 'There is nothing about Hephzibah's behavior that marks her as a mother or even a woman.' (Himmelfarb, 'The mother of the Messiah', 389).

114 Cf. Himmelfarb, 'The mother of the Messiah', 389.

115 Cf. ibid., 384.

116 Cf. Himmelfarb, 'Sefer Zerubbabel', 80.

117 The struggle against the Antichrist was also a central theme of Christian propaganda, and it was first and foremost the Archangel Michael who was engaged in this fight. Towards the end of the sixth century the Book of Revelation was very popular and, being available in various different translations, was adapted to reinforce such propaganda.

118 Cf. Himmelfarb, 'Sefer Zerubbabel', 68.

119 Ghaffar, *Der Koran in seinem religions- und weltgeschichtlichen Kontext*, 37.

120 Cf. ibid.

Qur'an cast a critical eye over it too. However, the fierce reaction of the *Sefer Zerubbabel* also speaks to the intensity of the polemical clash between Jewish and Christian propaganda in Late Antiquity, and shows how this could play out far from Constantinople.

It should also, however, finally be noted here that there were many instances where rabbinical Judaism assimilated mariological motifs perfectly amicably. Thus, in Jewish tradition, Miriam remained not just Moses's sister, as attested in the Bible, but also became the mother of Moses, a role in which from a typological perspective she followed in the footsteps of Mary.[121] And like Mary she sings a song in praise of God and is involved in saving a child in Egypt.[122] One can therefore see from such transformations that Mariology also had the capacity to be a thoroughly productive religious force within Judaism. From the Jewish side, only its political and imperialist supercharging was vehemently rejected, becoming at the same time a springboard for Judaism's own messianic fantasies of the Apocalypse. As Ghaffar has comprehensively shown, these apocalyptic fantasies, just like the corresponding Christian apocalyptic propaganda spread by Heraclius, are one of the key reasons why the proclaimer of the Qur'an takes a pronouncedly sceptical attitude toward all messianic claims and instead develops his own eschatological ideal of leadership.[123] Yet because our study is focused on Mary, we cannot follow this particular trail any further. Instead, we will now turn our attention to what the Qur'an has to say about Mary.

121 Cf. Askhar, *Mary in the Syriac Christian tradition and Islam*, 146.

122 Cf. ibid., 148.

123 Cf. Ghaffar, *Der Koran in seinem religions- und weltgeschichtlichen Kontext*, 57–110.

II

MARY IN THE QUR'AN

We shall now attempt to recall and clarify what the Qur'an has to say about Mary. Following the methodology of the historical–critical approach, we will consider in their diachronic sequence those individual verses of the Qur'an which refer to Mary and offer an interpretation of each of them within the literary context of the surah in which it appears, particularly where this furnishes us with some interesting interpretative angles. In addition, wherever it strikes us as being a meaningful approach, we will consult selected sources from the Muslim classical tradition of commentary on the Qur'an[1] in order to let this flow of tradition elucidate our

1 Our choice of commentators here is based on the following considerations: the exegete Abū l-Ḥaǧǧāǧ Muǧāhid ibn Ǧabr (d. 722) was one of the earliest reciters and commentators on the Qur'an. However, his commentary has not been preserved in the original, and is only available as a reconstruction. His work is characterised by metaphorical interpretations of the text of the Qur'an and had a profound influence on later commentators, including Ṭabarī. In his idiosyncratic commentaries, Muǧāhid frequently went back to Jewish and Christian sources, and he can be seen as the oldest representative of rationalistic Qur'anic exegesis. The exegete Muqātil ibn Sulaymān al-Balḫī (d. 767) was a traditional scholar of Islam, a commentator on the Qur'an, and a theologian. He wrote one of the oldest surviving commentaries to cover the whole of the Qur'an. However, as a result of his working method – he made no effort to properly trace the chain of sources and much of what he wrote is couched in a rather fanciful style – he remains a controversial figure. Yet the works of these two interpreters bring us very close to the period when the Qur'an was written. It is for this reason that we have chosen to cite them, even though they do not comment on all the verses that are of interest to us. The same is true of the following exegetes: Abū ʿAbdallāh Sufyān ibn Saʿīd ibn Masrūq aṯ-Ṯawrī (d. 778). He was a legal expert and a scholar of the Hadith, and is regarded as a highly authoritative arbiter in the realm of Qur'anic exegesis. Among many other roles, Abū Ǧaʿfar Muḥammad ibn al-Ǧarīr aṭ-Ṭabarī (d. 923) was a historian, legal scholar and commentator on

observations.[2] Above all, it is our intention to read the verses within the intertextual context of Late Antiquity, using especially the writings of the Syrian Church Fathers alongside biblical texts to form our interpretative framework. Indeed, this is the reason why we cited the works of Syrian patristics so extensively in Part I of this book. This is not by way of suggesting that the Qur'an has any literary dependency on those texts, but is merely meant as an aid to exploring the realm of discourse of the Qur'anic texts. It is important for us to highlight the prevailing perceptions, religious precepts and ideas to which the text of the Qur'an is responding while at the same time continuing to develop its own profile. Evidently, it was these very sermons of the Syrian Church Fathers and the liturgical texts that were influenced by them which were in widespread circulation on the Arabian Peninsula in the seventh century, and taking them into consideration when reading the Qur'an helps add an important dimension to our understanding.[3]

the Qur'an. Ṭabarī commented on the entire text of the Qur'an, verse for verse, primarily with regard to grammatical and lexical questions about the presentation of the historical background and the citation of traditional interpretations of the subject matter. His work is widely regarded as the highpoint of traditional exegesis and was therefore an essential point of reference for the present study. Maḥmūd ibn ʿUmar az-Zamaḫšarī (d. 1144) was a Qur'anic exegete and philologist. Although he was a Muʿtazilite, his work is also widely studied in the Sunni world. In his exegesis he concentrated on grammatical analyses of the verses as well as on a philosophical–dogmatic interpretation of the text. Muḥammad ibn ʿUmar Faḫr ad-Dīn ar- Rāzī (d. 1209) was an Ashʿarite theologian, philosopher and Qur'anic exegete. Gillot pointed to the centrality of these two exegetes (cf. Gillot, 'Kontinuität und Wandel in der "klassischen" islamischen Koranauslegung', 79, 94–96); this is a view that we are inclined to share. Finally, we have chosen to adduce one further exegete who, quite exceptionally, taught in an environment that was extremely religiously diverse: ʿAbdallāh Muḥammad ibn Aḥmad al-Qurṭubī (d. 1272). Qurṭubī was a scholar from the Maliki school of Islamic jurisprudence and a Qur'anic commentator who came from Muslim-controlled Spain (Al-Andalus). He analysed the Qur'an from a philological and stylistic viewpoint, with a particular focus on religious questions. He is a contentious figure, not least because of his occasional proximity to Christian conceptions.

2 For an overview of the evolution of Qur'anic exegesis, cf. Gillot, 'Art. Exegesis of the Qur'ān: Classical and Medieval', 99–124, and Wielandt, 'Exegesis of the Qur'ān: Early, Modern and Contemporary', 124–141.

3 Cf. Griffith, 'The poetics of scriptural reasoning', Chap. 4.

1

The Surah *Maryam*

Since the Surah *Maryam* is, from a diachronic perspective, the first surah of the Qur'an which mentions Mary,[1] we will begin with a thorough appraisal of the first part of this surah. And because the statements made about Mary in this surah are closely related to the story of Zechariah, we will start our investigation by examining the very first verse as well as providing a detailed analysis of how it sequences with Zechariah and John the Baptist.

a) Zechariah and John the Baptist (1–15)

[This is] An account of your Lord's mercy bestowed upon His servant Zachariah (Q 19:2).[2] Right at the beginning of the surah, mercy is introduced as the principal theme of this surah. The name given to God, *ar-Raḥmān*, which becomes prevalent in the Qur'an at this time, occurs sixteen times in the surah, 'the highest frequency for an individual surah'.[3] Here mercy is presented as a characteristic which the Lord displays towards his servant or slave Zechariah. The Arabic term *ʿabd*, which is translated here as 'servant',[4] is one of the standard designations used

1 Cf. Nöldeke, *Geschichte des Qorāns*, 130 f.; Neuwirth, *Der Koran 2/1*, 634 ff.

2 Our working method in this chapter will be to analyse Q 19:1–34 section by section. We will reproduce in italics various translated verses of the Qur'an; the translation broadly follows the copyright-free English text by Wahiruddin Khan and Farida Khanam (Goodword Books, New Delhi, 2009). In each case, the text of the Qur'an is followed by our interpretation of the respective verses.

3 Neuwirth, *Der Koran 2/1*, 605.

4 Special dictionaries which document pre- and early Islamic linguistic usage are an invaluable tool for gaining an insight through the use of language into the general environment and religious life around the time of Muhammad. We opted to use the work by Edward William Lane, *Arabic-English Lexicon*, 8 vols., Beirut 1968 (first published in Edinburgh in

in the Qur'an for people who are chosen and honoured by God. It is also widely applied to biblical figures, and basically denotes an elementary characteristic of the relationship between God and human beings. The Arabic term *rabb*, which is rendered here as 'the Lord', but can also be translated as 'creator', 'sustainer' or 'teacher',[5] is in the first instance the customary Arabic translation of the biblical name of God YHWH, which is also still commonly paraphrased nowadays in a Christian context as 'the Lord'. In other words, it is evident here, both through the concept of mercy (*raḥma*) and the concept of the Lord, that this verse alludes to the biblical notion of God and at the same time takes into account the conceptual world of pagan Arabs.[6] The subject being addressed is God's pronouncement to Zechariah, who also appears in the New Testament tradition as the father of John the Baptist. He is simply introduced by his biblical name without further explanation; clearly, the Qur'an is addressing an audience that was well-versed in the Bible. It is not attempting to tell any new stories, but instead integrating itself into an existing narrative context and setting new points of emphasis.

It is interesting that the Qur'an adopts the name Zechariah, which in its original Hebrew means 'God remembers'.[7] Thus, the name corresponds with the beginning of this Qur'anic verse, which uses a cognate word-stem to introduce into the surah the concept of God recalling mercy.[8] Over the course of the surah, the theme of remembering is taken up time and time again, virtually creating a framework for the surah's repeated recourse to a variety of prophetic figures. Yet whereas at other points in the surah, acts of remembrance are the subject of imperious demands by God, here remembrance functions more as a hermeneutic reading instruction. Evidently, this surah, whose name derives from Mary the mother of Jesus, is primarily about remembering God's history with individuals whom he has called upon, by whose example and through whom God wished to give evidence of his mercy.

1867) [hereafter abbreviated as Lane, *Lexicon*]. On the term *'abd*, see Lane, *Lexicon*, vol. 5, 1934–1936. The basic root verb means 'to serve, worship, admire, devote oneself to the service of God, obey God in humility and dedication, and to do what God wishes and wish for the things that God does'.

5 The basic verb *rabba* means 'to be a lord, owner, or master; to raise, sustain, nurture and support; and to guide a person until maturity'. Accordingly, a *rabb* would be someone whose character embraces all these qualities. For a more extensive treatment of the semantic field of *rabb* see Lane, *Lexicon*, vol. 3, 1002–1003.

6 Cf. Neuwirth, 'Eine "religiöse Mutation der Spätantike"', 203–232.

7 We are thinking here of the Arabic *ḏakara* ('to remember'), which has at its root the same Semitic verb as in Hebrew. Cf. Yehoshua M. Grintz, 'Zechariah.' In: *Encyclopaedia Judaica*, Volume 21, Wel – Zy 22007, 481 f.

8 Cf. Ghaffar, *Der Koran in seinem religions- und weltgeschichtlichen Kontext*, 45, note 33.

One is almost tempted to speak of *her* mercy at this point, inasmuch as the surah repeatedly uses mercy itself as the name of God, thereby reminding us that it would be reductive on our part to link God solely to attributes that are associated with masculinity. Especially with regard to Mary, within these verses a realm opens up which enables us to approach God through attributes associated with femininity, so broadening our conception of God. For the Arabic (and indeed the Hebrew) roots of the word 'mercy' (*r-ḥ-m*) are the same as those of the word for the womb *(raḥm)*.[9] The fact that in a diachronic perspective within the Qur'an, the first mention of God's mercy occurs in the surah *Maryam* (19:2) is extremely revealing as an initial pointer to the characterisation of Mary here. For in terms of the Qur'an, Mary is thus quite literally the very first person who, in direct speech, introduces the idea that God can be called upon as the Most Merciful or the embodiment of mercy (Q 19:18, 17:110 or 7:56).

While it would not be correct to claim that the designations *Allāh* or 'the Lord' do not appear at all in this surah – after all, as we have seen, 'the Lord' occurs even in this very first verse, and *Allāh* is used as a term for God with reference to Jesus as the servant or slave of God in 19:30 – mercy remains the keynote of the address by God that is repeatedly recalled here and which is illustrated precisely by the figure of Mary. It is quite evident that a primary aspect of the biblical image of Mary is being picked up and enhanced here – namely the idea that something of God's merciful philanthropy is channelled through her. Mary, who in the Church tradition becomes the God-bearer (*Theotokos*), appears here in the truest sense of the word as an embodiment of God's mercy, on the one hand by giving herself over entirely to God's mercy (Q 19:18) and on the other by lending this relationship with God human expression through her pregnancy and motherhood.[10] Of course, she cannot perform this role as mediator through her own efforts but only with God's help. Yet this was also exactly the same unreserved judgement we arrived at when examining how she was depicted as an individual in the Bible and by the Church. Consequently, associating Mary with the divine attribute of mercy is a key insight which forms a link between the Christian and Muslim traditions.

Looking at the rhyme structure of the Surah *Maryam*, it becomes apparent that

9 Cf. Lane, *Lexicon*, vol. 3, 1055–1057.

10 On the meaning of the concept of mercy cf. Lane, *Lexicon*, vol. 3, 1055–1057. It goes back to a verb which means to be compassionate, show sympathy, be gentle with someone, be inclined to help someone, and to forgive. On the gender-related issues that are associated with the term, cf. among others: Sa'diyya Shaikh, *Sufi Narratives of Intimacy. Ibn 'Arabī, Gender and Sexuality (Islamic Civilization and Muslim Networks)*, North Carolina 2012; Seker, 'Raḥma und raḥim', 117–131.

it is the name of Zechariah which defines the rhyme of the surah and sets its tone up to verse 33. In other words, the basic tenor of the surah, or at least its first part, is characterised by the same rhyme scheme which, in terms of content, brings the recollection of God's acts of redemption into relief and links this formally with the name of Zechariah. The same rhymes that occur in Q 19:1–33 reappear from verse 44 onwards, where the objective is to embed certain ideas that have been developed using the example of Mary within a prophetological context. However, this exposition need not concern us any further where the present study is concerned, since we want to concentrate entirely on the figure of Mary. As a result, we will confine our comments to verses 1–33 of the Surah *Maryam* here.[11]

Thus, following our brief initial look at the heading of the Surah *Maryam*, let us now consider how its narrative unfolds thereafter. *When he cried out to his Lord privately, saying, 'My Lord! Surely my bones have become brittle, and grey hair has spread across my head, but I have never been disappointed in my prayer to You, my Lord! And I am concerned about the faith of my relatives after me, since my wife is barren. So grant me, by Your grace, an heir, who will inherit prophethood from me and the family of Jacob, and make him, O Lord, pleasing to You!'* (Q 19:3–6). It would appear that Zechariah is here praying quietly and bashfully to God (Q 19:3) because he is childless and fearful that he will not be able to produce any heirs. This fear is not a private concern (Q 19:4), but results from his public role as a priest and representative of divinity and of God's calling, which finds linguistic expression in the Qur'an in the grace shown by God in choosing the children of Israel. The key concern here, therefore, is to ensure a successor who will be heir both to Zechariah's role as a priest and to Israel as a whole (Q 19:5). In the event that Zechariah had no child, from a typological viewpoint this would bring the danger that the Temple cult too might not be maintained and that Israel would thereby fall from God's grace.

If one compares the wording of Zechariah's prayer with Lk 1:5–12, it becomes clear that in the Qur'an version, it is Zechariah himself who presents his problems to God. He makes a point of stressing that his prayers have not gone unanswered hitherto (Q 19:4). Zechariah clearly has a profound relationship with God; he believes implicitly in an answering God, from whom he derives his own spirituality. In the Bible too, Zechariah and his wife Elizabeth are shown as devout and blameless (Lk 1:6). Yet their blamelessness here relates primarily to their observance of the Lord's commandments and not so much to the intensity of their life in

11 For an initial overview of the wider structure of the surah, cf. Mouhanad Khorchide and Klaus von Stosch, *Der andere Prophet. Jesus im Koran*, Freiburg – Basel – Vienna 2018, 120–124.

prayer. In the biblical version, Zechariah's spirituality is very strongly associated with his priestly function, which mainly consists of presenting burnt offerings in the form of incense (Lk 1:9). By contrast, Zechariah's sacerdotal role in the Surah *Maryam* is not even a topic of discussion in its own right. At all events, his particular service resides in prayer, and it is this praying on his part that elicits an answer from God.

If one thinks of the polemical texts of the Church Fathers from the period when the Qur'an was being compiled, the rejection of Israel,[12] against which the Qur'anic Zechariah implicitly directs his prayers, was one of the key leitmotifs of anti-Jewish polemics. Following this logic, from a typological perspective John the Baptist, as Zechariah's son, is called upon to continue the priestly function of his clan in order thereby to enact the representative service of Israel to God. Likewise, therefore, Zechariah's potential childlessness can be seen as a sign of God's rejection of Israel – a line of interpretation that was certainly not pursued by all the Church Fathers, but which nonetheless still represented an important strain of thought within the early church, and which the Catholic Church has only recently repudiated.[13] In view of the grisly death suffered by John the Baptist, in the eyes of many of the Church Fathers, even his birth to Zechariah could not alter the fact that the Jewish Temple cult was supplanted by the rise of the Christian Church. For John himself had no offspring, and in the biblical version of the story, he did not enter into the service of the Temple either.

It is only in relatively recent times that this problematic and unfortunately widespread substitution theory has been acknowledged and worked through by theologians.[14] As we shall presently see, the Qur'an takes its own very distinct view of these matters, an attitude which absolutely lends itself to interpretation as a rehabilitation of Israel in the face of sustained anti-Jewish Christian polemics in Late Antiquity.[15]

12 On the condemnation of Israel in patristic literature cf. Hruby, *Juden und Judentum bei den Kirchenvätern*, 27–54. Hruby identifies the collection of homilies 'Adversus Judaeos', traditionally attributed to John Chrysostom, as playing a key role in establishing this theme of the rejection of Israel – in addition to its other derogatory statements regarding Judaism.

13 Regarding the traditional Catholic attitude, see especially the dismissive declaration on the relation of the Church to non-Christian religions promulgated by the Second Vatican Council in 1965, 'Nostra aetate'.

14 Views differ on whether the retired Pope Benedict XVI plays a positive role here. Cf. Klaus von Stosch, 'Wechselseitig aufgehoben? Zum jüdisch-katholischen Verhältnis.' In: *IkaZ* 48 (2019) 202–215. One thing that is beyond dispute is that Benedict's statements on the theme of substitution theory are, to put it mildly, somewhat pedantic.

15 However, Islamic exegesis and theology swiftly levelled this progress on the part of the

The very fact that Zechariah prays 'privately' acts as a counterpart to Jesus's injunction against loud and self-righteous prayer (Mt 6:5f) – a favourite subject of early Christian commentators, who often associated this with the supposedly ostentatious practice of Jewish devotion. Thus, while in Christian eyes, Jews are readily regarded as legalistic, because they allegedly get carried away with the business of fulfilling external duties and perform these with excessive zeal and self-righteousness, Zechariah's prayer as depicted in the Qur'an appears as the prototype of what would be seen by Christians as 'righteous' prayer – from the mouth of a representative of the Jewish tradition. Of course, this assessment of Zechariah also has an important point of reference in the New Testament, insofar as the Song of Zechariah (the Benedictus) became established from early on as the centrepiece of the morning prayer service in the Church (Matins). Yet in this same process, Zechariah quickly came to be regarded as the prototype of Israel's role in pointing forward to Jesus Christ.[16] No consideration was given to the continuing independent significance of Israel and the Temple cult and hence of Zechariah's priestly function. Since the Qur'an does not take over the Song of Zechariah in this way, and above all continues to characterise him in his sacerdotal role, the text can be read as arguing for a new appreciation of the Jewish tradition, which is presented here as being on a par with Christianity and the emerging faith of Islam.

One element that is symptomatic of this new definition of interfaith relations is the mention of the divine scripture (*kitāb*) that is handed down to all three religions in the same way.[17] When, in Q 19:12, John the Baptist is exhorted to hold firmly to the scriptures, in view of his priestly role and his Temple service, this can surely only mean the Torah. But such an identification is out of the question in Q 19:16, when the Qur'an demands that Mary be mentioned in the 'book' – an exhortation to Muhammad or the Muslim community, which can only be interpreted as referring to the original word of God in the form of the Qur'an as scripture.[18] When Jesus is then given the scripture in Q 19:30, it is clear that the

---

Qur'an, by itself developing a kind of substitution theory, according to which Judaism was supplanted by Christianity and Christianity in its turn was supplanted by Islam. Cf. among others Seyyed Hossein Nasr et al. (eds.), *The Study Qur'an. A new translation and commentary*, New York 2015, 31 f.

16 In the context of exegesis of the Qur'an, when we refer to 'Jesus Christ', this is a translation of 'Īsā al-Masīḥ.

17 On the concept of the scripture in the Qur'an, see Neuwirth, *Der Koran als Text der Spätantike*, 120–181.

18 Geagea, *Mary of the Koran*, 116, sees in the repeated exhortations to the prophets to remember Mary (Q 19:16; 21:91) a challenge by God to Muhammad to be mindful of Mary. But in doing so he obscures what is clearly stated in the Qur'an so as to be able to interpret the

Surah *Maryam* is systematically embracing all three revealed scriptures of the great monotheistic sister faiths within the same term, and introducing them all in a similarly respectful and weighty manner. For all their superficial differences, all three scriptures can clearly be traced back to a common source, and according to our reading of the text it is Mary who holds them together in the Surah *Maryam*. For it is through her that the Qur'an is introduced here,[19] whereas the gospels are introduced through her son and the Torah through her father. In this way, Mary appears as a typological bracketing figure bringing together the three monotheistic faiths.

But let us return to Zechariah's silent act of praying. This does not simply signify his modesty and piety, but also his embarrassment and the threatening situation he finds himself in. Zechariah gives a convincing account of his distress and vulnerability and lays it before God (Q 19:4). Whereas the biblical text describes the plight of Zechariah and Elizabeth in a matter-of-fact manner (Lk 1:7), here it is presented in a moving way as an impassioned plea to God. And while the biblical Zechariah is almost entirely reduced to his function as a prefiguration of Jesus, the Qur'anic Zechariah stands for the continuing role of Israel, with which he struggles and whose fulfilment the Qur'an connects typologically with the redemptive role of Christianity and Islam. Even the heavenly response to the prayer is portrayed in a characteristically different way in the Qur'an than in the Bible. The relevant passage in the Qur'an runs thus: *'O Zachariah! Indeed, We give you the good news of the birth of a son, whose name will be John – a name We have not given to anyone before.' He wondered, 'My Lord! How can I have a son when my wife is barren, and I have become extremely old?' God replied, 'So will it be! Your Lord says, "It is easy for Me, just as I created you before, when you were nothing!"'* (Q 19:7–9)'.

Whereas the biblical Zechariah is interrupted by the angel of the Lord in the middle of performing his Temple rites and is duly startled (Lk 1:11f.), God responds to the Qur'anic Zechariah by engaging him in a direct dialogue. At least, no mediating figure is specially introduced, and the voice that answers Zechariah addresses him using the royal 'We'. Everything here speaks to a dialogue between Zechariah and God himself, and this once again serves to underline the intimacy

Qur'anic verse as an allusion to Mary's supposed connection to the favourite disciple of Jesus in Jn 19:26 f. This strikes us as somewhat bold.

19 Of course, we are well aware that the Qur'an is introduced earlier in the surah, via the story of Zechariah. But this does not alter the fact that the Qur'an is also introduced through Mary and that her figure is therefore associated in the surah with all three scriptures, making it possible to regard her as a bridging figure between the Abrahamic faiths.

and intensity of his relationship with God. When one considers that the Levites were left with no ritual function whatsoever after the destruction of the Temple, the portrayal of the priest Zechariah's relationship with God appears to be a thoroughly contemporary reappraisal of his role, which also holds up Zechariah as a role model for the mass movement of the faithful that the proclaimer of the Qur'an, at least during the Meccan period, was attempting to create.[20]

If one compares the words of the first reply given to Zechariah by the angel and by God himself in the Bible and the Qur'an respectively, promising him that his wife will give birth to a son, then one cannot help but notice that the Qur'an, in the Surah *Maryam*, has nothing to say either about the great joy that will be triggered by the birth of John (Lk 1:14) or about the fact that he will be filled with the Holy Spirit and lead an ascetic lifestyle (Lk 1:15). Likewise, no mention is made in the Surah *Maryam* about John the Baptist's successes in converting people and his role in preparing the way for Jesus (Lk 1:17). Instead, at this point the proclaimer of the Qur'an concentrates exclusively on showing that Zechariah's wish is fulfilled. The fact that God grants his wish for a successor can be understood typologically as confirmation in the Qur'an of the enduring redemptive significance of Israel. John the Baptist is thereby retrieved from the Christological referential context and appears as a lasting guarantor of the significance of Israel. In line with this, he is not known as John in the Qur'an but Yaḥyā – a name which according to the Qur'an's understanding was never given to a person before and was also indeed unknown prior to the Qur'an. Translated literally, it means 'he lives', thereby underlining the fact that John can be interpreted as a symbol of life and as a guarantor of the continuing significance of the Old Covenant (Q 19:7).[21] Furthermore, if one considers that an important soteriological title bestowed on Jesus by the Syrian Church Fathers was *maḥḥyānā* ('giver of life'), then it becomes

20 We concur with Fred Donner in seeing the Muslim community in Mecca as a *believers' movement* or more precisely, to quote Donner verbatim, as a 'strongly monotheistic, intensely pietistic, and ecumenical or confessionally open religious movement that enjoined people who were not already monotheists to recognise God's oneness and enjoined all monotheists to live in strict observance of the law that God had repeatedly revealed to mankind – whether in the form of the Torah, the Gospels, or the Qur'an' (Donner, *Muhammad and the believers*, 75). However, unlike Donner, we do not proceed from the assumption that this *believers' movement* was an eschatological movement with an imminent expectation of the end time. Finally, in contrast to Donner, who believes that Islam only emerged as a religious community in its own right during the Umayyad dynasty as a result of the imperial project of the caliphs (ibid., 194 f.), we take the view that the character of Muhammad's movement changed even during the Medina period and that Islam therefore already began to clearly emerge as a religion during the lifetime of the Prophet.

21 Cf. Ghaffar, *Der Koran in seinem religions- und weltgeschichtlichen Kontext*, 44.

abundantly clear that Jesus's Christological–livegiving role for the Old Covenant is implicitly being rejected here.[22]

After receiving the pledge of continuing life for his clan and his people, the first thing that Zechariah asks is how this miraculous promise might be realised. In other words, he reacts in a way that is completely analogous to Mary, whose first response to God's promise is to seek an explanation (Q 19:20). God's explanation is identical in both cases, pointing to the fact that such a powerful deed is a simple task for God (Q 19:9 and 21). This formulation is also found in the works of the Syrian Church Fathers,[23] meaning that a concept from the Christian tradition is clearly being affirmed here. Yet the first time this idea is encountered in the Bible is in reply to Mary's questions to the Angel Gabriel (Lk 1:37), whereas in this same tradition Zechariah initially has to come to terms with what has happened on his own. Indeed, generally speaking the biblical tradition deals rather roughly with Zechariah.[24] The questions he poses there, which are perfectly understandable, are literally silenced with a brusque invocation of God's authority and a divine show of power (Lk 1:19f.). By contrast the Qur'an even goes so far as to let Zechariah establish the conditions for God's reply. For just as it is easy for God to perform a miracle (Q 19:9), so Zechariah's prayer at the beginning is shown not to have been fruitless and therefore also easy to some extent (Q 19:4).[25] Praying is easy, and so is the response, an exhilarated and exhilarating harmony of simplicity between God and man and hence the precise opposite of the ritual ponderousness that Christians have so readily associated with Jewish religious observance.[26]

But that's not all: in the Qur'an, God also tries to win Zechariah round with argument. In response to Zechariah's doubts, he gives another indication of his creative power, something which is initially missing in his reply to Mary and is

---

22 Cf. Ghaffar, 'Kontrafaktische Intertextualität im Koran und die exegetische Tradition des syrischen Christentums', 20 f.

23 Cf. Ephrem the Syrian, Commentary on Tatian's Diatessaron, I,12 (136); Saint Ephrem (1963), Commentaire de l'Évangile concordant, I,12 (10).

24 On the clear agenda of Lk to show Jesus as outdoing John the Baptist, cf. Müller, *Mehr als ein Prophet*, 111 f.

25 *Šaqīy,* usually translated into English as 'disappointed', also means 'wretched', 'unhappy' or 'cursed' and is associated with the idea of difficulty. Conversely, in his prayer, Zechariah turns this idea on its head by describing his relationship with God as joyous, happy and blessed. From this, we may deduce that his relationship with God is an easy one.

26 The concept of easiness in no way questions the serious nature of prayer. On the contrary, appreciating the gravity and importance of prayer can be understood as a necessary prerequisite for overcoming any hindrances that might make it difficult for a person to pray.

only brought into play as an argument indirectly in the insertion[27] of Q 19:35, in other words outside the dialogue with Mary. Mary's doubts are clearly overcome more quickly than those of Zechariah. For in spite of this additional argument that God puts to him, Zechariah still requires another sign (Q 19:9). By contrast, for Mary, Jesus himself is already sign enough (Q 19:21). Even classical Muslim commentators recognised that Mary, in her faith, acts in a more exemplary fashion than Zechariah.[28] Yet the Qur'an refrains from any criticism of Zechariah and describes how God instils trust in him by giving him a sign:

Zechariah said, 'My Lord! Grant me a sign.' He responded, 'Your sign is that you will not be able to speak to people for three nights, despite being healthy.' So he came out to his people from the sanctuary, signalling to them to glorify God morning and evening (Q 19:11).

Zechariah's silence, which in the Bible and patristics is construed as a punishment for his unbelief,[29] is turned by the Qur'an into a beneficial sign to humankind. Behind this reinterpretation lies the Qur'anic theology of signs, which over and over again exhorts people to seek God's benevolent 'right guidance' even when they have suffered the most terrible blows of fate (Q 18:60–82); for even through apparent setbacks, God is intent upon leading us towards life in all its fulness. Zechariah requires a more practical concession on God's part than Mary for him to be able to place his unqualified trust in God.[30] The Qur'an characterises the three-day silence of Zechariah as this act of concession. Translated literally, in fact, one really ought to talk of an uninterrupted silence over three nights in the Surah *Maryam* (Q 19:10), whereas the Surah *Āl 'Imrān* refers to a silence 'for three days' (Q 3:41). The fact that reference is made within the Qur'an both

27 On the justification for regarding Q 19:34–40 as an insertion, cf. Neuwirth, *Der Koran. vol. 2/1*, 600, 618 f.

28 For example, Qurṭubī stresses the point that Mary, in contrast to Zechariah, needed no sign in order to trust in God's work. Cf. al-Qurṭubī, *al-Ǧāmi'*, vol. 5, 128.

29 Cf. Lk 1:20. How important this theme also was for the Syriac Church Fathers is demonstrated by Ghaffar, 'Kontrafaktische Intertextualität im Koran und die exegetische Tradition des syrischen Christentums', 5–8*. They were absolutely certain that this was a justified punishment for Zechariah's doubt.

30 At this point one might argue that a further sign is given to Mary without her asking anything more of God. As a result, we do not know how she would have reacted if, like Zacharias, she had been compelled in the first place to simply submit to God's omnipotence. On the other hand, the story is told in such a way that Zechariah cannot help but question God, while Mary does not, so that this of necessity gives rise to the impression outlined above. We will presently see that it is far from the Qur'an's intention here to draw any typological conclusions from this different response, to the effect that Judaism, as represented by Zechariah, is somehow being disparaged in comparison to Christianity, as represented by Mary.

to days and to nights indicates that the operative term here is most likely simply the number three, which is also significant in the Bible, rather than the actual times of day cited in the text. Clearly the Qur'an firmly assumes that a personal relationship with God operates at all times, and hence can also be symbolically interrupted, or newly qualified, at any time. It is a moot point which of these two conceptions is more appropriate for the Qur'an. The Qur'an does not explain the sign, but simply demands that Zechariah comply with it in its ritual form, while not making it clear how he is to derive any particular meaning from his enforced silence.

In any event, the sign does not absolve Zechariah from carrying out his priestly duties. Even while he is struck dumb, he is expected to lead the congregation in prayer (Q 19:11). It is interesting that in silently performing his role, he is still able to convey God's promise to the human race. For in his silence, he is able to impart divine revelation – *waḥy* in Arabic – and it is precisely in his silent state that he becomes receptive to this form of divine power. When *waḥy* shines forth from the silently performed priestly role of Zechariah, then it seems logical to assume that here too, the sacerdotal or liturgical role of Zachariah is being confirmed. While his silence in patristic exegesis typically illustrates the end of the old cult,[31] in the Qur'an it becomes the consummation of God's proclamation. Although *waḥy* can also come from the Devil in the Qur'an (Q 6:121), the common factor is that it always comes from beyond the human sphere. And in the story of Zechariah it is quite clear that it introduces a divine *waḥy* with the power to positively inspire him. Muslim exegetes class silence as a form of fasting and thus construe it as a means of visualising the nearness of God.[32] According to both biblical and Qur'anic texts, this proximity to God was from the outset a distinguishing feature of Zechariah's piety, and it is lent even greater intensity by the act of fasting. It therefore seems comprehensible that Zechariah should be able to give a sign pointing to God even without speaking and solely through his charisma.

It is interesting that it is only at the point under discussion here that it becomes clear for the first time that Zechariah is in the Temple when he engages in this dialogue with God. The Arabic word used here is *miḥrāb*,[33] which also reappears in Surah *Āl ʿImrān* in reference to Mary. This choice of vocabulary is noteworthy because, unlike in the episode of Muhammad's Night Journey or when speaking about the Jerusalem Temple, the Qur'an does not use the term *masǧid* (Q 17:7)

31 Cf. for example Pseudo-Ephrem the Syrian, *Commentary on the Diatessaron I*,10.

32 Cf. among others aṭ-Ṭabarī, *Tafsīr*, vol. 15, 517 f.; and ar-Rāzī, *Tafsīr*, vol. 21, 207.

33 This observation can also be found in Marx, 'Glimpses of a Mariology in the Qur'an', 542.

here. *Masǧid* (literally, 'the place of kneeling down') is a term that has become firmly established in Islamic tradition for a mosque, whereas *miḥrāb* ('place of dispute') actually denotes the prayer niche that is used by the prayer leader and which indicates the direction of Mecca, towards which prayers are directed. However, the term *miḥrāb* can also mean a separate room in a temple.[34] Therefore, its translation as 'temple' is not entirely compelling and the focus on Zechariah as a prayer leader simply within the context of his community remains unchanged. In the Qur'an he appears more as someone leading prayers than as a priest, and accordingly his mute form of prayer leadership is perfectly comprehensible.

Moreover, in the Qur'an's version of the story, Zechariah directly induces his congregation to participate in a devotional practice that was familiar from Christianity at this time. For in places in the Syrian region with smaller Christian communities during the period when the Qur'an was taking shape, communal prayer in the morning and the evening was seen as vitally important.[35] Though it cannot be proven, it is likely that people prayed in accordance with the liturgical tradition of the Benedictus and the Magnificat that is still in use nowadays and thereby cultivated a relationship with God together with Zechariah and Mary, so to speak. In linking Zechariah, who is styled as a priest, with this kind of liturgical tradition best known from Christianity, the proclaimer of the Qur'an was clearly shaping his activities in such a way as to bring about a convergence of Christianity and Judaism at this point too and attempting to break their antagonism. Praying twice a day was also customary in rabbinical Judaism;[36] it is therefore highly plausible that, in citing this invocation to morning and evening prayer, the Qur'an may well

34 On the lexical field of *miḥrāb* cf. Lane, *Lexicon*, vol. 2, 541. For example, the term is construed as being a straightforward synonym for 'Temple' in Reynolds, *The Qur'ān and its Biblical subtext*, 142.

35 As Robert Taft states in his – still authoritative – work on the historical evolution of the liturgy of the hours: '...in the second half of the fourth century [...] in Palestine, Syria, Asia Minor and Constantinople we see an already well-established cursus of cathedral offices celebrated by the whole community – bishop, clergy, and people. Matins and vespers were the two privileged hours of daily prayer' (Taft, *The Liturgy of the Hours in East and West*, 55). Most importantly, Theodoret of Cyrus testifies to the fact that daily communal prayer in both the morning and the evening was customary practice in Syria (and not just in the capital Antioch). Cf. Theodoret of Cyrus, *Historia Religiosa 30.1*, edited and translated by P. Canivet and A. Leroy-Molinghen (Sources Chrétiennes 257, p. 240), Paris 1979; cf. also the testimony offered by the 'Apostolic Constitutions', II.59, edited and translated by B. M. Metzger (Sources Chrétiennes 320, 329, 336), Paris 1985. These Church orders are thought to have been written in the Antioch region in around 380.

36 Cf. Berakhot 26a–26b. Whereas twice-daily prayer (morning and evening prayer) were mandatory, praying at other times of the day was optional.

have been surveying the ritual observances of Islam's two sister religions.

While verses 2–11 of the Surah *Maryam* are exclusively about Zechariah and the announcement that he will become the father of a son, there follow in verses 12–15 a number of reflections that are characteristic of the now-born John the Baptist. The role of Elizabeth, which is so important in the Bible, thus becomes invisible in the Qur'an[37] – a finding which fits in well with Angelika Neuwirth's observation that it is the family of Jesus where the female ancestors come to the fore, while the Jewish tradition is founded on strong male protagonists. However, we will examine Neuwirth's challenging thesis in detail in the chapter on the Surah *Āl ʿImrān*. For now, let us turn our attention to the Qur'an's characterisation of John the Baptist:

'O John! Hold firmly to the Scriptures.' And We granted him wisdom while he was still a child, as well as purity and compassion from Us. And he was God-fearing, and kind to his parents. He was neither arrogant nor disobedient. Peace be upon him the day he was born, and the day of his death, and the day he will be raised back to life! (Q 19:12–15).

From the very beginning, John is presented in his priestly or liturgical role and is exhorted to resolutely place the Torah at the very centre of his life (Q 19:12). Wisdom and integrity are in turn hallmarks of priests, which become immediately apparent as key characteristics of their actions – especially when those actions no longer have to do with performing the ritual observances that have been rendered obsolete by the destruction of the Temple. For wisdom in interpreting scripture and integrity in its implementation may well be the precondition for being able to enter credibly and authentically into the service of God. And here too we are dealing with qualities which the Christian tradition was not accustomed to associating with Jewish scribes.[38]

In the context of the Surah *Maryam* it is particularly significant that John is also characterised as possessing the qualities of empathy, compassion and a kind disposition, with the result that the fundamental theological concern of the surah is exemplified by him. It is interesting to note that the Arabic formulation *ḥanānan* in Q 19:13 highlights the virtue of compassion, which forms a constituent part of *yuḥannān*, the Arabic form of his name. The characterisation of John as *ḥanān* ('compassionate'[39]) serves to emphasise that the name change is not intended to

37 Elizabeth's story subsequently comes to the fore – however briefly – in the literature of Qur'anic exegesis. Cf. aṭ-Ṭabarī, *Tafsīr*, vol. 15, 491.

38 One need only cite here the many occasions on which Jesus decries the Scribes and the Pharisees (cf. Mk 12,38–40 par).

39 Cf. Lane, *Lexicon*, vol. 2., 652–654. This complex term has a number of different

question the accuracy of his classical Arabic name and the quality it represents, but rather to identify his actions (which are marked by empathetic compassion!) as having continuing validity. As we have already explained above, this is corroborated by his naming, insofar as the name he is given in the Qur'an, Yaḥyā, comes from a word root that means 'being alive'.[40]

However, the Qur'an does not come down in biased fashion on the Jewish–apologetic side; rather it is fully cognizant of how much the life and ministry of John the Baptist is interwoven with that of Jesus Christ, and to how great an extent Zechariah has his counterpart in Mary. It even leaves space for peculiarities of Mary and Jesus that distinguish them from Zechariah and John. Thus it is Mary who, in her trusting faith, finds herself more readily in accord with God than Zechariah – as we have observed above. And it is Jesus who is in a position to undertake his own characterisation, whereas John remains passive (Q 19:30–33). The fact that the traditions represented by the individual protagonists are shown to be of equal value does not, in the view of the Qur'an, in any way efface these differences. Thus, it is said of both John and Jesus that peace should be upon both of them at their birth, their death and the day of their resurrection (Q 19:15 and 33). This talk of peace is noteworthy because the Syriac Church Fathers tended to reserve this term for Jesus.[41] Now the term is expanded and comes to form part of the Jewish tradition with the same intensity of meaning. This is significant insofar as the mention of the endowment of peace as a way of bestowing distinction upon a person is familiar precisely from the rabbinical tradition. As Angelika Neuwirth has rightly emphasised, the expression 'Peace be upon him/me' represents a divine distinction, which in rabbinical practice and subsequently in Islam tended to manifest itself in special public privileged treatment of the individual thus honoured, whose name thenceforth was permanently linked with this expression. And yet it remains the case that, with regard to Jesus, this practice was introduced as a result of Jesus attributing it to himself. In this way, for all the parity that exists between Christianity and Judaism, a key difference is enshrined, founded in the fact that Christianity is essentially rooted in Jesus's statements about himself.[42]

Finally, it is also notable how great play is made of the deference John and

---

meanings, including: to be touched by someone or something, or to show sympathy and be merciful.

40 Cf. Lane, *Lexicon*, vol. 2, 679–693.

41 Cf. Ghaffar, 'Kontrafaktische Intertextualität im Koran und die exegetische Tradition des syrischen Christentums', 18.

42 Cf. Neuwirth, *Der Koran 2/1*, 618.

Jesus show, John to his parents and Jesus to his mother (Q 19:14 and 19:32). In the case of John, it is said that he was not arrogant or disobedient, while Jesus says of himself that he was not made to be arrogant or defiant. The Arabic text here could also be translated as Jesus claiming that he is not a tyrant. If one stops to consider that Jesus is speaking here as a child, then this statement might be taken as a deliberate counterpoint to the apocryphal stories (in the so-called 'Infancy Gospels') of Christ's childhood, in which tyrannical behaviour is ascribed to Jesus, for instance when he kills playmates whom he has bumped into while running.[43]

In general, in the portrayal of Zechariah and John it is significant that the violent end which both of them met goes unmentioned. For the Protevangelium of James, to cite just one source, ends with the murder of Zechariah (ProtEvJam 24,3), while the murder of John the Baptist is clearly attested in the Bible (Mk 6:17–29 par.). This omission effectively removes all grounds for talking about a shift towards salvation and the disinheritance of Israel, which some Church Fathers deduced from this violent end of the priestly caste.[44] Naturally, the authors of the Bible were well aware that Zechariah and John were not literally the last surviving Levites. Yet typologically both of them were regarded as such, which is why this reconfiguration of their fate by the Qur'an is so significant here.

b) Mary's withdrawal and the proclamation of Jesus's birth (16–21)

And mention in the Book, O Prophet, the story of Mary when she withdrew from her family to a place in the East, screening herself off from them (Q 19:16–17a).

Unlike the section concerning Zechariah, the section about Mary begins with an imperative. Nonetheless, one should be wary of making too much of this linguistic change in comparison with Q 19:2, since it most likely has to do with the stylistic device of chiasmus, which is used in the Zechariah section, and because

43 Cf. Klauck, *Apokryphe Evangelien*, 101, on the infancy gospel of Thomas: 'In Chap. 3 the son of the scribe Annas makes dammed-up water flow away, with the result that the ditches dry out. As a fitting punishment, his whole body "withers" (cf. Mk 11:20 f.), leaving his distressed parents with nothing to do but carry off his corpse. Another boy has the misfortune of bumping into Jesus while running through the village; he drops dead on the spot (4:1). When his parents complain to Joseph, Jesus causes them to go blind (5:1). These incidents are all meant to show the power of Jesus's words ('Where does this boy come from? Every word he utters is a *fait accompli*' (4:1; repeated in 17:2). Joseph, though, reacts angrily and twists the boy's ear. Jesus protests by delivering an enigmatic rebuke, but at least he refrains from hurting Joseph in retaliation (5:2 f.).' There could be no better description of tyrannical behaviour.

44 Cf. Ghaffar, *Der Koran in seinem religions- und weltgeschichtlichen Kontext*, 45.

this imperative also later reappears in reference to Abraham (Q 19:41). In any event, both sequences, and also the later one about Abraham, are joined together by the same word root and in this way, especially in this surah, they invite the reader to recall the respective figures from the Jewish and the Christian traditions. Without any mention of Mary's birth or any narrative conjunction of Mary's story with that of Zechariah, Surah *Maryam* launches straight into events and in the very first sentence broaches several revealing issues.

To begin with, it is striking that the text talks about 'a place in the East'. Classical Muslim commentary literature remained non-committal with regard to this reference.[45]

But if we enquire after some of the Christian and Jewish scriptures that have intertextual connections to the Qur'an, the deeper meaning of this location becomes apparent. The Eastern Gate of the Jerusalem Temple (the Golden Gate on the Temple Mount) was seen by both the Church Fathers and Jewish Apocalypticists as the gate through which the Messiah would enter.[46] And the Church Fathers associated the closure of this gate with Mary's virginity.[47] According to this interpretation, Mary – as the typological embodiment of the Temple and the Church – had the capacity to accept the Messiah into herself through the sealed Eastern Gate (i.e. in her intact state of virginity) and to bring him into the world. In a Christian–patristic context, talk of the Eastern Gate evolved as an allegory of the portals of heaven, through which our High Priest will descend to us – a typological interpretation which was applied in equal measure to the Virgin Mary

45 Ṭabarī for example offer the explanation that she withdrew from her family into the eastern part of the prayer niche, and associates this action with the Christian practice of praying while facing east (aṭ-Ṭabarī, *Tafsīr*, vol. 15, 483 f.). Zamaḫšarī also maintains that this Christian practice derives from Mary's withdrawal to the East and talks about an eastern place of worship or a free-standing house (az-Zamaḫšarī, *Tafsīr*, 633 f.). Qurṭubī states that the reason for the East being especially venerated is that the sun rises there, which therefore makes it the source of light (al-Qurṭubī, *al-Ǧāmi'*, vol. 13, 428). In the Arabic world, this compass direction was also associated with things that were good and close to God. In addition, it was thought that Christians faced east when praying because this was the position that Jesus was born in. Ṭabarī's explanations are succinctly summarised by Qurṭubī with words that he attributes to Ṭabarī: 'If there had been a better place than the East, then Mary would have given birth to Jesus there' – a formulation that is powerfully reminiscent of Jacob of Serugh's Marian hymns. Quoted in al-Qurṭubī, *al-Ǧāmi'*, vol. 13, 428, with reference to aṭ-Ṭabarī, *Tafsīr*, vol. 15, 484 f.

46 Cf. Neuwirth, *Der Koran 2/1*, 612: 'The closed Eastern Gate of the Temple, through which, according to Ezekiel 44:1 f. God exited Jerusalem; it has remained shut ever since and, according to Jewish and subsequently Christian tradition, should only open again to permit the entry of the Messiah.'

47 Cf. Ghaffar, *Der Koran in seinem religions- und weltgeschichtlichen Kontext*, 32.

and the Church, both of which were seen, like Jacob's Ladder,[48] as joining heaven and earth.[49]

If we consider the talk of a place in the East in the Surah *Maryam* against this background, it is evident that all the aforementioned implications of this designation are not invoked, although they surely must have been known about within the milieu of the Qur'anic community. Both Angelika Neuwirth and Zishan Ghaffar proceed from the premise that a de-allegorisation of the East is taking place here.[50] However, the East remains the place where, from a Qur'anic perspective as well, the Virgin Mary is informed that she will give birth to a child. Therefore, although one can certainly presume a decontextualisation of the East, whether a de-allegorisation is actually taking place strikes us as questionable. Still, it is noteworthy that, in an Old Arabic text of the poet Umayya ibn Abī ṣ-Ṣalt from the seventh century, which like the Qur'an takes issue with the Protevangelium of James, the 'place in the East' has entirely vanished and been replaced, probably deliberately, by the desert of Damdam.[51] This effectively cuts the ground from under the feet of the customary Christian allegory. But that is emphatically not the case in the Qur'an. There, the East at least constitutes a recollection of the interpretative traditions of the sister religions, and in a Christian reading leaves open the possibility of retaining Mary's mediating role in the conception and birth of Christ.

This possibility is underlined by a further detail. According to the Protevangelium of James, Mary (as described at greater length above) is assigned the task of helping to weave the Temple veil[52] – in colours reminiscent of the Passion of Christ (ProtEvJam 10:2). As patristics evolved, the cloth of the Temple veil increasingly became the subject of allegorical exegesis by the Syrian Church

48 The motif of the ladder reappears in the emergence of the Qur'an and the formation of Islam as an independent religion. Not only the terms *islām*, *salām*, and *muslim* belong to the family of words which derive from the basic word-stem *salima* (to be free, whole, hale and hearty) but also the term *sullam*, (ladder). In religious usage, the idea of a practical tool that can join heaven and earth shows a remarkable affinity to the concept of 'Jacob's Ladder' and the interpretation of Mary as a linking figure.

49 Cf. Schmaus, *Mariologie*, 294: 'The Church and the Virgin are the Ark of the Covenant, Jacob's Ladder, heaven's gate, and the Eastern Gate through which our High Priest will enter – the great gate that affords entry to the Lord of Israel.'

50 Cf. Neuwirth, *Der Koran 2/1*, 613; Ghaffar, *Der Koran in seinem religions- und weltgeschichtlichen Kontext*, 46.

51 Horn, 'Tracing the reception of the Protoevangelium of James in Late Antique Arabia', 130.

52 According to Neuwirth, she is chosen to perform the task through the drawing of lots. Cf. Neuwirth, *Der Koran 2/1*, 481. In the Qur'an, the only place where the motif of selection by lottery appears is when a husband/provider for Mary has to be found (Q 3:44); it does not feature as a theme in the Surah *Maryam*.

Fathers and is almost omnipresent in their interpretations. Even as early a commentator as Ephrem the Syrian saw the body of Jesus Christ as such a veil, covering Mary – and hence as supplanting the function of the fig-leaf covering that Eve has to make for herself. In other words, this motif is all about covering a person's own modesty.[53] The veil thus becomes Mary's raiment of glory and can also in this context be associated with her virginity. Ephrem, for instance, construes her virginity as a veil that envelops her or as a purple cloak protecting her,[54] and the metaphor of the door curtain is likewise related to Mary's hymen.[55] Yet in these interpretations of Ephrem, Mary is never the individual who has fashioned the veil for herself. This interpretative tradition is also found in the work of Jacob of Serugh, where mention is made of a veil that God has woven onto her pure motherly body – an allusion to her virginity.[56] Yet Christ too appears as a raiment of glory, which Mary has woven herself.[57] The role of the veil, or material, or curtain, is therefore manifold, but it always serves to protect Mary and symbolises either her virginity or her connection with Christ.

Yet in this instance too, Neuwirth takes the view that the Qur'an repudiates this tradition of allegorical interpretation. To quote her: 'As in the case of the "place in the East", so too in the case of the curtain, an image that has become established as an allegory in the Christian tradition is "de-allegorised". In the Qur'anic version, both of these details reoccur as everyday realities.'[58] But it is Neuwirth herself who has pointed out that, later in the Qur'an, the curtain is lent symbolic meaning by Q 42:51.[59] At this point, it is the veil or the curtain which

---

53 Cf. Ephrem, *Hymns on the Nativity*, 17,4. The Syriac word that is translated here as 'veil' is used quite unequivocally by another Syrian writer, Isaac of Antioch (active in around the first half of the 6th century), to denote the curtain in the Temple at Jerusalem (cf. S. Isaaci Antiocheni doctoris Syrorum, opera omnia, edited and translated by G. Bickell, vol. 2, *Gießen* 1877, V. 1736, 342). Consequently, in this sense of (a segregating or concealing) curtain, the word may have a connection to the hijab, even though there are other, more common Syriac terms that equate to hijab.

54 Cf. Ephrem, *Hymns on the Nativity*, 16,13. Like the aforementioned 'curtain', the word that is translated here as 'cloak' does not equate directly to the hijab. As regards its content, though, it does evoke similar associations.

55 Ephrem the Syrian, *Hymns on the Nativity*, 12,5. Furthermore, another metaphor that is used here is that of the seal, which plays a similarly important role in the Qur'an.

56 Cf. *Jacob of Serugh's homilies on the nativity. First Homily*, v. 285 f. The Syriac word is used here too.

57 Cf. Jacob of Serugh, *On the mother of God: Homily I*, 19. Again, the Syriac word that is used here is one that cannot readily be applied to the hijab.

58 Neuwirth, *Der Koran 2/1*, 613.

59 Cf. ibid., 649.

separates humans from the presence of God and precisely thereby enables communication to take place between God and man. The veil as a means of communication by God conceals and points to something at one and the same time. This ambiguous symbolism hints at a potential within the Qur'an to facilitate a dialogue with God.

However, this interpretation also applies to our passage in Q 19:17a. Mary screens herself off from her family by means of the veil, and also uses it to ensure she is protected and alone. It seems to us that the veil stands here for the experience of solitude and withdrawal from the demands of daily life, which appears to be the prerequisite for becoming sensitive and alert to the voice of God. This insight is common to all three sister religions. In the Qur'an, the extent to which the veil may also be practically associated with Mary's virginity is open to interpretation. In the text of the Qur'an, it is above all her presence in the Temple, and her worship there, which can be interpreted as vouchsafing her moral integrity. Yet the veil can also be understood as expressing that Mary has devoted her whole life to God and is keeping her distance from all human interactions, which of course would also logically include any intimate congress with a man. Consequently, Jesus is seen as the fullest expression of what occurs between Mary and God, an event that is encapsulated in the phrase 'Virgin Birth'.

If one reads the rest of this surah, it turns out to be the Christ child himself who defends Mary against persecution by her family, so that Jesus has a protecting function that can also be ascribed to the veil. And in addition the unassailable truth of Mary's virginity during the conception has the same protective function as the veil. Interestingly, the Qur'an does not use either of the terms that were thoroughly familiar in Arabic usage at that time – *bikr*[60] or *batūl*[61] – to describe Mary's virgin-

60 In the context of Mary's virginity, the semantic fields of *bakara a*nd *batala,* and hence linguistic usage on the Arabian Peninsula in general, are extremely enlightening and argue strongly in favour of an allegorical approach to the concept of virginity that transcends the physical dimension and which, as Neuwirth is keen to emphasise, does the hidden depths of meaning in the concept full justice. *Bakara* means to have an early start, to hurry oneself in the morning, while *bikr* denotes an unpierced pearl, and by extension a man or woman who has not yet had sexual intercourse, a woman who has not yet fallen pregnant or has not given birth or conceived her first child. Cf. Lane, *Lexicon*, vol. 1, 239–240. Although an association with biological virginity is certainly indicated in this lexical field, it is not nearly as prominent as the associations that have to do with the idea of a 'promising start'.

61 *Batala* means to detach oneself, withdraw from the world in order to serve God, or to live a chaste life, while *batūl* signifies the offshoot of a palm tree from the main trunk, independent of it; by extension a woman who has no husband, needs no spouse, or has no wish to have a husband; a virgin; the term *al-Batūl* thus denotes the Virgin Mary. Fatima, the daughter of Muhammad, is also given this designation, because according to tradition she was

ity. These words would take the physical aspect into account as well as hinting at other important dimensions such as a promising start and Mary's independence. As it stands, the uncertainty that is enshrined in the Qur'anic formulation 'the one who guarded her chastity' (Q 21:91) holds the possibility of a far more comprehensive depth of meaning that is quite intentional, in our view. As we see it, this provides another intratextual indication not to neglect the potential for allegorical interpretation of Mary's virginity and her veil. We therefore do not see how one can speak of a 'de-allegorisation' here. By contrast, the Qur'an does not contradict an allegorical interpretation of the veil, but instead puts it in a specifically Islamic context, which displays some striking intersections with Christian ideas.

In the Qur'an, the curtain that formerly protected the Holy of Holies can also be construed in such a way that it is transformed into a perfectly normal hijab, which Mary uses to protect herself from the young man who comes to visit her. In addition, one can also interpret the rest of the story in this same way: the fact that Mary takes the hijab is what makes it possible for God to send her an angel in the guise of a beautiful young man; in other words, the corresponding Arabic conjunction *fa-* cannot just be translated here as causative but also coordinate.

In any event it is the hijab which enables Mary to be 'set apart'[62] – a connotation of saintliness that continues to characterise phenomenologies of this term to this day.[63] The fact that the hijab has its ultimate origins in the curtain of the Temple that separated the Holy of Holies from the faithful, and that in the mindset of Late Antiquity God or monarchs could only address ordinary people from behind a curtain, demonstrates the special dignity that was associated with a veil. After all, even the Prophet Muhammad in older pictures was repeatedly shown with a veil in front of his face, in the same way as the Kaaba in Mecca is shrouded with black cloth as an indication of its sanctity. Mary's veil shows the special dignity that is ascribed to her, and chimes in well with her connection to Christ, whom the Church Fathers also regarded as having been given to her through the veil.[64]

---

distinguished from the other women around her by her powerful and intensive devotion to God. The fact that she was married and had children is not the decisive factor here. Cf. Lane, *Lexicon*, vol. 1, 150–151.

62 Likewise, according to Kuschel (*Juden, Christen, Muslime*, 483) the veil here symbolises 'concealing oneself, shutting oneself off from one's familiar environment.'

63 Cf. Evans, *The Sacred*, 32–47.

64 Cf. for example Ephrem, *Hymns on the Nativity 17.4*, 80: 'In her virginity Eve put on leaves of shame. Your mother put on, in her virginity, the garment of glory that suffices for all. I gave the little mantle of the body to the One who covers all.' Edmund Beck gives the following commentary: 'The garment of glory that suffices for all is the body of the redeemed and transfigured humanity with Christ at its head. The little mantle or, more accurately

The Mary of the Qur'an therefore deliberately heads to the East, as the place where heaven and earth join, and equips herself with a veil, the medium that protects her in her encounter with God and enables her to conduct a dialogue with God. All the same, she appears as a perfectly ordinary woman in the process, standing for every woman and every person who is open to hearing and receiving the word of God. The Qur'an does not therefore de-allegorise the images of the Christian tradition but rather interprets them inclusively and is intent on helping us put ourselves in Mary's position. After all, the Temple no longer stands just in Jerusalem and the curtain does not hang solely in the Temple, but is accessible to everyone. Only if we too repeatedly separate ourselves off and give God space to enter our lives will we become receptive to God's address, which the Qur'an attests for Mary and invites us to hear as well.

Then We sent to her Our angel, Gabriel, appearing before her as a man, perfectly formed. She appealed, 'I truly seek refuge in the Most Compassionate from you! So leave me alone if you are God-fearing.' He responded, 'I am only a messenger from your Lord, sent to bless you with a pure son.' She wondered, 'How can I have a son when no man has ever touched me, nor am I unchaste?' He replied, 'So will it be! Your Lord says, "It is easy for Me. And so will We make him a sign for humanity and a mercy from Us."' It is a matter already decreed (Q 19:17b–21).

We have already remarked that God's messenger appears to Mary in a very pleasing outward form. Interestingly, to begin with, there is no mention of an angel, and instead the figure's identity remains open to interpretation. The fact that a spirit of God is involved here indicates that in the Christian tradition, it is invariably the Holy Spirit who facilitates Mary's pregnancy – as already established in the Apostolic Creed.[65] Likewise, in the patristic tradition it is initially the spirit of God who creates Christ's human nature, even though this is then increasingly conveyed through the Trinity.[66]

In the classic commentaries on the Qur'an the spirit of God is, for the most part,

---

translated, the little (piece of) cloth is explained by the apposition that follows; it is the small body of the newborn child, given by the mother.' (Beck, 'Die Mariologie der echten Schriften Ephraems', 30; on this topic, see also Brock, 'Clothing metaphors as a means of theological expression in Syriac tradition', 11–38.)

65 We will presently see the problems that the Muslim commentary tradition has with this statement. By contrast, it is taken as read by the Islamic mystic tradition of Qur'anic exegesis. In this tradition it is axiomatic that: 'The Holy Spirit is the origin of the birth of Jesus.' (Yaşar, 'Maria und die Geburt Jesu im mystischen Korankommentar', 5)

66 Cf. Schmaus, *Mariologie*, 161.

identified without further ado with Gabriel.[67] However, in Fakhr al-Din al-Rāzi's great exegesis at least, there is a reflection to the effect that it is precisely the Spirit of God who enlivens all religions and fills us with love.[68] Thus, when Jesus is later described as the spirit of God, in Q 4:171, one might imagine that he too possessed this reviving power with regard to religion. According to Rāzi, the spirit is to be understood here as a metaphor for God's love, and he substantiates this relationship by citing contemporary Arabic linguistic usage.[69] And if it is the Spirit of God which enables the Virgin Mary to give birth to Jesus, this only emphasises how much the reviving, renewing power of God is needed for this to take place.

The spirit of God approaches Mary in the form of a person, and Mary's reaction can scarcely be interpreted as anything other than an indication that the apparition before her takes the shape of a man. Otherwise, why would she feel obliged to appeal to his God-fearing nature? Ṭabarī, for instance, explains her anxiety as a fear that this man – Ṭabarī and the whole tradition take him to be Gabriel – might want something immoral from her. In the Qur'anic text, she therefore makes a point of reminding the figure that appears to her in the form of a man of his 'human', good side, so that he might distance himself from any base desires by calling to mind his fear of God.[70]

Nonetheless, the historical appropriateness of this widespread interpretation is open to question. For instance, in the writings of the Church Fathers – unlike in the period when the New Testament was being compiled – angels were always genderless, and were often portrayed in icons as androgynous figures. Ephrem, though, does not appear to fully trust this interpretation and instead characterises the angel as an old man, who is by no means young and beautiful, in order to thereby to exclude any sexual connotations from the outset.[71] The text of the Qur'an is open to interpretation here and does not exclude a sexual challenge on

67 Cf. among others aṭ-Ṭabarī, *Tafsīr*, vol. 15, 485–486 and az-Zamaḫšarī, *Tafsīr*, 644.

68 Cf. ar-Rāzī, *Tafsīr*, vol. 21, 197 and az-Zamaḫšarī, *Tafsīr*, 686.

69 Cf. ibid., 686.

70 Cf. aṭ-Ṭabarī, *Tafsīr*, vol. 15, 485. If, like Ṭabarī and many other commentators, one assumes that the spirit is to be identified with Gabriel, then the appeal by her to this angelic figure to leave her alone once more underlines Mary's chasteness, for unlike the people of Sodom and Gomorrah she does not want to have intimate contact even with angels.

71 Cf. Ephrem, *Hymns on the Nativity 2.19*, 16: 'For Gabriel appeared as a transfigured, venerable old man, and greeted her (thus) in order that she should not be fearful, and in order that the chaste Virgin should not behold a youthful countenance and be troubled (by it)'; cf. the almost certainly later (i.e. post-Qur'anic) *History of the Virgin Mary*, edited and translated by E. Wallis Budge, London 1899, 20, in which Gabriel appears before Maria 'like an aged, chaste man' – these two adjectives (i.e. 'aged' and 'chaste') are customarily applied in Syriac literature to elderly monks.

Mary's part. However, it would be wrong to therefore assume that advances of a sexual nature by a male angel do not have any bearing whatsoever on her alarm. In Rāzi's view, Mary's fear is because she immediately recognises him as an angel and is afraid of this irruption of the transcendent realm into her life[72] – a view that is fully consonant with her shock as recounted in the Bible (Lk 1:29).[73]

This interpretation of Mary's alarm as depicted in the Qur'an as fear of the irruption of divine transcendence is borne out by the typically apotropaic formula that she uses in Q 19:18 – albeit with the telling difference that she does not take refuge in an appeal to God's power, but instead to his compassion. Mary thereby introduces a personal address to God and qualifies the ambiguous situation of the meeting with God's messenger by signalling her trust in God's all-embracing compassion.[74] She therefore places the dialogue with God's emissary from the outset under the heading of mercy and so divests it of its terror – a creative theological achievement, which is not directly traceable back to a biblical provenance, but was certainly familiar to the Muslim tradition.

Thus, according to Ṭabarī, with this prayer Mary demonstrates her assumption that wisdom and reason must be inherent in the God-fearing character that she attributes to Gabriel.[75] For she tries to defend herself by using an argument with religious connotations, and at this point appears self-assured and not at all passively submissive. Ṭabarī's fundamental point here seems to be that being God-fearing is not to be equated with blind fear, but rather should be thought of in conjunction with a shrewd alertness that is closely akin to the application of reason. For Mary demands this use of reason from Gabriel by tapping into her own understanding of what being God-fearing entails. In applying her critical questioning and creative intellect, Mary is thus seen to point beyond the biblical text while at the same time to take her cue from it.[76]

72 Cf. ar-Rāzī, *Tafsīr*, vol. 21, 199.

73 The text of the Bible also attributes her shock to being addressed as 'You, who are highly favoured' (Lk 1:29), a greeting that only exacerbates the disturbing nature of her encounter with the angel. This kind of encounter and selection of Mary does not occur in the Surah *Maryam* (cf. Neuwirth, *Der Koran 2/1*, 614) – though it certainly does in the Surah *Āl 'Imrān*, as we shall presently see (cf. Q 3:42).

74 Cf. al-Qurṭubī, *al-Ǧāmi'*, vol. 13, 429.

75 Cf. aṭ-Ṭabarī, *Tafsīr*, vol. 15, 487.

76 As a point of contact for our reflections here, we might cite our earlier comments on Lk 2:19 and 1:29 (see above, 'Mary in the Bible'). Precisely because of this critical, questioning and alert intellectual capacity that Mary displays in the Surah *Maryam*, we find implausible Neuwirth's assertion that Mary is – similar to her role in the Protevangelium of James – 'more the passive instrument for a divine plan rather than its active protagonist in the Qur'anic version of her story that is recounted in Surah 19' (Neuwirth, *Der Koran 2/1*, 646).

So many divergences are apparent here in comparison with the biblical text that we cannot treat them all. Nazareth as a setting (Lk 1:26) has been dropped, as has the figure of Joseph and the famous beatitude spoken to Mary by Gabriel at the beginning of the dialogue. But what is primarily absent are the Christological interpretive statements found in Lk 1:32f. Instead, all that is mentioned is a 'pure son'. Yet if we also draw in the Protevangelium of James for comparison, we notice that we should not be too hasty to draw conclusions from the absence of these details. For the Christological statements are entirely lacking there, and Mary's encounter with the angel is highlighted with none of the familiar context from Lk 1:26–33 (ProtEvJam 11:2 f.).

While the Protevangelium rescinds some of Mary's further questioning of the angel in comparison with Lk 1:34, the questioning by the Qur'anic Mary in Q 19:20 is almost identical to the biblical text, and forcefully confronts us with the biological virginity of Mary. For just like the biblical formulation 'seeing I know not a man', the Qur'anic phrase 'no man has ever touched me' uses the specific term referring to the legal, legitimate congress of a married couple; in both cases, this means that Mary is asking how she can have a child without intimate contact with a man. Because the proclaimer of the Qur'an evidently already had in mind various examples of polemical literature against Mary, he put in her mouth the further defence 'nor am I unchaste', thus making it clear that she will not only have no legal, legitimate contact, but no illegitimate intimate congress either. Although the Bible takes this latter point as read, it is referred to repeatedly in the apologetics of the Syrian Church Fathers.[77] Mary's persistent questioning of Gabriel in the Bible and the Qur'an – more persistent than in the apocryphal literature – once again underscores her discursive inclination to reason, but at the same time also her intensive and dialogic relationship with God, a feature that is strongly reminiscent of Zechariah.

As mentioned, the parallelism with the situation of Zechariah is also expressed in God's reply, which once again consists of the statement that this powerful deed is an easy undertaking for God (Q 19:21). This reply also casts Mary's dialogue with God into the same sphere of ease that characterises Zechariah's dialogue with God. The biblical answer given by the angel, that nothing is impossible for God (Lk 1:37), which in turn refers back to the birth of a child to Abraham and his aged

77 Cf. *Jacob of Serugh's homilies on the nativity*, 78, and Jacob of Serugh, On the mother of God, 66: 'If Mary had revealed the divine mystery, she would have been scorned, hated, calumniated. She would have been slandered, persecuted and stoned; she would have been regarded as an adultress and a liar.'

wife Sarah (Genesis 18:14), is thus taken up in conjunction with formulations of the Church Fathers and furnished with even greater effortlessness.

From a Christian point of view, it is remarkable that the idea of the sign that is so central, say, to the Gospel of John, and which was also so important for the theology of the Syrian Church Fathers,[78] is picked up in a positive way by the Qur'an and related to Jesus. Here, Jesus is clearly a sign for all people and Mary is the first human being to be convinced by this sign. For the birth of Jesus, conveyed through this sign, is a foregone conclusion. Admittedly, Mary's *fiat*, which is so prominent in the Bible, is missing at this point.[79] But we will presently see that this topic is picked up elsewhere in the Qur'an (namely in Q 66:12); as a result, from a Christian perspective its absence here should not be overstated in theological terms. Clearly, God's address alone, plus the sign that Jesus Christ himself represents, are enough for Mary to cease her questioning and place her trust in God.[80] It is also significant – especially in the context of the theology of the Surah *Maryam* – that Jesus is seen as a sign of God's compassion (Q 19:21). By implication, it is God's mercy that Mary has invoked shortly before and which in this surah qualifies the relationship with God that is expressed through Jesus. The insight that this importance accorded to compassion is not just a purely Christian affair,[81] but precisely through this surah becomes an abiding concern of Islam too, can be seen from the Qur'an's characterisation of Muhammad alongside Jesus as a symbol of mercy. Nevertheless, the verse in question, Q 21:107 could also mean that Muhammad was sent out of compassion, whereas in Q 19:21 Jesus unequivocally

78 Cf. Griffith, 'Disclosing the mystery', 53 f.

79 Angelika Neuwirth ascribes the absence of Mary's *fiat* in the Surah *Maryam* to the fact that the account of Mary given in this Surah was heavily influenced by the Protevangelium of James, and that this apocryphal text likewise does not acknowledge any self-assured *fiat* on Mary's part (cf. Neuwirth, *Der Koran 2/1*, 646). Yet for one thing Mary's *fiat* most decidedly is contained within ProtEvJam 11,3, and for another we might question whether the Surah *Maryam* really is so strongly influenced by this text as Neuwirth claims. In any case, direct references to ProtEvJam are far more evident in Q 3 than in Q 19, as we shall later see.

80 The question of a more precise understanding of Jesus's role as a sign at this point also occupied the Muslim commentary tradition. Muqātil identifies it as a lesson or an instructive example *(ʿibra)* for humans (cf. Muqātil, *Tafsīr*, vol. 2, 624) and claims that not all people comprehend as quickly as Mary does, simply by virtue of being touched inwardly by the Word of God. More often, it requires the more arduous path of teaching, which is likewise the reason why God sent Jesus to earth.

81 Compassion – *raḥmē* – also forms the centrepiece of the theology of Jacob of Serugh, for example. Jacob and many of the Syriac Church Fathers firmly believed that: 'In his mercy, God created humanity, in his mercy he redeemed it through the sacrifice of his son, and in his mercy God will return at the end of days and ultimately restore humanity in all its glory' (Ghaffar, *Der Koran in seinem religions- und weltgeschichtlichen Kontext*, 51).

embodies God's compassion.[82] This embodiment, which Mary feels in her conception, makes it possible for her to assent to this sign from God and to acquiesce in God's goodwill toward herself and all humans.

At this point one might expect, from reading the Gospel of Luke, a connection to be made between the stories of the birth of John the Baptist and Jesus through a meeting between Mary and Elizabeth. But this does not occur in the Surah *Maryam*, because it aims to link the stories of Zechariah and Mary through their parallel structure rather than through their individual narrative elements. Even the classic Muslim commentary tradition did not always tolerate this literarily powerful silence on the part of the Qur'an. Thus, in his analysis of Lk, Ṭabarī writes that Mary and her sister,[83] the wife of Zechariah,[84] tell one another that they are pregnant, whereupon Zechariah's wife testifies that the child in her womb bows before the child that Mary is carrying.[85] By contrast, the Surah *Maryam* skips over such details and the hierarchisation associated with them, because its intention is quite openly to honour the Christian and Jewish traditions in equal measure.

c) Pregnancy and birth (22–26)

So she conceived him and withdrew with him to a remote place. Then the pains of labour drove her to the trunk of a palm tree. She cried, 'Alas! I wish I had died before this, and was a thing long forgotten!' So a voice[86] *reassured her from below, 'Do not grieve! Your Lord has provided a stream at your feet. And shake the trunk of this palm tree towards you, it will drop fresh, ripe dates upon you. So eat and drink, and put your heart at ease. But if you see anybody, say, "I have vowed silence to the Most Compassionate, so I am not talking to anyone today"'* (Q 19:22–26).

---

82 Certainly, Muqātil for one also sees Muhammad himself as an embodiment of the principle of compassion. Cf. Muqātil, *Tafsīr*, vol. 2, 624.

83 We will say more in our comments below on Q 19:28 on the theological significance of the family relationship between Mary and Elizabeth. It should simply be noted here that this sisterly relationship is presented fully in line with Qur'anic interpretation and in contradiction to the Syrian patristic viewpoint, whereas the biblical text is open to interpretation.

84 Qurṭubī sees Elizabeth as a maternal aunt of Hannah (cf. al-Qurṭubī, *al-Ǧāmiʿ*, vol. 13, 108), whereas Ṭabarī and others identify her as Hannah's sister (cf. aṭ-Ṭabarī, *Tafsīr*, vol. 15, 491).

85 Cf. aṭ-Ṭabarī, *Tafsīr*, vol. 15, 491.

86 One possible translation here could involve replacing 'it' with 'he'. In addition, one canonical reading has at this point *'fa-nādāhā man taḥtahā' instead of 'fa-nādāhā min taḥtihā'*, which further argues in favour of translating the subject as 'he' rather than 'it'.

As Karl Josef Kuschel has rightly remarked, Mary's withdrawal to a remote place has a parallel in the Protevangelium of James.[87] However, her sojourn there is an enforced one in ProtEvJam 16:2. The High Priest Annas uses the time that Mary and Joseph spend in the wilderness to verify her claim of virginity. By contrast, in Q 19:22 Mary's withdrawal is portrayed as a freely willed action on her part, in order to protect herself from malicious gossip within the family, which does indeed later arise.[88] Whereas in Lk 1:39–45, Mary receives support from her relative Elizabeth just a few days after the Annunciation and as a result – strengthened by her stay with Elizabeth – is able to sing her famous hymn of praise, the Magnificat (Lk 1:46–56), in the Qur'an Mary is left to her own devices. She receives no support whatsoever, either from the religious institution of the Temple or her husband (unlike in the ProtEvJam), or even from her family (unlike in Lk), but is left utterly alone in a far-flung location.

And in this situation of total forsakenness, while sitting against the trunk of a palm tree, she is suddenly overcome by labour pains and wishes she were dead. From a biblical point of view, she finds herself in a very similar situation to that of the Prophet Elijah just prior to his most intensive and intimate encounter with God on Mount Horeb. Elijah, too, is at his wits' end, and so walks off into the desert and longs for death (1 Kings 19:4). And just like Elijah, Mary hears the voice of an angel telling her to eat and drink (1 Kings 19:5–8).[89] But to begin with she is in an even more precarious situation than Elijah. For precisely her closest friends and confidants – and not just, as in Elijah's case, a malevolent queen (Jezebel) – have shunned her. And in addition she suffers labour pains all on her own, without any

87 Cf. Kuschel, *Juden, Christen, Muslime. Herkunft und Zukunft*, 482. This supposition can also be found in Riße, 'Maria, die Gottesfürchtige', 37 f., 44.

88 We would agree with Angelika Neuwirth that Mary's abandonment in the wilderness is reminiscent of Hagar 'who suffers a similar fate in Genesis 21:19–21' (Neuwirth, *Der Koran 2/1*, 647). Yet Hagar and Ishmael were expressly banished by Abraham (Genesis 21:14) and have no other choice but to flee into the desert. The parallels between Hagar and Mary therefore more likely derive from a narrative that was well-known throughout the Arabian Peninsula, which recounted Hagar and Ishmael's sojourn in the desert and the direness of their situation, which is miraculously relieved by the sudden appearance of a spring at Ishmael's feet. No motif of banishment appears in the Qur'an.

89 Monks who live in the desert are also entirely dependent upon God for everything and according to patristic thinking are provisioned by God in the wilderness. Accordingly, this need not be a specific reference to Elijah here. The idea that God encourages people to keep going and find courage within themselves by providing food and water is well embedded in the biblical tradition from Exodus onwards and shaped the faith of many people in Late Antiquity. The parallels between Mary's and Elijah's situations reside in the fact that this faith is challenged in both him and her alike by their critical predicament.

professional or empathetic support. The setting of this scene in the desert, as an inhospitable place of solitude, loneliness and barrenness, only serves to further underline her complete exposure.

The stress that the Qur'an places on Mary's labour pains intervenes in a debate that was a somewhat contentious topic within Christian circles in Late Antiquity. Certainly, we have seen above how Ephrem, Jacob and other Syrian Church Fathers affirmed that Mary experienced birth pains, in order to emphasise the very real actuality of Jesus Christ being born as man. And we have indicated how various writings of Jacob of Serugh presuppose that Mary had labour pains.[90] And yet these same works also proceed from the assumption that Mary suffered no ill effects from giving birth, and indeed one of our principal findings above was that there are other texts, surely of only secondary importance, which deny the existence of any birthing pains. Likewise the early Christian texts known as the Odes of Solomon, which also come from the Syrian tradition, contain a denial of Mary's labour pains too.[91] Consequently, the heavy emphasis on Mary's birth pains in the Qur'an is remarkable. In the modern period, it has in all probability become self-evident within Christianity as well to assume that Mary experienced labour pains. In any event, this would have the effect of bringing her closer to us humans and our real problems. And even if the Arabic wording is not entirely unambiguous and may perhaps denote only the physiological reality of the birth and not the pains associated with it,[92] its translation here as 'labour pains' is still the most probable, and moreover fits in well with the flow of the narrative, which starkly confronts us with the drama of Mary's desolate situation.

This situation is also acknowledged in the classical literature of commentary on the Qur'an. Ṭabarī recognises that Mary has to flee from her family here, since she has perceived them as a threat. He sees her withdrawal as a *hijra*, which in

90 Cf. Jakob von Sarug, *Die Kirche und die Forschung*, 18.

91 To quote the Odes verbatim: 'And the Virgin became a mother in great compassion and went into labour and bore a son. Yet she suffered no pain, because her labours were not in vain' (Odes of Solomon, Ode 19).

92 Significantly Geagea, *Mary of the Koran*, 143, highlights this possible way of translating the Arabic, attempting thereby to once more corroborate the unfortunate tradition in Christianity of denying that Mary experienced labour pains. In his view, the term *maḫāḍ* does not necessarily denote pains, but merely describes the contraction of the embryo. Correspondingly, Mary's pain might also be spiritualised here, he claims, which is indeed what most commentators of the Qur'an allegedly do (Geagea, *Mary of the Koran*, 144). However, this claim does not seem to us to be accurate. Rāzī for instance talks in very graphic terms about her loss of blood, while the water and dates she consumes are meant as practical means of combating the physical weakness she experiences as a result of giving birth. Cf. ar-Rāzī, *Tafsīr*, vol. 21, 207.

some regards anticipates the *hijra* of Muhammad.[93] He explains her death wish as a response to her sense of having brought shame on her people by conceiving a child with no father.[94] And indeed, this explanation is not only perfectly plausible in Late Antiquity's reading of the story but also as regards its historical origins. In a patriarchal society that reacts to a child born out of wedlock with draconian sanctions, a young woman who tries to talk her way out of the situation by claiming that she has conceived her child from God without a biological father finds herself not only in a very lonely position – this would also be the case nowadays – but also in danger of her life. One need only think of the punishment of extra-marital sexual intercourse with death by stoning which is attested not just in the Old Testament but in Sharia Law as well.

In this situation of threat and loneliness, Mary is in sore need of help and support. In our Qur'an story, she receives this initially from nature and then from her newborn child. Nature's help is expressed firstly in the image of the palm tree, which provides her with fruits, and the stream that flows beneath the tree. Here, therefore, it is not an angel that supplies her directly with food and drink – as with Elijah in 1 Kings 19 – but rather God himself who helps her in a creatively mediate way. Thus, Ṭabarī explained that, although the tree would have been dried out since it was winter, it would have still borne fruit, which fell when Mary shook the trunk. Furthermore, he maintained, dates were the very best food for women in labour.[95] Rāzī too speculates that Mary, having lost a large amount of blood while giving birth, would have had an even greater need of the dates than the water as a way of building up her strength again.[96] This once again emphasises that the Muslim commentary tradition also saw the birth of Jesus as a completely natural occurrence – with all the perils and pains that such an event entails for women, especially when there is no-one to help them with the delivery.

Scholars are divided over whether the story of Mary giving birth under a palm tree had pre-Qur'anic antecedents that it drew upon.[97] Suleiman A. Mourad, for

93 Cf. aṭ-Ṭabarī, *Tafsīr*, vol. 15, 496.

94 Cf. ibid., 498.

95 Cf. ibid., 511. Ṭabarī specifically discusses the precise circumstances of the story with the palm and the dates. In his view, to yield up its dates the palm tree lowered its crown rather than having to be cut down – yet another indication that the natural world was intrinsically at Mary's service (cf. ibid., 512–514).

96 Cf. ar-Rāzī, *Tafsīr*, vol. 21, 207.

97 The fact that the concept of a palm frond which can exist independently of the main trunk and the term denoting Mary as a virgin are rendered in Arabic by exactly the same word *(batūl)*, indicates that in all probability palms were associated even in pre-Qur'anic times with femininity and (spiritual) fertility, and that there must have been a fund of familiar stories

example, attempts to show that the Ancient Greek myth of the labour pains suffered by Leto in giving birth to the god Apollo forms the background of the story that is found in the Qur'an and in corresponding Christian apocryphal texts.[98] The tale of Apollo's birth beneath a palm tree on the island of Delos was, Mourad claims, known far and wide in the Hellenistic and Roman worlds and had been in circulation in a whole series of different versions.[99] Common to both traditions, he maintains, was the narrative of a miraculous appearance of a palm tree with water at its roots.[100] For instance, Herodotus cited an Egyptian version of the story, in which the infant Apollo was said to have been hidden by his nurse Leto from the ravaging giant Typhon.[101]

Historically speaking, however, it is a very bold assertion to claim that an Egyptian version of a legend from antiquity could have exerted an influence in Arabia in the seventh century. In this respect, it is true that Mourad himself also assumes that the ancient story must have been taken up in Christian traditions. The possible source of this Christian adaptation of this myth may have been the Christians of Nağrān, who revered a palm tree as their ritual cult site prior to their Christianisation.[102] Cornelia Horn picks up this idea[103] and argues that a lost Syrian original of the Arabic apocryphal Gospel of John,[104] which may well have contained a general account of the life of Mary,[105] influenced the account which appears in the Qur'an.

Karl-Josef Kuschel has pointed to a parallel in the Gospel of Pseudo-Matthew, which however to the best of his knowledge is thought by scholars to postdate the Qur'an.[106] In addition, in PsMt 20:1 f. the palm tree appears during the Flight to Egypt of the Holy Family. Generally speaking, the PsMt is an updating of ProtEvJam, but the scene with the palm tree is new. Here, the narrative tells of Mary stopping to rest in the shadow of the palm out of sheer exhaustion and

---

relating to this that the Qur'an was able to tap into. However, the Qur'an actually uses a different term for palm tree at this point (*naḫla*) – possibly precisely in order to lay to rest any associations with such stories. Cf. footnote 64 above.

98 Cf. Mourad, 'From Hellenism to Christianity and Islam', 206–216.

99 Cf. ibid., 210.

100 Cf. ibid., 209.

101 Cf. ibid., 212.

102 Cf. ibid., 214 f.

103 Cf. Horn, 'Intersections', 133 f.

104 Cf. Horn, 'Tracing the reception of the Protoevangelium of James in late antique Arabia', 138.

105 Cf. ibid., 140.

106 Cf. Kuschel, *Juden, Christen, Muslime: Herkunft und Zukunft*, 482.

longing to eat some of its fruit, which is unfortunately hanging far too high for her to reach. So, the child Jesus orders the palm to bend and the whole family is able to enjoy the refreshing dates (PsMt 20:2).[107] Before Jesus's intervention, Joseph is astonished by Mary's extraordinary wish and makes it clear that it would be more appropriate to wish for water. Yet as a result of the miracle, they are later supplied with water as well (PsMt 20:3).

Meanwhile, in more recent research, the almost unanimous assumption has been that the post-Qur'anic Gospel of Pseudo-Matthew might ultimately date back to a pre-Qur'anic apocryphal Christian tradition. For the story of the palm tree miracle also occurs in the *Book of Mary's Repose* (the oldest account of Mary's Dormition). A fragment of this work is preserved in a Syrian palimpsest manuscript from the late fifth century.[108] Yet this does not provide any connection to the story of Jesus's birth. At this point, it should be mentioned that Michel van Esbroeck long since postulated a link between the miracle of the palm tree and the birth of Christ.[109] This alternative tale of Jesus's birth was, van Esbroeck claims, subsequently supplanted by Luke's narrative. However, there is not a shred of historical evidence to corroborate this interpretation. Therefore it remains the case that the story of the miracle of the palm tree, which relates to the childhood of Jesus, may have a putative pre-Qur'anic date, but that in any event the tale is only of limited relevance to the story in the Qur'an.[110]

107 Ṭabarī also reports that the palm tree bent for Mary. Cf. aṭ-Ṭabarī, *Tafsīr*, vol. 15, 512–514.

108 In addition, certain details of the text content argue in favour of a very early dating, such as the angel Christology of the 'Book of Mary's Repose', which was actually already obsolete by the fourth century. Cf. Shoemaker, Mary in Early Christian Faith and Devotion, 101 ff. and 127; cf. B. Müller-Kessler, *Obsequies of my Lady Mary: Unpublished Syriac Palimpsest Fragments from the British Library* (BL, Add 17.137, no. 2); on the angel Christology cf. Shoemaker, *Mary in Early Christian Faith*, esp. p. 106.

109 Cf. Michael van Esbroeck, 'Apocryphes géorgiens de la Dormition.' In: *Analecta Bollandiana* 92 (1973) 69–73.

110 Neuwirth, *Der Koran 2/1*, 615, even goes so far as to state: 'The context is very different: in Pseudo-Matthew, it is a collective experience in which Joseph, Mary and the infant Jesus, who by this stage is capable of action, all actively participate, whereas the Qur'an depicts the confinement of a lone female figure cut off from all human company and provisioned by supernatural forces. This story is of little relevance as a point of reference for Q 19.' One might also add that the other apocryphal stories are likewise far from indispensable for interpreting the situation presented in the Qur'an. For the miracle of the palm tree is perfectly comprehensible within the plot of the narrative and in the context of the message the Qur'an itself seeks to convey. Nonetheless, in the light of recent research findings, it is not so easy to dismiss the relevance of the Christian intertext as vehemently as Neuwirth does in her commentary.

Let us now examine a further problem for the interpretation of the passage of text under discussion here, which has been of concern above all for the Muslim commentary tradition. The text of the Qur'an leaves it open as to whence, or from whom, the voice comes which instils Mary with hope and which reassures her that she will be provided with dates and water. The only thing that is clear is that it comes from below and hence from a direction that is not customarily associated with God or God's word in the Qur'anic context. Rather, people's words of praise rise *up* to God (Q 35:10), or his words are sent *down* to humanity (Q 3:3, 4:113). Consequently, the only possibility that is entertained throughout the Muslim commentary literature is that Jesus himself or the Angel Gabriel is the one who is speaking here.[111] Interestingly, most commentators do not decide on this matter, but simply bring both possibilities into play.[112]

In the event that Jesus himself is the speaker, then some commentators proceed from the assumption that his birth has taken place immediately prior to this scene and that it is therefore the newborn infant Jesus who is speaking, while others do not want to commit themselves and even deem it possible that the voice is emanating from Mary's womb. Regardless of whether it occurred shortly before or after his birth, an utterance by Jesus at this point would also explain on a narrative level why Mary is subsequently so certain that the Baby Jesus can speak and take her part. Through this reading it would also become apparent that Mary's death wish in Q 19:23 actually accompanies her labour pains and that the voice from below represents Jesus's first sign of life. From a purely grammatical perspective, this solution appears perfectly self-evident, as Ṭabarī argued.[113] For the last person to be mentioned in the course of the story, and the one to whom the male personal pronoun could refer, is Jesus himself, whereas the final speech of the angel already occurred several verses beforehand, and above all nothing is said about the angel accompanying Mary into the desert. Although she is described in Q 3:37 as being provided with food by angels, the whole dramatic thrust of the Surah *Maryam* is to depict Mary's loneliness – without a husband, family members, friends and also without an angel. In this situation it is only the sign of God himself and of his mercy, namely her child Jesus, that instils her with new courage and hope. Only

111 Even the earliest commentators could not agree on this point. While Muqātil hears the angel calling here (Muqātil, *Tafsīr*, vol. 2, 624), Muǧāhid takes the view that Jesus calls Mary from below during the birth. Cf. Muǧāhid, *Tafsīr*, 455. For his part, Ṯawrī does not settle the dispute, opting instead to simply cite both alternatives, Gabriel or Jesus. Cf. aṯ-Ṯawrī, *Tafsīr*, 183.

112 Cf. aṭ-Ṭabarī, *Tafsīr*, vol. 15, 500; ar-Rāzī, *Tafsīr*, vol. 21, 205; az-Zamaḫšarī, *Tafsīr*, 635.

113 Cf. aṭ-Ṭabarī, *Tafsīr*, vol. 15, 501.

through Jesus, and not mediated by other messengers or signs, does she begin to turn her life around and gain new confidence.

The main problem with this interpretation is that it is hard to comprehend how a newborn child could speak. Yet we may be guilty here of importing modern sensibilities into the culture of Late Antiquity. For it evidently presented no problem to the Syriac Church Fathers that Mary should ask her embryo for help even when it was still in her womb.[114] Besides, this problem would arise anyway, since the Baby Jesus delivers a speech of his own at the latest in Q 19:30–33. Consequently, if one attributes the voice to an angel at this point, one is only avoiding addressing the inevitable problem.

Let us therefore investigate how the voice of Jesus in these verses can be understood as an intervention on the part of the newborn infant. In classical terms, one might perhaps assume that God had endowed the child with superhuman powers and given him the gift of speech, which of course is possible in view of God's omnipotence. On the other hand, the Qur'an is repeatedly at pains to reduce everything miraculous from biblical stories to their function as signs, and even Muslim commentators tend to explain miracles as natural occurrences. In consequence, one might perhaps also interpret the voice of Jesus as a power that was given to Mary by Jesus. This power puts her heart at ease (Q 19:24) and allows her to notice the little stream where she can quench her thirst. It is also this same power that emboldens her to shake the palm tree and so find sustenance (Q 19:25). At most, it is the final verse of this speech that presents difficulties. For here it is not a question of Mary's being emboldened by the voice, but of its also issuing her an order relating to her fasting (Q 19:26).

Certainly one could also say here that giving birth to her child not only emboldens Mary but also instils in her an inner need to fast in a particular way. Nonetheless, even in a Christian context, the idea of not speaking to anyone is a very unusual method of fasting, and it is hard to understand how the experience of giving birth might give rise to such an imperative in a person.[115]

In any event, as regards the pragmatic business of storytelling, the act of fasting performs two important functions. To start with, it links Mary with

114 Cf. Jacob of Serugh's homilies on the nativity, 86 (= *First Homily*, v. 673).

115 This form of fasting is also the subject of discussion in the Muslim commentary tradition. Thus, Ṭabarī for example believes that Mary and no one else was permitted to fast in this way (aṭ-Ṭabarī, *Tafsīr*, vol. 15, 519). The obvious objection that Zechariah was also required to fast in this way can be answered by pointing out that Zechariah does not actually fast but rather is given a sign by God in order to inspire confidence in him. For him, remaining silent is not a voluntary decision or the result of an inner struggle, but is imposed upon him by God.

Zechariah and provides another indication that the Qur'an intends to break the customary relationship between the old and the new covenants. While the Church Fathers interpreted Zechariah's enforced silence as a punishment for his doubt, the ground is cut away from beneath this interpretation by the Qur'an. Now that Mary must also be silent, and this silence is interpreted as fasting and hence as a meritorious act, it becomes fully evident that Zechariah's fasting should likewise not be seen as negative. Zechariah's doubt, which links him to Mary, is therefore rehabilitated, and the two protagonists from Judaism and Christianity are thereby put on an equal footing. And once again from a pragmatic narrative point of view, this injunction to keep silent is the prerequisite for Mary's being able to point silently at Jesus and let him defend her. After all, Mary would not have fled in a pregnant state from her family if she had possessed her own ways and means of defending herself discursively against the accusations of her relatives. As a result, it is very plausible that God here enables Jesus himself to take matters into his own hands and proceed to take over her defence. Anyway, he is a prophet and clearly even as a newborn child has the God-given power to turn God's will into tangible reality.

But if at this juncture one were to contend that newborn infants simply cannot talk, then one might nonetheless also quite happily concede that God or an angel would certainly not speak in the same way that we do. The fact is that God can communicate through all manner of messengers, such as prophets – and even, if he so chooses, through a newborn infant too. In acknowledging this, we do not need to presume that the infant speaks directly. One could also speculate that an encounter with God might result in humans, thanks to God's power, being able to receive a divine message and, as it were, be spoken to by God in a non-verbal way.[116] Aside from this passage, the proclaimer of the Qur'an also has the earth speak (in Q 99:5) as well as the hands and feet of men (Q 36:65), and in those instances likewise, we are not expected to picture the earth or people's hands and feet literally delivering a speech. Whenever the Qur'an has protagonists speak, they are fulfilling a particular purpose and clarifying something. The intention is to conjure up an image, an impression, a composition. The interplay between the various elements generates a truth that has an effect – regardless of whether

116 Cf. aṭ-Ṭabarī, *Tafsīr*, vol. 15, 518 f. Islamic exegetical literature contains the formulation *bi-lisān al-ḥāl* (literally 'with the tongue of the situation'). When applied to our problem of the speaking infant, this means that Jesus's speech can be understood both as actual speaking and as a form of non-verbal communication. On the use of this term, cf. for example az-Zamaḫšarī, *Tafsīr*, 598. There, he understands the glorification of God by the heavens and the earth (Q 17:44) by means of their very being *(bi-lisān al-ḥāl)*.

we assume these to have a literal or an allegorical meaning. In this sense, the proclaimer of the Qur'an is inviting us not so much to disengage the speech of the newborn Jesus from its pragmatic context and see it as a miracle, as to let the image that is thereby evoked have its effect on us.

We do not want to labour this point any further here, but believe that we are fully justified in hearing the voice of Jesus already in Q 19:24–26, instilling Mary with courage and leading her back to her family. Jesus comes to her unexpectedly from below; he is the prophet who humbles himself and makes God's presence known and approachable from an angle where we do not expect to find God.[117] This all fits so neatly with the specifically prophetic calling of Jesus that even the assignment of these verses to him makes perfect sense.[118]

Yet if we assume that verses 24–26 really were spoken by an angel, then this would mean that this angel was Mary's constant companion during her sojourn in the desert. God's mercy would manifest itself in the fact that God himself comes to her from below through the mediation of the angel and instils in her a new hope of life. The angel would accompany and guide Mary on all her journeys. In this way, Mary would become somewhat less independent and her relationship to Jesus less momentous. This interpretation is possible, but in our view not very plausible. For as Qurṭubī's commentaries on these verses demonstrate, Mary's devotion to God does not manifest itself in a passive acceptance of events. In a moving dialogue between Mary and Jesus, Qurṭubī shows the fears and anxieties of Mary when she thinks of the confrontation with her clan, and one can almost hear a reproachful tone when she identifies the existence of Jesus as the source of

117 Strictly speaking, the effect of God's presence cannot of course be determined as working in any particular direction. The fact that the Qur'an speaks at many points of its message being 'sent down' or of words of praise 'ascending' to God should not mislead us into simply concluding that God's location can be pinpointed as somewhere up in the sky. Systematic theology has therefore quite rightly concluded that God cannot be fixed in space and time. Thus – insofar as no limits can be set to God's presence – God's immanence can also be one that supports and nurtures from below. Associating such manifestations of God's presence with lowliness and smallness is a particular defining characteristic of Christian theology and faith. As such it is easy to understand why the Islamic tradition has such difficulties with talk of God being present within a figure of lowly stature.

118 Ṭabarī also points out that many people believe the little stream or spring that God makes flow underneath Mary to be Jesus himself (cf. aṭ-Ṭabarī, *Tafsīr*, vol. 15, 509). While this kind of interpretation of Jesus as flowing water or the fount of life is of course perfectly plausible, the text here does not appear to warrant it. Yet because verse 26 expressly exhorts Mary to eat and drink, the literal reading that she is being sanctioned to take a drink from a stream is to be preferred here over a more speculative Christological interpretation.

all her problems.[119] But in Qurṭubī's account, Jesus also has the capacity to confront Mary in such a way as to give her the strength and courage she needs to meet her people. Here, the ease in the relationship with God, which we described above in relation to Zechariah, finds its complementary counterpart: Mary finds it hard to carry the burden of what has happened to her, and indeed this is no easy load for her to bear. While we may learn from Zechariah that communication between God and man can and should be experienced as a easy phenomenon, like a natural stream, we can see from Mary that it is also possible to have an encounter with God of a kind that requires some courage to accept – specifically the courage to give God space in one's life. The consequences of this are not always clear and, as one reading of Mary's story shows, not always comfortable either.[120]

d) Mary's conflicts and Jesus as the bringer of peace

*Carrying her child, she brought him to her people. They said: 'O Mary, you have indeed done something terrible! Sister of Aaron, your father was not an evil man, nor was you mother an unchaste woman!' She pointed to the child. They said: 'How shall we talk to someone who is a child in the cradle?' But he said: 'I am God's servant (*ʿabd allāh*)! He has given me the Book and made me a prophet. He has made me blessed wherever I may be and has enjoined upon me prayer and almsgiving throughout my life. He has made me dutiful toward my mother, and He has not made me arrogant or wicked. Blessed was I on the day I was born, and blessed I shall be on the day I die and on the day I am raised to life again!'* (Q 19:27b–33).

After giving birth, therefore, Mary returns to her people. According to our interpretation it is Jesus himself who has opened the way for her to undertake this return. Consequently, it emphasises once more the paradoxical situation to which Mary has exposed herself, in having to support the very person on whose intercession she is counting. The relationship of mutual dependency between Mary and Jesus that the Syriac Church Fathers often discuss at some length is neatly encapsulated here in a simple image: Mary carries to her people the only one who can help her regain acceptance there and avoid punishment for her supposedly illegitimate sexual intercourse.

And indeed, no sooner has she arrived than Mary is bombarded with

119 Cf. al-Qurṭubī, *al-Ǧāmiʿ*, vol. 13, 436–440 including Ṭabarī's commentary, and also aṭ-Ṭabarī, *Tafsīr*, vol. 15, 518–519 as an explanation of verses 23–26.
120 Cf. ibid..

reproaches. She is charged with having done something outrageous (Q 19:27). She is reminded of her family honour, as a sister of Aaron, and of the rectitude of her parents (Q 19:28). Clearly this concerns the notion that she has dishonoured the entire family by engaging in illegitimate intimate physical congress. All in all, what the proclaimer of the Qur'an is doing here is reporting accusations that were also well rehearsed by the Syrian Church Fathers[121] and which constitute a typical subject-matter of Jewish polemics in Late Antiquity.[122] Evidently, this 'monstrous slander' (Q 4:156) against Mary was a topic of repeated concern in the Qur'an, presumably because, following the intensification of Marian devotion in the fifth and sixth centuries – around the time when the Qur'an came into being – such calumnies became especially virulent in the debates that raged in Late Antiquity.

Naturally, though, polemical questioning of the theologoumenon of the Virgin Birth was not a new phenomenon generated by the debates in Late Antiquity, but had dogged Christianity ever since its inception. In Part I of this book, we have already seen that Mary's virginity may even have been a bone of contention within the Bible. But what is clear at the very least is that it was questioned right from the outset. Thus, according to Mt 1:20–25, Joseph is only persuaded to believe Mary after an angel appears to him in a dream – a story which, with some embellishments, reappears in ProtEvJam 13 f. and which clearly made a deep impression on certain classical commentators of the Qur'an.

Thus, according to Ṭabarī, Joseph was one of the first people who, in the light of her pregnancy, refused to believe that she was a virgin, and who challenged her by asking if a fruit could be produced without a seed and so whether a child could possibly come into existence without a father. In Ṭabarī's view, Mary defended herself eloquently and fearlessly by pointing out that God (too) created the first fruit without a seed, and through his power caused a tree to grow without any rainfall, and also that it was possible for Adam and Eve to be created without parents. Eventually Mary manages to convince Joseph, who in a typically Qur'anic manner declares that God in his power can create anything he wishes.[123]

121 Cf. for example Ephrem the Syrian, Hymns on the Nativity, 12,9. On other texts from the Syrian hagiography cf. the remarks in Neuwirth, *Der Koran 2/1*, 617.

122 Cf. Schäfer, *Jesus in the Talmud*, 15–24.

123 aṭ-Ṭabarī, *Tafsīr*, vol. 15, 494–496. Very similar debates between Mary and Joseph are reported by Rāzī (ar-Rāzī, *Tafsīr*, vol. 21, 202 f.). According to Zamaḫšarī Joseph at first wanted to flee with Mary when she was accused of adultery. However, acting on a sudden impulse he then decides to kill her, and it is only the angel of God who manages to placate him and persuade him that the Holy Spirit impregnated Mary (cf. az-Zamaḫšarī, *Tafsīr*, 634). On the Muslim tradition regarding this passage, cf. also Ashkar, *Mary in the Syriac Christian tradition and Islam*, 157–163.

Embellishments of this kind, however, have no real bearing on the actual wording of the Qur'an. Joseph does not appear anywhere in the text, nor do we gain any insight into the discussions that Mary has with her clan. In any event we can only speculate about Mary's attempts to defend herself, since they are not documented in the Qur'an. All that has been passed down is the fact that accusations were levelled at her and that the baby Jesus speaks in her defence. Yet the exegetical embellishments do certainly represent an answer to questions by the Muslim faithful, to whom (in place of Joseph) the miraculous elements of Mary's pregnancy had to be made plausible here.

From an intertextual point of view, one very interesting aspect is the fact that Mary is addressed as the 'sister of Aaron' in Q 19:28.[124] Zishan Ghaffar sees this as an example of counterfactual intertextuality, in other words a clear rejection of the genealogy that most of the Syriac Church Fathers subscribed to. These early Christians never sought to prove that Mary came from the Aaronite line, but rather that she descended from the House of David.[125] One must tread somewhat carefully at this point, however, since it is not the proclaimer of the Qur'an himself who is speaking in Q 19:28 but the enemies of Mary who are having their say. Yet presumably these enemies of Mary come from her own family, which means that they would scarcely have fabricated her membership of the Aaronite clan. Nonetheless, it might be the case that they are establishing this similarity between themselves and Mary here while omitting to mention that she is also of David's line. In other words, although the form of address used in the Qur'an makes it clear that from the Qur'anic standpoint Mary is also an Aaronite, this in no way precludes her from also being descended from King David.[126]

---

124 This unusual form of address to Mary was also remarked upon by classical Muslim commentators, though they did not arrive at any theologically relevant insights as a result. Thus Rāzī and Ṭabarī cite traditions which seek to explain this form of address by claiming that Mary really did have a brother of this name (cf. ar-Rāzī, *Tafsīr*, vol. 21, 209 and aṭ-Ṭabarī, *Tafsīr*, vol. 15, 522). Ṭabarī also suggests that Mary may have belonged to the clan of Saleh, because the name Aaron was very common there. Ṭabarī finally comes to the conclusion that Mary's designation as the sister of Aaron meant that there was an Aaron in the clan to which her family belonged. Yet he firmly rejects the idea that this Aaron was the brother of Moses (aṭ-Ṭabarī, *Tafsīr*, vol. 15, 523). Qurṭubī on the other hand explores the argument that Mary was addressed thus because she came from the same lineage *(min naslihī)* as Aaron (Cf. al-Qurṭubī, *al-Ǧāmi'*, vol. 13,334).

125 Cf. Ghaffar, 'Kontrafaktische Intertextualität im Koran und die exegetische Tradition des syrischen Christentums', 23–32. Wilde also speculates about Syrian influences on Q 19:28 and concludes that the Qur'an was reacting here to the typological mindset of the Church Fathers (Wilde, 'Jesus and Mary', 297 f.).

126 Generally speaking, the assertion that Mary has an Aaronite lineage need not necessarily

In relation to this matter, there is no question of the Bible claiming Davidic descent for Mary at any point. Thus, in the genealogy given in Mt 1:1–16, Jesus's Davidic lineage is shown to come from his stepfather Joseph's side. From a legal standpoint, this adoption by a man from the line of David was absolutely sufficient to establish Jesus's Davidic ancestry, thereby making the question of Mary's ancestry irrelevant. At the same time, the family relationship between Mary and Elizabeth which comes to light in Lk 1:36 suggests that Mary had Aaronite ancestry. This Aaronite ancestry also fits well with the typological identification of Mary with the Temple in patristic exegesis, since the Aaronites were traditionally the foremost priestly caste, responsible for sacrifices. This association of Mary with the Temple later formed the basis for seeing her as a prefiguration of the Church, as we have seen above.

Even so, in spite of these arguments for Mary's Aaronite descent, from an early date the Syrian Church Fathers clearly felt it vitally important to reinterpret the biblical evidence in such a way that Mary could also be regarded as a descendant of the House of David. Thus, Ephrem the Syrian saw it as highly significant that in Lk 1:36 Mary was not called the 'sister of Elizabeth'; in his eyes, this raised the distinct possibility that she might be descended from David, since more distant family relationships between the various clans were conceivable.[127] Elsewhere, the Syrian Church Fathers expended a great deal of effort arguing repeatedly that not only Joseph but also Mary descended from the line of David.[128]

However, this opinion was in no way confined solely to the Syrian Church Fathers. From Origen onwards, this interpretation, which to begin with had not been very plausible, became axiomatic for many Church Fathers, especially those writing in the Alexandrian tradition. Syrian translations of the Bible, which had manipulated the text of the Bible in the way explained above, were cited as the authorities for this reading. And even as late as the twentieth century, conservative Catholic theologians such as Dibelius and Gaechter took the view that the original text of Lk 1:26 f. proved that Mary too came from David's line, or at the very least that Lk 1:32 indirectly identified Mary as being of the House of David.[129]

be directed against Christianity, as Reynolds, *The Qur'ān and its Biblical subtext*, 145 f. demonstrates.

127 Cf. Ephrem the Syrian, *Commentary on Tatian's Diatessaron*, I,25; Ephrem, *Commentaire de l'Évangile concordant*, I,25 (24).

128 Cf. Pseudo-Ephrem the Syrian, *Marian hymns*, 28,1; Pseudo-Ephrem the Syrian, *Commentary on the Diatessaron*, 1, 25 f.; Jacob of Serugh, *On the mother of God: Homily II*, 47; see also Puthuparampil, *Mariological thought of Mar Jacob of Serugh*, 168.

129 Cf. Schmaus, *Mariologie*, 190, who justifies his support for the latter interpretation in the

Indeed, this insistence by parts of the Christian tradition does make the interpretation of a negative intertextuality between the designation of Mary as the sister of Aaron (Q 19:28) and the assertion of a Davidic ancestry appear more plausible. Having said that, at the time when the Qur'an was being compiled, an attempt was made in the East Syriac tradition to mediate between the two positions, by seeing Mary as the heir to Levi and Judah at the same time, thus leaving open the question of whether Mary and Elizabeth were actually sisters or not.[130] This East Syriac tradition should be seen as influential inasmuch as the same idea recurs in the West Syriac context as well, in writings that are traditionally attributed to Ephrem.[131] As a result, one should not be too hasty in claiming that the Qur'an adopts an anti-Davidic interpretation of Mary. At least the Surah *Maryam* would also be open to a mediating interpretation linking Mary with both a Davidic and an Aaronite heritage. Even so, we will presently see how the Qur'an at large does indeed reject Mary's Davidic genealogy (cf., for example the anti-Davidic leanings of Q 38, which will be discussed in greater detail below, 161 ff.), though at the same time it may nonetheless stop short of simply affirming her Aaronite origins.

From a theological perspective, this interpretation strikes us as being extremely helpful precisely with regard to the debates that were taking place in Late Antiquity, as well as being fully consonant with the conciliatory atmosphere informing the Surah *Maryam* as a whole. For as we have seen above, the surah's aim is to give equal weight to the Aaronite tradition that is linked to Zechariah and the Christian tradition associated with Jesus, which for Christians is linked to the Davidic genealogy. The Qur'an avoids explicitly tracing the genealogy back to David, for reasons that we will go into in greater depth presently and which have to do with the political exploitation of Davidic messianology by the Emperor Heraclius. Yet neither does the Surah *Maryam* completely exclude it, instead allowing it to continue to resonate with the reader. For if Mary were exclusively an Aaronite, there would be a danger that, in her position as heir to this priestly tradition, she

---

following terms: 'When the angel says that the Lord God will give the throne of his father David to Mary's son, the most obvious meaning of this is that Jesus is related to his ancestor David through Mary. The remark made in Luke 1:36 that Mary is related to Elizabeth, who belongs to the priestly line of Aaron, does not present an insurmountable obstacle to also assigning Mary to a lineage other than the Aaronites, namely the house of David. For marriages from one clan to another were not entirely out of the question. Moreover, Jesus was legally counted as belonging to the house of David through his foster father Joseph.

130 Cf. *Cause of the Commemoration of Mary*, 54.

131 Cf. Pseudo-Ephrem the Syrian, *Commentary on the Diatessaron*, I, 26.

might introduce it into Christianity. Come what may, in the works of the Syriac Church Fathers, Mary is identified with the Temple; she comes, so to speak, as 'the embodiment of the Church into the inheritance of the Temple.'[132] When Mary is now identified as Aaron's sister in this interpretative tradition, it allows us to see her as both the heir to this tradition and at the same time as the '"sister" of the founder of the Temple cult, Aaron.'[133] From this, Neuwirth concludes that the aim here is a 'supplanting of the paradigm of service to the Temple by a new form of devotion inspired by the idea of mercy.'[134] Yet we have noted above that the deeds of Zechariah already anticipate this new form of devotion. And indeed, by Late Antiquity, the sacrifice of praise in synagogue services had long since taken the place of the old Temple cult. Thus, the proclaimer of the Qur'an does not see the Jewish tradition as an old practice that needs to be overthrown and replaced by Christianity or the Qur'an. Rather, Christianity and Judaism are seen to be related within the new theology of compassion, which now also manifests itself in the Qur'an. This conciliatory theology has its decisive protagonist in Mary, who can thus be understood at one and the same time as both the Christian heir to the Temple legacy and the sister of its updated Jewish iteration.

Let us return, however, to the narrative plot of the Surah *Maryam*. Mary and her newborn baby find themselves exposed to the hostility of her family. Because she has been tasked by the mysterious divine inspiration with remaining silent, and since she also knows from the speech delivered by her infant that Jesus is able to intervene to help her, she says nothing in her defence but instead points silently at Jesus.

This silent act of pointing at Jesus is strongly reminiscent of the iconographic tradition, which offers numerous depictions of Mary and her son in which Mary is shown pointing wordlessly at her offspring.[135] This so-called *hodegetria* depiction is even the standard version of icons of Mary and Jesus in the Eastern

132 Neuwirth, *Der Koran 2/1*, 648; Cf. Marx, , 559.

133 Neuwirth, *Der Koran 2/1*, 617.

134 Neuwirth, *Die koranische Verzauberung der Welt*, 140.

135 Muqātil does not find the silent gesture made by Jesus's mother sufficient at this point and so deems it necessary to introduce the figure of Zechariah, who appears here as a mediator and calls upon Jesus to speak and defend his mother before her family (Muqātil, *Tafsīr*, vol. 2, 626). From the perspective of the Qur'an, this embellishment is entirely fictitious and is unhelpful for an appropriate understanding of the passage. According to Ṭabarī, Mary points to Jesus because Jesus – and in another interpretation God directly – requires that she does so (aṭ-Ṭabarī, *Tafsīr*, vol. 15, 526). This interpretation is particularly persuasive if one regards Q 19:24–26, as we have done above, as a speech delivered by the infant Jesus.

Church,[136] and also, according to Serafim Seppälä's analysis, constituted the driving force behind verse 19:29 of the Qur'an.[137] Such visual representations were present not only in lectionaries containing relevant pictures,[138] but were also found on bottles, medallions, seals, rings and coins.[139] This means that we can safely assume that these images were also well known on the Arabian Peninsula in the seventh century. Seppälä even attributes Joseph's absence in the Qur'an to the fact that he was not present in standard iconographic treatments of Christian motifs in Late Antiquity.[140] However, other theologically more profound reasons may be cited for Joseph's absence in the Qur'an. For Joseph is suspect to the proclaimer of the Qur'an precisely because of his role as the lineage holder of Jesus's Davidic ancestry. Accordingly, even without this highly unconventional thesis of Seppälä's, it is possible to explain why the Qur'an makes no reference to Joseph.[141]

However, we will pick up the iconographic trail suggested by Seppälä once more subsequently, given that it is an extremely controversial topic in light of the aforementioned use of icons in the wars conducted by Heraclius.[142] We should merely take note of it here. But we should also recall at this point our earlier interpretation of the scene at the Wedding at Cana described in Jn 2:5. It is true that Mary speaks here, and Jesus is already a grown-up. Yet here too she holds back entirely and points to her son as the person who should take charge of the situation. The relationship between mother and son is inverted here, because the truly protecting, caring and direction-giving mother now places herself in her son's hands with complete trust. In the Qur'an, this paradox is accentuated because it also characterises the relationship between the mother and her son while he is still in the cradle. This challenging recasting of the mother–child relationship in the Qur'an certainly does not involve the mother asking her son to perform a miracle to help a bride and groom out of an unfortunate predicament during a wedding.

---

136 Cf. Seppälä, 'Reminiscences of icons in the Qur'an', 5.

137 Cf. ibid., 10.

138 Cf. ibid., 6.

139 Cf. ibid., 7.

140 Cf. ibid., 14. Consequently, Joseph does not appear in any icons throughout the entire first century.

141 The polemical clash with Judaism might provide another explanation for Joseph's absence (cf. Reck, 'The Annunciation to Mary', 370 f.).

142 Generally speaking, it is reasonable to assume that Heraclius's war propaganda was well known on the Arabian Peninsula because Christian Arabs who had made common cause with him were involved in the battles against the Sassanids (cf. Tesei, 'Heraclius' war propaganda and the Qur'ān's promise of reward for dying in battle', 244).

Rather, in the Qur'an, Mary's sheer survival is at stake, and in this situation of extreme existential threat she trustingly invests all her hope in the infant Jesus. In his commentary, Ṭabarī also indicates that Mary finds solace in Jesus.[143] To begin with, however, she does not want to get involved in this undertaking and falls prey to doubt. She can picture the possible scenarios all too clearly in her mind's eye when she imagines appearing before her family as a single mother. In his commentary, Zamaḫšarī emphasises that Mary's 'despondency' relates to her insight into God's wondrous treatment of her and Jesus (*lahā umūran ilāhīyan*). This seems to her to be a miracle (*mu'ǧiza*), which leaves her in a position so far removed from what might commonly be expected that she dare not entertain any hope that her family will give her a sympathetic hearing.[144] As Ṭabarī reports, Jesus assures her that his existence alone will be a sufficient argument to counter their expected recriminations, and ultimately Mary ventures to place her trust in his words.

And Jesus does not disappoint her. He takes his mother under his wing and demands that she be shown respect (Q 19:32). By calling himself a servant of God and a prophet, who is already engaged in proclaiming God's message to humanity, he also clearly implies that the extraordinary circumstances of his birth were also occasioned by God.

In addition, this first speech of Jesus contains a whole series of Christologically revealing points, which admittedly are somewhat out of place here,[145] but which nonetheless throw the special nature of this person's birth into sharp relief and hence help put Mary in the right light. It is at least worth noting here that Jesus's presentation of himself in the Qur'an as a peace-bringer (Q 19:31) has a close correlation with the speech delivered by the host of angels in Lk 2:14, who on the occasion of Jesus's birth foretell 'peace to those on whom his favour rests'.

e) Mary as the mother of Jesus and as a prophet?

In historical–critical exegesis of the Qur'an, it is generally assumed that Q 19:34–40 represents a later insertion into the Surah *Maryam*, since the rhyme structure here is markedly different, while in terms of the content of these verses, it is evident that no immediate connection to what has preceded them can be identified. And because detailed critical analysis of this insertion is of relevance to

143 Cf. aṭ-Ṭabarī, *Tafsīr*, vol. 15, 509–510 and 517–520.
144 Cf. az-Zamaḫšarī, *Tafsīr*, 635.
145 Cf. Khorchide and von Stosch, *Der andere Prophet*, 107–113.

Christology but not to Mariology, it is best treated elsewhere.[146] For our study in this book of the figure of Mary in the Qur'an, just one aspect of it is of interest, which we should discuss here, albeit briefly. At the beginning of the insertion in Q 19:34, Jesus is described as Mary's son for the first time. This title is picked up again during the Meccan period, in Q 43:57 and Q 23:50 – or alternatively, if one goes along with Angelika Neuwirth's analysis, it originates in Q 43 and is then retrospectively applied to the insertion in Q 19.[147] The close connection between Jesus and Mary that it expresses is also significant for our assessment of Mary; as a result, we should briefly investigate the meaning of this title.

In the lyric hymns of Ephrem the Syrian, talk of Jesus as the son of Mary serves to express the tension that is inherent within his divinely human nature. To quote Ephrem verbatim:

'My mouth knows not how I shall call You, O You Child of the Living (God)! For to venture to call you as the Child of Joseph [*bar yōsep*], I tremble, since You are not his seed: and I am fearful of denying the name of him to whom they have betrothed me. […]

'2. Since You are the Son of One, then should I be calling You the Son of many? For ten thousand names would not suffice You, since You are the Son of God [*bar alāhā*] and also the Son of Man [*bar nāšā*], the Son of Joseph [*bar yōsep*], David's Son [*bar Dāwid*], and the Son of Mary [*brāh d-maryam*].'[148]

From a Christological standpoint that is not yet finely nuanced, one can simply see Jesus as being merely the son of man and the son of Joseph, whereas it is only a soteriological perspective that reveals him to be the Son of God and the Son of David. But it is his designation as the son of Mary [*brāh d-maryam*] that binds these two perspective together. For Ephrem, Mary is also the daughter of David, and as such expands the biological to the soteriological viewpoint.

Thus, when the Qur'an now acknowledges Jesus as the son of Mary, it is applying an honorary title that we may presume was already well known; furthermore, it is one which both incorporates Mary's function of joining together Christian figures of hope with the Jewish tradition and epitomises her enormous significance for the integration of the Christian and Jewish prophetic traditions. In the light of this special acknowledgment of Mary, we should consider in conclusion here whether the Qur'an in the mid-Meccan period regarded Mary as a prophet. We will presently see that, by taking into account the Surah *Āl 'Imrān*, it

146 Cf. ibid., 113–120.

147 Cf. Neuwirth, *Der Koran vol. 2/1*, 600.

148 Ephrem, *Hymnen de Nativitate*, VI, 1–2,5.

is possible to reflect upon whether Mary might not, through Jesus as the Word of God, have been assigned a book (*Kitāb*) in her own right and hence been accorded the status of a prophet.

Right now, however, we wish to turn our attention to two further verses from the mid-Meccan period, which are probably dateable to shortly after the composition of Q 19:1–33, and which both in their own way might corroborate the idea of a prophetic role for Mary. This is most clearly the case in a verse from the Surah *Āl Anbiyāʾ* (Q 21). This surah as a whole concerns prophets, and indeed takes its name from them.[149] It begins by developing its own prophetology and then proceeds to recall figures from the biblical tradition who can be definitively characterised as prophets, such as Moses and Aaron (Q 21:48), Abraham (Q 21:51–71), Isaac and Jacob (Q 21:72), Lot (Q 21:74 f.), Noah (Q 21:76 f.), David and Solomon (Q 21:78–82), Job (Q 21:83 f.), Ishmael, Idris and Dhu al-Kifl (Q 21:85 f.). In verses 89–90 of this surah, Zechariah is counted among their number, followed in verse 91 by Mary and Jesus. Mary is therefore included here within a group of outstanding servants of God, almost all of whom are explicitly designated by the Qurʾanic proclamation as prophets. Consequently, this textual evidence would appear strongly to suggest that Mary too should be regarded as a prophet.

Before we come to examine the wording of this verse more closely, in view of the intertextuality of these verses from the Qur'an, let us first consider whether Mary is even considered to be a prophet from a Christian perspective. As far as the Church Fathers are concerned, the answer to this question is an unequivocal 'yes'. From a patristic viewpoint, her honorary title of prophet was completely self-evident.[150] 'As the Church Fathers emphasise, clearly referring to the Magnificat, Mary is the "prophet of Christ". Whenever she appears, the talk is of Christ and the Word of God is accentuated.'[151] Joseph Ratzinger maintains that Mary is clearly a prophet, since she is someone 'who can harken to people's hearts, and who therefore truly appreciates the meaning of the Word and can proclaim it anew to the world.'[152] Yet it is rare to find her being identified as a prophet after the fourth century, because by then her role as the Mother of God had eclipsed all other designations. The title of prophet for Mary can be found in the writings

149 Within the surah itself, people who subsequently act as prophets in the Qurʾan are still designated as emissaries and admonishers. As a result, the phrase 'development of a prophetology' is only legitimate in this surah from a synchronic perspective.

150 Cf. Mußner, *Maria*, 102.

151 Gerwing, 'Mariologie', 415 f.

152 Ratzinger, '"Du bist voll der Gnade." Elemente biblischer Marienfrömmigkeit.' In: H. U. von Balthasar, *Maria*, 53–70, 63.

of Origen and Basil the Great in the East, and Jerome and Augustine in the West, but above all in the works of the Syriac Church Fathers, initially in the writings of Aphrahat, and thereafter in Ephrem, Severus of Antioch and Jacob of Serugh as well.[153]

But if we are really to read Q 21:91 as stating that Mary is to be thought of as a prophet, then in the light of Q 21:89, one must also do the same for Zechariah. Even that would not be unusual from a patristic point of view, for the Church Fathers also saw him as such. Generally speaking, a positively inflationary use of the term 'prophet' can be identified in their works, whereas from a rabbinical perspective the notion of prophecy was to be treated with caution and so was consciously applied only very sparingly.

The proclaimer of the Qur'an therefore appears to be operating within the Church Fathers' tradition of prophetology when he names prophets and outlines what happened to them in a typological fashion, and then locates himself within this tradition. But is Mary to be included among this group? Let us take a closer look at the verse in question. Here, Mary is introduced as 'the one who guarded her chastity.' The surah then says of her: '*So We breathed Our spirit into her, and made her and her son a sign for all people*' (Q 21:91).

The first thing to note here is that Mary is addressed by an honorary title: *allatī aḥṣanat farǧahā* ('who guarded her chastity'). This honorary title is reminiscent of 'a liturgical eulogising of Mary in the liturgy of the Feast of the Dormition.'[154] At any rate, it once again brings her virginal chastity more sharply into focus and makes it into an essential marker of Mary's identity. Considering this virginity in the context of the theology of the surah, it can also be combined with the theme of purity or the struggle for purification. For, as Ashkar has already explained, the life stories of many of the other prophets revolve time and again around the theme of purification in the sense of an external or internal struggle. Thus, Abraham struggles against defilement through idolatry, Job fights against impatience and Mary, according to Ashkar, against the desires of this world.[155] In this view of things, Mary's virginity can be seen as a prophetic sign of her struggle to attain purity. But even if one does not want to go so far as to talk in terms of a prophetic sign here, one would have to concede in any event that a classically patriarchal

153 Cf. Seppälä, 'Is the Virgin Mary a prophetess?', 369–372.

154 Neuwirth, *Der Koran 2/1*, 646.

155 Cf. Ashkar, , 245: '(1) Abraham, fighting against idolatry; (2) Lot, fighting against injustice; (3) Job, fighting against impatience and want of self-confidence; (4) Isma'il, Idris, and Dhu al-Kifl, fighting against want of steady perseverance; (5) Dhu al-Nun, fighting against isolation; and (6) Mary, fighting against the lust of this world.'

interpretation of Mary as a passive figure is out of the question in the Surah *Āl Anbiyā'*. For the context of the surah constantly stresses the active nature of the people to whom God provides answers, so that Mary's chastity is clearly being presented here as an individual achievement of hers.

In addition, another noteworthy feature of Q 21:91 is that not just Jesus but also Mary is now being acknowledged as a sign. In view of the aforementioned major significance accorded to the theology of signs in the Qur'an, which is prominently concentrated on Jesus in Q 21:91, the elevation of Mary to act with Jesus as a sign to all people of the world represents a quite extraordinary accolade for this woman,[156] which might possibly indicate that she is to be seen as a prophet.

The talk here of a sign that functions 'for all people' is particularly unusual. According to standard Qur'anic diction, this signifies the inhabitants of all worlds both visible and invisible, in other words also including both angels and jinnis – creatures that from a Christian perspective would not be the first one would call to mind when considering those to whom the message of Jesus Christ is addressed. Because angels and jinnis are immortal, the emblematic function of Mary and Jesus is rendered not just spatially but also temporally unlimited by this reference to other worlds. Correspondingly, it makes sense to see this as confirmation that their emblematic function is valid not just for this world but also for the hereafter. However, if one stops to consider that this surah of the Qur'an also uses the same phrase to express the significance of Jerusalem for all people (Q 21:71), it becomes clear that this distinction applied to Jesus and Mary should not be construed as exclusively reserved for them. Instead, the by-now familiar balance between Christianity and Judaism is once again observed here.

It is therefore significant that the labelling of Jesus and his mother as a sign is also found in another surah from the mid-Meccan period (Q 23:50). Many Muslim commentators have seen this verse as an allusion to the flight of Mary and her child to Egypt.[157] Literally, the verse reads: *We made the son of Mary and his mother a sign and gave them shelter on a peaceful hillside watered by a fresh spring* (Q 23:50).

If one examines this surah with an interest-based hermeneutics that places the question of Mary front and centre, then its composition reveals the following exciting lines and connections. The surah begins with an encouraging message

156 Seppälä, 'Reminiscences of icons in the Qur'an', 5, points out that across the whole of the Qur'an, this distinction is only bestowed upon Jesus and Mary. While numerous prophetic figures are referred to as 'signs of God', the term 'a sign to all people of the world' is one that is used exclusively of Jesus and Mary.

157 Cf. Ashkar, *Mary in the Syriac Christian tradition and Islam*, 178.

from God to all those who faithfully believe in him (Q 23:1–11). One of the previously mentioned Marian motifs is introduced in the indication that it is precisely the faithful who are able to preserve their chastity (*li-furūǧihim ḥāfiẓūn*; 5). This reveals the special nature of Mary in her virginal chastity; for the Qur'an, the paradigmatic aspect of Mary resides first and foremost in her chasteness.

Over the course of the ensuing text, God shows himself to be a provider and creator (Q 23:12–22), and this is then linked to a recollection of the story of Noah (Q 23:23–31), to an unnamed prophet (Q 23:32–41), and to various other prophets (Q 23:42–44), as well as to the story of Moses's and Aaron's dealings with the Pharaoh (Q 23:45–48). God, it turns out, repeatedly encounters human stubbornness, inasmuch as messengers of God are sent time and again to warn people or to deliver divine promises. The reproach with which all the prophets in this overview find themselves confronted by those to whom they speak is that they are mere humans. People's scepticism that a fellow human could ever experience transcendence and communicate it in a reliable and trustworthy manner is therefore what constitutes the principal contradiction of God here.

An intensification is evident in the list of examples cited here. To start with, the example of Noah establishes the idea of a person communicating prophetically with God for the benefit of his fellow human beings, and this communication is described as being clearly intelligible as a sign of God's benevolence (Q 23:30).[158] Many other messengers then follow, but their messages, like Noah's, also fall on deaf ears. Then (*ṯumma*), the text recounts, God sends Moses and Aaron to Pharaoh, once more with a sign from God (Q 23:45). They are not given a hearing. Then – virtually at the mid-point in the composition of this surah – Jesus and Mary are named (Q 23:50), following on from the beginning of the surah which indirectly recalls Mary in the motif of chastity. The increasing intensity with which God tries to make his purpose known to man by means of signs delivered by humans is illustrated in the fact that Jesus and Mary do not now appear with a sign but instead, as the text of the Qur'an records, are themselves the sign. As such, they appear particularly transparent to the reality of God. In both of them it is patently obvious how God is trying to make things especially easy for humans through Mary and Jesus, so as to overcome the human, all-too-human, tendency to gainsay the existence of a transcendent reality.

158 In this sense, Noah is commonly regarded as the first prophet to recall the ancient covenant with God. He was awakened as a prophet among his own people and was tasked by God with proclaiming the truth. In the Qur'anic account of Adam as the story of humanity, in the logic of the story no other people yet existed to whom he could have been sent as a prophet.

Over the further course of the surah, through encouragement to lead a good life and to believe in the one God, the aforementioned stories of the prophets are brought together, with the intention of showing how the individual communities of the previously named prophets might be reflected in a single community united by its faith in the one God (Q 23:51 f.). However, this theological ideal, which links a good life with a harmonious coexistence of all people under the aegis of monotheistic faith, is then again overtaken in the rest of the surah by the all too frequently evident empirical reality of disunity and denial. Warnings and promises by God are now interwoven through dialogue with human failures and successes in heeding God's truth (Q 23:53–90). Then, after a preparatory preamble in verses Q 23:88–90, an injunction appears, exhorting people not to attach a son (*walad*) to God or to ascribe a rival potency to other deities beside God (Q 23:91) – an idea that would certainly not be entertained by Christians, given that Augustine's axiom of *opera trinitas ad extra indivisa sunt* ('the outward works of the Trinity are indivisible') precludes any notion of the three different elements of the triune God having competing potencies.[159] This human aberration in ascribing divine power to entities other than God once more points thematically to the heart of the surah (Q 23:51) and to the key issue it is driving at, which is exemplified especially, as outlined above, by Jesus and Mary. Their pre-eminent acknowledgment of God is precisely designed to secure faith in the one God and at the same time make possible unification into a single community.

The conclusion of the surah is introduced by way of the divine imperative to Muhammad to ward off evil with all that is best and most beautiful (Q 23:96–98). This pivotal passage is then followed by descriptions of paradise and hell (Q 23:99–115), and after having once again thematised the unique power of God (Q 23:116) the surah draws to a brilliant close by auspiciously recalling God's readiness to forgive and his mercy. This now leaves us in a position where we can provide a remarkably comprehensive answer to the question of what the composition of this surah can tell us about Mary (Q 23:118). For the conclusion of the surah also obliquely though quite manifestly recalls Mary; as we have had cause to note already about the Surah *Maryam*, any mention of the mercy of God also points indirectly to Mary. Key concepts in the surah can be linked to Mary and defined in terms of her. The power and mercy of God, the idea of a life lived well and peacefully that resonates in the surah, and also the absolute need for chastity – all of these themes unfold as a panorama that can easily be connected to the figure of Mary.

159 Cf. Klaus von Stosch, *Gott – Macht – Geschichte. Versuch einer theodizeesensiblen Rede von Gottes Handeln in der Welt*, Freiburg – Basel – Vienna 2006, 338.

The unconventional designation of Mary and Jesus as a sign in Q 23:50 was naturally also remarked upon in the Muslim commentary tradition. Scholars drew particular attention to the grammatical form of the verse, which eschews the dual form we might really expect and talks instead about a sign in the singular. Ṭabarī explains this by stating that both of them together constitute evidence or a sign of God and his majesty.[160] Qurṭubī also interprets the use of the singular in a similar vein and substantiates this by claiming that the concerns and life stories of Mary and Jesus belong together,[161] insofar as both have had an existential experience of God's miraculous deeds and also, one might add by way of further explanation, have symbolically exemplified that experience through their own lives.

Another explanation for why Mary and Jesus belong together as a unit might once again be provided by Christian iconography. We referred earlier to the tradition of icons of the *hodegetria* type. The substantial presence of such icons in the Eastern Church in Late Antiquity prompts Serafim Seppälä to identify them as the basis for this unusual grammatical formulation in the Qur'an. Such icons are, he claims, a sign of God in their quite literal togetherness of Mary and Jesus. The fact that these signs would have been ubiquitously present gave rise to their designation as a visible sign for all people.[162] However, in view of the deeper meaning of the theology of signs in the Qur'an and the close connection with their models in Syriac patristics,[163] this interpretation seems to us to fall somewhat short. We find it more plausible that Mary is being acknowledged as a sign of God here precisely in her role of pointing to Jesus and her indissoluble relation to him. The orientation of this function 'for all worlds' or 'for all people of the world' expressed in Q 21:91 might even be intended as an echo of talk in the Bible about the peoples of the world and be designed to emphasise that the sign was also valid for the Gentiles.[164] In this case, the verse would make clear that Mary and Jesus were primarily focused on establishing a new covenant and did not wish to replace the old one, as well as stressing anew Mary's linking function. We will presently see that it is exactly this aspect which is lighted upon and further developed in the Surah *Āl ʿImrān*.

160 Cf. aṭ-Ṭabarī, *Tafsīr*, vol. 16, 392.

161 Cf. al-Qurṭubī, *al-Ǧāmiʿ*, vol. 14, 281.

162 Cf. Seppälä, 'Reminiscences of icons in the Qur'an', 11.

163 Cf. Griffith, 'The poetics of scriptural reasoning', Chap. 4.

164 Cf. Ṭabāṭabāʾī, *al-Mīzān fī tafsīr al-Qurʾān*, vol. 1, 21. This interpretation is unusual, however. Normally, this verse is read not as denoting different peoples but different ontological entities – in other words people, angels, jinns etc. On this classical interpretation, cf. for example Ṭabarī's exegesis of Q 1:2, in which the term *al-ʿālamīn* appears for the first time in the Qur'an (aṭ-Ṭabarī, *Tafsīr*, vol. 1, 144).

We have therefore been able to identify two pieces of evidence supporting the hypothesis that Mary has a prophetic role in the surahs of the Qur'an from the mid-Meccan period. Her emblematic function resides precisely in the interweaving of her testimony with the life story of her son, but also keeps in mind her independent achievement of chastity and acknowledges her virginity. In accordance with this, the classic commentators on the Qur'an also strive to express Mary's specialness by virtue of her virgin conception of Jesus. Thus, on the basis of the Virgin Birth a whole series of them accord her the honorary title *salāmun ʿalayhā* ('Peace Be Upon Her'), which is otherwise the mark of a prophet.[165] Qurṭubī even uses this honorary title from the very beginning[166] and expressly argues that she should be designated a prophet, because God speaks to her through an angel and because she has a mission (*irsāl*), which finds its expression, as Qurṭubī's declaration specifically identifies, in the figure of Jesus.[167] Rāzī, meanwhile, discusses what form of miracle has been bestowed upon Mary[168] – a line of enquiry that we will pursue further in Part III. Rāzī discusses the view that Mary has witnessed a great miracle and that she can therefore be regarded as a prophet. As a result, we may fairly presume that this line of tradition was already familiar within Islam at this stage. We can surmise that it must have been the view of a number of serious commentators, even though Rāzī himself follows another line of interpretation.[169]

Taken as a whole, however, these voices are insufficiently representative to substantiate the talk of Mary as a prophet.[170] But at least they do furnish us with some initial indicators, which we can pursue when considering the rest of the text of the Qur'an. Accordingly, in the following pages we will turn our attention to the Surah *Āl ʿImrān*, which provides an extensive commentary on the Surah Maryam from the perspective of the Medina period and lends more precise theological shape to many of its statements. The background to these recastings is formed by the theologically closer relationship between the Qur'anic community and Christian and Jewish groups in Medina, which made a more precise theological language possible and essential.

165 Cf. among others Muqātil, *Tafsīr*, vol. 3, 624; ar-Rāzī, *Tafsīr*, vol. 22, 202.
166 Cf. al-Qurṭubī, *al-Ǧāmiʿ*, vol. 13, 428.
167 Cf. ibid., 428 f.
168 Cf. ar-Rāzī, *Tafsīr*, vol. 22, 218 f.
169 Cf. ibid. Rāzī speculates at this point whether Mary knew that Jesus would speak for her, and entertains the idea of a divine inspiration (*waḥy*). Cf. ar-Rāzī, *Tafsīr*, vol. 21, 209.
170 Ashkar, *Mary in the Syriac Christian tradition and Islam*, 186 cites other Muslim voices who accord Mary the status of a prophetess primarily because of her sinlessness and because she was chosen by God, as for example the testimony of Ibn Ḥazm. We will examine this question in greater detail in Part III.

f) Summary

Before we deal with how talk of Mary is transformed in the further course of the Qur'anic message, we should first summarise the findings of our deliberations thus far by highlighting the key salient points. In the surahs from the mid-Meccan period, talk of Mary helps broaden the conception of God, which begins to take account of metaphors like mercy that have connotations of female qualities. It therefore becomes perfectly plausible for feminist issues to be connected to the figure of Mary, even in the Qur'an.

But above all Mary is the first person who calls upon God as a compassionate deity. In other words, she is looking for a quite particular intensity in her relationship with God and is exemplary in the way in which she conducts a dialogue with him. For all her humility, Mary comes across as a shrewd and theologically innovative thinker with a critical, questioning and creative intellect, who is engaged in an intensive relationship with God based on dialogue.

In comparison with the Jewish tradition, in the Qur'an Mary appears as a linking figure who connects the three monotheistic religions. It becomes apparent at many points that her intention is not to play these religions off against one another but to unite them in her own way. The proclaimer of the Qur'an's estimation of Zechariah and the Jewish tradition that he represents is correspondingly high.

For the mid-Meccan period surahs, Mary is a perfectly ordinary woman, who through her trust in God's power comes to focus entirely on God in the figure of her son; together with Jesus, this orientation towards God makes her a symbol for humanity. On the one hand, she stands for every woman and every person who wants to hear and receive the word of God. On the other hand, she finds herself in a unique situation, and only becomes a symbol of God's mercy in conjunction with her son Jesus. In a situation of absolute desolation and complete vulnerability, in which even her family turns against her, she places her trust in God's help through her newborn baby, and it is precisely through her act of pointing to Jesus that they together become a prophetic sign of God.[171]

171 Therefore, one may justifiably claim that Mary's special nature in the Qur'an is consistently founded upon her relationship with Jesus (cf. Geagea, *Mary of the Koran*, 154).

2

The Surah *Āl ʿImrān*

The Surah *Āl ʿImrān* forms part of the Medinan (or Madni) surahs of the Qur'an, and it is likely that its time of writing can be dated to the first half of the period that the Prophet spent in Medina.[1] For the Medinan period it is highly probable that, after a time, the relationship between the Prophet and his community on the one hand and the Jewish tribes resident in Medina on the other began to turn into one of competition or even tension.[2] The aim of the surah that is of interest to us here is evidently to intensively weigh up the relationship with both Judaism and Christianity. Interestingly, in this situation the proclaimer of the Qur'an chooses to undertake a re-evaluation of the story of Mary. We intend to subject this re-evaluation to a thorough examination by studying it first against the background of the Surah *Maryam*, but then going on to look at how it relates to the Protevangelium of James and other relevant intertexts, especially from the Syriac Christian tradition.

Considering the surah in the round, from a literary-critical perspective its core section undoubtedly comprises Q 3:1–62, meaning that the passage concerning Mary belongs to the oldest part of the surah.[3] Angelika Neuwirth has suggested on several occasions that Q 3:7 should be regarded as a hermeneutically important reading instruction for the whole surah. The passage that interests us runs as follows in translation: *It is He who has sent down the Book to you. Some of its verses are clear and precise in meaning – they are the foundation of the Book – while others are ambiguous. Those with deviation [from the truth] in their*

1 On the difficulties involved in dating this surah, see Nöldeke, *Geschichte des Qorāns*, 189–194.

2 On the new circumstances in Medina, see Sinai, 'The Unknown Known'.

3 Cf. Neuwirth, 'The house of Abraham and the house of Amram', 506.

hearts pursue the ambiguous, so as to create dissension by seeking to interpret it. However, no one but God knows its meaning. Those who are firmly grounded in knowledge say: 'We believe in it. It is all from the Lord.' (Q 3:7). In this translation, therefore, only God knows the meaning of the ambiguous verses, and it is counted as a virtue for interpreters to simply put up with the ambiguity of the verses and accept them as God-given. If one understands this verse of the Surah *Āl ʿImrān* in this way, then it really does not seem far-fetched to see it as a tribute to the rabbinical tradition of exegesis,[4] whose principal concern is to take ambiguity as a given and simply allow different readings to co-exist alongside one another. Angelika Neuwirth sees this verse as signalling the discovery of ambiguity by the Qurʾanic community, which it adopted from rabbinical traditions in Medina.[5] Nonetheless, this is a controversial interpretation, as she herself admits. For the verse could also mean that not only God knows the meaning of the ambiguous verses but also those who are firmly grounded in knowledge. The grammatical structure of the sentences admit of two different possible variations in punctuation at this tricky point, one of which enables this second reading.[6] According to this reading, it would precisely *not* be a virtue for exegetes to accept ambiguity, and the meaning would instead be that they were being exhorted to gain firm foundations for their knowledge and hence arrive at an unambiguous interpretation.

It is interesting, then, that the Qur'an's commentary on ambiguous verses is itself ambiguous. It leaves us uncertain whether an ambiguity is to be endured as something God-ordained or to be overcome through exegetical effort. This ambiguity of ambiguity appears to the present authors to justify our enquiring with all the exegetical means at our disposal after the historically and theologically correct meaning of the individual verses, in the case of the Surah *Āl ʿImrān* too, and not to accede too hastily to an 'anything goes' hermeneutical approach. At the same time, however, we cannot exclude the possibility of persistently ambiguous verses. For the Muslim–Christian analysis of the Qurʾan that we are attempting to provide in this book, this means that it is perfectly possible for there to be several legitimate readings of the same verses from a Qurʾanic perspective and also documented in the tradition of Islamic exegesis.

---

4 Marx, 'Glimpses of a Mariology in the Qur'an', 551.

5 Neuwirth, 'The house of Abraham and the house of Amram', 518.

6 Cf. ibid., 515: 'Verse 3:7 is a *crux interpretum* that has been the subject of numerous debates since the expression *ar-rāsikhūna fī l-ʿilm*, "those firmly rooted in knowledge," can be construed both as the end of the sentence preceding it, and as the beginning of the one following it, thus either reserving the prerogative of exegesis to God or attributing it to both God and the learned.'

a) On the genealogy of Mary

God chose Adam and Noah and the family of Abraham and the family of 'Imrān above all his creatures. They are the offspring of one another. God hears all and knows all (Q 3:33 f.).

The passage on Mary in the Surah *Āl 'Imrān* begins with a programmatic placing on an equal footing of the houses of Abraham and Amram, who from the perspective of the surah may stand for Judaism and Christianity respectively. According to Exodus 6:20, Amram – the biblical form in Hebrew of the name that is rendered in Arabic by 'Imrān – is the father of Moses and Aaron, and according to Numbers 26:58 f. is also the father of Miriam. This is the same Miriam who was frequently identified typologically with Mary, even by the Church Fathers.[7] Thus, when Mary is already referred to in Q 19:28 as the sister of Aaron, this corresponds with the biblical portrayal of the Old Testament prophetess Miriam, while in another place in the Qur'an there is mention of a sister of Moses, albeit without any name being given (Q 28:11). Yet in view of the typological identification of various Mary figures in Late Antiquity, it is not uncommon for the mother of Jesus to also be regarded as the sister of Aaron and the daughter of Amram. As such, she is construed as belonging to the clan of the Levites and hence closely associated with both Zechariah and John the Baptist. Thus, when the proclaimer of the Qur'an emphasises that God has chosen both the house of Abraham and the house of Amram, the house of Amram as the house of the father of Mary stands for Christianity, whereas the house of Abraham stands for Judaism. At least, this is how Angelika Neuwirth interprets this connection.[8] She points to the fact that, even in the surah that bears his family name, Amram actually plays no part whatsoever, but that only the women are of significance – that is, both the unnamed mother of Mary and Mary herself. The genealogy of Jesus therefore consists solely of two female protagonists, and in this interpretation is set alongside the far more patriarchal Abrahamic tradition.

According to an interpretation that was first developed by Angelika Neuwirth, the Surah *Āl 'Imrān* represents a politicised rereading of the Surah *Maryam*, which accords the tribe of Amram its own independent status alongside Judaism, which traces its roots back to Abraham.[9] In this interpretation, the proclaimer of

7 Cf. Severos of Antioch, *Homiliae cathedrales*, ed. Maurice Brière, Patrologia Orientalis 20, Paris 1927, 420; Gregory of Nyssa, *Traité de la virginité*, ed. Michel Aubineau (SC 119), Paris 1966, 484–488; *Anonymus dialogus cum Iudaeis: saeculi ut videtur sexti*, ed. José H. Declerck (CCSG 30), Turnhout 1994, 39.

8 Cf. Neuwirth, *The house of Abraham and the house of Amram*, 507 f.

9 Cf. Marx, 'Glimpses of a Mariology in the Qur'an', 535.

the Qur'an was concerned to balance out the Jewish conception of God's chosen people,[10] which is here disengaged from the exclusivity of the male Jewish patriarchs and extended to include a purely female genealogy of the chosen people.[11] Michael Marx too sees the surah as being about establishing the equal status of the successors of Abraham and the successors of Amram, who all descend from Adam and Noah.[12]

And yet the question remains whether these two houses can really be said to represent Judaism and Christianity. Accordingly, other commentators like Karl-Josef Kuschel, for example, place the surah within a purely Jewish context.[13] Although this interpretation can itself be questioned in view of the large amount of space devoted to Mary in the surah, it is interesting to keep in mind that the house of Amram was primarily a Jewish house and that it is therefore different Jewish groups that are under consideration here. Amram is, after all, also the father of Moses, the principal ancestor figure in Jewish self-identity. Indeed, it is perplexing that Moses is not actually mentioned by name at this point.[14] However, this might simply have to do with the fact that the proclaimer of the Qur'an had Christian patterns of argumentation in mind.

It is striking that, in naming the houses of Abraham and Amram, the Qur'an invokes a genealogy that ultimately leads to Mary and Jesus and which begins with Adam and Noah. All four of these figures stand for decisive steps in God's connection with Israel, which were analysed both by the Christian Church Fathers and subsequently by the Qur'an. Adam represents the very first instance in which God turns to man, while Noah stands for the renewal of God's commitment to all people in the wake of the first cosmic catastrophe. In both the Bible and the Qur'an, the story of both individuals demonstrates God's devotion to all humans, which still holds good even when humans turn away from God (as Adam was the first to do). Whereas Adam and Noah enter into the covenant with God rather as individuals and are hence still not regarded as representatives of Israel, but instead simply stand for God's covenant with all people, Abraham represents the patriarchs who according to the Qur'an's testimony do not belong to a particular religion but who in equal measure lay the foundations of Judaism, Christianity and Islam (cf. Q 3:65). For in the Qur'anic interpretation, Abraham was not a Jew or

10 Cf. Neuwirth, *The house of Abraham and the house of Amram*, 526.

11 Cf. ibid.: 'Mary's story is retold in order to support a female-dominated genealogy of elects.'

12 Cf. Marx, 'Glimpses of a Mariology in the Qur'an', 549.

13 Cf. Kuschel, *Juden, Christen, Muslime*, 486.

14 Cf. Marx, 'Glimpses of a Mariology in the Qur'an', 547.

a Christian but an 'upright man' (Q 3:67) and as such he established a new form of religiosity. It would therefore be wrong to see him solely as a representative of Judaism. Instead – just like Adam and Noah – he is the forebear of Mary and Jesus, just as he is also the forebear of the Jewish tradition and the new Muslim community.

Yet Jesus's and Mary's origins are also traced back to the house of Amram and hence to the priestly caste, the tradition of the prophetesses of Israel and the Mosaic tradition. The genealogical concept of the Qurʾan therefore unifies seemingly opposing elements of Judaism and Christianity into a single family tree and emphasises how mutually interdependent their origins are and how fruitless it is to try and play them off against one another.

It is informative to compare this genealogical perspective of the Qurʾan with the biblical genealogy as exemplified by the family tree cited in the Gospel of Matthew. As we have already seen in the section on the biblical foundations of Mariology, Jesus's family tree derives his genealogy from the families of Abraham and David:

> This is the genealogy of Jesus the Messiah the son of David, the son of Abraham: Abraham was the father of Isaac, Isaac the father of Jacob, Jacob the father of Judah and his brothers [...] and Jesse the father of King David. David was the father of Solomon, whose mother had been Uriah's wife, [...] and Jacob the father of Joseph, the husband of Mary, and Mary was the mother of Jesus who is called the Messiah. Thus there were fourteen generations in all from Abraham to David, fourteen from David to the exile to Babylon, and fourteen from the exile to the Messiah (Mt 1:1, 2, 6, 16, 17).

The house of Abraham is therefore expressly introduced in Mt 1:2. By contrast, there is no mention of Amram, Moses, Aaron or Miriam. Still, four women whom we have already discussed in detail in Part I do appear in the family tree. Thus, when the Qurʾan places the female genealogy of the house of Amram in the foreground, this ties in very strongly with the biblical genealogy. However, the proclaimer of the Qurʾan is at pains to avoid any dubiousness surrounding the female figures, and so portrays the mother of Mary as an ideal type. Any suspicion that Mary might have been an adulteress or even a prostitute is thus nipped in the bud.

If one considers the other genealogy of Mary in the Qurʾan, the first thing that strikes one is that there should be a genealogy of Mary at all. Although Mary does appear in the genealogy of Jesus in Mt 1, she does not play any genealogical role. Jesus's ancestry runs exclusively via his adoptive father Joseph; Mary is irrelevant here from a genealogical point of view. This changes with the Syrian Church Fathers, who also assume a Davidic line of descent for Mary as well, as we have noted above. However, this idea was not exclusive to Syrian patristics, but was also evident in the writings of other Church Fathers after Justin Martyr.[15] It is intriguing that the proclaimer of the Qur'an goes along with this shift of emphasis in patristic exegesis and even intensifies it by eliminating Joseph entirely as the father. This surely has to do with the fact that the Qur'an – quite at variance with the classical Muslim commentary tradition[16] – does not make Jesus's lineage from the house of David a topic. Yet this also means a revaluation of Mary as a woman, who against the customary patriarchal thinking of the time is seen by the Qur'an as a fully fledged element in the genealogy of Jesus. While women only appear in Mt in a supplementary role, in Q 3 it is the men who are given the minor roles or who disappear completely from the picture – at least as regards Jesus's immediate background and hence also as regards the house of Amram.[17]

Looking at the Qur'anic genealogy of Mary as a whole, it therefore becomes clear that Mary is not just the sister of Aaron and hence a member of the house of Amram, but is also an Abrahamite. She therefore stands for all facets of Judaism, the priestly side as well as the prophetic, and that of the patriarchs as well as that of the strong prophetic women. She is simply – as the Surah *Maryam* made clear – a figure of integration, who even within her family tree brings together rather than divides different traditions. Only the Davidic dimension, which was so important to the Church Fathers and which is also the decisive one for the genealogy of Jesus, is disregarded. Clearly the legitimation of this new tradition functions even without messianic borrowings, which constantly incur the danger of unduly narrowing down the full breadth of the biblical legacy and which also, through being

15 Cf. Luz, *Das Evangelium nach Matthäus*, 137.

16 Cf. Muqātil, *Tafsīr*, vol. 4, 380. Here Muqātil presents an extensive genealogy of Mary, which he traces back to Abraham via David. Cf. also Ashkar, Mary in the Syriac Christian tradition and Islam, 151. Ṭabarī's commentary on the Qur'an adopts a large section of the genealogy from Mt 1,6–11, with the result that Jesus's descent from David in confirmed *de facto*, and Amram is identified with Joseph. Cf. Mourad, 'Mary in the Qur'ān', 164; with regard to aṭ-Ṭabarī, *Tafsīr*, vol. 3, 234. According to Ibn Isḥāq, even Mary belongs to the house of David (cf. Mourad, 'Mary in the Qur'ān', 165).

17 There is an interesting parallel to the Prophet Muhammad at this point. His children too (who were approaching adulthood) were all girls, forcing him to establish a female genealogy. This may well have made easier for him to understand the message proclaimed here, and may also explain why that message becomes more important in Medina than it was in Mecca.

aggressively misused for imperialistic ends under Emperor Heraclius, become problematic for the proclaimer of the Qur'an.[18]

b) Mary's birth and childhood – the connection with Zechariah

Remember when the wife of 'Imrān said, 'My Lord! I have dedicated what is in my womb entirely to Your service, so accept it from me. You are the One who hears and knows all.' When she gave birth, she said, 'My Lord! I have given birth to a girl,' and God knew full well what she had given birth to – and a male is not like a female. 'I have named her Mary, and her and her offspring in your protection from the accursed Satan.' So her Lord graciously accepted her and made her grow in goodness by entrusting her to the care of Zachariah. Whenever Zachariah visited her in her sanctuary, he found her supplied with provisions. He exclaimed, 'O Mary! Where did this come from?' She replied, 'It is from God. God provides for whoever He wills without measure' (Q 3:35–37).

After mentioning her genealogy, the Surah *Āl 'Imrān* proceeds to describe Mary's birth and childhood – an account which has no precedents either in the Bible or in the Surah *Maryam*. Because the Protevangelium of James was especially influential for the Christian tradition where this topic was concerned, it is worthwhile scrutinising the following verses of the Surah with particular reference to this text. If one compares the Surah *Āl 'Imrān* with the Protevangelium of James, one notices straight away that the proclaimer of the Qur'an does not touch upon the lead-up to Mary's conception of Jesus – namely, the pleas and laments of Joachim and Anne from ProtEvJam 1–3 hold as little interest for him as the angel's announcement of the birth of Mary (ProtEvJam 4:1). Instead, the Qur'an commences directly with the reply given by Mary's mother, who remains nameless, and reports this answer in a somewhat abbreviated fashion, albeit while retaining the basic content. The character of her vow is also preserved.

Whereas one gains the impression from ProtEvJam that it is first and foremost Joachim's prayers that are being answered (ProtEvJam 4:2 f.), the Qur'an focuses entirely on the mother of Mary and her relationship with God. She is portrayed as having a particular intimacy with God, which is why she wants to dedicate her child to him. According to the classical commentary tradition, in this she is

18 Cf. Ghaffar, *Der Koran in seinem religions- und weltgeschichtlichen Kontext*, 57–74. In his analysis of the mid-Meccan Surah *Ṣād* (Q 38) Ghaffar indicates that even at this stage the proclaimer of the Qur'an will not accept a Davidic Messiah. Since in all likelihood Emperor Heraclius began spreading his propaganda about a Davidic Messiah as early as the 610s, it therefore makes sense that the proclaimer of the Qur'an should repeatedly react here.

following God's inspiration,[19] which makes it clear that her development, and hence the development of Mary and Jesus too, will take place from the outset under benevolent divine providence. The lines of communication between God and Mary's mother appear straightforward and direct, and bespeak a great closeness and familiarity.

Her first utterance ends with an echo of the way God is introduced by the Qur'an in the preceding verse; she acknowledges God as all-hearing and all-knowing. But while it remain unclear in Q 3:34 why the account of Mary's genealogy should culminate in a proclamation that God hears and knows everything, here these predications are given a practical meaning. They are, so to speak, translated from a Dominican statement into a Franciscan one, to cite an important distinction drawn by Eleonore Stump.[20] That is to say, the statements of God's omniscience are no longer just abstract utterances spoken in the third person; instead, they have now become part of an address to God, a dialogue. This is expressed linguistically in the fact that God's hearing and seeing are first presented adjectivally, and so come across as general and abstract as a result of appearing without a definite article, while in the concrete relational dialogue they appear as an integral part of God's name and have an article placed in front of them. If God is the All-Hearing, then this now means that Mary's mother can turn to him in full confidence. The proclaimer of the Qur'an does not even need to have her spell out her wish to bear a child, since this is already known to God the All-Knowing anyway. As the All-Hearing, God is already aware of all her desires; he knows of her concerns and is compassionate towards her. In addition, the naming of God, which occurs at the end of the verse, emphasises that she can be sure that her wish will not go unheard and come to nothing. By contrast, in the Qur'an her husband only appears as the person who gives his house its name. We learn nothing at all about his relationship with God.

In ProtEvJam 7:1 it is Joachim who takes the initiative in having Mary accepted for service in the Temple while she is still only a young girl, and his wife Anne delays taking this step until Mary has reached the end of her third year. By contrast, in Q 3:36 it is solely at her mother's instigation that Mary is placed under God's special protection. It is she who of her own volition dedicates her child to God; according to the clarifications offered by tradition, it is her prayer of supplication which ensures that Mary and Jesus remain immune to Satan. Interestingly, this prayer of supplication is not about God granting this special protection

19 Cf. ar-Rāzī, *Tafsīr*, vol. 8, 27.
20 Cf. Stump, *Wandering in darkness*, 39–64.

at all, but solely about him accepting her devotion. Yet the all-hearing and all-knowing God identifies in it her yearning to have her child protected, and acts accordingly. In his commentary on this passage, Ṭabarī uses a particular turn of phrase to describe God accepting (*taqabbala*) what the mother of Mary desired (*arādat*),[21]and this points up especially clearly God's amenability to dialogue and reciprocity; in his deeds, he meets a person's wishes and gets involved with that person. Mary's mother appears here as the instigator or at least the catalyst of a miraculous story of human–divine interaction. The fact that Ṭabarī does not choose the Arabic verb *šāʾat* to express Mary's mother's wish but instead uses the term *arādat,* which has connotations of single-mindedness and intent, indicates that he wanted to emphasise her strength of will,[22] which is what prompts God to heed her supplication.

While Anne in ProtEvJam 5:2 learns the sex of her child from the midwife, in Q 3:36 Mary's mother is in the know herself, without any mention of outside help, and informs God that it is a girl. Of course, God must know in advance what gender the child will be, and factored this in when answering Mary's mother's prayers. From the Qurʾanic perspective, it is clearly not a problem at all for God that his special protection should be accorded to a woman. A woman too can be dedicated to the special service of God.

This insight is especially remarkable inasmuch as certain influential Christian churches, even nowadays, have a major problem with the idea of consecrating women to the service of God and in conferring priestly duties on them.[23] From the

21 Cf. aṭ-Ṭabarī, *Tafsīr*, vol. 5, 345.

22 In her encounter with God and in praying to him, the mother of Mary thus observes a particular etiquette, which Muhammad later formulated in terms of advice to his community, namely not to equivocate bashfully when praying in supplication, but to articulate one's wishes clearly and self-assuredly. Cf. at-Tirmiḏī, *Ǧamiʿ*, Hadith No. 3479, Book No. 45 (*Kitāb ad-daʿwāt*), 198.

23 Ṭabarī explains Anne's wish for her child to be a boy by pointing to the restrictions that are imposed on women in serving the Church (aṭ-Ṭabarī, *Tafsīr*, vol. 5, 337). In other words, even at this stage, Ṭabarī is no longer referring to the context of the Temple, but identifying that women are placed at a distinct disadvantage in the Christian churches. Yet it was also the case in Jewish temples in antiquity that women were not permitted to undertake any ritual activities. Although this ban may not have been couched in the form of an express proscription in ancient Judaism, many factors lead us to conclude that such a ban did exist *de facto*: the periodical ritual 'uncleanliness' of women (i.e., through menstruation), which would render them unsuitable for Temple service; the total absence of any female priestly figures in biblical texts (and by contrast their presence in Hittite texts, cf. Marsman, *Women in Ugarit and Israel*, 487–489); the negative appraisal of women in 2 Kings 11 and 1 Kings 16–21 as well as 1 Kings 15:13, who were admittedly not priestesses but queens, yet who nonetheless played an active part in religious life, albeit in different faiths; and finally, as Marsman emphasises, the

Qur'an's viewpoint, Mary is the decisive counterargument to this position, whose example clearly shows that women too are worthy of being dedicated to God. In its lobbying efforts to secure the ordination of women, the German Catholic women's movement 'Mary 2.0' would therefore do well to refer to the Qur'an's portrayal of Mary. Yet the idea of ordination for women does not find much favour in the Muslim community, so within Islam it would actually be inappropriate to talk in terms of Mary being consecrated. What the Qur'an is picking up on here, rather, is simply the Jewish tradition of making children available for Torah study and service in the Temple.[24] Yet precisely against this background, it is of abiding interest that, in Jewish culture, this kind of service was actually only intended for male children. And in Christianity, although it was possible for women to spend an ascetic life of devotion in a convent, it was unthinkable for them to be ordained as priests, so that it was also challenging for the Islamic commentary tradition to interpret these statements of the Qur'an appropriately. Rāzi interprets the passage in such a way that Mary is here freed from worldly matters to focus on obedience to God – an idea that would be entirely fitting for a monastic life. He also considers whether it might not also be about the freedom to study the word of God[25] – a thought which in turn is instructive for the rabbinical context, insofar as devoting one's life to the study of the Torah was also traditionally considered a privilege reserved for men.

If one looks at the rest of what the mother of Mary says, one notices that it is she alone who take it upon herself to name her daughter (Q 3:36). For all her humility, she is very determined at the same time; she seems to have a clear vision for her daughter and guides her destiny in the direction she desires by giving her a name and praying for her – subtly and yet unequivocally.[26] It is also noteworthy that all the miraculous elements of the Protevangelium have been expunged from the story: the Qur'an neither mentions Mary's ability to walk at just six months

desire to block women's access to priestly roles, lest such roles became identified with the role of the spouse of a god (primarily Asherah) and led to women assuming a position of power, cf. Marsman, *Women in Ugarit and Israel*, 572. Where the Bible is concerned, the passages Exodus 40:13–15, which speak of the sons (but not daughters) of Aaron as the successors to their priestly father, as well as Leviticus 15:14 and 15:29, where both men and women are expected to take part in ritual cleansing and sacrifice, but only men may approach the Lord, only serve to corroborate such a *de facto* ban.

24 Cf. aṭ-Ṭabarī, *Tafsīr*, vol. 2, 476 f.

25 Cf. ar-Rāzī, *Tafsīr*, vol. 8, 27.

26 According to Rāzī, the name 'Mary' denotes a servant whom God preserved from iniquities in both this life and the hereafter. Cf. ibid., vol. 8, 29.

of age,[27] nor does it directly take up the idea that she allowed nothing unclean to pass through her (ProtEvJam 6:1). Everything is concentrated on her relationship with God. Mary now enters into this special relationship and is placed, together with her offspring, under God's special protection.

This protection of Mary and her children from Satan was also a topic of interest for the Muslim Hadith tradition. Thus, in one hadith it is said that only Jesus and Mary were left untouched by Satan at their respective births.[28] In saying this, the hadith tradition awakened echoes of the Catholic doctrine of original sin,[29] which also maintains that it is exclusively Jesus and Mary who were born without original sin and who are therefore protected from Satan. It is interesting that the Qur'an extends this protection to the whole of Mary's family, and thereby symbolically to all Christians or all believers. This makes it clear that the motif of protection is not meant to indicate some miraculous immaculate conception, or to signal a special privilege on the part of Jesus and Mary, but rather simply a special connection between God and the Christian communities or believers as a whole, as represented emblematically by Jesus and Mary. The story of Mary and her son brings to light something that applies to all worlds. It is precisely for this reason that the two of them are used to symbolise all the peoples of the world, as we discussed earlier.

It is positively exciting that Mary's and hence Jesus's special role is made possible in the Qur'an by a prayer offered up by Mary's mother. This aspect too is treated in the Hadith tradition and emphasised by the classical commentators on the Qur'an.[30] According to the relevant traditions, in response to the prayer of supplication by Mary's mother, God placed a veil between Mary and Satan right at the moment of her birth. Here we see the reappearance of the image of the cloth or veil, which played such a significant role as a means of protecting Mary in the

27 Despite the Qur'an itself taking a very critical stance toward miraculous embellishments of the story of Mary's childhood, the Muslim commentary tradition seems on occasion all too happy to recount such tales. Thus, according to Qurṭubī it was even the case that Mary was able to grow more in an hour than her contemporaries were in a whole year. Al-Qurṭubī, *al-Ǧāmi'*, vol. 8, 101 f.

28 Cf. al-Buḫārī, *Ṣaḥīḥ*, Hadith No. 4548, Book No. 65 (*Kitāb at-tafsīr*), 1114 f. Ṭabarī too refers to this hadith: 'There is no soul that is born which does not feel the sting of Satan except Mary, the daughter of 'Imrān, thanks to the prayers her mother offered up…' (aṭ-Ṭabarī, *Tafsīr*, vol. 5, 339–342).

29 Cf. Anawati, 'Islam and the immaculate conception', 447, 457. Ultimately, Anawati comes to the conclusion that it might represent a deliberate strategy on the part of Catholicism to try and identify corresponding echoes in the Qur'an and the ahadith (ibid., 461). We doubt whether this is a fruitful line of enquiry.

30 Cf. ar-Rāzī, *Tafsīr*, vol. 8, 26.

Surah *Maryam*. The Surah *Āl 'Imrān* therefore makes it clear from the Qur'an's standpoint how important the prayers of one's own mother are in shielding a person from the forces that might separate them from God.

If the verses Q 3:35 f. are focused entirely on Mary's mother and her relationship with God, then from Q 3:37 onwards the relationship of Mary with God is brought to the fore, and her mother is no longer mentioned. Instead of her parents, Zechariah now cares for her, because God makes him her guardian. The two stories of Mary and Zechariah, which remained without any direct connection in the Surah *Maryam*, are now interwoven with one another by means of this bridging verse.[31] On a narrative level, the close connection between Mary and the Temple serves to link her both with the clan of Aaron and with the new Temple, namely the Church – connotations which were of course known about in the milieu in which the Qur'an came into being.[32] As a result, they are consciously alluded to here, and once more reveal Mary as an interlinking figure.

However, one must take care when interpreting this talk of the Temple. In our analysis of the Surah *Maryam*, we have already noted that the Arabic text of the Qur'an does not actually refer to the Temple but rather to the *miḥrāb*. Accordingly, the Muslim commentary tradition conceives of this as a separate room, which however was definitely located within the Temple. Yet at this point in the Qur'an, Zechariah hardly appears any longer as a servant of the Temple, but becomes instead Mary's guardian, who has to act as a substitute for her deceased father.[33] As a variety of exegetes point out, the only way to access this separate room in the Temple was by climbing a ladder, and Zechariah has locked Mary away behind a door. Ṭabarī and Rāzī even talk in term of seven locked doors, but they too are in agreement that the *miḥrāb* constitutes a closed discrete space whose purpose is to shield Mary from the outside world.[34]

Fantasies of this kind are far removed from the text of the Qur'an. It is difficult to decide whether their aim is to defend Mary's chastity and integrity against any reproaches, or whether an urge to exert control over excessive female independence is perhaps influencing the viewpoint of the male exegetes here. However, we do not need to agonise over resolving this question, since the Qur'an is crystal clear on this point: Mary is not growing up here in a room with multiple locks under the supervision of her guardian, but is experiencing a pleasant upbringing'.

31 Cf. Neuwirth, 'The house of Abraham and the house of Amram', 512.
32 Cf. Marx, 'Glimpses of a Mariology in the Qur'an', 551.
33 Cf. al-Qurṭubī, *al-Ǧāmi'*, vol. 5, 108.
34 Cf. aṭ-Ṭabarī, *Tafsīr*, vol. 5, 359 und ar-Rāzī, *Tafsīr*, vol. 8, 32.

In philological terms, the Qur'an's phrasing here is interesting in the way the active and passive voices relate to one another, since the text literally states that God 'caused Mary to be brought up in a pleasant way'. The Qur'an's choice of grammatical form here can be interpreted as an indication of the connection between grace and freedom, which characterises the way Mary conducts her whole life,[35] and which marks her out in the Qur'an as the paradigm of the faithful believer. Therefore it is not a question here of a young woman being kept under surveillance by her guardian but rather of this young woman paradigmatically devoting her life to God away from her family. Genealogically, she is not subsumed within the family of Zechariah. Despite the fact that Zechariah and Mary belong to one and the same house of Amram and hence have a genealogical connection, the 'women's power' of Mary's mother and Mary herself cannot simply be assigned to the men of the same clan. Instead, an independent female genealogy is actually established here, which then goes on to form the basis of Jesus's prophetic ministry.

In ProtEvJam 7:2, the priest remains nameless and the parents simply hand their daughter over to the Temple in general. The priest also immediately points to Mary's soteriological role for Israel when he announces: 'In you, at the end of days, the Lord will manifest His redemption to the sons of Israel.' In other words, the priest plays only a subsidiary role here and is merely present to point to the Church's precedence over Israel. By contrast, in the Qur'an Zechariah is on a par with Mary: on the one hand, he is placed above her as her guardian, but on the other God provides for her directly, meaning that Zechariah is clearly not indispensable for Mary, but rather acknowledges with wonder her proximity to God, which he finds miraculous and special.

Thus, God himself provides Mary directly with food (Q 3:37). The Muslim commentary tradition also acknowledges this aspect of being cared for by God and highlights its miraculous nature. For if Mary is being shielded behind seven locked doors, as Ṭabarī and Rāzī maintain, it really is a mystery where she gets

35 In the formulation *anbatahā nabātan ḥasanan* ('made her grow in goodness') from Q 3:37 the verb is in the fourth base form and is transitive and hence signifies that someone (here God) causes the thing that is denoted (growing) to happen. In this case, one would expect the ensuing accusative to also derive from the fourth base, given that a verb–accusative construction via the same root is a common grammatical construction. However, the fact that the accusative object is in the first base form and hence is an intransitive construction points grammatically to Mary's active cooperation. Here too, therefore, just as we found with regard to Mary's mother's prayer, the correlationship between God and humans through dialogue can be identified right down to the level of linguistic subtleties.

her food from.[36] On the contrary, the Qur'an is concerned to show that Mary is not dependent upon her guardian but that she orientates herself entirely towards God. It is God who preserves her and provisions her. She does not need any overseer for this. In the same way that, in the Christian liturgy, Mary is repeatedly given sustenance by angels,[37] and just as in the Protevangelium of James it is an angel who brings Mary food (ProtEvJam 8:1), so too in the Qur'an it is God's care that ensures she is provisioned.[38] On a narrative level it is therefore easy to see how Mary's special trust in God might arise and how she can later instantly recognise the figure of the angel. After all, she has been used to being provided for by an angel since her childhood.[39] Whether, as the Christian tradition suggests,[40] she really was presented in the Temple at Jerusalem as a consecrated individual who dwelt within the sanctuary, or whether her devotion to God unfolded in a different religious context and took the form of a service she chose herself, is not of key importance here. The only thing that is of significance in this context is that Mary gives herself entirely to God of her own free will and that God accepts her into his care without her requiring any protection from a man. If one construes Zechariah here as the typological representative of the Jewish priestly tradition, it is interesting that it is precisely this tradition which is provided to her for her support.

Thereupon Zachariah prayed to his Lord, saying, 'My Lord! Grant me by your grace righteous offspring. You are the Hearer of all prayers.' So the angels called out to him as he stood praying in the sanctuary, 'God gives you the good news of the birth of John, who will confirm the Word of God and will be a great leader, chaste, and a prophet among the righteous.' Zachariah exclaimed, 'My Lord! How can I have a son when I am very old and my wife is barren?' He replied, 'Such is the will of God. He does what He pleases.' Zachariah said, 'My Lord! Grant me a sign.' He said, 'Your sign is that you will not be able to speak to people for three days except through gestures. Remember your Lord often and glorify Him morning and evening' (Q 3:38–41).

In comparison with the Surah *Maryam*, it is apparent here that Zechariah, albeit with a different stress, likewise alludes to his advanced age. There is also

36 Cf. footnote 34 of p. 220.
37 Marx, 'Glimpses of a Mariology in the Qur'an', 554, citing Beck, *Nachträge zu Ephrem Syrus*, 32.
38 Geagea, *Mary of the Koran*, 72, sees the angel's provisioning of Mary as a sign that God takes very special care of Mary – right from the moment of her birth onwards.
39 The term *rizq* covers the provision of both material and spiritual comfort. Cf. Lane, *Lexicon*, vol. 3, 1076.
40 Kuschel, *Juden, Christen, Muslime*, 489.

a similarity in the typically Qur'anic hope for righteous offspring, which closely associates the quality of this offspring with its devotion to God (cf. Q 19:6). The same intimate relationship between Zechariah and God is in evidence, and likewise Zechariah's confidence that God will hear his prayers. And while in the first instance, the response now no longer comes from God but from the angels, the function of the angels here is to act as door openers, so that after their initial entrance in Q 3:39, the communication from the next verse onwards takes place between God and Zechariah directly. The same pattern recurs with Mary. Here too, communication begins with the angels, yet like Zechariah Mary reacts directly to God's address, and thereafter God starts to lead the conversation in her case too. In this way the proclaimer of the Qur'an clearly wishes to emphasise that angels are not there to prevent humans from intimate contact with God but actually want to facilitate it.

In the rest of the surah, there is also talk of many angels. In other words, the Annunciation scene, which we will discuss in greater detail presently, also sees the appearance of a number of angels. In the Muslim tradition, the host of angels is justified by the fact that the Holy Spirit or Gabriel is wont to appear at the head of a heavenly council, that is accompanied by other, lower-ranking angels, who therefore do not need to be individually named, and who can be understood as speaking with a single voice.[41] However, the spirit of God from the Surah *Maryam* is not mentioned in the Surah *Āl ʿImrān*, which means that the passages of the Qur'an that are adduced here as analogies are only of limited instructive value. They would tend to suggest that the angels here also denote the same spirit which appears in the Surah *Maryam* – hence perhaps the angel Gabriel, but here with an entourage. That is certainly possible, though it does not explain why the talk now is of a multitude of angels.

One reason for the plurality of angel figures at the moment of the Annunciation may be to remove any grounds for suspecting any intimate relationship between the heavenly figure and Mary. Because the proclaimer of the Qur'an clearly intends to draw a structural parallel between the scenes of annunciation to Mary and Zechariah as a way of countering the customary Christian hierarchisation of the two scenes, it is incumbent upon him to also have several angels appear to Zechariah. In at least one text of pre-Qur'anic Syrian patristics, Gabriel

41 Cf. among others Muqātil, *Tafsīr*, vol. 1, 275. For Rāzī just one angel is active, who is identified, analogous with Surah *al-Qadr* (Q 97), as Gabriel (ar-Rāzī, *Tafsīr*, vol. 8, 46). However, the flaw in this reading is that neither Gabriel nor the Holy Spirit are mentioned in Q 3. Frequently, Q 81:21 is also read as evidence that Gabriel has a kind of entourage. Cf. aṭ-Ṭabarī, *Tafsīr*, vol. 24, 164.

is symbolic of Mary's husband. In accordance with this, at this point his name ('the man of God') is interpreted in such a way that it becomes clear that he is a symbol of Mary's husband. In this way, a special connection between Mary and Gabriel is established on a symbolic level, which in the pagan environment where the Qur'an arose might have led to sexual misinterpretations.[42] So the proclaimer of the Qur'an simply cuts the ground from underneath this potential misreading with his talk of a host of angels.

Another striking feature of the re-evaluation of the Surah *Maryam* is the greater weight that is now given to the Temple as a stage on which the scene with Zechariah unfolds. The Temple plays no part in the dialogue between Zechariah and God in the Surah *Maryam*. The first mention of it comes when Zechariah communicates with the community. By contrast, in the Surah *Āl ʿImrān*, Zechariah is already active in the Temple when he receives the answer of the angel – albeit with the proviso that one is prepared to translate the term *miḥrāb* as 'Temple'. Q 3:39 does not provide any grounds for interpreting Zechariah's prayers as a ritualistic act. In some respects, one might even say that the Qur'an already presupposes that the Temple has become the synagogue and that sacrificial duties have now been supplanted by the offering-up of prayers.[43] As a result, the priest is no longer a priest in the cultic sense but instead a prayer leader, and the Temple is no longer a cultic site but a prayer room. If we take seriously the hypothesis that this change had also already taken place within the Jewish community after the destruction of the Second Temple, but that Christian polemics were based on the premise that the Church was the true 'new' Temple, then it would be perfectly in keeping with the desire of the proclaimer of the Qur'an (which we have already noted in the context of the Surah *Maryam*) to view Judaism and Christianity as equally valid to present Zechariah as praying in the prayer room/Temple. In this way, he is explicitly shown operating within the same space where Mary grows up, and so is moved even closer to her. It must remain a matter of speculation whether the addition of these details was made necessary by Jewish, Christian or pagan intervention. Whatever the case may be, they underline the intention that

42 For the complete context here and the relevant passages from the Syriac Church Fathers, see Ghaffar, 'Kontrafaktische Intertextualität im Koran und die exegetische Tradition des syrischen Christentums', 14.

43 Cf. Marx, 'Glimpses of a Mariology in the Qur'an', 554: 'It is noteworthy that Zachariah in ecclesiastical memory is presented as the last of the priests who according to Luke still fulfils sacrificial duties. The Qur'an goes a step further by picturing the temple service as being already a prayer service and accordingly has Zachariah no longer perform sacrifices, but depicts him as praying in the Temple (Q 3:39).'

is already evident in the Surah *Maryam* of placing Zechariah and Mary on an equal footing as a matter of principle, which is now completed by the motif of a common bond.

This requirement is also apparent in another element of the narration, the assignment of names. Unlike in Q 19:7, the special meaning of the name 'John' is not explicitly mentioned, nor is the name the subject of another introduction; instead, the angels simply accept the name as a given, ordained by God (Q 3:39). John is therefore treated in exactly the same way as Jesus, whose name is simply introduced without more ado in the Surah *Maryam* by the proclaimer of the Qur'an and whose name is now determined here as well not by the mother of Jesus but by God. In Q 3:45 it is once again the angels who introduce this name. Thus, in the matter of the choice of names too, pre-existing differences between Zechariah and Mary are erased, and their relationship to the same angel figures is underscored – another indication of how closely the Qur'an means to associate the roles of Zechariah and Mary and hence of the clear convergence between the typological figures representing Judaism and Christianity respectively.

At the same time, the role of John the Baptist is also described in greater detail.[44] He is now introduced as an ascetic, a prophet, and as one of the righteous (Q 3:39) – all labels that do not appear in the Surah *Maryam* and which on the one hand chime in with the portrayal of John the Baptist in the Gospels, but on the other give no room to the hierarchical relationship between the two figures that is assumed in the Bible. Even so, Jesus is later acknowledged as the Word of God (Q 3:45), and this particularity of Jesus is anticipated here in the fact that John is portrayed as the person who is to meant to confirm a Word from God. Here, then, the roles of John and Jesus are clearly distinguished, and it is also difficult to read their relationship at this point as simply being one of equal status. Yet because the present book is about Mary and not Jesus, we need not seek to clarify this question, but instead should reflect on the implications the way Zechariah is presented have for Mary.

---

44 Apart from in the Surah *Maryam* and the passage cited here, the only other place where John the Baptist appears in the Qur'an is in the late Meccan Surah *al-An'ām* (Q 6). There, he is named in conjunction with Zechariah, Jesus and Elijah (Q 6:85). Neuwirth quite rightly sees this as a sign of the typologically close connection with Jesus (Neuwirth, *Der Koran 2/1*, 611). At the same time, the mention of Elijah in this group of four is revealing, given that Jesus is, after all, first identified by his disciples as a new Elijah. Evidently, the preacher of the Qur'an does not find such an analogy absurd and so underlines the prophetic role played by Jesus and John. One might also be able to deduce an argument by the Qur'an in favour of seeing Mary as a prophetic figure from the fact that Zechariah is included in this group and is so unequivocally placed on a par with Mary.

And here the parallels are obvious. Q 3:40 repeats the question posed in Q 19:8, which expressed the doubts of Zechariah in a way that was very similar to those uttered by Mary (Q 19:20). The Surah *Āl 'Imrān* echoes this parallelism (Q 3:47), which is, after all, primarily to be understood as a rehabilitation of Zechariah, as we have seen, and which broadly stresses that it is completely legitimate to question heavenly voices that seem to be irrational. In a very similar way to the Bible, the Qur'an also warns us about blindly following instructions that are seemingly issued from above and invites us to pose searching questions. Both traditions thus paint a picture of a God who wants to win humans round through dialogue and who is prepared to make himself understood in a rationally comprehensible way. Likewise, the content of the angel's answer corresponds to that of the spirit of God in Q 19:9, though now only a very abbreviated reason is given: the angel merely replies that God can do what he wants, rather than reprising the theme of the straightforward nature of God's actions. Zechariah's reaction is a word-for-word repetition of Q 19:11, while the angel's response to this echoes the reply given in Q 19:11 in slightly modified form. In other words, the rest of the conversation broadly follows the instructions given by the angel in the Surah *Maryam*, thus making any further comment here unnecessary.[45]

Even so, this new reprise of the Zechariah scene naturally alters its meaning. Especially when one considers that the Surah *Āl 'Imrān* discusses the Protevangelium of James in such detail,[46] it is intriguing to observe how important the figure of Zechariah remains. For Zechariah really only makes an appearance in ProtEvJam 23 in order to be killed. He is of no consequence in relation to Mary, and typologically he swiftly becomes for the Church Fathers a symbol of the end of Judaism or the reassignment to Jesus Christ of the promises that God originally made to Israel. At this point it is significant that the proclaimer of the Qur'an emphasises the enduring importance of this typological representative of Judaism, and even facilitates a new synagogal interpretation of his service in the Temple.

c) The first Annunciation scene

And remember when the angels said, 'O Mary! Surely Allah has selected you and

45 Louis Massignon's theory that Q 3:41 contains an allusion to the Immaculate Conception, untainted by any contact with the Devil, does not seem persuasive to us (see Ashkar, *Mary in the Syriac Christian tradition and Islam*, 246, citing Louis Massignon, *'Le Signe marial'*, *Rhythmes du monde*, 1947, 9). As a result, we do not intend to pursue it here.

46 A comparable verse-by-verse analysis of Q 3:42–47 and ProtEvJam 1,1–3 can be found in Reck, 'The Annunciation to Mary', 365.

purified you. He has chosen you over all women of the world. O Mary! Be devout to your Lord, prostrate yourself in prayer and bow along with those who bow down.' This is an account of the unseen that We reveal to you [O Prophet]. You were not with them when they drew lots to decide who would be Mary's guardian, nor were you there when they argued about it (Q 3:42–44).

After the scene with Zechariah, the proclaimer of the Qur'an returns to Mary and now describes the actual Annunciation scene – that is, the scene with which the Surah *Maryam* begins the story of Mary. However, the Surah *Āl 'Imrān* does not simply reiterate once more the withdrawal of Mary to the East but launches straight into the angel's address. This serves not only to bring out more vividly the parallels between the events here and the annunciation to Zechariah, but also to render certain mariological references, which we have discussed above, invisible. Yet we will see straight away that this does nothing to reduce Mary's special distinction, but instead merely highlights it in a different way. For the angel's speech is clearly more focused on Mary than even the speech of the spirit of God in the Surah *Maryam*. Whereas the proclamation of Mary's conception of Jesus was immediately placed at the centre of the Surah *Maryam*, the focus of the Surah *Āl 'Imrān* is initially on Mary herself. She is addressed as the one chosen and purified by God; indeed, she is acknowledged as the woman who has been selected over all the women of the world (Q 3:42). In the first place, this is a bold statement which ties in directly with the distinctions accorded to Mary in Christianity, without repeating them verbatim. To some extent, what we are dealing with here is a condensed version of the salutations that are repeatedly addressed to Mary in Christianity and of what the angel expresses in Lk 1:30 when he tells her that she has found favour with God. Of course, the intensity of the distinction bestowed on Mary at this point was not lost on early Muslim commentators of the Qur'an, and it has played a major part in ensuring that the high esteem which Mary enjoys in Islam remains unchallenged. Let us examine the individual elements of this distinction one by one.

To start with, the angels proclaim that Mary has been chosen by God. This accords her the same distinction as that applied to Adam, Noah, the house of Abraham, and the house of Amram at the beginning of the surah – a qualification that once more puts Mary close to being a prophetic figure. In his commentary on the Qur'an, Rāzī sets especially great store by the sequence of God's actions at this point. According to the text of the Qur'an, God begins by selecting and purifying Mary, before the focus then shifts once more to the question of selection. Rāzī interprets this first selection as indicating that God accepts her as exempt from sin despite the fact that she is a woman. In his view, this happened only in her case.

He does not see it as being in any way a statement about the potential for women in general to be chosen. Correspondingly, it is also important for him to stress Mary's extraordinary nature in being provided for by God right from the outset. In this way God has freed her, and so to speak divested her, of anything that might distract or prevent her from devoting herself completely to God and his service. In Rāzī's estimation, God has thus enabled her to become the recipient of special divine favours (*laṭā'if*). In turn, these are for Rāzī the prerequisite for being able to see Mary as guided entirely by righteousness, since her communication with God, he concludes, was never broken and she remained attentive to God right down to the subtlest of signs. Perhaps we can construe this as Rāzī interpreting this aspect of isolation and focus on God as the force that enables Mary to be especially receptive to God's special favours. On the basis of its semantic field, the following theologically significant and for this context highly relevant meanings are associated with the concept of *laṭā'if*: a gentle, friendly and subtle divine disposition towards the human race, which in its turn, by virtue of the gentleness of this approach, is only able to appreciate this disposition insofar as it is receptive and sensitive to it in the first place.[47] Mary appears to fulfil this criterion to the highest degree.

Following the Qur'anic listing, Rāzī goes on to explain that God purified Mary both where ritual observance was concerned as well as in a religious-spiritual and an ethical sense; in other words, he comprehensively cleansed her.[48] Rāzī comes to the conclusion that Mary should be understood as free from all sin (*'iṣma*) – once again, a totally unique distinction in his view.[49] Taking the text of the Qur'an as his basis, Rāzī paints a picture of a person whom he considers to have given herself over to the religious-spiritual realm in the most comprehensive way imaginable,

---

47 The word family of *laṭufa* comprises the following meanings: to be fine and delicate, or elegant and graceful, ethereal, imperceptible to the senses, friendly and good-natured, to caress, to stroke, to mitigate, to be good to someone through having a precise knowledge of their circumstances, to treat a person in a friendly and gentle manner, coax someone, win someone round, to beg, to give someone a gift; it is denotes the opposite of leaving someone in the lurch. *Luṭf* is defined as: friendliness, politeness, kindness. The adjective *laṭīf* embraces the meanings: to be friendly, subtle and gentle, to be attentive and perspicacious, to be wise on the basis of having all the facts at one's disposal. As a name for God, *Al-Laṭīf* means the 'sensitive one, who encompasses all dimensions'. Cf. Lane, *Lexicon*, vol. 8, 310, and al-Iṣfahānī, *al-Mufradāt fī ġarīb al-qur'ān*, 466.

48 According to Rāzī, the things that make a woman unclean are being touched by a man, menstruation, lack of faith and disobedience, blameworthy deeds and repugnant habits. He also defended Mary against the accusations, calumnies and lies of her opponents. Cf. ar-Rāzī, *Tafsīr*, vol. 8, 47.

49 Cf. ibid. 47.

and who appears to live entirely for God and free from all earthly necessities. It is particularly noteworthy that he applies to her the concept of being totally free of sin, which is otherwise reserved for prophets. In general, she seems to have been transported from the realities of contingent existence; clearly an ideal of piety and spirituality is being applied to Mary here which breaks the bounds of what women are normally deemed capable of.

It is at this point that Mary's selection by God is mentioned for the second time. According to Rāzī, this denotes the second phase of her life that is of interest to the Qur'an, In this phase, God sent Mary Jesus without the involvement of any man in order to make her and her son into a sign for all the peoples of the world.[50] On the basis of what is written in the Qur'an, Rāzī ascribes to Mary the character traits of an exemplary believer. The most exciting of these from an intertextual point of view is the distinction which emphasises Mary's purity. From a Christian perspective, one naturally immediately thinks here of Mary's purity from sin and hence of the intactness of her relationship with God. And indeed, aside from Rāzī, other commentators on the Qur'an also construe this purity as freedom from sin.[51] By contrast, Zamaḫšarī sees the motif of purity simply as a way of protecting Mary from attacks on her character by Jews.[52] In this case, therefore, purity would not relate generally to Mary as a person but to the attacks on her by her family prompted by the suspicion that she had conceived her child as a result of sex out of wedlock. But if this were truly the meaning of purity here, then it would be hard to understand why Mary is so lauded in the latter half of the sentence.

Most commentators therefore, like Rāzī, see Mary's purity in a more wide-ranging sense. For Qurṭubī, God not only cleansed Mary of unbelief, but also of everything that was thought of at the time as impurity, such as menstruation, puerperium, etc.[53] This interpretation thus saw ritual aspects of Mary's purity once again come into effect in the Muslim commentary tradition; these were also important to the Church Fathers and made her sacerdotal role plausible. We do not know whether such a characterisation of Mary was really intended in the Qur'an. But in any event, pre-existing talk of Mary's purity was taken up and linked back to theocentric ideas.

For it is God who has made Mary pure, whereas the Syrian Church Fathers set great store by Mary's selection as being explained by the fact that she was

50 Cf. ibid. 47.
51 Cf. Muqātil, *Tafsīr*, vol. 1, 275, and aṭ-Ṭabarī, *Tafsīr*, vol. 5, 392 f.
52 Cf. al-Zamaḫšarī, *Tafsīr*, 172.
53 Cf. al-Qurṭubī, *al-Ǧāmiʿ*, vol. 5, 126.

already so spotless that God chose her for that very reason. In the Maronite Christian liturgy too, Mary's purity is the reason she is selected by God.[54] At the same time, Mary's freedom from sin is ultimately christologically based for the Syrian Church Fathers, as we have already noted. Mary is free from sin through having been baptised in Christ. And this baptism takes place through her conception of Jesus Christ. By contrast, the proclaimer of the Qur'an stresses that it is not Christ but God who makes Mary's purity possible.

At this point, from the point of view of the Qur'an, the foundations of Christian Marian devotion begin to crumble. If it is not God's grace that explains Mary's selection, and if it is not the purifying power of God that sets her relationship with God on the right track, then from a Qur'anic standpoint this amounts to a quite fundamental misunderstanding of the relationship between the creator and his creation. The proclaimer of the Qur'an is therefore perfectly willing to grant the greatest of all conceivable distinctions to Mary just as long as that distinction does not compromise her status as a created being. It is important to him that these distinctions do not derive from human merit but are the result of divine acts of salvation. Humans do not gain God's attention and election through their own efforts; rather, it is the case that election by God and cleansing set a person free and grant him or her beauty and purity. In the Qur'an's eyes, this is unreservedly true of Mary too, and even from a Christian standpoint – with all due deference to the Marian devotion of the Syrian Church Fathers – one can only agree with this. Indeed, the Church Fathers themselves would in all likelihood have concurred with the Qur'an's critique here if they had been asked for their expert theological opinion. Only their poetic texts tend to be misleading if they are not studied very precisely in context, and can lead in popular religious observance to the kind of consequences that are deplored by the Qur'an.

Of course, this does not mean that Mary is just a puppet in God's hands, devoid of any free will. The very next verse shows that Mary is called by God, not coerced by him. But her free commitment to God and the purity and beauty expressed therein do not in the final analysis arise from her, but are originally created by God. In consequence, she remains God's creature, set apart from him and bound to show him devotion and adoration.

Admittedly, among her fellow human beings, Mary is accorded a very special place of honour. In the Qur'an's view, she is chosen over all women of the world. Qurṭubī, for example, sums up the Qur'an and the Hadith tradition by pronouncing

54 Ashkar, *Mary in the Syriac Christian tradition and Islam*, 131: 'God has chosen you from among all people because he saw you the purest and the most devout of those who were born.'

Mary simply the best woman of all time – from Eve to the woman of the last hour.[55] Indeed, he positively rhapsodises about her and asks rhetorically where there has ever been a woman among the daughters of Adam who displayed such outstanding qualities and virtues. For Zamaḫšarī too, the selection of Mary leads to her being exalted above all other women.[56] And Ṭabarī speaks of Mary having been chosen from all the women of her times and of her being superior in paradise even to Fatima[57] – a distinction that is based on a hadith.[58] Yet this hierarchical classification of Mary in relation to other women is not without controversy within Islam. Thus, the singling out of Mary for distinction is also widely understood as distinguishing her from all other women of her time. In this interpretation, women from other periods – such as the women surrounding the Prophet – are thus not ranked below Mary.[59] Instead, women from the milieu of the Prophet Muhammad and Mary are readily identified typologically with one another;[60] the Shiite tradition thinks primarily of Fatima in this context, whereas Sunni traditions point to Aisha. Alternatively, hadith are cited which identify religious perfection not just in Mary but also in Pharaoh's wife, as well as in Aisha or Fatima.

Clearly, one can only find the idea of Mary's election before all other women in a somewhat watered-down form in the Islamic tradition, despite its being so clearly enunciated in the Qur'an. However, it is interesting that – for all the disagreement within Islam over the status of particular women from the milieu of the Prophet – there is broad agreement across denominations about Mary's outstanding importance. Mary therefore serves not just as a figure of reconciliation

55 Cf. al-Qurṭubī, *al-Ǧāmi'*, vol. 5, 128.

56 Cf. Ashkar, *Mary in the Syriac Christian tradition and Islam*, 170.

57 Cf. ibid. 170.

58 Cf. ibid. 181; and aṭ-Ṭabarī, *Tafsīr*, vol. 5, 392. The hadith, handed down by Tirmiḏī among others, states: 'Umm Salama recounted that on the day Mecca was conquered, God's Prophet called Fatima to him and spoke to her, whereupon she began to cry. The he spoke some more and she smiled. When the Prophet died, I asked her [sc. Fatima] why she had cried and then smiled, and she told me: "The Prophet said to me that he was going to die, and I started crying. Then he told me that I am superior to all the other women who dwell in Paradise, except for Mary, the daughter of 'Imrān, which made me smile."' at-Tirmiḏī, *Ǧāmi'*, Hadith No. 3873, Book No. 49 (*Kitāb al-manāqib 'an rasūli llāh ṣalla llāhu 'alayhi wasallam*), 489.

59 This determination of ranking may also be based on a hadith: 'Sufficient for you among the women of the earth are Mary the daughter of 'Imran, Khedijah the daughter of Khuwailid, Fatima the daughter of Muhammad and Asiya the wife of the Pharaoh' (at-Tirmiḏī, *Ǧāmi'*, Hadith No. 3878, Book No. 49 (*Kitāb al-manāqib 'an rasūli llāh ṣalla llāhu 'alayhi wa-sallam*), 492. Cf. also al- Buḫārī, *Ṣaḥīḥ*, Hadith No. 3815, Book No. 62 (*Kitāb faḍā'il aṣḥāb an-Nabīyi ṣalla llāhu 'alayhi wa-sallam*), 934.

60 Cf. Ashkar, *Mary in the Syriac Christian tradition and Islam*, 186 f.

between the Abrahamic faiths, but can also be called upon to bring about rapprochement within Islam. For in the conflict between Sunni and Shia Muslims, it is a major bone of contention whether female relatives of the Prophet such as his daughter Fatima are accorded distinctions (as happens in the Shiite tradition) or rather those who were bound to him in love like his wife Aisha (as in Sunni Islam). Mary, though, stands above this conflict, being neither a wife of Muhammad nor a blood relation.

Yet regardless of whether only Mary or other women too are to be seen as perfect in a religious sense, it is highly significant in itself that the Islamic tradition should even talk in terms of Mary's being considered a perfect woman in the first place. For this designation fulfils an important necessary criterion for her prophetic significance from the standpoint of Islamic scholastic theology. It is also exciting that she is able to attain this perfection without being married. To be sure, the Muslim tradition has no truck with the concept of the perpetual virginity of Mary, nor is there any religious ideal of perfection that entertains the idea of perpetual virginity. Instead – much like in Judaism – all men and women are expected to get married. On the other hand, neither the Qur'an nor the Muslim tradition turns Mary into a happily married woman surrounded by a clutch of children; rather, she remains, at least in the Qur'an, unmarried and alone before God. In the Islamic mystical tradition, Mary's virginity is even regarded as a sign of her fundamental holiness.[61] Building on this tradition, perhaps Mary might one day be rediscovered in her virginity even within Islam, as a protagonist for Muslims who wish to resist the pressure that is brought to bear on them by their families and to stay unmarried. On this point, although the Qur'an makes it clear that, in doing so, one may potentially leave oneself open to terrible calumny, it does nonetheless defend Mary in her virginity – at least where the conception of Jesus is concerned. This is the sole matter of interest for the Qur'an, nor has the Muslim tradition ever been interested in going beyond this. That is all too understandable given Christianity's great veneration of virginity. Even so, as a figure that straddles both religions, in the modern world Mary might have the potential to become a figure who could raise awareness and understanding even within Islam of a lifestyle that refuses to be confined within bourgeois ideals and which in its radical devotional nature points to the immanence of God. Certainly, even the Qur'an voices its special admiration for monks, who express their devotion and attachment to God through their humility (cf. Q 5:82).

Conversely, however, the Qur'an also conveys a keen awareness of the dangers

61 Cf. ibid., 167; Yaşar, 'Maria und die Geburt Jesu im mystischen Korankommentar', 4.

of a celibate lifestyle (cf. Q 57:27) and above all of the risks involved in venerating people who choose to pursue this way of life (cf. Q 9:31). Accordingly, we do not mean to suggest here that the proclaimer of the Qur'an directly advocates the ideal of perpetual virginity. But on closer inspection he does without question allow more wiggle room and grey areas in this matter than might appear at first glance. So, perhaps the image of Mary presented in the Qur'an might become a reason for Muslims to entertain in some measure the possibility of a person remaining unmarried 'for the sake of the kingdom of heaven' (Mt 19:12) as a viable life plan, and conversely to invite Christians to recognise the susceptibility of this ideal to abuse and not to make it an end in itself. From a historical perspective, the proclaimer of the Qur'an thus indicates a middle path between the Christian esteem of the monastic way of life and the rabbinical obligation to marital cohabitation – and hence once again points out a way to overcome conflicts between Christianity and Judaism.

Let us return, however, to the Annunciation scene in the Surah *Āl 'Imrān*. Immediately after the angel's remarkable eulogy to Mary, she is called upon by the angels to show humility and submission before God. Then she is expected to bow her head in communal prayer. At this point, the Qur'an is clearly alluding to Islamic ritual prayer, which involves both the act of bowing one's head and ritual prostration. However, the text inverts the usual sequence of the ritual prayer, by having the act of self-prostration precede the bowing. The Muslim commentary tradition acknowledges this peculiar feature without being able to convincingly explain it. Thus, Rāzī surmises that the closest one can get to achieving the goal of being near to God is through prostration, which means that prostration is the noblest part of prayer. Accordingly, he maintains, it is a distinction for Mary that this particularly important element of prayer is first mentioned in relation to her.[62]

As regards this question, a more convincing approach than these ultimately somewhat forced explanations seems to us to be an interpretation against the background of the Syriac intertexts of the Qur'an, which were in all probability not known to Muslims at the time of Rāzī, or were possibly ignored. This interpretation has only recently been put forward by Ghaffar. As he demonstrates, it had become commonplace among the Syrian Church Fathers to believe that the angel must have prostrated himself before Mary during their encounter, because as the *Theotokos* she was ranked above the angels in the hierarchy. In Jacob of Serugh's writings, for example, Gabriel has to prostrate himself in adoration before Mary before he announces God's promise to her. The verb that is used for prostrating

62 Cf. ar-Rāzī, *Tafsīr*, vol. 8, 48.

oneself is identical in both Jacob and the Qur'an (Syriac *sged*/Arabic *sağada).*[63] If one visualises this scene, it becomes clear that the Qur'an carries out an inversion here which is meant to remind us that Mary is a human being created by God. Here, therefore, the proclaimer of the Qur'an is criticising the patristic and imperial veneration of Mary and is attempting to sustain the idea of reverence for Mary while at the same time retaining her human nature and her humble subordination to God. His remedy is to take her into the community of believers. She should not be a separate entity before whom people prostrate themselves but should become part of the whole community that bows before God.

In much the same way as happened at the Second Vatican Council, this reading effectively liberates Mariology from Christology and soteriology and transforms it into part of the doctrine of the community of believers. As one of the faithful, Mary is expected to perform the ritual prayer and prostrate herself before God like the rest of us. Once again, Mary appears as the ideal type of the believer, a fact now also made evident in her observance of prayer and spirituality. Interestingly, in the Qur'an her devotional practice does not take place in the privacy of her home – which is otherwise common practice for women. She also has no children to look after, which would prevent her from attending ritual prayers within the community. Instead, she is united with those praying beside her. And these fellow supplicants are designated in Arabic with the generic masculine noun, so that we can envision here a communal prayer session involving both men and women,[64] of the kind that still takes place today in Muslim communities during the *hajj*. In this respect too, Mary might also become a bridging figure – this time between the sexes, leading to a prayer practice that could bring together men and women more visibly than is currently the case in many places.

In Q 3:43, therefore, Mary is addressed as the typical Muslim woman, performing the same ritual prayer observances as her fellow supplicants. In other words, the Ave Maria is picked up and Mary's special honour is voiced, but this acknowledgement is not used as a springboard for praying to Mary, but rather for praying alongside her. To some extent this also picks up the idea of Mary as the archetype of the Church, except that she now no longer stands for just the Church

---

63 Cf. Ghaffar, 'Kontrafaktische Intertextualität im Koran und die exegetische Tradition des syrischen Christentums', 15 f.

64 Most Islamic commentators also assume that a Muslim communal prayer is being referred to here (cf. for example al-Qurṭubī, *al-Ǧāmiʿ*, vol. 5, 129). Moreover, before Ghaffar, the parallels with Muslim prayer practice were also noticed by Kuschel, *Juden, Christen, Muslime*, 491; on the basis of this, he talks about there being 'basic elements of a theocentric Mariology in the Qur'an.'

but for every godly person. It is intriguing to note that, despite being incorporated into the community of believers, and for all the stress that is placed on her as a human being, she still remains the person whom the angels address as having been selected over all women and purified by God. One need not therefore immediately see in her the Queen of Heaven. But it is already striking that, although she does prostrate herself before God on the orders of the angels, conversely the angels proclaim her special distinction over all other women.

After the theologically highly charged Annunciation scene, by way of contrast the Qurʾan turns its attention to motifs from the Protevangelium of James that relate to the question of who should act as Mary's guardian (Q 3:44). Once more, in characteristic fashion, the Qurʾan resolves this in a different way to the ProtEvJam. The text of the Qurʾan assumes that a dispute arose over who should look after Mary, albeit without entertaining the possibility of marital cohabitation. Instead, the question here is one of guardianship. The Muslim commentary literature further develops this motif, explaining that the dispute over Mary's guardianship arose among other things from her descent from the house of Amram.[65] In contrast, in ProtEvJam 9:2 it is the case that Mary's care is guaranteed above all in the form of marriage. Yet in the ProtEvJam, Joseph is reluctant to take Mary as his wife and is worried that he will be ridiculed for having a wife who is so much younger than him. He only finally agrees to take Mary on after being threatened by the High Priest. He duly takes her home, only to then immediately leave her on her own, having been called away on business (ProtEvJam 9:3). Evidently, the ProtEvJam does everything to try and prevent any thoughts of marital intimacy between Mary and Joseph from even arising in the first place. And Joseph is completely exonerated of the suspicion that he agreed to marry her out of erotic desire for her beauty.

However, such thoughts run the risk of questioning any connection between marriage and sexuality, and indeed from such precepts there developed in the Catholic tradition the practice of the 'Josephite marriage', which posited an enduring marital bond on a purely spiritual level. If married men want to become priests, then in agreement with their wives, they can pledge to refrain from any form of intimate physical contact in order to be admitted to the priesthood. But the proclaimer of the Qurʾan cuts the ground from underneath any such practice simply by virtue of not portraying Mary as married to begin with; this consequently also sidesteps the dilemma of having to sketch out a legitimate form of marriage that is not conducted on a physical level. From the point of view of the Qurʾan, therefore,

65 Cf. ar-Rāzī, *Tafsīr*, vol. 8, 51.

it is crystal clear that, however perfect people might be, marital love will – and indeed should – always find physical expression.

In the passage we are examining here, we can see how closely the proclaimer of the Qur'an is in dialogue with the Protevangelium of James from the way he adopts the idea of drawing lots, albeit without going into the precise circumstances of how Mary's caregiver was selected by this method. In ProtEvJam 9:1, there is a description of the widowers of Israel all taking their rods to the Temple and drawing them out of a bundle held by the High Priest, and Joseph's rod miraculously producing a dove, which settled on Joseph's head, thus making it clear that he was the chosen one. In Rāzī[66] and Qurṭubī's[67] commentaries, this story is modified in such a way that Zechariah wins the competition to become Mary's guardian in an unusual way (by casting lots). In this case, the lots are cast into a river – some commentators identify it as the River Jordan – and the owner of the rod that miraculously advances against the current wins the competition to see who should look after Mary. In this instance it is Zechariah.

The business of drawing or casting lots is thus recontextualised by the commentary tradition and no longer focused on marrying off Mary The text of the Qur'an can be interpreted in a number of ways here, because it it is announcing the revelation of a previously hidden story. There is much evidence to suggest that the appointment of Zechariah as Mary's carer in the Temple is once again being retrospectively thematised here. But from the pragmatic point of view of the narrative, marriage to Joseph at this point would also make sense, but then again his designation as a 'caregiver' would not argue in favour of the Qur'an's having in mind for him a happy and physically fulfilled marriage with Mary. Perhaps, then, one should probably get away entirely from the biblical idea of a marriage and instead proceed from the assumption that the scene is about finding a guardian for Mary.

d) The second Annunciation scene

*Remember when the angels proclaimed, 'O Mary! God gives you good news of a Word from Him, his name will be Christ Jesus, son of Mary; honoured in this world and in the next, and he will be one of those granted closeness to God [*muqarrabīn*]. And he will speak to people in his cradle, and as a grown man, and will be one of the righteous.' 'My Lord!' Mary wondered, 'how can I have a*

66 Cf. ar-Rāzī, *Tafsīr*, vol. 8, 50.
67 Cf. al-Qurṭubī, *al-Ǧāmiʿ*, vol. 5, 131.

child when no man has ever touched me?' An angel replied: 'Thus will it be. God creates what He wills. When He decrees a thing, He need only say "Be!" and it is! God will teach him writing and wisdom, the Torah and the Gospel' (Q 3: 45–48).

After the depiction of the Annunciation scene that ends with the drawing of lots to determine who should be Mary's guardian, in the Surah *Āl ʿImrān* the proclaimer of the Qurʾan, unlike in the Surah *Maryam*, moves on to the birth of Jesus. The traditional story of Mary experiencing the miracle of the date palm tree in the desert is omitted, without any replacement, as is the account of her labour pains. Likewise, her family's reproaches find no room here. Instead, the angels offer a theological interpretation of the conception of Jesus, and thereby present a kind of Qurʾanic Christology. For now explicitly Christological titles are taken up and put in a new context and thus reinterpreted. We cannot expand further on this topic here because it diverts us away from Mary. We intend to simply note what implications the information given on Jesus has for the status of Mary.

Let us begin with the first mariologically controversial key word, namely the talk of Mary's son as a 'Word from God'. Ṭabarī does not apply this specialist term 'Word' (*kalima*) to Jesus; instead, in his interpretation, the 'word' is the imperative 'Be!' which is cited later and with which God creates Jesus.[68] In Ṭabarī's reading of the text, God brings Mary the good news (Jesus) by means of a message (*risāla*) and a word (*kalima*), which God instructs to meet Mary in order that he can create from this encounter a person, completely without the agency of any husband. However, the possessive pronoun 'his' in the following sentence clearly refers to *kalima*, yet it is in the masculine, despite the fact that *kalima* is a feminine noun. Accordingly, most commentators, even in the classical Muslim tradition, proceed from the assumption that *kalima* and Jesus are one and the same.[69] Whether *kalima* is a suitable translation of the Greek term 'Logos' is open to different interpretations.[70] But even if one were to assume that the proclaimer of the Qurʾan is using precise terminology here to allude to the Christian doctrine of the Logos, this does not mean that he is also appropriating its content. Rather it is a case of his picking up the doctrine in a terminologically exact way precisely in order to be able to attach his own meaning to it. Again, though, we are precluded from pursuing this train of thought because it would entail our discussing the Qurʾan's conception of Jesus at exhaustive length.[71]

68 Cf. aṭ-Ṭabarī, *Tafsīr*, vol. 5, 407.
69 Cf. for example ar-Rāzī, *Tafsīr*, vol. 8, 55.
70 In our opinion, many factors speak in favour of this assumption. Cf. for example the argument put forward by Geagea, *Mary of the Koran*, 82.
71 Cf. Khorchide and von Stosch, *Der andere Prophet*.

For Mary the characterisation of Jesus as a Word of God in Q 3:45 means that she receives physical contact with the Word of God. It touches her, so to speak, from within, is permitted to grow inside her, and is brought into the world with her help. Mary thus appears as a prophet who brings the Word of God to the human race. Her direct contact with the angels, which is again made explicit here, also supports this contention. In the classical commentary tradition, Qurṭubī for one is of the opinion that Mary actually sees the angel in exactly the same way as Muhammad did.[72] And yet – unlike in the Surah *Maryam* – there is no mention of her seeing the angel, only of her hearing his voice.[73] Chiming in with this is the fact that several angels speak, so that this annunciation becomes an echo of the company of the heavenly host in Lk 2:14, which takes the opportunity of the birth of Jesus to glorify God. It is precisely this theocentric motif of the choir of angels that the proclaimer of the Qur'an picks up, and contextualises a number of the most important Christological titles in such a novel way that they once again serve the purpose of glorifying the One God.

Thus, when the Qur'an states that 'his name will be Christ Jesus, son of Mary', at first glance, the Arabic text appears to suggest that only Jesus is being presented as a name, whereas 'Christ' performs the role of a title here. For 'Christ', in Arabic *al-masīḥ*, is written here with the definite article, and hence appears to function as an adjective or attribute. Therefore, strictly speaking, in this case one would have to translate as follows: 'His name, in other words the name of the Word that is the Messiah, that is Jesus.' However, the definite article is used every time the title of 'Christ' is mentioned even when, during the late Medinan period, the name 'Jesus' is omitted entirely and he is only spoken of as 'the Christ'. This then clearly argues against the thesis that 'Christ' is being introduced as a title here. Rather, it appears that 'Christ Jesus' is being presented here as a name, in order to thereby relieve it of the soteriological function that Christianity assigns to it.

In the classical commentary literature, though, this point is disputed and there are even some commentators who do indeed choose to regard 'Christ' as a title and not just a name[74] and who make a whole series of suggestions for interpretation

---

72 Cf. al-Qurṭubī, *al-Ǧāmi'*, vol. 5, 129. According to Muqātil (Muqātil, *Tafsīr*, vol. 1, 276) and Rāzī (ar-Rāzī, *Tafsīr*, vol. 8, 52) it is once more Gabriel alone with whom Mary communicates. We have already reflected above on the question of whether one or more angels visit Mary.

73 Cf. Kuschel, *Juden, Christen, Muslime*, 492.

74 In common with many other exegetes, Zamaḫšarī for example understands *al-masīḥ* as a *Laqab* (the part of an Arabic name that is a nickname, title or family name) and so regards it as being a title as opposed to a given name (*ism*). On the basis of the lexical sense of the word, he

that are highly interesting from a Christological standpoint.[75] There is no need for us to try and resolve this dispute here.[76] Even so, it is worth bearing in mind that in the patristic tradition even the name 'Jesus' was more than just a name and was meant to characterise the person thus designated.[77] For the Syrian tradition in particular, it was very important that 'Jesus' was not just a mere name, but that it stood for 'the Saviour'.[78] For this reason, the Syrian tradition contended 'that the angel did not say that Jesus will become the Messiah and the giver of life; rather, Jesus has always been the Messiah and the Redeemer as a result of his whole way of being. One might also add that "Messiah" and "Life-giver" are no ordinary titles, but instead are ones that naturally attach to him by virtue of the fact that he combines within himself a human and a divine nature.'[79] Yet precisely at variance with this interpretation, the proclaimer of the Qur'an is adamant that 'Jesus Christ' does not stand for a being who in his very nature is different from us, but that it is simply the name of an entirely human manifestation of God's caring Word.

For our Mariological investigation, it is of prime interest that the name of Christ is linked with the label 'son of Mary'. This underlines once more that the person who is being acknowledged as a human manifestation of God's caring Word was given birth to by Mary. It strikes us as being highly probable that the

---

proposes that its meaning is that Christ is the 'Blessed One'. Cf. az-Zamaḫšarī, *Tafsīr*, 172.

75 In accordance with the meanings of its word family associated with the term and texts in the tradition, Ṭabarī understands *al-masīḥ* as expressing the idea that God stroked Jesus (on the head) and in so doing absolved him of all sin (*ḏunūb*). Another explanation on which Ṭabarī speculates is that Jesus is given this title because he is the one who confirms the truth (*ṣiddīq*) (aṭ-Ṭabarī, *Tafsīr*, vol. 5, 409). Rāzī also presents several potential explanations as to why Jesus is so called. The common denominator of all of them is that it was an integral part of Jesus's nature to touch and be touched. In the latter instance, this would involve being anointed with pure consecrated oil like all prophets. Alternatively, according to another explanation, Jesus was touched by Gabriel and has this name or title bestowed upon him as a result (ar-Rāzī, *Tafsīr*, vol. 8, 54). Yet another explanation regards the term as synonymous with 'king' (kings were traditionally anointed when ascending the throne). Finally there is also an interpretation that lights upon another aspect, seeing the term 'Messiah' as synonymous with 'friend' (*ṣadīq*).

76 Khorchide and von Stosch, *Der andere Prophet*, 79 f., continue to argue that 'Christ' should be interpreted as a title. This view strikes us as no longer convincing.

77 The basis for this theological interpretation was the etymological derivation of the name Jesus, which to this day is still construed as meaning 'God's help', literally: 'YHWH is help' (Luz, *Das Evangelium nach Matthäus*, 142). Even in the Bible, the name 'Jesus' is charged with soteriological significance (Matthew 1:21 'She will give birth to a son, and you are to give him the name Jesus, because he will save his people from their sins'.

78 Pseudo-Ephrem the Syrian, *Commentary on the Diatessaron I*, 25.

79 Ghaffar, 'Kontrafaktische Intertextualität im Koran und die exegetische Tradition des syrischen Christentums', 20.

Qur'an is here making a direct allusion to Mary's Christian title as the Mother of God or the *Theotokos*. Without directly criticising this title, the Qur'an does define it more narrowly, inasmuch as it makes it clear that Mary does not give birth to the uncreated, unchanging, eternal God, but simply imparts to us a Word from him, which then assumes human form in Jesus Christ. This serves to stress Mary's special role, but at the same time to counter any deification of Mary or Jesus.[80]

So that we may continue to focus our attention on the figure of Mary, we will refrain from commenting on the other statements that are made about Jesus in the verses Q 3:45–46 and proceed directly to considering Mary's reaction instead. In very similar fashion to Q 19:20, in Q 3:47 Mary asks how her pregnancy is even possible given that she has never had intimate relations with another human being. In contrast with the form of words used in the Surah *Maryam*, it is noticeable here in Mary's defence of herself that no stress is placed on her ethical integrity. After the angels have proclaimed Mary's purification (Q 3:42), the question of whether Mary might possibly have prostituted herself no longer needs to be broached in the Surah *Āl ʿImrān*. By this stage Mary has been elevated beyond all question, and accordingly the conflicts with her family are no longer made a topic of discussion either. Mary's questioning is therefore no longer intended as part of her own defence, but as a way of highlighting God's miraculous deeds. It is God who is giving proof of his power here when he makes possible Mary's motherhood in spite of her never having touched another human being.[81]

If we compare the phraseology in both surahs with Lk and ProtEvJam, we can see that the Surah *Maryam* clearly adopts the Lucan conception of virginity. Whereas Mary's virginity presents a narrative problem in Lk and places in question how she might bear a child, in ProtEvJam virginity appears as a virtue that has to be preserved even after the birth.[82] The Surah *Āl ʿImrān* offers a third way here. It is no longer interested in the problem of virginity and accepts Mary's intactness

80 By contrast, Zamaḫšarī assumes that Mary learns indirectly, through her son's being designated the 'son of Mary', that she will bear her son without a father, because he would otherwise be called the son of a man. Certainly, the question she poses in Q 3:47 makes it clear that Mary does not at this stage understand how this birth might be possible without a man being involved. In other words, this explanation does not provide an answer to what for her is the decisive existential question (az-Zamaḫšarī, *Tafsīr*, 172).

81 Here, 'touched' is a technical term for intimate physical congress. The Arabic term that is used here to denote 'human being' is *bašar*, a word that has the same root as the term for 'gospel' (*bušrā*); this means that in Mary's case it is God's 'good news' which assumes the essential role customarily taken by a man.

82 Cf. Mary F. Foskett, 'Virginity as purity in the Protoevangelium of James.' In: Levine (ed.), *A Feminist companion to Mariology*, 67–76, here 68.

as a foregone conclusion. The principal focus, rather, is on the power of God, whose Word takes shape in Mary. Ultimately, the angel's reply here places God's creative power more firmly in the centre than the corresponding formulations in Q 19:35 and Q 19:21. Here, God does not simply make or decide whatever he wants, as in the Surah *Maryam*. Instead, God now creates what he wants. The formulation 'When He decrees a thing, He need only say "Be!" and it will become so! (*kun fa-yakūn*)'[83] from Q 19:35, which is repeated verbatim in Q 3:47, thus becomes God's word of creation, with the result that Jesus appears as a new creation of God and Mary's virginity becomes a sign of God's acts of creation.[84]

Here too, the proclaimer of the Qurʾan is once more engaged in a dialogue with the Syrian tradition of Christianity. Thus, Ephrem the Syrian emphasises that God's creative word is precisely not expressed through the imperative 'Be!' but rather in the formulation 'Let it be!' But above all, Ephrem is concerned to stress that God's creative word is carried out through Jesus Christ.[85] But it is this very possibility that the proclaimer of the Qurʾan excludes when he makes the birth of Jesus the result of an order issued by God in the imperative. In the Surah *Āl ʿImrān* it is once again stressed that the word which is enacted in Jesus derives from God's creative power. This gives Christians the possibility of seeing in him God's new creation. At the same time, however, it is clear that Jesus is a created being and is not himself involved in God's acts of creation. For Mary's virginity, this means that it too is meant to underline God's creative power. As such, therefore, it is just as little a miracle as the creation of the world per se. For God's word entered history in Christ Jesus, as God exercised the creative power of his spirit and in so doing enabled Mary to conceive and give birth to his Word. At this point, we will break off our reading of the Surah *Āl ʿImrān*, since its focus in the verses that follow leads us completely away from Mary. Jesus gets a chance to speak at such length in these verses that it is evident that his birth must have taken place by this stage. The Surah *Āl ʿImrān* thus considers it superfluous to portray Mary's

83 We have chosen to translate the Arabic *kun fa-yakūn* as 'Be! And *it will become so*' as a way of retaining the potential interpretation that, in performing his act of creation, God implicitly involves man in his actions. For a process of becoming implies the possibility of involvement on the part of the created entity.

84 According to Q 3:59, at this point Jesus resembles Adam, and like Adam is created directly by God. In saying this, the proclaimer of the Qurʾan confirms the theology of Lk that we treated explicitly in the section above on Mary in the Bible, which begins the genealogy of Jesus with Adam thanks to the perceived affinity of the Virgin Birth with God's creation of Adam.

85 Cf. Ghaffar, 'Kontrafaktische Intertextualität im Koran und die exegetische Tradition des syrischen Christentums', 35.

confinement and the birth of Jesus, and instead has the annunciation of the angel to Mary run straight on into the pronouncements of Jesus himself.

e) Other verses from the Medinan period prior to the confrontation with Byzantium

...they denied the truth and uttered a monstrous slander against Mary (Q 4:156).

This verse occurs in the middle of a list of accusations levelled at the Jews (Q 4:155–157). Where our context is concerned, we do not need to go into these accusations in detail, or to explain why some Jews were being accused of unbelief at this point. From a mariological point of view only the second half of the verse is of interest, since the proclaimer of the Qur'an demonstrably takes Mary's side here and defends her against enmities and vilification. It is not possible to determine from the context the precise nature of these slanders. But it seems reasonable to assume that, as in the Surah *Maryam*, the point at issue was whether Mary had indulged in extramarital intercourse. This accusation had indeed played a role in Jewish apologetics of Late Antiquity, meaning that it is highly plausible that the Qur'an should respond here. Most classical commentaries of the Qur'an also interpret the verse in this way.[86]

The repetition of Mary's defence at this point makes it clear that this polemical context remained a hot topic even in Medina. Indeed, in the dispute between the Abrahamic faiths, which was conducted through competing apologetics, it seems to have taken on even greater importance, since by the Meccan period it is only Mary's relatives who are seen making accusations against her, without their religious affiliation being a subject of discussion (Q 19:27).[87] By contrast, in Q 4:156, it is the 'People of the Book' in general who are under attack (Q 4:153), and from the context it is clear that this can only mean the Jews.[88] Consequently, the attack on Mary is now revealed to be a religious polemic, and so her defence is a defence not only of her person but also of her religious significance, which the proclaimer of the Qur'an has described at length in the interim. It is interesting that this *de novo* rehabilitation of Mary and her religious role should occur in a surah whose main subject is legal provisions concerning the relation between the genders, and

86 Cf. aṭ-Ṭabarī, *Tafsīr*, vol. 7, 649; az-Zamaḫšarī, *Tafsīr*, 273; ar-Rāzī, *Tafsīr*, vol. 11, 100.
87 Of course, it might be also be the case here that only the Jews are meant. Yet the polemical religious context is not specifically thematised in the Surah *Maryam*.
88 God's covenant with Moses, recollection of the breaking of the covenant by the worship of the Golden Calf, recollection of the Sabbath commandment and recollection of the killing of prophets (Q 4:153–155) are all topoi that are clearly associated with Judaism.

which is therefore entitled *an-Nisāʾ* ('The Women'). This context allows us to see Mary's religious role as also having paradigmatic importance for the rights of women – a line of enquiry that has assumed great significance within contemporary Christian feminist theology, and which has recently been the subject of positive treatment in Islam as well.[89]

Another verse in the Surah *an-Nisāʾ* also contains a small fragment that is of Mariological interest: *People of the Book! Do not go to extremes in your religion. Speak nothing but the truth about God! The Christ Jesus, son of Mary, was only a messenger of God and His word, conveyed to Mary, a spirit from Him. Therefore believe in God and his messengers and do not say: 'Trinity!' Desist, for your own good. For God is the one and only God. His holiness is far above having a son. To him belongs whatever is in the heavens and whatever is on the earth. And God is sufficient as a trustee* (Q 4:171).

Mary appears here as the addressee of the Word of God, which is embodied within Jesus Christ. She therefore comes into contact with God, through Christ, only inasmuch as she is touched by one of his Words. The sole agent here is God; he ensures that his Word comes into contact with Mary and is directed at her.[90] This therefore reiterates the reading of God's word of creation as being an imperative, which according to Q 3:47 and Q 19:35 was what made Mary's conception of Christ possible, and once again God's prerogative is emphasised in his actions towards Mary through Jesus. Yet this verse also makes it clear that Mary has direct dealings with God and that she is touched by him – a distinction which once again suggests that we should see her story as the fulfilment of a prophetic mission.[91]

Whereas both verses from the Surah *an-Nisāʾ* are fully in keeping with the picture of Mary that was developed in the Surah *Āl ʿImrān* and also do not add any new elements to the Qurʾan's critical analysis of Judaism and Christianity, an

89 See here Tanner, *Divine words, female voices*, 121–155. We will discuss the Islamic approach to Mary in feminist theology in greater detail in Part III.

90 Qurṭūbī for instance stresses that it is God alone who created Jesus's soul and sent this soul to Mary when Jesus Christ was destined to be born into this world (Al-Qurṭubī, *al-Ǧāmiʿ*, vol. 7, 231).

91 Our talk of direct contact with God is not intended to repudiate the idea that this contact could have been mediated by angels. Accordingly, in the classical commentary literature it is important that God speaks through the angels here (cf. for example aṭ-Ṭabarī, *Tafsīr*, vol. 7, 703). Even so, the interpretation of the spirit of God in Q 19 as an angel is not obligatory, and indeed in Q 4:171 there is no longer any talk of one or several angels. As a result, perhaps one should after all seriously entertain the idea of the Word of God, which comes to Mary in the form of Jesus, entering Mary directly, notwithstanding the fact that angels set the scene for this process and are present when it takes place.

entirely new debate is indicated in the Surah *at-Taḥrīm*/'The Prohibition' (Q 66). However, this still does not point clearly enough to Byzantine Mariology to justify our including it within the section on the Qur'an's conflict with Byzantium. To begin with, therefore, all we will attempt to do is to gain an overall impression of the surah in order to better understand the context within which Mary is being spoken about here.

Tradition tells us that the subject matter of Surah *at-Taḥrīm* comprises two marital disputes between Muhammad and his wives (Q 66:1–5) that are comprehensively discussed in the classical commentaries on the Qur'an, and which end in a thematically similar way, namely with teachings concerning marital relations that are characterised by conflict (Q 66:10 f.). The citing of Mary in this context in Q 66:12 is surprising insofar as, according to the Qur'an, she had no husband to begin with. But because precisely this was a major cause of discontent in her clan and her people, the topic is not out of place in this listing. A number of markedly different situations are discussed in the closing passage of this surah. These include on the one hand religiously corrupt wives with religiously righteous husbands (Q 66:10) and on the other a religiously righteous woman with a religiously corrupt husband (Q 66:11). Mary occupies this position of religious and ethical integrity, but appears to be unique in this.

In the opening verses of the surah, Muhammad's wives are criticised for being lacking in obedience towards God (Q 66:5), and they are invited to make their connection with God stronger by showing repentance and offering up more fervent and devout prayers. In a patriarchal context, the danger would arise of the will of a man becoming identified with the will of God, and correspondingly that obedience to God would actually be enacted through obedience to a husband. And indeed, a male prophet might well be particularly prone to such behaviour. Yet, as we will presently see, this is not the point the Qur'an is seeking to make here.

Following on from this, the verses Q 66:6–8 contain direct addresses to believers (male and female alike) in which they are exhorted to show ethical behaviour. These exhortations climax in a direct address to the Prophet, who is given the task of enacting strict measures against those who deny the truth. The surah ends, as we have seen, by invoking women who might serve as warning examples, or models to be followed, to men and women. These instances show women as cautionary or inspirational examples or figures to be imitated or followed by men as well, and it is extremely interesting to see how prominent Mary is here, indeed how she forms a crowning conclusion to this list.

When, in the penultimate verse of the surah, a woman who defies her husband is praised (Q 66:11), it is clear that in the final analysis obedience is always owed solely to God. If a prophet is accorded reverence and obedience, then this is due to his special mission from God, not because of his role as a man. If a woman is as honourable and upstanding as the Pharaoh's wife and at the same time her husband played as nefarious a role as he did, the relations between the sexes are turned on their head and, to follow the Qur'an's logic, it would actually be the man who owed obedience to his wife in this case. For at root the main thing is never obedience to a person but always obedience to God, but this is exactly what the Pharaoh refuses to show, meaning that his wife is obliged to set herself apart from him. And as far as supplanting the idea that a woman has to obey her husband and to follow him through thick and thin is concerned, Mary is ultimately held up as an example. As a single woman left to fend for herself, she embodies on the one hand a supreme instance of independence, which at the same time does nothing to change her humble surrender to God's will (Q 66:12). As a result, Mary's example can help accord independence to women and surmount men's fear of such independence; we have already seen this in our reading of the commentaries on the Qur'an which dealt with Mary's incarceration in the Temple behind a series of locked doors.

Following this contextualising preamble, let us look more closely at the verse on Mary in this surah of the Qur'an: *There is also the example of Mary, 'Imrān's daughter, who preserved her chastity. We breathed Our spirit into her, and she testified to the words of her Lord and His Scriptures, and was one of the truly devout* (Q 66:12).

As in Q 21:91, Mary has the name of one who guarded her chastity – just as her virginity also become part of her personal name in Christianity ('the Virgin Mary'). The Virgin, or the 'one who preserved her chastity', is clearly Mary even when she is not mentioned by name. In the English translation, even the phrasing that follows this introduction is identical to Q 21:91. However, there is a significant difference between the two in Arabic. In the Surah *at-Taḥrīm*, it is stated that the spirit is not simply breathed into Mary, but into 'him'. Because, in Arabic, the private parts (*farǧ*) are grammatically a masculine noun, what this verse appears to be saying is that the spirit of God was breathed into Mary's vagina.

However, because of its sexually charged connotations, this statement was apparently extremely disagreeable to a large part of the Muslim classical commentary tradition.[92] And these associations were all the more unwelcome precisely

92 Nevertheless, the sexual connotations are counteracted by the fact that there is no mention of procreation. If it is correct that the formulation about breathing into the vagina in place of any talk about procreation is designed to play down a sexual interpretation, then this might

because the tradition deemed the spirit to be the comely figure of the Angel Gabriel. As a result, scholars searched for other masculine subjects that might conceivably be intended as the object of the act of breathing here. Most exegetes believed they had found the answer in Mary's robe and so explained the passage as stating that Gabriel breathed into Mary's robe.[93] Although this does not make much sense theologically, it at least has the virtue of not evoking any indecent associations.

And yet the sense of this passage in the Qur'an is perfectly self-evident when we recall the patristic interpretations of Jesus's conception. As shown above, the Church Fathers repeatedly emphasised that the conception of Jesus took place through Mary's ear.[94] Just as Eve brought evil into the world by means of the ear, so Mary receives salvation and the turnabout in human history through her ear. In Christian art, right up to the Middle Ages, this interpretation gave rise to images, for instance on church doorways, that we would find bizarre nowadays. These portrayals show the infant Jesus being sent by God down a slide into the ear of Mary. However amusing this idea might seem, it nonetheless interferes with the notion of the real humanity of Mary and Jesus, and turns the act of his conception into a totally asexual piece of magic. In opposition to this body- and sex-hostile and ultimately docetic tendency, which lends the conception of Jesus miraculous connotations, the proclaimer of the Qur'an insists upon the fact that Mary conceived perfectly normally through her vagina. For all the specialness of the emergence of Jesus, which in the Qur'an too is also brought about solely by God, at least the starting point of a person who comes into being as the result of an extraordinary new act of creation on God's part remains the one foreseen in the natural order of things. From a typological viewpoint, this of course hampers the interpretation of Mary as the new Eve, most probably because this carries with it the considerable burden of downgrading Eve, which is avoided in the Qur'an's version of the story of the Fall of Man.

When Mary is described by the Qur'an as testifying to the words of her Lord and his scriptures, then it seems to us that the most plausible interpretation is that this is another allusion to her aforementioned integrative role. For she does not just believe in the one Word of God, which she herself brings into the world, and

also explain the rejection of any idea of procreation in Q 112, though one should be wary of assuming that an attack on the Christian faith is the intention here (cf. Woyke, 'Mit Jesus ist es vor Gott wie mit Adam' (Sure 3,59), 143).

93 Cf. ar-Rāzī, *Tafsīr*, vol. 30, 50; al-Qurṭubī, *al-Ǧāmi'*, vol. 21, 106. Still, Ṭabarī and Zamaḫšarī do acknowledge that Gabriel actually breathed into Mary's vagina (cf. Yaşar, 'Die Schwangerschaft Mariens und die Geburt Jesu aus der Sicht islamischer Theologie', 13).

94 Cf. Brock, 'Introduction', 10.

hence not merely in the Gospel that is embodied in Jesus. Instead, as a Jew, she continues to believe in the Torah and, as the epitome of the devout believer, in all the words and scriptures of God as well.[95] We misunderstand Mary if we reduce her to simply being a mascot or a partisan figurehead of Christianity, and we sell her belief short if we see it as relating solely to Christian articles of faith. For it is she, the person who was closer to Jesus than anyone else, who understands the Word of God that is imparted to her through him as being inclusive, and in so doing also opens herself up to other words and scriptures of God.

In classical exegesis, this integrative role of Mary is overlooked for the most part, and in consequence commentators search for other ways to explain the plural form of 'words' and 'scriptures' here, say by identifying the words (*kalimāt*) with Jesus and the scriptures that were sent down to him,[96] or by construing the words as those of the Angel Gabriel.[97]

This latter interpretation is actually very sensible and helpful where the first part of the verse is concerned; in other words, it could well be the case that 'words' might refer to the words of the angel in the Annunciation scene and that one would therefore have to discount the possibility that the scriptures should be understood in the integrative sense that we have just outlined. If the words affirmed by Mary mean the words of the angel, then Mary's reaction here would represent the *fiat* of Mary that Christians are usually so keen to point out is missing in the Qur'an. In other words, she is here declaring her faithful readiness to follow God's annunciation to her.[98]

This interesting line of interpretation can be reinforced if one takes a closer look at the verb describing Mary's activity here, which Hartmut Bobzin renders as 'believed'. Yet the translation 'testified to/attested to' strikes us as being more appropriate here, and classical exegetes like Rāzī even go so far in their interpretation as to have Mary make the words come true.[99] This would therefore mean that

95 From the Qur'an's perspective, even Noah has faith in all of God's emissaries, despite the fact that as the first of those emissaries, he cannot yet know the others. Consequently, in the eyes of the Qur'an, Mary can also be relied upon to know all of God's scriptures, even though they were not all available in written form in her lifetime. This is not a question of supernaturally conveyed knowledge, but of the unity underlying all of God's scriptures and emissaries, which are clearly attested prophetically by Mary here.

96 Cf. az-Zamaḫšarī, *Tafsīr*, 1123.

97 Cf. al-Qurṭubī, *al-Ǧāmi'*, vol. 21, 106.

98 Qurṭubī also points in this same direction. Cf. ibid., 128.

99 '… so that she made the Words and Scriptures come true (*ǧa'alat al-kalimāta wa-l-kutuba ṣādiqatan*), which means that she distinguished them with truth (*ya'nī waṣafatha bi-ṣ-ṣidq*)' ar-Rāzī, *Tafsīr*, vol. 30, 50.

through her *fiat*, Mary makes possible the actions that God undertakes with and through her. One might also speculate whether she might not through her *fiat* bring about the fulfilment of the Old Testament word of the covenant in Jesus Christ in the first place. In this context, the Old Arabic formulation *tasdīq bi-ʿaynihī* signifies that she achieves this fulfilment through herself. This in turn might point to the fact that it is the physical realisation of the conception and birth of Jesus Christ that manifests God's Word in all its truth and makes it accessible – an interpretation that already goes a long way towards approaching the position of Christian Mariology. Classical Qur'anic exegesis attempts to forestall these kinds of excessively Christian associations by interpreting the 'words' that are affirmed here by Mary simply as assurances that she is acting in good faith (*šarāʾiʿ*). According to this interpretation, therefore, all that is being stated is that Mary did not utter untruths or give a lie to the truth through contradictory actions.[100]

At the end of this verse, Mary, in being termed 'one of the truly devout' (*mina l-qānitīn*) is given the same title as the virtuous (married) women in Q 4:34 (*qānitāt*) and also from this same surah, Q 66:5, who just like Mary are called upon to show their submission to God (*qunūt*).[101]

Mary appears as a model for women and leads an exemplary life, which is also expected of the wives of the Prophet and indeed of all (married) women. Moreover, this central religious expectation has nothing to do with a woman's behaviour towards her own husband, but solely with her attitude to God. In this, it accords with the behaviour that is exemplified by other prophets such as Adam, Noah and Abraham[102] – a parallel which once more assigns Mary a prophetic role. Mary is thus not only a role model for women but also for all men. In purely philological terms, this is already evident in the grammatical form used at the conclusion of Surah 66. If Mary were just an exemplar for women, then a grammatically feminine participle (*qānitāt*) would appear here, and not the form which in grammatical terms encompasses both the masculine and the feminine (*qānitīn*).[103]

Let us examine this emancipatory, exemplary nature of Mary's attitude a little

---

100 Cf. ibid., 50.

101 When the same verse, according to most readings, talks of women's obedience to man, it uses another word in Arabic, which does not reappear in relation to Mary. In other words, humble submission always refers solely to a person's attitude to God.

102 Cf. Ashkar, *Mary in the Syriac Christian tradition and Islam*, 122.

103 Cf. Ali, 'Destabilizing gender, reproducing maternity', 94: 'Rather than being among "devoutly obedient" women – *qāniṭāt*, which has a particular resonance in the Qur'ān, appearing in the context of marital relationships (Q Nisā' 4:34) — Mary is "among the *qāniṭīn*," those people or men who show *qunūṭ*, devout obedience (Q Taḥrīm 66:12); thus, the only specific woman identified as having *qunūṭ* has no husband.'

more closely by reconsidering the behaviour shown by the wife of the Pharaoh in the preceding verse (Q 66:11). In the Muslim commentary tradition, the seriousness of the rift between Āsiya, as the Pharaoh's wife is known in this tradition, and her husband is explained by the fact that the Pharaoh has subjected Āsiya to the worst kind of torture to try and make her renounce her faith. For Āsiya only believed in the one God and refused to worship her husband. She called on God for help, and before she died God showed her paradise. God saved her in the most magnificent way, by raising her up to be near him.[104]

In some ways, one might also say that Āsiya represents a warning to all women not to deify their husbands. In her we find someone, perhaps the only female martyr figure in the whole of the Qur'an, who bears witness to her belief and trust in God through her suffering and death. The text of the Qur'an does not tell us a great deal about her. But what we do know is that she talks to God directly using the familiar form of address, and God, at least in the accounts given by Ṭabarī and Zamaḫšarī, is constantly by her side.

The name Āsiya, which is not actually mentioned in the Qur'an but which the commentary tradition invented, comes from a word root meaning 'having a peaceable nature', 'being patient', 'giving solace', 'healing', while also conveying the sense of 'being sad' and 'suffering'.[105] The exegetes therefore encapsulated the message of the life of the Pharaoh's wife in this constellation of associations that are reminiscent of Mary and tried to express her essential qualities in her very name. Like Mary, Āsiya is in close communication with God, like Mary Āsiya has also suffered, and like Jesus and Mary she was raised up to heaven by God. It is interesting that the Muslim tradition here draws an even stronger connection than the Qur'an itself between Christian traditions concerning Mary (and Jesus!) and a prominent female figure who has distinct affinities with Mary and so appropriates her under new auspices.

In conclusion, however, let us return to Mary and provide a brief overview of what we have learnt thus far about the image of Mary that is presented in the Qur'an.

f) Summary

We have seen that the Surah *Āl 'Imrān* picks up and expands upon the concept of Mary as a figure of bridging and integration, an idea already developed within

104 Cf. az-Zamaḫšarī, *Tafsīr*, 1123; al-Qurṭubī, *al-Ǧāmi'*, vol. 21, 104.
105 Cf. Lane, *Lexicon*, vol. 1, 60–61.

the Surah *Maryam*. Now, though, it is no longer simply a question of bringing together Judaism and Christianity, but also priestly and prophetic traditions, men and women, and – through the tradition literature developed for this purpose within the classical canon of exegesis of the Qur'an – even Sunni and Shia Muslims. And countering any devaluation of the cultic tradition of Judaism, the role of ritual observance in religion is also rehabilitated.

However, in the Surah *Āl 'Imrān* not just Mary but also her mother is portrayed as being a particularly close confidante of God. It is Mary's mother who dedicates Mary to the Temple and whose prayer of intercession is offered up to God. It is through her that Mary's line of descent is established, as her husband (i.e. Mary's father) drops out of the picture on a narrative level. The same then holds true for Mary, who enters into a special intimacy with God. In addition, she is provisioned directly with all she needs by God and his angels, and so needs no male provider. Evidently, through his mother and grandmother, a large measure of women's power is passed on to the infant Jesus, but above all this intimate relationship of direct dialogue with God.

From a Christian viewpoint, what is especially remarkable is the characterisation of Mary as specially chosen and purified, indeed the distinction accorded to her as the woman who is selected above all other women of the world. From the point of view of the Qur'an, God has cleansed Mary of everything that might distract or impede her, with the result that she is entirely focused on God and her service to him. In the process, she is highly sensitive to the subtlest signs of God's favour to her and hence to the gentle and friendly pointers that God gives her in her life. For all the emphasis he places on God's prerogative, the proclaimer of the Qur'an recognises Mary's special sensitivity and receptiveness to his words, which is what enables her to have this loving, attentive attitude in the first place. And for all her classification as one of the community of believers and all the stress placed on her status as a created being, in the Qur'an Mary remains the one whom the angels address as elect before all women and as purified by God. Mary is thus clearly presented as the most outstanding example of human and female independence, precisely because she submits with such radical humility to God's will, but also because she wishes to make God's benign will a reality through her service.

If one wants to get to the heart of what makes Mary special, then one may perhaps use a formulation that picks up on and transforms the Christian idea of Mary's role as the mother of God. This involves seeing Mary as a prophetic figure, who is touched inwardly by the Word of God. She allows it to grow within her and brings it into the world. The person who on numerous occasions in the Qur'an is acknowledged as a human corporeal manifestation of God's benevolent word is given birth to by Mary. And for this reason, we may reiterate that it is precisely she, who was closer to Jesus than anyone else, who understands the Word of God that is imparted to her through him as being inclusive, and in so doing also opens herself up to other words and scriptures of God. In saying this, we have returned once more to the idea of Mary as a bridging figure who promotes inter-faith dialogue.

3

The Surah *al-Mā'ida*

With the Surah *al-Mā'ida* ('The Table') we enter the final phase of the message conveyed by the Qur'an. For the most part, both traditional exegesis and more recent historical–critical studies tend to consider this surah as one of the final surahs of the Qur'an. As a result, the general assumption has been that it was written sometime after Heraclius's victory over the Persians in 628 and in addition almost certainly after the relic of the True Cross had been brought back from Iran to Jerusalem in 630. Therefore, we may well expect to find traces in the surah of the power-political antagonism that begins to develop around this time between the movement led by Muhammad and the Byzantine Empire. It would therefore not be surprising if the image of Mary in the Qur'an were also to undergo a change, and for the political Mariology we described previously to become the main focus of attention for the proclaimer of the Qur'an. And it is indeed the case that the very first verse of the surah which has to do with Mary hints at a connection with the imperialist Mariology promoted by Heraclius.

a) Criticism of the political Mariology of Byzantium

Unbelievers indeed are those who say 'God is Christ, the Son of Mary'. Say: 'Who then has the power to prevent God, if he so desired, from destroying Christ, son of Mary, and his mother and everyone else on earth, altogether?' The kingdom of the heavens and the earth and everything between them belong to God. He creates whatever he will. God has power over all things (Q 5:17).

To begin with, we want to turn our attention to the section after the first sentence in this verse. It confronts us with the idea that neither Jesus nor his mother Mary has power over God. Both can be destroyed by God at any time if he so wished. In other words, calling upon them does not afford a person any protection whatsoever from God's wrath. Dominion over the heavens and the earth and everything in-between belongs to God alone. For the heavens and the earth and everything between them was created by God alone (Q 15:85), and everything in the heavens and the earth and in-between belongs only to him (Q 20:6). From the point of view of the Qurʾan it is therefore true to say that, even if Jesus and Mary, as a result of their faith in God and their close connection to him, are largely exempted from the limitations of human existence on earth and appear to be closer to heaven than to the earth, they nonetheless remain God's creatures and are subject to God's commands. He is the sole authority who holds the course of the world in his hands.[1]

The first thing to note is that this would also appear self-evident to Christians. In the Christian faith, too, the Son and the Holy Spirit have no power that is independent of God the Father. And Mary, as a mere human being, is in any case subject to God's will. But let us recall for a moment the imperial Mariology that became widespread in Byzantium after the successful breaking of the siege of the city in 626. For in this form of propaganda, it was indeed Mary who – seemingly all by herself – guaranteed the emperor's triumph. It was she who, as a military commander, put Byzantium's enemies to flight in the field. In the eyes of the imperial historiographers, it was her invincibility, strength and power that were solely responsible in and of themselves for vanquishing the enemy. When Theodore Synkellos, for example, claims that there was no force that could withstand the Virgin, then the proclaimer of the Qurʾan now retorts that no one has power over God and that Mary especially, as a created being, is entirely dependent upon him.

In the eyes of the proclaimer of the Qurʾan, Jesus too is a creature of God and was only created because God so ordained it. In stating this, Q 5:17 adopts the phraseology from Q 3:47 – in other words, the verse that specifically alludes to the creation of Jesus and which, in the context of the second part of the Annunciation scene, defines the role of Jesus Christ. In Q 3:40, it was sufficient to simply point out that God does what he pleases. The fact that the nature of Jesus as God's creature is now emphasised so clearly may well have to do with the Christian belief that the Word (Logos) that was made flesh in Jesus Christ was 'begotten, not made'. In Byzantine imperial theology, this conviction led to the power of

1 We are not convinced by the interpretation of Henninger, 'Mariä Himmelfahrt im Koran', 289, who believes that the fact that God can still destroy both of them signifies that they live on in paradise and therefore that not only Jesus but also Mary was taken up body and soul to heaven. From the viewpoint of the Qurʾan, it would be more appropriate to state that heaven is also part of God's domain and that he could destroy Mary there too whenever he wanted.

Jesus Christ taking on a life of its own that was seemingly wholly independent of God.[2]

We may also gauge from the final verses of the surah how ever-present the imperial theology of Byzantium was in the mind of the proclaimer of the Qur'an during this phase of imparting his message. Thus, the surah ends with the declaration that the kingdom of the heavens and the earth and everything in them belongs to God and that he has power over all things (Q 5:120) – a clear rejection of all attempts to shore up imperial power by invoking Mary or Jesus. The general thrust of the final verse in this direction is made even clearer somewhat earlier, when it is stated with regard to the Christian community: *If You* [i.e. God] *punish them, they are surely Your servants, and if You forgive them, You are surely the Mighty and Wise* (Q 5:118). Hence, both Jesus and Mary are subject to the prerogative of God, who alone guides the destiny of the world. And it is God alone whom men should serve (Q 5:117). The idea that calling upon Mary makes her into an authority that can determine the course of history is clearly rebutted. In the Qur'an's view it was thus not Mary, but God and no one else, who saved Constantinople – provided, that is, one assumes that supernatural forces played a role at all in this, something which was taken for granted by the inhabitants of Byzantium in Late Antiquity. Byzantine theologians too would no doubt have come down strongly in favour of God's prerogative if they had been called upon to determine theologically the principal agent of human destiny. But this did not alter the fact that the emperor, his court historians and also the Byzantine Patriarch all preached in such a manner as to create the impression that Mary had at her disposal an independent power to which people could entrust themselves when they needed help.

Yet this runs the risk of selling short Mary's true humanity – and indeed the genuinely human nature of Jesus. In this misreading, both are endowed with

2 Zishan Ghaffar indicates that, as early as the mid-Meccan period, the Qur'an also identified this danger and therefore began to argue against this attempt by Heraclius to co-opt the ideal of the Davidic Messiah into his ideology of rulership. For example, in the context of the dispute with the Queen of Sheba over Heraclius's imperious conduct, Ghaffar claims that in Q 27:30 the Qur'an responds by citing the *Basmala* ('in the name of God, the Most Gracious, the Most Merciful') as the ruling motto of Solomon (cf. Ghaffar, *Der Koran in seinem religions- und weltgeschichtlichen Kontext*, 105). However, it strikes us as improbable that Heraclius would appear this early as the focus of attention of debates within the Qur'an. A simpler explanation would be that the Qur'an is here presenting a stylised image of the devout ruler in marked contrast to rulers of southern Arabia such as Abraha – an interpretation that even Ghaffar himself deems likely (ibid., 106). In any event, it is clear that the Qur'an, from an anti-imperial standpoint, consistently displays a high degree of scepticism towards any form of messianically charged theology (cf. ibid., 110). As yet, Mary plays no part in these early Qur'anic verses concerning anti-imperial theology.

divine powers and hence, from a Qur'anic point of view, are no longer appropriately acknowledged as God's creatures. Let us therefore take a closer look at the first sentence of Q 5:17, which we initially chose to skip over; although this relates solely to Jesus Christ, it nonetheless opens a theological front that will also prove instructive for our examination of Mary.

b) Criticism of the imperial downplaying of Mary's humanity

Unbelievers indeed are those who say 'God is Christ, the Son of Mary' (Q 5:17).

This unconventional phraseology is repeated verbatim once more in Q 5:72. The phrasing is unusual insofar as one would actually expect the sentence to have the word order reversed. To state that Jesus Christ possesses a divine nature and that he therefore can in a sense be designated as a God or at least as God-like is a familiar sentiment to which the proclaimer of the Qur'an might easily relate. The Council of Chalcedon, for example, issued a Definition which expressly declared that Jesus Christ was 'perfect both in deity and in humanness; this selfsame one is also actually God and actually man' – leading to the obvious conclusion that we should see him as divine or accord him a divine nature. Instead, the proclaimer of the Qur'an reverses the word order and does not talk in terms of Christ being God, but of God being Christ.

The overwhelming majority of Christians – both in Late Antiquity and nowadays – would surely object to this intensification. For even though they would agree that Christ is God's essential Word, and hence to that extent that God is inherent within him, that does not however mean that God can be reduced to the figure of Jesus Christ. From a Christian perspective, God has a trinitarian structure and cannot be reduced to one of the persons. Consequently, not only for Late Antiquity but also for us nowadays, this formulation in the Qur'an is extremely odd.

This peculiarity was also noticed by classical Muslim commentary literature. Some commentators speculated that there might perhaps be some Christians, for example the Christian community of Nağrān,[3] who spoke about God in this way, albeit without providing any proof to back up this statement. Others admitted that Christians did not say such a thing directly, but took the view nonetheless that it was implicitly contained within their religion,[4] for instance in the article of faith which claims that Jesus is a creator in his own right and can give life, bring death

3 Cf. Muqātil, *Tafsīr*, vol. 1, 463.
4 Cf. ar-Rāzī, *Tafsīr*, vol. 11, 195.

and affect the destiny of the world.[5] Yet because Christians make a special point, in the theory of the hypostatic union and trinitarian theology, of repudiating any simple identification of God with Christ, it is questionable to attribute this kind of belief to them.

One can certainly try to explain this formulation as a deliberate misrepresentation of Christian beliefs by the proclaimer of the Qur'an for polemical purposes. But although the polemical intention behind twisting an opponent's words in this way is to expose them to ridicule, it loses its impact if it is based on a credo that is not even accepted by Christians in the form in which it is cited. Plus, if we accept that the Qur'an is the Word of God, it also reduces the Muslim faith to absurdity. For it would be truly strange to think of a God whose polemical intent was to traduce the beliefs of others by twisting their words. As a result, it seems more pertinent in our view to investigate the question of who might possibly have expressed the relationship between God and Christ in such a way in Christian Late Antiquity. Who then really claimed that God is Christ? Or whose theology might have given this impression, leaving aside any polemical distortion of the truth?

Interestingly, our hunt for clues on this score takes us back to Byzantium, more specifically to the Theopaschite controversy, namely the dispute over whether God himself suffered on the Cross and whether God is therefore capable of suffering. In the 530s, Justinian, first in his role as the military strongman behind the then-emperor Justin I and subsequently as emperor in his own right after 532, attempted to promote the position of Scythian monks, who maintained that one of the Trinity had genuinely suffered in the flesh on the Cross.[6] Fully intending to remain faithful to the Roman interpretation of the Chalcedonian Definition, these monks developed a theology of the suffering God, who is entirely present in the Word and hence also present at the Crucifixion, where he reveals himself. Joannes Maxentius, the leader of the Scythian monks, was adamant that God had really become Christ in this context.[7] As such, this formulation is certainly somewhat unusual, containing as it does the inverted sequence evident in the Qur'anic text. Even so, in the light of the formulation that continued to be commonly used in patristics, namely that God became man, it could undoubtedly be interpreted in such a way as to cause little offence within the Christian community. Yet when

5 Cf. az-Zamaḫšarī, *Tafsīr*, 283.

6 Cf. Uthemann, 'Kaiser Justinian als Kirchenpolitiker und Theologe', 21–23.

7 Cf. ibid., 20. On the exact formulation presented in Joannes Maxentius, *Libellus fidei*, see: F. Glorie (ed.), *Maxentii aliorumque Scytharum monachorum ...opuscula (CChr.SL 85A)*, Turnhout 1978, 5–25.

taken together with the talk of the real suffering of God on the Cross, it does actually give rise to the kind of interpretation that the proclaimer of the Qurʾan is criticising here. At this point it seems anything but wilful to take the utterances of the Scythian monks as meaning not just that Christ is God, but also that God is the person whom he has become, namely Christ.

Theologically this inversion of the usual sequence of the Christian credo strikes us nowadays as of little use, even under Christian auspices, but Emperor Justinian seems to have consistently defended the position of the Scythian monks. In saying this, one should also be aware that Justinian's rule, as well as that of his successors – a period which included the time when the Qur'an came into being – was defined by a dispute within Christianity regarding the Council of Chalcedon (451). While Justinian and his successors defended Chalcedon and its decision that Jesus Christ possessed two natures, there arose within the Church throughout the Near and Middle East an oppositional movement, which gained steadily in strength and which insisted that Jesus Christ could only have one nature. During Justinian's reign, this led to a schism within the Church, and the so-called Eastern Churches formed their own hierarchies, each of which was opposed to the doctrinal developments that had taken place since Chalcedon. Anti-Chalcedonian, so-called Miaphysite Christology, which rejected the Two Natures doctrine, was extremely well established in the Near East before Justinian's uncle and predecessor Justin ascended the throne in 518 and proceeded to implement unequivocally pro-Chalcedonian ecclesiastical policies. Prior to this, under the pro-Miaphysite Emperor Anastasius (r. 491–515), the scholar Philoxenus of Mabbug was undoubtedly the most influential disseminator of this Miaphysite Christology. He was insistent that it really was God himself who shouldered the burden of the Cross and who suffered and died for us.[8] The idea of God's suffering and hence the belief that it is God himself who is Jesus Christ became the trademark of Philoxenus's theology and also the confessional shibboleth of the Miaphysite movement.

Furthermore, this idea became widespread after the Miaphysite Patriarch of Antioch Peter the Fuller, a close confederate of Philoxenus, altered the *Trisagion* ('Thrice Holy') chant that was repeated in all liturgies – 'Holy God, Holy Strong, Holy Immortal, have mercy on us' – by inserting the words 'who was crucified

8 Cf. Viezure, 'Philoxenus of Mabbug and the controversies over the "Theopaschite" Trisagion', 139: 'Philoxenus argues that the strong formulations "God the Word died", "God died", "the Immortal died", "One of the Trinity died" are needed in order to maintain the uniqueness of subject in Christ and to uphold orthodoxy.'

for us' directly after 'Immortal'.[9] This new liturgical acclamation – the so-called Theopaschite *Trisagion* – reworked to reflect the theology of God's suffering, became so much the hallmark of Miaphysitism that, when the pro-Chalcedonian Emperor Anastasius attempted to introduce it in Constantinople, the pro-Chalcedonian (and hence anti-Miaphysite) faction was able to foment a massive, bloody uprising against it.[10] When the Scythian monks now adopted this theology of the suffering God, but at the same time interpreted it within the framework of the Two Natures doctrine, in Justinian's eyes they were providing an opportunity for reconciliation between the two opposing groups within the Church.

It was for that very reason that, in 533, Justinian made the phrase 'One of the Trinity', a formula used by the Scythian monks in order to express the suffering of this one person of the Trinity (*unus ex trinitate passus est*), the official title of Christ. Of course, this title also contained resonances of Philoxenus's idea that God is this 'One of the Trinity' and that he himself suffered and died.[11] An edict made the use of this title mandatory throughout the empire and in 534 Justinian also persuaded Rome to adopt it.[12] But to assume that it is the immortal God who suffers on the Cross and dies only validates the accusation that this simply identifies God with Christ, and that God is therefore Christ. If one is aware of the factual connection between the title 'One of the Trinity' and the accusation that God is Christ, which is thereby justified in this context, then it is fascinating to note that both formulations are reproduced and attacked in the text of the Qur'an.

Unbelievers indeed are those who say 'God is Christ, the Son of Mary.' For Christ himself said: 'Children of Israel, serve God, my Lord, and your Lord.' If anyone associates anything with God, God will bar him from entering Paradise and the fire of Hell will be his only place of refuge. The wrongdoers shall have no helpers. Unbelievers are those who say: 'God is one of three.' There is only One God! If they do not desist from such talk, a painful punishment will be bound to befall the deniers of the truth (Q 5:72 f.).

According to Sidney Griffith, the Arabic phrase *ṯāliṯu ṯalāṯatin*, translated here as 'God is one of three', is a loan coinage from Syriac that picks up on the title of

9 Cf. Viezure, 'Philoxenus of Mabbug and the controversies over the "Theopaschite" Trisagion'; Halleux, 'Le Mamlelā de "Ḥabbīb" contre Aksenāyā', 67 f.; Abramowski, 'Aus dem Streit um das "Unus ex trinitate passus est"', 570–647.

10 Cf. Meier, *Staurotheis di'hemas*, 157–237.

11 Cf. Philoxenus Mabbugensis, 'Dissertationes decem de uno e sancta trinitate incorporato et passo.' Edited by Maurice Brière and François Graffin, *Patrologia Orientalis* 15, Paris 1920 and *Patrologia Orientalis* 38–41, Turnhout 1977–1982.

12 Cf. Uthemann, 'Kaiser Justinian als Kirchenpolitiker und Theologe', 34 f.

Christ as one of the Trinity just mentioned above.[13] Behind this title, rejected by the Qurʾan, is a Theopaschite tendency which accords well with the new Chalcedonian theology that was prevalent at the time and which stands in the tradition of Cyril of Alexandria – more specifically in the tradition, so to speak, of the right wing of the school of thought that bears Cyril's name, which was widespread in Constantinople, but which also resonated with some Syrian theologians. For Philoxenus of Mabbug, for example, as we have already noted above, it was clear that it was God himself who had died on the Cross. This extreme theological position, which even nowadays a majority of Christians would reject – notwithstanding the prominent place which Jürgen Moltmann accords to it[14] – became a distinctive mark of identity for West Syrian Christians, primarily as a way of distinguishing themselves polemically from East Syrians and Chalcedonians. And it was convenient for imperial theology to try and adopt this distinguishing feature when it was keen to bring the West Syrians back into the Byzantine fold. Thus, the Christian theology so roundly rejected in Q 5:72 and Q 5:73 is official imperial theology, to which the proclaimer of the Qurʾan finds himself in opposition not merely from theological considerations. In theological terms, this imperial theology is difficult to understand, not just according to modern criteria but also the conventional philosophical theology of Late Antiquity.

As a result, the adverse reaction in the Qurʾan is especially vehement, and drastic threats are issued against anyone espousing these views – including severe retribution and the fires of Hell. The accusation of 'associating anything with God' in Q 5:72, which the proclaimer of the Qurʾan does not otherwise level at Christians, is particularly dramatic. Indeed, those who make such associations are frequently mentioned in lists that also name Christians, thus indicating that these two groups are seen as quite distinct from one another. Yet in Q 5:72, those who are being threatened with exclusion from the garden of paradise, and hence from God's presence, are clearly those who identify God with Christ and hence follow Byzantine imperial theology. For if one reduces God to Christ, he effectively becomes his own factioneer and is also laid open to exploitation in military contexts, thus paving the way for military triumphalism – and this is precisely what the proclaimer of the Qurʾan wants to warn against. But in his eyes, Justinian's tactical relationship with the truth that is already revealed by such an approach

13 Cf. Griffith, 'Al-Naṣārā in the Qurʾān', 317; for a more extensive account, see Griffith, 'Syriacisms in the "Arabic Qurʾān": Who were "those who said 'Allāh is the third of three" according to al-Māʾida 73?', 100–108.

14 Cf. Moltmann, *Der gekreuzigte Gott*.

would appear to be especially striking. For he is seen to be employing counter-intuitive and irrational formulations that he himself would not normally use from his own theological standpoint, but from which he expects to gain political capital. The talk of God therefore enters the service of vested political interests. At this point, the proclaimer of the Qur'an draws a clear line of demarcation. The aim of religion must always be devotion to God, and everything else must be subordinate to this objective. If theological proclamations are developed with the aim of ensnaring political opponents, and a tactical relationship with the truth gains ground, then this places the core of faith in serious jeopardy.

Yet Mary still plays no role whatsoever in the verses treated thus far here. This only changes at verse 75, which at the same time reveals a new theological context, pointing to an imperial theological project of reconciliation instigated by Justinian. Let us first examine the verse in question in its immediate context.

c) On the significance of Mary's eating

Christ, the Son of Mary, was no more than a messenger. Many messengers had come and gone before him. His mother was a virtuous woman and they both ate food! See how We make the signs [āyāt] *clear to them* [nubayyinu]*! Yet see how they are deluded!* (Q 5:75).

The first statement about Mary here identifies her as a virtuous woman. Another possible translation of the Arabic is that Mary was a woman of truth. Commentators in the classical tradition speculate whether this might mean that Mary trusted Gabriel's message to her,[15] or that she bore witness to the truth through her actions.[16] According to Rāzī, the Qur'an bestows on Mary the soubriquet 'the virtuous one' because, as he puts it, she is so far removed from showing any disobedience to God and engages joyously in service to God and in venerating him.[17] Whatever the precise meaning of this first phrase describing her, it certainly harmonises well with the Christian interpretation of Mary and demonstrates that she is held in high regard in Islam.

This makes it all the more perplexing when the next thing said about her is that Mary and Jesus ate food (Q 5:75). Our puzzlement derives from the fact that, from the Wedding at Cana in John 2 onwards, eating and drinking by Mary and Jesus play a large part in the New Testament, thus making it hard to understand why the

15 Cf. Muqātil, *Tafsīr*, vol. 1, 495.
16 Cf. aṭ-Ṭabarī, *Tafsīr*, vol. 8, 582.
17 Cf. ar-Rāzī, *Tafsīr*, vol. 12, 65.

proclaimer of the Qurʾan should feel the need to remind Christians of this. And when one considers that Christian remembrance of Jesus Christ in the Eucharist is first and foremost a recollection of his role in the Last Supper, this statement in the Qurʾan is utterly mystifying.

Nor is the classical Muslim commentary literature of much help on this score. It simply chooses to ignore any potential Christian objection and declares the passage in the Qurʾan as a necessary corrective aimed at bringing Christians to their senses. Commentators are unanimous in postulating that eating is to be seen here as a token of created beings' dependence upon their creator. The fact that Jesus and Mary have to eat thus underlines their human nature and their dependence upon God.[18] However, Christians would naturally retort here that they were fully in agreement with this and that Jesus and Mary in their humanness are unquestionably created beings,[19] making it perfectly normal they should require food. So what is the point of the Qurʾan's reminder?

To begin with, one might be tempted to search here for an unorthodox Christian viewpoint with which the Qurʾan is taking issue, to the effect that Jesus and Mary did not need sustenance. And it is true that, in the fifth and sixth centuries, there existed on the Arabian Peninsula a widespread Christian grouping whose doctrines have largely been forgotten but who might conceivably fit the bill here.[20] Moreover, from the early sixth century onwards, Bishop Julian of Halicarnassus (died c. 527) did indeed develop a doctrine that denied the necessity of eating in Jesus's case.[21]

According to Julian, before the Fall of Man people knew neither hunger nor death nor suffering. At the same time, he was adamant that Jesus was born without

18 Cf. Muqātil, *Tafsīr*, vol. 1, 495; aṭ-Ṭabarī, *Tafsīr*, vol. 8, 582–583; az-Zamaḫšarī, *Tafsīr*, 303; ar-Rāzī, *Tafsīr*, vol. 12, 65.

19 Qurṭubī accuses Christians of becoming muddled in their doctrinal statements, and in so doing blurring the clear distinction between God and created beings (al-Qurṭubī, *al-Ǧāmiʿ*, vol. 8, 101). The Christian response, of course, would be to point to the Council of Chalcedon and insist that a divine nature and a human nature coexisted, unalloyed and unchanged, in Christ. However consistent one judges the Two Natures doctrine to be, one would at least have to concede that it is not meant to signal an intermingling of the divine and the human, and that the human Jesus had to eat in the same way as we do.

20 On the spread of Julianism on the Arabian Peninsula from the sixth to the eighth century, see Debié, 'Les controverses miaphysites en Arabie et le Coran', 145–148. Interestingly, the oasis town of Naǧrān appears to have been a major centre of Julianism.

21 The following account of Julianism basically summarises the central ideas of Khorchide and von Stosch, *Der andere Prophet*, 37–45, and in the process cites some formulations verbatim. However, we have also changed and expanded upon some of that work's findings, in addition to correcting certain errors.

sin and therefore remained unaffected by the consequences of the fall from grace. But the fact that, in spite of this, Jesus was still forced to starve, suffer and perish was not a result of his nature but instead because he wished it so. Nonetheless, in Julian's eyes, Jesus was a real person – albeit one endowed with the prelapsarian attributes of a human being.[22] Therefore, Julian was in no way seeking to deny that Jesus really did grow weary or feel hunger or that he suffered repeatedly. Like us, Jesus sustained his physical being by eating and drinking.[23] His incorruptible body assumed a genuinely human nature.[24] To this extent, Julian does not mean to deny the reality of Jesus's suffering, but is simply insistent that, even in his suffering, Jesus was exercising his free will. That is, Jesus remained by nature essentially immune to suffering, and it required a voluntary act of will on his part, free from any human constraint, for him to experience it.[25] Julian was therefore at pains to emphasise Jesus's complete freedom and sovereignty – in his Passion as well as in the matter of eating and drinking. Thus, when Jesus returns after forty days of fasting in the wilderness, he only experiences hunger to the extent he does because he wants to show solidarity with us.

However, the fragments of Julian's doctrine that have been preserved do not give any indication that he extended his thesis to also incorporate Mary.[26] Certainly, it would seem obvious from a Catholic point of view to include her in Julian's doctrine, since – as we have seen above – she is deemed in the dogmatic definition of the Immaculate Conception formulated in 1854 to have been born free from original sin. Yet it is a matter of contention how widespread this belief was in Late Antiquity. In any event, Julian does not appear to have espoused it, nor was such a view represented among the Syriac Church Fathers as we noted above. Even so, it was already the case in their view that Mary was cleansed of all guilt by the birth of Jesus Christ and hence was thought to be free from original sin. Consequently, Jacob of Serugh likens Mary from that moment on to Adam before the fall from grace and applies this to her giving birth to Jesus.[27] Even though no direct statements by the

22 Cf. Draguet, *Julien d'Halicarnasse*, 119.
23 Cf. ibid., 160.
24 Cf. ibid., 161.
25 Cf. ibid., 187.
26 For the fragments of Julian's writings, Cf. ibid., *Appendix: Iuliani Halicarnassensis fragmenta dogmatica*. The early church father Severus of Antioch, for example, who was strongly inclined toward the idea of the incorruptibility of Jesus's body, although he would later become the most vehement opponent of Julian's doctrine of Christ's incorruptibility prior to the Resurrection, was clearly of the opinion that this was not the case for Mary (Moss, *Incorruptible bodies*, 120).
27 Cf. Jacob of Serugh, *On the mother of God: Homily I*, 36.

Syriac Church Fathers on the matter of Mary's partaking of food after the birth of Jesus can be found, at least with regard to Jesus it is clear to Ephrem the Syrian that he only felt hunger and thirst because he wanted to.[28] For him, the hero Jesus must first learn how to feel these sensations because such a thing was not inevitable in his human nature, which was untouched by original sin.[29]

Therefore, the notion of Jesus having no necessity to eat or drink was not peculiar to Julian, but was also widespread among the Syriac Church Fathers. Furthermore, it is interesting to note that in sixth-century Byzantium, the important court theologian and representative of the new Chalcedonian doctrine of enhypostasis, Leontius of Byzantium, wrote a work in opposition to other Chalcedonians in the city who advocated a form of Julianism, but that he nonetheless found himself in full agreement not only with the Julianists (as well as the Chalcedonian Aphthartodocetes) but also with all Christian theologians of that time in assuming the *de facto* incorruptibility of the physical body of Jesus even before the Resurrection, namely during his entombment. The essential difference, though, lay in the question of whether this *de facto* incorruptibility was an inherent property of the pre-Resurrection body of Christ (the Julianist position) or the result of a miracle or a divine act of free will (the anti-Julian position).[30] The idea that Jesus, by dint of the union of his human nature with his divine nature, did not actually need to eat or drink anything unless he felt like doing so, was therefore well established in Byzantium too. Indeed, even the great church father Maximus the Confessor, who was active at the time when the Qur'an was emerging, was of the opinion that Jesus did not feel hunger and thirst in the same way that we do, 'but instead in a superior way to us, namely voluntarily.'[31]

Generally speaking, among the Greek Church Fathers there were two schools of thought whose theological beliefs led them to the assumption that Jesus did not have to eat anything. Both schools were influential but did not represent the totality of opinion. In other words, there were many church fathers – most notably Diodorus of Tarsus, Theodore of Mopsuestia and John Chrysostom, together with the representatives of Eastern Syrian theology – for whom it was absolutely beyond dispute that Jesus needed to eat and drink just like us, though even they took the view that the combination of human and divine nature within Jesus Christ, and hence a hard-to-define participation of his human nature, with its physical needs,

28 Cf. Ephrem the Syrian, *Hymnen de nativitate*, 11,5.

29 Cf. ibid., 11,8.

30 Cf. Uthemann, 'Kaiser Justinian', 80.

31 Maximus the Confessor, *Disputatio cum Pyrrho*, 297D, quoted in Bausenhart, 'In allem uns gleich außer der Sünde', 203.

in his divine nature, which had no such needs (the so-called *communicatio idiomatum*), always had to be borne in mind. The first of the schools mentioned above believed simply that Jesus did not have to eat thanks to his divine nature. With this in mind, Maximus for example was of the opinion that the hypostatic union altered Christ's relationship with the natural requirements of human nature. This theological interpretation is certainly not applicable to Mary, and also seems to have been the driving force behind Leontius's arguments.

By contrast, the other school of thought, which first and foremost characterised Julianism but was also strongly reflected in certain positions taken by Maximus, maintained that the physical body itself should be seen as a result of the fall from grace. Its proponents pointed to the loincloth which according to Genesis 3:7 Eve and Adam are required to make for themselves in order to cover their nakedness. Typologically, this cloth becomes a symbol of the body, which becomes a given fact in its customary biological functions only after the Fall of Man; consequently it is also only from that point on that it requires food. This viewpoint, which was represented by Origen and Gregory of Nyssa,[32] is largely in accordance with Julianism. It also seems to us to lie at the root of the comments made by Ephrem the Syrian, and basically amounts to making biological bodily functions the subject of an act of free will on Jesus's part – in other words, in this theological doctrine Jesus only has to eat because he wills himself to require food. On the basis of the story of the Fall of Man and the conception of Jesus as the new Adam, this doctrine also becomes applicable to Mary, who, as we have seen earlier, is regarded as the new Eve by the Church Fathers almost without exception. All the same, this application is not well attested.[33] Although we do not have any

32 Cf. Gregory of Nyssa, *De anima et resurrectione*, ed. by A. Spira (Gregorii Nysseni Opera 3/3), Leiden-Boston 2014, 113, 20–114, 7; See also Nellas, *Le vivant divinisé*. On the pioneering – though in itself less than unequivocal – position taken by Origen or the Origenists, cf. *Selecta in Genesim (fragmenta e catenis), Patrologia Graeca 12*, 101A-B; see also Guillaumont, *Les ‚Képhalaia Gnostica' d'Évagre le Pontique et l'histoire de l'origénisme chez les Grecs et chez les Syriens*, 109, f. 131; Thunberg, *Microcosm and mediator*, 159.

33 Nonetheless, we have been able to find at least two instances. A letter written to Severus of Antioch, the principal opponent of Julian of Halicarnassus, contains explicit criticism of heretics who regard Mary, like Jesus, as being incorruptible (cf. Brock, 'A letter from the orthodox monasteries', 39). In his commentary, Brock maintains that there is no other evidence of anyone adopting such a position (ibid., 43). Another instance is when Leontius asks his Julianist interlocutor whether, in the light of his argument, he does not consider Mary's physical body to be incorruptible as well. Though his adversary denies that, he does at the same time admit that other followers of Julianism believe it to be true (cf. Leontius of Byzantium, *Complete Works*, ed. Brian E. Daley, Oxford 2017, 350–352).

sources corroborating the existence of Julianist ideas on the Arabian Peninsula in the seventh century, we should beware of setting too much store by this lack of evidence, since we can still identify a positive surge in Marian devotion throughout the whole of the Byzantine Empire in the century prior to the emergence of the Qurʾan. Put quite simply, it seems highly likely that theologians, no matter whether they were broadly associated with Julianism or opposed to it, came to include Mary within the doctrine of the incorruptibility of the body of Christ. Indeed, one can even read Q 5:75 as historical evidence of this development. And the fact that we noted above of Mary's clothes after the siege of Constantinople in 619 also being venerated for their indestructibility[34] – as if the incorruptibility of Mary's body had somehow been transferred to her garments – is at least an indication that, beyond the realm of scholarly theology, a popular belief in the incorruptibility of Mary's body was also widespread in Byzantium.

In any event, it appears to have been this form of theology – at least as regards the person of Jesus Christ – that also became a constituent part of official imperial theology towards the end of Justinian's life. In an edict to the Romans published in late 564 or early 565, Emperor Justinian defended the position that the body of Jesus Christ was incorruptible, and in so doing voiced a central theme of the doctrine of Julian of Halicarnassus. The church historian Evagrius Scholasticus (d. 600), who was born in Syria, thus reported that the emperor, shortly before his death, embraced the Julian heresy, which Evagrius characterises as claiming 'that the Lord ate in the same way before his Passion as he did after his resurrection.'[35]

However, this characterisation does not do justice to Julianism, and we have already seen that Leontius of Byzantium adopted the central tenet of Julianism that is criticised here. The context of Justinian's espousal of this theological idea may be that the emperor was seeking to further lower the temperature in religious politics. Thus, not long before, he had also entered into negotiations with the Nestorians and explored the possibility of compromises with them.[36] Perhaps Justinian was now attempting to find some rapprochement with the Armenians, who had also espoused Julianism.[37] Certainly, the incorruptibility of the body of Christ was an idea that was also defended by other supporters of the Council of

34 Cf. once again Wenger, 'Les interventions de Marie', 424.

35 Quoted in Uthemann, 'Kaiser Justinian', 79; see also Grillmeier, *Jesus der Christus im Glauben der Kirche*, vol. 2, 492.

36 Cf. Uthemann, 'Kaiser Justinian', 77 f.

37 Cf. Michael van Esbroeck, 'The Aphthartodocetic Edict of Justinian and Its Armenian Background.' In: *Studia Patristica* 33 (1997) 578–585.

Chalcedon, as the aforementioned work of Leontius of Byzantium proves.[38] This position was attractive where the politics of religion were concerned, because its doctrine offered the possibility of circumventing the irresolvable internal contradictions in the Two Natures doctrine that the Anti-Chalcedonians had highlighted: both the full divinity as well as the full humanity of Jesus Christ appeared to be preserved, insofar as the human nature of Adam *before* the Fall was understood to be the true definition of humanness.[39] As a consequence, it is perfectly possible to also see the Julian position as a politically interesting theological attempt at mediation, and it is conceivable that the emperor, who took a lively interest in theological matters, was keen to adopt it. But equally, it could simply have been that the emperor, who had a natural bent towards asceticism, found it an utterly intolerable notion that the earthly Jesus should have eaten food in the same way we do, and hence also had a digestive system just like ours. According to this way of thinking, even his earthly body appears to be like the pneumatic body of the Risen Christ, which according to the testimony of the gospels could pass through walls and so was not subject to the same earthly constraints as our bodies.

We can only speculate on this point; we have no idea whether Justinian also saw Mary's body as being similarly incorruptible. One thing that is apparent here is that the proclaimer of the Qur'an once more targets a theological doctrine in which Byzantine imperial politics try to gloss over theological contradictions with questionable formulaic compromises. Here, too, the implication is that the emperor has a tactical relationship with the truth. He certainly takes a position that is open to numerous misunderstandings. For if the human nature of Jesus is conceived in such a way that it is imperishable, it is easy to imagine that it shares in God's indestructibility and could therefore offer effective protection in situations of military threat as well. This would bring us back to the exploitation of the figure of Mary to military ends, a misappropriation of which Emperor Heraclius was demonstrably guilty, and which has definite affinities to the theological positions outlined here. For if Mary's body is thought of as indestructible, and her

---

38 On the idea of the incorruptibility of the bodies of prophets in the Islamic tradition, cf. Abū Dāwūd, *Sunan*, Hadith No. 1047, Book No. 2 (*Kitāb aṣ-ṣalāh*), Vol. 1, 612 and on the immortality of Muslims who died in the Battle of Uḥud starben cf. Malik ibn Anas, *al-Muwaṭṭa'*, Hadith No. 50, Book No. 21 (*Kitāb al-ǧihād*). English translation: Bewley, *Aisha Abdurrahman, Al-Muwaṭṭa' of Imam Mālik ibn Anas. Arabic & English*, 566 f.

39 Cf. Kate Adshead, 'Justinian and Aphthartodocetism.' In: Stephen Mitchell and Geoffrey B. Greatrex (eds.), *Ethnicity and culture in Late Antiquity*, London 2000, 331–336, here p. 333.

cloak likewise, it seems reasonable that her image would also be able to protect the walls and gates of Byzantium. Her course was thus set to become the *de facto* tutelary goddess of imperial politics.

Contrary to such delusions, the proclaimer of the Qur'an reminds us of the true symbolic function of Mary and Jesus (Q 5:75), and insists that God alone is the All-Seeing and the All-Knowing (Q 5:76). In saying this, the proclaimer of the Qur'an picks up on the profession of faith that was already made prominently by Mary's mother in the Surah *Āl 'Imrān* (Q 3:35) and which in general can be said to serve as a heading to the whole story of Mary (Q 3:34). The proclaimer of the Qur'an wants to lead us back to this biblical–Qur'anic Mary, and thus divest her of Heraclius's imperial propaganda. Thus, in opposition to imperialist propaganda, the Qur'an posits a theology of signs, into which it integrates Jesus and Mary.

In addition, the proclaimer of the Qur'an endeavours throughout to accommodate the theological intuitions of his Christian audience. For the Surah *Āl 'Imrān* had already conceded the essential purity of Mary (Q 3:42). At the same time, Mary was shown as having been constantly provided with sustenance by the angels when she was a child. While other people – from a biblical standpoint, as a result of the fall from grace – were forced to obtain their food by the sweat of their brow (Genesis 3:17–19), God or his angels provide directly for Mary (Q 3:37) and so preserve her from that which Christians regard as the consequences of the Fall of Man. Also during her confinement, as portrayed in the Surah *Maryam*, dates are provided for her without any effort on her part (Q 19:25 f.). Mary is therefore consistently described as someone who is protected and accompanied by God and thus preserved from sin and its consequences. However, this does not mean that her human nature is altered in any way.

Furthermore, this theological insistence on the real humanity of Mary and Jesus is of central importance for Christian theology. For in the Christian doctrine of salvation, everything depends upon God truly touching all human hardships and transforming them in a beneficial way. The position of Christian theology must therefore inevitably be that if Jesus did not really know at first hand what it was like to be exposed to hunger, then he would be incapable of saving us from such afflictions. And if Mary did not truly know human pain, she would hardly be the *mater dolorosa* with the capacity to comfort us in our distress. Accordingly, the Qur'an's theology of signs is far closer to the testimony of the Bible than the imperial utilisation of Christology and Mariology to promote Heraclius's political and military ambitions.

d) Limits and opportunities of the presentation of Mary in the Surah *al-Mā'ida*

In conclusion, let us briefly discuss the closing passage of the Surah *al-Mā'ida* (Q 5:109–120). Structurally, these last eleven verses of the surah form the counterpoint to the first eleven verses. The surah begins with verses that were revealed to Muhammed at the end of his life and which in terms of their content have something of a concluding character in the manner of a bequest. Parallel with this, the surah ends with verses in which Jesus's farewell and bequest to his community come into play. The miracles Jesus performed are called to mind (Q 5:110) and the convening of the Last Supper is vividly depicted (Q 5:112–113). This is followed by another warning against deifying Jesus and his mother. To quote this passage verbatim: *When God says 'Jesus, son of Mary, did you ever ask people to worship you and your mother beside God?', he will answer: 'Glory be to You! How could I ever say what I had no right to say? And if I had said such a thing, you surely would have known it; for you know what is in my mind, while I do not know anything that is within Yours.' You alone are the Knower of unseen things* (Q 5:116).

This scene clearly plays out on the Day of Judgement, and God poses a purely rhetorical question here when he enquires of Jesus if he ever instructed him to set himself and his mother up as deities beside God. Even the classical commentators of the Qur'an recognise the purely rhetorical nature of this question. Of course, Jesus did nothing of the kind. The question is not therefore intended as an attack on Jesus but as a criticism of all those who might disagree with this.[40] But which Christians is the Qur'an referring to here, Rāzī is one of the first to ask, given that no Christian would conceivably claim that Jesus and Mary were deities or question the divinity of God?

Rāzī explains the entire passage by stating that Christians believe that Jesus and Mary were themselves responsible for bringing about the miraculous things that happened to them. In this interpretation, therefore, Christians take the view that Jesus's miracles were his own doing and not God's.[41] It is for this very reason, Rāzī claims, that the proclaimer of the Qur'an insists that Jesus only performed his miracles with God's permission (Q 5:110). Yet we do not know of a single Christian theologian who would disagree with this statement. Of course, the momentous deeds that Jesus performed and the signs he gave can only have happened with God's permission and power. And self-evidently, he obtains his power from God alone. Indeed, from a Christian viewpoint, the defining feature of his

40 Cf. ar-Rāzī, *Tafsīr*, vol. 12, 132.
41 Cf. ibid., 132.

existence is that his entire life derives from God and provides living testimony to God's presence. Yet it would certainly still be pertinent to enquire whether the Christian doctrine of the Trinity was not after all open to misinterpretation on this point and to ask whether Jesus was in fact acting on his own authority. In all likelihood, it may even have been characteristic of the historical Jesus that he took it upon himself to forgive sins and in so doing arrogated divine authority to himself. In response to this, one would undoubtedly have to add the caveat, gleaned from the theology of the Trinity, that even the intratrinitarian Son derives every last vestige of his authority from God and that he is therefore never an autonomous agent. Nonetheless, one would also have to concede that a number of questions remain open on this score.

It is far less easy to see how any questions could remain regarding the position of Mary. This is why Qurṭubī, for example, explicitly queries Mary's inclusion in the reproach delivered by the Qurʾan here; the conclusion he arrives at is that, in venerating Mary as the 'God-bearer' (*Theotokos*) Christians implicitly rank her alongside God.[42] Yet it would be to grossly misconstrue the doctrine of Mary as the *Theotokos* outlined earlier if one were to attempt to infer from it that it establishes Mary as a deity on a par with God. Instead, a Christian would contend, all that is happening here is that Mary, in her willingness to make herself entirely into a servant of the Lord, is facilitating his effectiveness through her actions, with the result that she becomes a conduit for God's liberating reality to be conveyed to the world. In this, she can in no way be interpreted as standing alongside God; rather, it is precisely by virtue of her complete subordination to God that she becomes the one who paves the way for him.

However, this matter takes on an entirely different complexion if we recall Heraclius's political theology. Here, Mary almost morphed into a goddess of war, and the impression is given that she made his military successes possible through her own initiative. We have investigated this question earlier at some length. Another factor was that the veneration of icons of Mary originated in Byzantium. While it is true to say that there was also a strong tradition of Marian veneration in the West Syrian Church, the veneration of icons appears to have spread much more widely throughout the Byzantine Church and to have been far more pronounced than in West Syrian Christianity during the period when the Qurʾan was emerging.[43] Such veneration was especially evident in imperial and military contexts. However, from the outside, the veneration of an icon can easily be

42 Cf. al-Qurṭubī, *al-Ǧāmiʿ*, vol. 8, 301.
43 Cf. Kremer, 'Bildverständnis, Bilderverbot und Bilderverehrung in den syrischen Kirchen', 301.

mistaken for worship, which may have constituted further grounds for criticism of Byzantine theology.

It therefore seems to us highly plausible that it is once more the imperial Christology and Mariology of Heraclius that the proclaimer of the Qur'an is attacking when he accuses Byzantine Christians of having placed Jesus and his mother *de facto* alongside God. It may be possible to identify a connection here with the almost contemporaneous verses of the Surah *at-Tawba* ('Repentance'), in which the Byzantines are castigated as atheists (Q 9:29) for having taken Christ and their ecclesiastical office holders as their lords in God's place (Q 9:31). Whenever people install a created being beside God and in so doing dare to associate another entity with God, in the Qur'an's eyes the human relationship with God is permanently disrupted, and human interests start to supplant the devotion to God that is truly required. Furthermore, when these human interests are allied with an imperial agenda, the proclaimer of the Qur'an objects vehemently, reminding us of God's saving grace. Although this grace is made tangible reality in the persons of Jesus and Mary, no simple law of cause and effect is in operation here.

In accordance with this, the following passage appears a little earlier in our surah: *And God will say 'Jesus, son of Mary, remember my favour to you and your mother, how I strengthened you with the Holy Spirit so that you could speak to people in your infancy and adulthood; and how I taught you writing, wisdom, the Torah and the gospel'* (Q 5:110).

Here too, right at the end of the Qur'an's proclamation, it is made clear that not only Mary, but also Jesus in the gospel is not conveying a new message but instead repeating what had already been laid down in the Torah and then reiterated in the Qur'an. The unifying view of Jesus and Mary is thus maintained. This is a message that concerns Jews and Christians alike. In keeping with this, the formula that is used at the beginning of the verse – 'remember my favour to you' – is an expression that is used time and again for the children of Israel.[44] The concept of grace is thereby wrested from a narrow Christomonistic context and appears rather as part of a Jewish–Christian heritage, which becomes tangible reality in Jesus and Mary in a special way. Of course, this is also a heritage to which the proclaimer of the Qur'an is eager to lay claim for his community as well (Q 1:7). It is comforting that this conciliatory endpoint to Mariology is placed at the start of the closing passage of the Surah *al-Mā'ida*, a clear sign that the proclaimer of the Qur'an was prepared right to the very end to bear witness to Mary's bridging role and her productive religious significance.

---

44 Cf. among others Q 2:40, 2:47, 14:6.

III

MARY IN THE CONTEXT OF ISLAMIC SYSTEMATIC THEOLOGY

In this part of the book, working from the findings we have obtained from exegesis of verses in the Qur'an, we will investigate what impact the insights we gleaned about the figure of Mary from those verses might have on the Muslim faith. In the process we will provide a comprehensive analysis of what contemporary Islamic systematic theology (or Islamic theology at those points where it intersects or overlaps with Islamic systematic theology) has to say about Mary. If at this juncture we do not devote as much attention to classical school theology, then the primary reason for this is that the questions posed by systematic theology have changed fundamentally since the days of scholastic theology. We see systematic theology in both Islam and Christianity as an instrument for the articulation and the critical ongoing development[1] of faith in the context of the demands of the

1 The adjective *critical* comes from the Greek *krinein*, which means 'to distinguish'. In other words, in a critical connection, the intention is not to malign tradition, but to distinguish what strands one can adopt and at which points one can identify the need for further developments. Precisely this form of critical relationship to tradition has always been the criterion of Islamic scholastic theology. Otherwise, it would never have been able to find theological grounds for questioning the keeping of slaves and polygamous marriage. Cf. the concept of critical traditionalism, which was largely introduced by Ebrahim Moosa: Moosa, 'Transitions in the "progress" of civilization', 123 f.

Late Modern period.[2] And it is these demands above all that have changed in comparison to classical times.

Another factor to bear in mind is that Mary scarcely makes an appearance in classical scholastic theology. The hadith tradition likewise has little to say about Mary beyond pointing to her special status.[3] It is often the case that Christian traditions are taken up and appropriated or are deliberately misrepresented for polemical purposes. While this is extremely interesting for the history of theology, our concern here is not to give an appraisal of Mary's reception in the history of Islamic theology[4] but rather to enquire what role she might play nowadays, if we accept the results of the exegesis of the Qur'an that we presented in Part II.

We have attempted to demonstrate the impressively nuanced and precise way in which the text of the Qur'an reveals itself as evidence of a sophisticated exchange of theological ideas within the Late Antique realm of discourse. The example of Mary should serve to demonstrate how this exchange might currently also have groundbreaking significance for a systematic study of the teachings of the Islamic religion, and also be a source of stimuli for practising the faith. Our intention is to explore a total of five thematic areas, each of which will begin with a brief look back at the exegetical conclusions we came to on that topic. We will then review the current state of debate in systematic theology before finally sketching out some tentative suggestions of our own on the way forward.

---

2 In using the term 'Late Modern period' we are denoting a form of modernity that has become conscious of the irresolvable contradictions of its own aspirations for the future and of the dialectic of the Enlightenment, but which still holds to a belief in the emancipatory potential of the modern period.

3 For this reason, we have repeatedly invoked hadith texts as supplementary evidence, but have not chosen to devote a separate part of the book to them. In so doing we do not mean to insinuate that Islamic systematic theology should only rely upon the Qur'an and should not also treat seriously its second mainstay, the record of the traditions of the Prophet Muhammad. This approach is also sensible and advisable in relation to other topics of systematic theology on the basis of the source material as it relates to the body of tradition, and the analysis of hadith texts – founded on a rigorous historical–critical study of the hadith – should form an integral part of this. Yet in examining the figure of Mary, such an approach does not appear promising enough to us to warrant a part of the book to itself. Accordingly, we have chosen instead to insert individual insights from the record of traditions into various strands of argument in this part where appropriate.

4 Cf. George-Tvrtković, *Christians, Muslims, and Mary.*

1

The Qurʾanic Mary as an Impulse for Prophetology

In the course of our observations on the exegesis of the Qurʾan, we have already remarked on the fact that even classical commentators on the Qurʾan treated the question of whether Mary could be seen as a prophet. In modern theology, especially Islamic feminist theology, approaches of this kind are readily seized upon, offering as they do a way of corroborating the possibility of the existence of female prophets in antiquity, based on the example of Mary. In light of this, it seems reasonable to once more briefly rehearse the arguments in favour of recognising Mary as a prophet. We will do this under heading c) below; this will reveal that the question of whether Mary should be distinguished in such a way is by no means easy to decide.

It is therefore important to consider carefully what the real significance of Mary's being thought of as a prophet – or at least of something approaching a prophetic nature being ascribed to her – might be. In this chapter, then, our first task will be to enquire what would or could actually change for Islamic theology – or more precisely for the Islamic doctrine of the prophets (*nubūwa*; 'prophetology') – if Mary, as she is portrayed in the Qurʾan, were to be placed in this context. Our question will therefore be: what new stimuli for prophetology might result from including Mary (a)? We will see that, in this matter, the key concept of vulnerability takes on a central significance; accordingly, as a second step, we will examine this question in greater detail (b). Only then will we pose the question of whether these stimuli can be incorporated into Islamic theology in a theologically legitimate manner and consequently whether it can be viewed as a responsible move to see Mary in a prophetic role (c).

a) The portrayal of Mary as an impulse for Islamic prophetology

The necessity of incorporating Mary into prophetology is often associated with the need for gender equality. We will treat this important aspect presently, in Chapter 3 below. For the theme of gender equality is naturally a major topic for systematic theology in all religions, and can readily be associated with the figure of Mary. However, in this first chapter we are not primarily concerned with Mary, but rather with what substantive characteristics she might contribute to the overall image of prophets if one were intent on seeing her as a prophet. In this first pass, we will develop three ideas that can be summarised by the key terms compassion, corporeality and tolerance of ambiguity.

In our analysis of the Surah *Maryam*, we have already seen that the broadening of the concept of God through metaphors such as that of compassion, which is customarily associated with female character traits, was promoted by this particular surah as well as through Mary's relationship with God as revealed by the text of the Qur'an in general. Yet this is also an influence that is prevalent in prophetology, characterising for example the image of the Prophet Muhammad that is presented in the Qur'an (cf. Q 21:107). Of course, from an Islamic perspective, one would be wary of ascribing maternal qualities to God. But this has more to do with concerns about attaching excessively anthropomorphic associations to the concept of God than with any wish to neglect such aspects. And indeed, as a consequence, in this particular regard nothing much would change as a result of seeing Mary as a prophet. Nor do these motherly qualities serve to emphasise in any characteristic way Mary's critical, questioning and creative mental power or her dialogic relationship with God. Although they may be cited as arguments for construing Mary as a prophet, they do not represent an innovative stimulus for prophetology.

By contrast, the emphasis placed on Mary's corporeality is an aspect that is otherwise scarcely thematised in descriptions of the prophets' relationship with God.[1]

1 Loren Lybarger ('Gender and prophetic authority in the Qur'anic story of Maryam', 258) points to the fact that, through Mary, the womb becomes a metaphor and matrix for prophetic power. She extrapolates from this that the role of prophet thereby becomes intimately associated with the emergence of life, conception and new creation (cf. ibid., 266). We remain unconvinced that these ideas, interesting though they are, are really corroborated in Qur'anic theology. While not wholly misguided, her reflections are somewhat wayward when, regarding the parallel drawn in the Qur'an between Jesus and Adam, she casts Mary in the role of the soil from which Adam is created (cf. ibid., 266). If this were the case, it would represent a point of contact in the Qur'an for the Christian association of Mariology with paganism's veneration of Mother Earth. It would be clear that such an adoption and integration of pagan traditions would only be legitimate if Mary remained clearly visible as a created being and that

Mary carries within her a Word of God and is also depicted very explicitly in desperate physical straits – including her labour pains. She convinces less through her words than through the signs she conveys in her very being. Not for nothing is her silence the visible sign of her abstinence and not for nothing does she point, at the height of her distress, to her son (the *hodegetria*). Indeed, in this situation her whole body acts as a signpost to him and to the divine message he has to impart.[2] Just as in the Christian tradition, so too in the Qur'an Mary communicates through gestures and through her body, and in so doing introduces the dimension of corporeality into the relationship with God.

In this way she renders the relationship with God approachable and physically tangible. The linguistic style of the Surah *Maryam* also matches this intention. For example, Hosn Abboud has drawn attention to the fact that the story of Mary in the Surah *Maryam* unfolds through dialogue which is couched in very familiar expressions and phrases in Arabic that are widely used in both everyday speech and literature. According to Abboud, the atmosphere of linguistic directness they create is meant to help the reader connect emotionally with the story.[3] In its narrative development, the story of Mary therefore assumes the same qualities that are exemplified by the figure of Mary herself, which all point in the direction of greater approachability and tangibility. In using this stylistic device, the proclaimer of the Qur'an wants to make Mary – and himself – appear approachable. At the same time, this device also emphasises that Mary should not be seen as a detached ascetic and an exceptionally pious woman who is elevated above all other men and women. Approachability by means of language is designed in general to facilitate a theological approachability to the person of Mary and the other agents in the story. And this approachability is established in the fact that Mary speaks through her body and thereby underlines the significance of corporeality in the human relationship with God.[4]

One final aspect seems important to us here. The Qur'an does not portray an ideal image of a family or a perfect world in which Mary can pursue her ideals. Instead, it reveals with unsparing honesty the tensions and conflicts in which she becomes embroiled as a result of her surprise pregnancy. In fact, one might even say that the Qur'an as a whole has no interest in idealisations, since these tend to

---

the transcendence and the uniqueness of the Creator was thereby preserved.

2 Cf. Gilis, *Marie en Islam*, 16 f.

3 Cf. Abboud, 'Qur'anic Mary's story and the motif of palm tree and the rivulet', 272.

4 The aspect of corporeality in the relationship with God also makes itself apparent in the rites associated with the Islamic celebration of faith, such as the act of bowing in ritual prayer, fasting and going on pilgrimage.

place a veil in front of reality and are inclined to make people inflexible because they are only capable thereafter of seeing the world through the filter of those idealisations. The figure of Mary presents an unfiltered image of the fragility of reality and of its essential ambiguity. She has to grapple with her fate and to repeatedly pose questions, and generally speaking it is this unvarnished view of reality and its ambiguity that prophets in the Qur'an ask human beings to confront. In this respect, Mary implicitly demands that people display an appropriate measure of tolerance for ambiguity. As with the other prophets, including the Prophet Muhammad, in Mary's case too, the Qur'an paints an unembellished picture of conflict with her family.[5] And yet it may be that she in particular exemplifies more clearly how fragile and vulnerable a person can be despite the support she receives from God and his angels. Precisely through having to engage with God's word with such intense physicality, she also makes herself especially vulnerable and gives us an insight into vulnerability as a defining characteristic of those who are called upon to impart God's message.

b) On the meaning of vulnerability in the relationship with God

Taking their cue from Paul Ricœur, leading pioneers of comparative theology like Marianne Moyaert have repeatedly stressed how important the quality of vulnerability is for understanding others – and hence also for understanding matters that lie far beyond our normal comprehension. Moyaert demonstrates convincingly how Ricœur departs from the Cartesian intellectual tradition in the importance he accords to a corporeally constituted, vulnerable and fragile Self, in order to thereby turn the virtue of vulnerability into fertile ground for hermeneutics and introduce it as a key element into interfaith dialogue. The evolution of a person's own identity and subjectivity is thus presented as a never-ending task, in which each and every individual is reliant upon otherness.[6] The way in which Moyaert treats this hermeneutics, derived from Ricœur, as a plea for the centrality of the categories of fragility and vulnerability within theology, is truly inspiring.

On the one hand, according to her observations, vulnerability is often associated with weakness and defencelessness; accordingly, it is seen as characterising a person who is weak and open to attack.[7] Constantly resonating within this

5 Cf. Abboud, 'Is Mary important for herself or for being the Mother of Christ in the Holy Qur'an?', 28.

6 Cf. Moyaert, *In Response to the religious other*, 13–44.

7 Cf. Tatari, 'Vulnerabilität', 19–24.

definition, Moyaert claims, is a suggestion of the potential for being hurt and feeling pain – in other words the idea of being helplessly prey to external forces, combined with the possibility of suffering misery and loss as a result. According to Moyaert, people who are described thus generally seem in need of help and require support.[8] From this standpoint, vulnerability is regarded as a lack of something that should be there. Consequently, the imagined ideal is that of invulnerability. This quality is commonly associated with strength and independence, along with the capacity to be self-sufficient and free of doubt. An invulnerable person therefore has every situation under control, and no one can stand in their way. As a result, invulnerability is generally prized as a desirable quality, while vulnerability by contrast is classified as an undesirable character trait and hence is all too often projected onto others.

However, looking again at the term reveals an inherent ambiguity that is clearly of great interest not only in a sociological but also a theological context. Moyaert links the concept of vulnerability to the capacity to feel joy and to experience contentment in the company of others. In her eyes, it is emblematic of an awareness of being incomplete, an openness to learning, being challenged and challenging oneself as a necessary precondition for change; as such, it forms the basis of every kind of creativity. Vulnerability, Moyaert maintains, denotes the ability to be touched and to touch, to be loved and to love. It is therefore an essential prerequisite for a reciprocal relationship and that indispensable capacity which makes a person a social being who is able to engage responsibly and in a caring fashion with other people on the basis of shared, fundamental human experiences and empathy. By contrast, invulnerability signifies a rejection of change, an unfeeling insensitivity and a refusal to take responsibility. Anyone who is not vulnerable shows themselves at the same time to be aloof. The conclusion that Moyaert comes to in her reflections based on the work of Ricœur is that, where the category of vulnerability is concerned, the one cannot exist without the other. It therefore requires courage to yield to this trait of vulnerability – in her eyes a fundamentally human quality – in order to lay oneself open to the potential that this quality conceals within itself.

In hermeneutics, Moyaert and Ricœur are not alone in their re-evaluation of vulnerability. Erinn Gilson also stresses the extent to which vulnerability should be seen as a fundamental quality underlying our capacity for love, joy and learning. Vulnerability, she claims, is therefore not just a limiting factor, it is an

8 Cf. also Moyaert, 'On vulnerability', 1144–1161.

enabling one too. It conveys openness and breadth, says Gilson.[9] This element of weakness and vulnerability as a prerequisite for receptivity, as described by Moyaert and Gilson, can be identified in some central motifs of Islamic history, and among other things also embodied within the person of the Prophet Muhammad. Yet nowhere it is displayed quite as openly as in the figure of Mary and the account of her pregnancy and the birth of Jesus. When she is shown all on her own in the desert, pregnant and deprived of any human assistance, when she is attacked by her own family without any friends coming to her aid, and above all when she becomes pregnant without having been touched by a man, a measure of vulnerability becomes apparent in all these elements that could scarcely be more eloquently expressed by the narrative.[10] And at the same time, all these factors are linked with the greatest possible receptivity on Mary's part for the word of God.

The parallels between Mary and Muhammad, which feminist Islamic theology is very keen on drawing in this context, and which we will examine in greater depth (see below, 'Mary and Muhammad', 251 ff.), also help throw Muhammad's vulnerability into sharper focus.[11] Of course, this vulnerability also comes through in the biographical details about the Prophet Muhammad that have been handed down.[12] But these tend to be relegated to the background when his prophetic gifts are under discussion, as a result of the Muslim tradition likewise being afflicted by the same notions of invulnerability as an ideal of perfection that Moyaert criticises.[13] That is why the profile of the figure of Mary presented in the Qur'an can help

9 Cf. Gilson, 'Vulnerability, ignorance and oppression', 310: 'Being vulnerable makes it possible for us to suffer, to fall prey to violence and be harmed, but also to fall in love, to learn, to take pleasure and find comfort in the presence of others, and to experience the simultaneity of these feelings. Vulnerability is not just a condition that limits us but one that can enable us. As potential, vulnerability is a condition of openness, openness to being affected and affecting in turn.'

10 Cf. Kaltner, *Ishmael instructs Isaac*, 232.

11 Cf. Abboud, 'Is Mary important for herself or for being the Mother of Christ in the Holy Qur'an?', 28 f.

12 On the various stages in the Prophet's life – becoming first a half- and then a full orphan, being placed under the protection of his grandfather and then dependent upon his uncle, the cruel twist of fate in the death of his wife Khadīja and much more, through to his championing of the cause of the poor and the needy, see the relevant accounts in diverse works of biography. Cf. for example the authoritative biography by Ibn Isḥāq, available in English as *The Life of Muhammad*, trans. Alfred Guillaume, Pakistan 1989.

13 Beyond any doubt, however, is the authenticity of the impressive accounts which tell how Muhammad found the sheer power of God's revelation to him physically hard to bear, which shook his being to the very core and rendered him vulnerable.

us put the significance of vulnerability in our relationship with God and our fellow human beings into a proper perspective – on the level of prophetology as well. At the same time, the vulnerable, exposed and approachable Mary of the Qur'an represents a logical antithesis to the imperial Mary that we encounter in the guise of a military commander in the propaganda of Heraclius. Clearly the Mary of the Qur'an is far closer to the testimony of the Bible than the picture presented by her Christian interpreters at the court of the Byzantine emperor. And it is equally apparent that the prophetology of classical school theology could learn a thing or two if the character traits of Mary that we have uncovered were used to alter the traditional ideal image of a prophet. Yet is such a suggestion even legitimate? Is it permissible from the Qur'anic perspective to see Mary as a prophetic figure?

c) Was Mary a prophet?

Whenever this question is broached, certain figures from the Islamic tradition are invoked in defence of this proposition, while – just as predictably – counter-arguments are put forward to supposedly prove that this would be a false track to pursue. Let us begin by looking at the classical sources that support Mary's designation as a prophet.

The most frequently cited source on this matter is the scholar Ibn Ḥazm (d. 1054) from al-Andalus.[14] The basis for his contention that Mary, the Pharaoh's wife Āsiya, Sarah and the mother of Moses were all prophets lies in the form distinction he draws between the words *nabīy* and *rasūl*,[15] in other words the Arabic term that is primarily used in the Qur'an as a designation of biblical prophets, and the term that is employed more generally for messengers sent by God. In the case of the most important prophet figures, both terms tend to appear together, but in Islamic scholastic theology they were often differentiated hierarchically, with the result that in this tradition, greater importance is accorded to the term denoting a messenger than to that signifying a prophet. It is a matter of debate whether this distinction drawn by scholastic theology is a true reflection of what the Qur'an actually says.[16] Yet come what may, it clearly makes it easier for Ibn Ḥazm to assign this category of lesser theological and social importance to a woman.

14 Ibn Ḥazm's plea for the recognition of Mary as a prophet even made it into a number of Catholic handbooks on Mariology. Cf. Beinert, *Maria*, 13, with reference to Annemarie Schimmel, *Jesus und Maria in der islamischen Mystik*, Munich 1996, 141 f.

15 On this and the following, cf. Ibrahim, 'Ibn Ḥazm's theory of prophecy of women', 75–100.

16 For an introduction to this terminology, cf. Ghaffar, 'Einordnung in die koranische Prophetologie', 178 f.

With regard to the role of Ibn Ḥazm, it is instructive to note that he took a critical stance in his theology towards all interpretations of the Qur'an that he regarded as too rationalistic. In consequence, he even opposed the use of argument by analogy in textual exegesis. Instead, he set great store by as literal an interpretation of the Qur'an as possible, and it was precisely this path of literal Qur'anic exegesis that led him to recognise Mary as a prophet. In doing so, he defined prophecy as the selection of a person by God. According to his definition, a person in this position received a special message from God, which was accompanied by miracles. This message was conveyed by an angel or some undefined power imparted to the human soul.[17] Quite clearly, these exact criteria were fulfilled by Mary, since an angel addresses her and she receives a word of God in the form of Jesus via the miracle of the Virgin Birth. Whether Ibn Ḥazm was thereby imbued with a special admiration for Mary, he does not say.

This was decidedly not the case for his fellow Andalusian Qur'anic exegete al-Qurṭubī, whose great enchantment with the figure of Mary we have already illustrated through extensive quotations in Part II of this book. It is striking that some of the most prominent defenders of the idea that Mary was a prophet came from al-Andalus. Alongside these two scholars who designate Mary as a prophet, Maribel Fierro also names the mystic Muḥy ad-Dīn Ibn 'Arabī (d.1240) and the legal scholar of the Maliki school Abū Bakr Muḥammad ibn Mawhab at-Tuǧībī al-Qabrī (d.1015),[18] who likewise both hailed from al-Andalus. It was said that the controversy about Mary's status as a prophet had intermittently got so out of hand in Muslim Spain that the Umayyad caliph Al-Manṣūr ibn Abī 'Āmir (d.1002) found himself obliged to banish some of the proponents of the idea, as well as a number of its opponents, from the country in order to restore public order.[19] Whether Mary should be seen as a prophet was clearly a highly charged question

17 Cf. Ibn Ḥazm, *al-Iḥkām fī uṣūl al-aḥkām*, Vol. 1, 40: 'Prophethood [*an-nubūwa*]: God marks a man or a woman out from other people by making known to them something that they did not previously know through an angel or a power which he imbues them with and which enables them to transcend their customary existence [the laws of nature]. Such acts are miracles [*mu'ǧizāt*] and they culminate in Muhammad.' It is noteworthy that Ibn Ḥazm also associates the concept of miracles (*mu'ǧiza*) with prophets (*anbiyā'*) and not solely with divine emissaries (*rusul*).

18 Fierro introduces him under this name. In other sources he is known as Abū Šākir 'Abd al-Wāḥid Muḥammad ibn Mawhab at-Tuǧībī al-Qabrī. Cf. Manuela Marin, *Estudios onomástico-biográficos de Al-Andalus*, Volume 1. See also aḏ-Ḏahabī, *Siyar a'lām an-nubalā'*, Vol. 19, 149.

19 Cf. Fierro, 'Women as prophets in Islam', 184.

within the Muslim community during the Golden Age of al-Andalus, with scholars coming to very different conclusions.

Fierro has established that debate about Mary's role as a prophet came to a head in al-Andalus at the same time as the most conversions from Christianity to Islám were recorded. It is her thesis that the Christians who converted to Islam imported their veneration of Mary into Islam.[20] Perhaps one might also simply say that Mary was such a beloved figure in the popular piety of the period that the Qur'an's articulation of Mary's special status should have made it, or actually did make it, easier for Christians to convert to Islam. In any event, it appears that in mediaeval al-Andalus, a significant site of intersection for Islamic–Christian relations, there were already moves afoot within Islam to interpret the points of reference in the Qur'an in such a way as to recognise Mary as a prophet. However, mediaeval Muslim Spain was not only a special location for interaction between the faiths, it was also a place that was especially progressively minded in the matter of women's rights.[21]

These historic examples from Muslim Spain might act as a spur for a new appraisal of the situation in present-day Europe, which is likewise and to an even greater degree characterised by moves toward female emancipation and interfaith dialogue. At the same time, one might enquire how the Islamic tradition's attitude to Mary manifested itself in regions that lay farther to the east and were not so strongly shaped by encounters between the great Abrahamic faiths.

Purely by way of example, therefore, let us examine a remarkable theological classification of Mary that transcends the Andalusian context. In his work *Ǧawāhir al-qur'ān* ('Jewels of the Qur'an'), one of the most influential theologians in the history of Muslim scholarship, Ġazālī (d. 1111) presents six hermeneutic approaches (the 'jewels' of the title) to grasping the meaning of the verses of the Qur'an. His fourth approach presents the stories of 'those who have followed in God's path and those who have deviated from it'. As belonging to the former group, he names exclusively and explicitly 'the stories of Adam and Noah, Abraham and Moses and Aaron, Jesus and Mary, David and Solomon, Jonah and Lot, Idris and Ḫiḍr, Šu'ayb and Ilyās, Muhammad (ṣ), and the angels Gabriel and Michael and the other angels (*ġayrihim*)'.[22] For Ġazālī, these stories all have the common aim of demonstrating God's actions and providing pointers to profound

20 Cf. ibid., 194.

21 Cf. Viguera, 'Aṣluḥu li 'l-Ma'ālī. On the Social Status of Andalusī Women', 709–724, plus additional information in Abboud, *Mary in the Qur'an*, 134.

22 Al-Ġazālī, *Ǧawāhir al-Qur'ān*, 31.

religious and theological insights. In his reading, the figures he names are the greatest protagonists of the Qur'an and as such are theologically all on a par. Certainly, the sequence is interrupted after his naming of Muhammad as the 'seal of the prophets', and a new category ensues, that of the angels. Yet the figures named up to that point clearly all belong in the same group. Ġazālī gathers all those named under the heading *Qiṣaṣ al-anbiyāʾ wa-l-awliyāʾ* ('Stories of the prophets and the friends of God [*awliyāʾ allāh*]').

One striking feature is that, from the perspective of scholastic theology, all those named except Mary are prophets (*nabīy/anbiyāʾ* or *rasūl/rusul*). Rāzī notes that most of the scholars named, including the mysterious figure of Ḫiḍr cited by Ġazālī, are classified as prophets. The compassion with which God endows him in the Qur'an is interpreted by Rāzī by means of cross-references within the Qur'an, as a sign of his prophetic nature.[23] And Qurṭubī likewise makes the case for designating Ḫiḍr as a prophet by arguing that no one can possess more knowledge than a prophet and that, on the basis of the knowledge that God imparted to him, Ḫiḍr was able to demonstrate to the Prophet Moses that he (Moses) possessed only limited powers of insight; because he therefore showed himself to be more knowledgeable than even Moses, then by definition he must also have the status of a prophet (cf. Q 18:60–82).[24] Ġazālī also appears to share this view, since in his listing he links Ḫiḍr with Ilyās (Elijah), whose status as a prophet is undisputed. But how does Mary fit within this list? Why does he name her at all, given that he omits to mention so many other prophets at this point?

It is likely that Ġazālī appended the addendum about the 'friends of God' here so as to keep in step with scholastic theology and to steer clear of the debate about Mary, and thereby avoid becoming embroiled in the controversy over Mary's status. It is our view that Ġazālī remained deliberately vague when composing this section of his work. It is impossible to determine whether this really was his intention. But certainly, the way he has composed his literary work gives due cause for speculation, plus we can establish without doubt that Ġazālī included Mary, in some guise or another, in a list of those who were in his view the great, indispensable prophets of the Qur'an.[25]

23 Cf. ar-Rāzī, *Tafsīr*, Vol. 11, 149.

24 Cf. al-Qurṭubī, *al-Ǧāmiʿ*, Vol. 13, 324 f.

25 At this point the following tradition would doubtless also have played a role, in which Muhammad names those who will be among the first (men/*riǧāl*) to enter paradise, namely: Abraham, Ishmael, Isaac, Jacob, al-Asbāṭ [i.e., the 12 sons of Jacob], Moses, Jesus and Mary, and the daughters of ʿImrān (cf. al-Qurṭubī, *al-Ǧāmiʿ*, Vol. 5, 128). For the tradition in question, cf. among others aḍ-Ḍaḥḥāk, *al-Āḥād wa-l-maṯānī*. Vol. 1, 56.

Thus, other examples can be found outside al-Andalus of Mary being accorded special honour. Another aspect which speaks in favour of a reappraisal of Mary in the context of prophetology may be that the narrative of the Qur'an repeatedly endows her with the typical attributes (*topoi*) of a prophet's biography. So, like Moses in the Sinai Desert or Muhammad in the cave at Mount Hira, Mary too learns of her calling by God or her encounter with the angel in the solitude of the wilderness. Similarly, her early experience of loneliness in childhood is reminiscent of the story of Muhammad.[26] And the stream or spring that wells up at Mary's feet may be likened to the experience of Moses, who strikes a rock with his staff to obtain water, or to that of Ishmael, who scraped his feet on the ground for so long that a spring appeared in the desert.[27] In any event, one can at least say with certainty that Mary's role as the only girl in the Temple and the ensuing distance from her parents engendered in her an emotional, intellectual and spiritual independence – qualities which appear time and again in depictions of prophetic figures.[28]

When Mary is introduced in the Qur'an as the sister of Aaron and is thereby typologically merged with Aaron's sister Miriam, as we have already remarked upon in Part II, this too might constitute an argument for honouring her as a prophet. For in the tradition of biblical exegesis, Miriam soon became an archetype of the female prophet, just as Moses became the archetype of the male prophet. The reference in the Qur'an might therefore be understood as transferring this prophetic function to Mary as well.[29] While all these arguments are certainly not compelling in and of themselves, they do nonetheless provide hints that could be used to corroborate the veneration of Mary as a prophet.

Why, then, has the tradition in the vast majority of cases inveighed against Mary's being included within the ranks of the prophets? The counterarguments that are deployed here generally begin by questioning whether Mary really did experience a miracle. For the time being we will let this counterargument rest, since it requires a more detailed analysis of scholastic theology in order to understand this point. We will cast a closer eye over this question in the next chapter. It suffices at this juncture for us to simply indicate the high degree of plausibility attaching to an outcome which consists in classifying Mary's virginity as a miracle and which is hence able to produce the attestation argument required in traditional apologetics.

---

26 Cf. Buisson, 'Subversive Maryam or a Qur'anic view on women's empowerment', 451.

27 Cf. ibid., 452.

28 Cf. ibid., 451 f.

29 Cf. Abboud, 'Qur'anic Mary's story and the motif of palm tree and the rivulet', 270.

A second counterargument maintains that Mary was not in fact the recipient of a message aimed specifically at her. However, if one gives credence to the idea that Jesus should himself be regarded as the word of God, then one must conclude that Mary both received this word and conveyed it on to humanity. Furthermore, given that the angel communicated direct messages from God to Mary, one might even ask whether Mary should be designated as a messenger (*rasūla*) in her own right. At any rate, one would be hard put to demonstrate that she should not be recognised as a prophet.

It may also be possible to read the Qur'an's version of Mary's story in the following way. The account given in the Qur'an of Mary's despair and longing for death during the birth of Jesus can be interpreted as a moment of weakness, as we have already explained in Part II. Her weakness resides in the fact that she is at odds with herself over God's plan and is minded to reject it – in just the same way as the biblical and Qur'anic prophet Jonah (at least initially) refused to become a prophet among his own people. Mary can anticipate that the confrontation with her family might be conflictual and even – given her status as a single mother – life-threatening for her. Analogous with this, the Qur'an recounts the experience of prophets who were subjected to ridicule, persecution, attacks and even attempts on their life (cf. Q 2:91; 38:20; 3:21; 4:155).

Mary feels deeply insecure because she lacks any support from her family and friends and because she is struggling to comprehend her extraordinary fate. As a result, she wishes herself dead (cf. Q 19:23). Like Jonah, she could have considered not going to her people but instead simply remaining in lonely isolation. After all, as the account in the Qur'an shows, she can rely on God continuing to provide for her. Yet she clearly sees it as her duty to return to her people and so lay herself open to their accusations and threats. For only in this way can Jesus impart his message.[30] And so her silence also thereby becomes explicable. For just as Muhammad does not add any of his own words to the message of the Qur'an, so Mary does not add any words to the word of God which she conveys to humankind and which manifests itself in Jesus.

We will come back to reviewing a number of other reference points that can be read as parallel in the lives of Muhammad and Mary (see below, 251 ff.). Here, we first want to follow another train of thought. It was only in Mary's state of exclusion and exposure that the essential vulnerability and weakness of serving

30 Cf. Kaltner, *Ishmael instructs Isaac*, 226: 'In order for this part of the revelation to be fulfilled, she must bring the child back to her community so they can see the sign and experience divine mercy.'

as a prophet could become tangible reality. Thus, Mary also had to bring her own message to her people[31] and in addition another that is still relevant to us today, perhaps particularly relevant to those of us living in the Late Modern period. For considering the paradoxes that inhabit all great stories,[32] perhaps it is only nowadays that a prophet can come across as more convincing by showing vulnerability, weakness and brokenness while also conveying authenticity, resilience and devotion in their relationship to God than by exuding success and strength.

The third and most important counterargument consists of a verse of the Qur'an which explicitly refers to men (*riǧāl*) as the recipients of revelations (Q 12:109), an idea that is also expressed in a similar vein in Q 16:43 and Q 21:7. However, there are convincing arguments for construing the context of these passages from the Qur'an as meaning that men rather than angels are the recipients of revelations and can therefore be called messengers – at least this was the construction that was placed upon these passages in the classical period, with good reason.[33] In other words, these passages are not about choosing men as opposed to women.[34] Elsewhere in the Qur'an, the Arabic term *raǧul* that is translated here as 'men' is also used to distinguish the beings thus designated from angels, and in all likelihood refers to humans in general as opposed to angels, rather than primarily to their biological gender (cf. Q 6:9).[35]

---

31 For this reason it does not seem legitimate to us either to conflate the Mary of the Qur'an entirely with Jesus and thereby construct a transgender prophet figure. In this, we are once again at variance with Lybarger, 'Gender and prophetic authority in the Qur'anic story of Maryam', 241, 249 f.

32 Cf. Jean-François Lyotard, *Das postmoderne Wissen. Ein Bericht* [*The Postmodern Condition: a report on knowledge*] ed. P. Engelmann, trans. O. Pfersmann, Vienna 1994 (Edition Passagen; 7).

33 In his work on the reasons behind the revelation, Wāḥidī dates the verse to the Meccan period, in which Muhammad's role as a prophet was still not accepted by the majority of people. In rejecting his claim, they contended that God was far too great to send just a single man to proclaim his message, and consequently they called on God to send an angel (cf. al-Wāḥidī, *Asbāb nuzūl al-Qur'ān*, 463). Ibrahim thus logically concludes: 'It is therefore reasonable to argue that by "men" *(rijalan)*, the Qur'an intended "human beings" as opposed to "angels", proposed by the sceptics and rejecters' (Ibrahim, 'Ibn Ḥazm's theory of prophecy of women', 83).

34 Cf. Abboud, *Mary in the Qur'an*, 157.

35 In his dictionary *Muḫtār aṣ-ṣiḥāḥ* Rāzī places the Arabic term for woman (*imra'alniswa*) under the root *raǧila*. While on the one hand maintaining that the terms for woman and man denote opposites, at the same time he states that some women can also be described through derivations of the root *raǧila*: namely women who have distinguished themselves by standing on their own feet, as the word root indicates (*raǧila* = to go on foot). For example, according to Rāzī, in this sense Muhammad's wife Aisha, who was known for her keen intellect, would be designated as *raǧla ar-ra'y* [*ra'y*: reason]. Cf. ar-Rāzī, *Muḫtār aṣ-ṣiḥāḥ*, 99. We are

Besides, every verse without exception that is adduced as evidence of the supposedly exclusive maleness of the role of prophet refers to messengers (*rusul*) rather than to prophets (*anbiyā'*).[36] Consequently, Ibn Ḥazm contends that the verse should not be used to deprive women of the possibility of prophethood (*nubūwa*). The whole matter is further complicated by the fact that the Qur'an designates humans and angels alike as messengers. That is to say, as a general principle the argument cannot be used to lay down rules regarding who is permitted to be a prophet and who is not. For this reason, there are a number of voices in contemporary Islamic systematic theology arguing in favour of recognising Mary as a prophet, while at the same time reminding us that this is a contentious issue.[37]

We do not intend to delve any deeper into this subject here. However, it should already have become clear that the existing sources are anything but unequivocal on this matter and that it depends heavily on exegetes' view of humanity and the sexes as to how they interpret the relevant verses. At any rate, even in classical times, it was clearly a matter of great concern for the exclusively male exegetes to determine whether men and women had spiritual experiences in the same way and could be taken into service by God. The conclusions they came to are manifestly conditioned by the times and the civilisations in which they lived. This does not mean that we would be justified in simply jettisoning these conclusions as culturally relative. They are part and parcel of the Muslim tradition. These conclusions therefore need to be subject to a constant process of critical re-evaluation, informed by a sense of epistemic humility, and in full cognisance of the fact that we have never hitherto been in a position to conclusively grasp God's word, nor will we ever be in the future. It is interesting just how ambiguous the testimony of the Qur'an is on this point and how diversely it can be interpreted. With regard to this confusing situation, Kecia Ali talks in terms of a certain 'messiness' within

---

indebted to Jasser Auda for revealing the inherent potential within Arabic for inclusive linguistic usage for men and women via the word root *rağila*. See http://www.khotwacenter.com/woman-in-the-mosque.

36 Interestingly, it is indeed the case that the term 'prophet' in the Qur'an is reserved for figures who are already known from the Bible. Non-biblical prophets are generally referred to in the Qur'an as messengers. The only explicit exception to this is the Prophet Muhammad, who from the Medinan period onwards was also regarded as a prophet and so was included within the biblical tradition. On implicit exceptions cf. Q 7:49–94. These verses serve to demonstrate how dynamic the evolution of terminology was and how the Qur'an does not operate with hard-and-fast concepts.

37 Cf. the conclusion to this effect in Schleifer, Mary the blessed virgin of Islam, 95; Yitik, 'Die Jungfrau Maria und ihr Haus bei Ephesus', 3 f.

the Qur'an[38] – admittedly a rather shocking phrase, yet one which clearly draws attention to the ambiguity inherent in the text of the Qur'an, which cannot help but refer to man in all his human, all too human, limitations.[39] The promulgation of the Qur'an's message never occurs neutrally in a laboratory atmosphere, but always against the backdrop of the worldviews of exegetes and systematic theologians. If a theologian, as a man, believes that women cannot be prophets, then he justifiably interpret the 'messiness', openness and ambiguity of the Qur'an so as to corroborate this conclusion.

Yet the opposite interpretation also seems perfectly legitimate to us, especially in view of the fact that the Surah *Āl ʿImrān*, which has a lot to say about Mary, accords women religious rights and possibilities that were hitherto only granted to men, such as giving a newborn child its name, taking part in religious services and engaging in communal prayer. These rights and duties, which up till then had been the exclusive preserve of men but which were now practised by Mary and her mother, should encourage us to consider new possibilities of interpretation here. In consequence, one might actually be able to concur with Abboud in seeing a spiritual equality between men and women in the Qur'an. At all events, any attempt to discern a hierarchy at this point would be hard pressed to justify itself.

Yet if, out of respect for tradition, one were to come to the conclusion that Mary should not be endowed with the title of prophet, which is formally reserved for men, then it could at least be established that she had the most intimate contact with God and his angels and in the process was touched by holiness and taken into God's service. She was the recipient of a heavenly message and revelation and was, like the prophets, singled out and honoured.[40] Perhaps one must nevertheless find other terms to describe the honour that is bestowed upon her. In keeping with tradition, one could for example describe Mary as a 'friend of God' or a 'saint/holy woman' (*walīya*) or 'the truthful one' (*siddīqa*).[41] But perhaps it is less

38 Cf. Ali, 'Destabilizing gender, reproducing maternity', 109. Schleifer, on the other hand, resolves the vagueness she encounters in the Qur'an in the following terms: 'As she had the attributes and experiences of prophets, and there is no satisfactory argument against her having achieved their status, she should logically be classified a prophetess, although this should not be regarded as proven beyond dispute' (Schleifer, *Mary the blessed virgin of Islam*, Cambridge 1998, 95).

39 On the problem of the impossibility of imposing an authoritative interpretation upon the text, cf. Abou el-Fadl, *Speaking in God's name*, 145–150.

40 Cf. Abboud, 'Is Mary important for herself or for being the Mother of Christ in the Holy Qur'an?', 27.

41 Cf. Seppälä, 'Is the Virgin Mary a prophetess?', 375 f.

important that Mary actually be designated as a prophet, and more that her personality traits be included in ideals of feminine, and above all masculine, perfection. In any event, it is beyond question that this woman is esteemed in a very special way by the Qur'an for her relationship with God. And for this reason, she is able to assume a role-model function in anthropology too.

2

The Qur'anic Mary as a Stimulus to a Traditional Understanding of God's Actions

We have already seen in the preceding chapter that a key argument against seeing Mary as a prophet figure was that people were loath to concede that she had performed any major miracle. We did not investigate this point any more closely at the time, because it required a somewhat more detailed insight into the traditional debates surrounding God's actions.

a) Distinctions in the perception of miracles in classical scholastic theology

Two different Arabic terms are used in classical scholastic theology when discussing the perception of miracles. Although neither of these terms appears in the Qur'an, they are nonetheless important in the logic of scholastic theology for the conception of prophetology. The term *karāma* generally denotes charismatic symbolic acts, which are performed by 'friends of God' (*awliyā*) with divine help. The acts in question are typically minor miracles in the physical world, such as prophecies or interpretations of secrets of the heart.[1] They are by definition strictly confined to the personal realm, and do not occur in public. They are meant to remain secret and can therefore in no way be taken as an indication of prophethood. Rationalistic scholastic theology, or *mu'tazila*, regarded *karāma* as nothing more than tricks performed by charlatans, and warned against these potentially

1 Cf. Louis Gardet, 'Art, Karāma.' In: Emri van Donzel, Bernard Lewis and Charles Pellat (eds.), *Encyclopaedia of Islam*, vol. 4, Leiden 1997, 615 f.

manipulative forces. By contrast, classical mainstream Sunni scholastic theology, or *aš'arīya*, firmly adhered to a belief in *karāma*, pointing to God's omnipotence in all things.

A greater kind of miracle, which is the exclusive preserve of prophets, is known as *mu'ǧiza* in classical scholastic theology. For the most part, the criteria for a miraculous event to be categorised in this way are as follows: it must take place publicly (in other words, in front of witnesses), be proclaimed in advance, and implicitly involve a challenge to others to perform similar deeds. The futility of ordinary people attempting to perform such miracles on their own (*'aǧaza*) should, then, make apparent the prophet's superior position and his divine mandate. For rationalistic scholastic theology, the category of *mu'ǧiza* is the only form of miracle that it deemed valid. It is strictly and exclusively reserved for prophets and its sole purpose is to establish the true nature of their mission.[2]

In Islamic philosophy, on the other hand, Ibn Sīnā (Avicenna; d. 1037) for example placed the *mu'ǧiza–karāma* discussion in the context of necessary and consciously willed emanations, and here too the categories are used to justify making a distinction between prophets and the 'friends of God', namely the righteous. According to Ibn Sīnā, the *awliyā* can also, by undertaking ascetic exercises, put themselves in a state where they too are capable of performing miracles, but they are still fundamentally operating on a lower level than prophets.

These brief explanations should suffice to show that the concepts of *karāma* and *mu'ǧiza* in classical scholastic theology share a common trait inasmuch as they both breach the laws of nature. Having said this, though, it is clear that they work at different levels of intensity and differ from one another primarily as regards their public exposure. Since the question of what caused Mary to conceive cannot by definition be proved publicly, because an intimate encounter that is not consummated simply has no public profile, classical exegesis self-evidently deems the miracle she performs to be an example of *karāma*.

Thus, for example, Rāzi rejects Mary's designation as a prophet by arguing that she did not perform a publicly verifiable and observable miracle. In addition, he claims, she did not actively perform the miracle herself; instead, it happened to her. In any event, he concludes, in view of the lack of any public transparency, Mary's virgin conception of Jesus is to be classified merely as *karāma*.[3]

Interestingly, an exegete such as Qurṭubī, who defends Mary's prophetic role, avoids the categories of *karāma* and *mu'ǧiza* altogether. In all likelihood, this was

2 Cf. Zamaḫšarī's exegesis of the Surah *al-Ǧinn* (Q 72:26–27): Az-Zamaḫšarī, *Tafsīr*, 1149.
3 Cf. ar-Rāzī, *Tafsīr*, Vol. 21, 199.

because he did not rate his chances of being able to successfully argue his case for Mary being a prophet in this realm of scholastic quiddities, and so chose to steer away from miracles and concentrate instead on other criteria of prophecy that he saw her as fulfilling, such as communicating with angels, the message that is imparted to her, and the arguments advanced in the authoritative traditional sources that count Mary among God's perfect creatures.[4] Zamaḫšarī, on the other hand, opts for a quite different way of connecting the miraculous events surrounding Mary with Mary herself, namely by maintaining that she herself was a miracle. This effectively makes her no longer potentially the transmitter of a content, but the content itself.[5] How far such a categorisation can be applied here would surely call for a wider discussion, which cannot be conducted at this juncture, since it touches upon the whole question of God's methods of communication, in other words the theme of revelation. Such a vast topic would require a volume of its own to do it justice, given that the question in particular of the relationship between form and content in the act of revelation nowadays has quite different parameters to those which we customarily applied to it when our thinking was trammelled along the lines of scholastic theology.[6]

Returning to the problem raised at the outset, we find that the classical quiddities applied by Islamic scholastic theology are mirrored very closely in Christianity. In Christian theology too, a miracle is normally construed as a publicly verifiable occurrence, and official recognition of miracles by the Catholic Church is based even to the present day on legal proceedings, which run through a set of publicly verifiable criteria and apply them to the case in hand to determine whether they have been fulfilled. Accordingly, medical or scientific knowledge is to an increasing degree injected into the proceedings when it is a question of ascertaining whether a miracle has taken place. And even though no search for miracles with an eye to establishing prophethood is conducted in the Catholic Church, public proof of two miracles forms an integral part of every canonisation process. Here too, therefore, it is not about private actions on God's part but publicly verifiable transgressions of the laws of nature.

We can presume that this perception of miracles most likely also obtained

---

4 Cf. al-Qurṭubī, *al-Ǧāmi'*, Vol. 5, 126 f. and 428 f.

5 Az-Zamaḫšarī, *Tafsīr*, 635: 'Mary and Jesus are two miracles (*mu'ǧizatān*).'

6 For an ambitious attempt to square the Muslim concept of revelation with the findings of modern philosophy, cf. Ahmad Milad Karimi, *Hingabe. Grundfragen der systematisch-islamischen Theologie*, Freiburg – Berlin – Vienna 2015. On the questions arising from this topic for Muslim faith reflection, cf. the reappraisal of the current status of the debate in: Klaus von Stosch, *Offenbarung*, Paderborn 2010.

during Late Antiquity. Consequently, the process that we examined in Part I, whereby Mary's virginity came to be interpreted as perpetual virginity, can also be seen as a need by Christian communities to have their belief in Mary's virginity corroborated in theological argument. For instance, in the Protevangelium of James, it is no coincidence that it is a Hebrew midwife who inserts her finger into Mary's vagina in order to verify her virginity (cf. ProtEvJam 19:3). As a result of being designated as a Hebrew woman, she is placed in the ranks of the principal sceptics of Late Antiquity who challenged the Christian belief in Mary's virginity, and this makes her testimony all the more impressive. In addition, the narrative is at pains to stress that she is not Mary's usual wet-nurse, meaning that external expertise has been adduced. Of course, the whole procedure described bears witness to a shocking objectification of the conception of virginity and a highly problematic – and in empirical terms, verifiably false – equating of virginity with the intactness of a woman's hymen. Yet it also demonstrates how acutely Christians felt the need to construe Mary's virginity not as *karāma*, but instead to manufacture a public scenario, thus enabling them to some extent to present the event as an instance of *muʿǧiza*.

Yet for all the sympathy which the proclaimer of the Qur'an displays for the figure of Mary and the belief in her virginity, he nonetheless correctly identifies this path as a fallacy, and so the Qur'an remains free of all objectified indications of Mary's virginity during her labour. At the same time, however, this means that her virginity is thereby divested of any form of public verification, and the classic route taken by Christian apologetics to vindicate its belief is blocked. In this way, Mary's virginity is turned into a private occurrence, and although for the faithful the truth of the event is vouched for by its attestation in the Qur'an, at the same time it cannot itself assume any legitimising role for Mary. Against this background, it is easy to see why Islamic scholastic theology could not get involved in recognising Mary as a prophet by applying the aforementioned perception of miracles in the sense of *muʿǧiza*.

All the same, this classical perception is based on the premise that there exist publicly verifiable breaches of natural laws, which can become the basis on which the phenomenon of prophecy is legitimised. Islamic scholastic theology in the Middle Ages held this view in common with both Christian and Jewish scholasticism. And yet precisely this conception has become open to question to us in modern times – meaning that this once conclusive argument against Mary's role as a prophet is ripe for reconsideration.

b) On the crisis of the classical perception of the concept of miracles in the modern period and its consequences for the distinctions drawn by classical theology

This is not the place to discuss at length the challenge posed by a modern critique of religion to the classical stance of apologetics in defending a belief in miracles.[7] Purely by way of summarising, two matters which have fundamentally changed the whole nature of apologetics should be noted here. Firstly, it is the case that the latest research findings in the natural sciences have made the possibility of a divine agency in the contingent opening up of natural laws seem plausible. The re-evaluation of natural laws that this has facilitated makes it conceivable that a special (miraculous) agency of God might lie hidden within the statistical range of variation in the laws of nature, with the result that it eludes any public verifiability.[8] Secondly, it has become a widespread and central tenet of Christian theology, when defending a belief in God in the face of all the suffering that exists in the world, to point to the fact that God never disrupts the laws of nature in a manipulative fashion. According to this way of looking at things, there would be absolutely no justification for believing in the possibility of a publicly verifiable intervention on God's part in the course of nature when faced with phenomena such as Auschwitz. If God can change the course of nature and save lives, then it would be wholly indefensible for God not to have used this potential for intervention in view of the great catastrophes in the history of mankind, as exemplified most forcefully in the last century by the atrocities that occurred at Auschwitz.

If at this point the classical rationalistic scholastic theology of all religions were to point out that God only acts in an interventionist way when legitimising his prophets, then this too could be seen as problematic even from simply a scholastic theological perspective, inasmuch as this would imply for one thing a limitation of God's actions, given that this idea could hardly be reconciled with the customary scholastic theological concept of God's omnipotence – at least if

7 On the presentation of the current status of this problem and defence of talk of God's specific actions in the world from a Christian theological perspective, cf. Klaus von Stosch, *Gott – Macht – Geschichte. Versuch einer theodizeesensiblen Rede von Gottes Handeln in der Welt*, Freiburg – Basle – Vienna 2006. On the Muslim standpoint on this question, cf. Tatari, 'Eine muslimische Perspektive auf das Handeln Gottes', 35–53.

8 Cf. Klaus von Stosch, 'Gottes Handeln denken. Zur Verantwortung der Rede von einem besonderen Handeln Gottes im Gespräch mit den Naturwissenschaften.' In: Georg Gasser and Josef Quitterer (eds.), *Die Aktualität des Seelenbegriffs. Interdisziplinäre Zugänge*, Paderborn and elsewhere 2010, 55–80.

one does not wish to argue from a rationalistic viewpoint.[9] In addition, arguing in this way entails the assumption, equally questionable for traditional scholastic theology, that an interventionist agency on God's part was restricted to a period up to and including Muhammad, as the world's last prophet.

And yet rationalistic scholastic theology would regard precisely this restriction as a strength of the concept being described. Consequently, in our context, it is another aspect, already hinted at above, that is far more important. The conviction that God can intervene in human history, and that this therefore forms part of God's plan for creation, but that he would then confine himself to enacting this powerful intervention only in the case of prophets, is highly suspect in view of the shocking extent of man-made catastrophes in history. Why, for example, should God protect the Israelites from persecution by the Egyptians by performing a miracle (the parting of the Red Sea), yet at the same time condemn countless other peoples to death? In the light of the horrific death of so many people, is it really simply enough to accept the idea that this miracle serves to authenticate Moses's role as a prophet as an argument that excuses everything else? In this instance, could one really exonerate a belief in God from the suspicion that it is nothing but acquiescence in despotism? At this point any theology that wishes to cleave to a belief in classical interventionism would necessarily have to abandon its attempt to develop rationally verifiable systems of thought and take refuge instead in the idea of the ineffable mystery of God's will. However, the price of this theological emergency exit would be very high: after the catastrophes that have taken place in the history of humankind, and most especially those of the twentieth century, a theodicy of this nature is only possible if one builds into one's theology a large measure of apathy and wordless indifference on the part of God. In the interim, such an approach has been comprehensively discredited within Christianity, and we would not recommend it for Islamic systematic theology either.

Yet the scholastic theological notion of the concept of miracles also appears problematic to us in another regard. For a key consideration in our eyes is that, if miracles are verified as such, then this in principle leaves humans no potential for coming to a rational decision either for or against believing in God. And it was precisely this effect of miracles that was important to theologians of the scholastic period. It was intended to reveal God's power and man's impotence and to make clear that prophets were individuals whose mission and authority should be seen as deriving from God alone. As the root of the Arabic term

9 Current Sunni scholastic theology would reject the kind of rationalism classically espoused by *mu'tazila*.

suggests, miracles are overwhelming experiences: the *mu'ǧiza* renders those who witness it *'āǧiz* ('powerless') and thereby positively compels them to believe in God. At least this is certainly the case if a miracle is publicly verifiable and hence irrefutable. Such an event is compelling not just for prophets but also for everyone who bears witness to the miracle – and it is precisely this aspect which distinguishes it from *karāma*.

However, in common with many other theologians of modern times, the two authors of this book strongly favour a liberation-theological approach and take the view that the Bible and the Qur'an should be understood in such a way that God in his actions does not annul human freedom. Failing this, we would be at a loss as to how to rationally affirm the existence of God in the face of all the evil in the world. For notwithstanding that it seriously compromises any supposition of a theodicy, an argument that posits human free will is nonetheless an indispensable component of any modern theology.[10] How else could one explain the fact that God makes no effort to convert tyrants who inflict untold misery on large numbers of people? In the absence of a firm belief in the autonomy of God's creatures, what is one to make of the fact that infants with multiple disabilities and other innocent beings are forced to suffer grievously to the end of their days? The idea that God uses evil people as his tools and that suffering can be justified in theological terms as a test or an educative measure is increasingly becoming the subject of polemical debate, even within Islam.[11] In reaching this conclusion, however, we are not seeking to deny that a certain subjective, healing reality and truth can be ascribed to those verses of the Qur'an which, for example, talk about suffering as a test – as we will explain below.

Where the whole concept of miracles is concerned, we want to ask whether rejecting the idea of a miraculous intervention by God – a position that we have

10 Cf. von Stosch, *Theodizee*, 70–111; on the need to supplement this kind of argumentative theodicy with a practical and authentic one, cf. Tatari, 'Ein Plädoyer für die Klage vor Gott', 279–285.

11 On initial attempts to sound out a plurality of standpoints on this topic with Islam, see: Andreas Renz et al. (eds.), *Prüfung oder Preis der Freiheit? Leid und Leidbewältigung in Christentum und Islam*, Regensburg 2008 (Theologisches Forum Christentum – Islam). As regards the question of the death of small children, in the story of al-Khidr the preacher of the Qur'an appears to entertain one further way of identifying a theodicy in operation here – namely the possibility that such a death might actually be to the benefit of children, since they might otherwise run the risk of growing up to commit grave sins and so being cast into Hell (cf. Q 18:80). Such logic is perfectly understandable and was also widespread in Christianity in Late Antiquity and the Middle Ages. In modern times, however, it is not regarded as a plausible solution of the theodicy problem, since it begs the question of why God did not then kill people such as Hitler when they were still children.

argued for above – implies a fundamental criticism of the notion that God intervenes beneficially in creation. We firmly believe that it does not. A root-and-branch rejection of a God who can perform miracles is by no means a compelling solution either within history or for the end of history, assuming one wishes to leave open the possibility, firmly anchored in the Islamic tradition, that God can personally turn to the individual human being and guide his or her destiny. We therefore argue here in favour of taking seriously the personal experience of believers and cannot imagine any reason why we would reject the notion of God performing miracles, which is widely attested in the Islamic, Jewish and Christian traditions – provided that these are understood as personal testimony and not as facts which can be scientifically verified by people. In this approach, defining an event as a miracle could not be established without taking into account the subjective perspective of the viewer and hence would express something about that event only within the context of this relationship. Thus, enquiring about the existence of an interventionist action on God's part would be to ask the wrong question in the first place, since it does not ultimately matter whether God breaches natural laws or not,[12] but instead whether he turns to a person in such a way that the divine presence becomes a comprehensible and beneficial reality to the individual concerned.

As a result of this change in the concept of miracles within modern theology that we have just described, the traditional distinction between the concepts of *karāma* and *mu'ǧiza* has lost its cogency. For miracles in the modern sense only gain their cogency from the fact that the signs (Arabic: *āya*) they give are intelligible to me as an individual. In this view of things, God must enthral and convince me on a subjective level. Certainly, my faith community and the tradition that it imparts can also be of assistance to me in this. Our aim is not to wrench the testimony of faith from its anchorage within the community. And yet this common anchorage generates only communal structures of plausibility rather than any truly compelling contexts. And, according to our take on things, I too as an individual can never be subject to compulsion. Otherwise, this would constantly beg the question of why God has not compelled miscreants and tyrants to cease their murderous activities and turn anew to him. What we are trying to do, therefore, is to present a picture of a God who woos, invites and calls us, as opposed to one who coerces and oppresses. But if it is indeed the case that, even in miracles, God's

12 And perhaps God does indeed breach the laws of nature. It may be that increasing awareness of the complexity of natural processes does not permit us to come to a definitive conclusion on this question. In any event, for the reasons that we have cited, it would certainly seem that any assumption that such a breach of natural laws should be publicly verifiable needs to be abandoned.

actions always leave human beings room for manoeuvre, then it follows that there cannot be any objective proof of prophethood of the kind demanded by tradition in the category of *muʿǧiza*. And so even prophetic testimony remains contentious and ambiguous – what other interpretation could one otherwise put on the oft-attested repudiation of prophets in the history of religion?

c) A reappraisal of our understanding of miracles through the Qur'anic Mary

In Part II, on exegesis of the Qur'an, we saw that the Mary of the Qur'an is clearly in a dialogic relationship of freedom with God, and we repeatedly stressed the dimension of freedom that existed within this relationship. Of course, at first glance one might well ask oneself how a person who comes face to face with an angel can still be thought of as free. Yet the narrative in the Qur'an makes it unmistakably clear that Mary is not simply overawed.[13] There remain warning signs that make her reflect and question. Of course, she knows the angel of God so well that she ultimately has good cause to trust. Nor should we imagine her frantically turning the matter over in her mind and wrestling with her decision. There is nothing of this in the text of the Qur'an. But as a consequence of the angel appearing in the form of a young man, the scene remains ambiguous and questionable and is not clarified from an objective external viewpoint. The only clarity that does emerge here comes through Mary's developing and clear-sighted relationship with God – in other words not from outside but solely from within her subjective religious devotion. Mary's experienced eye enables her to place a fresh interpretation on a situation which from an external standpoint appears highly ambiguous and to steer it in a subjective, unambiguous direction.

Much the same can be said of the other signs that occur in Mary's life and which accompany and strengthen her on her path of devotion. Particularly striking in this regard are the meals that she is provided with by angels time and again throughout her childhood. Classical religious scholars are divided over how to interpret these *karāma*. As a general rule, they concede that these meals are of supernatural origin and that this divine care represents a special distinction and honour where Mary is concerned, which has to do with her status of being 'favoured above all

13 Cf. Ali, 'Destabilizing gender, reproducing maternity', 101: 'In theory, Mary, like the earth in the eyes of exegetes, could have rejected God's breath that imparted his spirit into her body ... While God could have created Jesus in Mary's womb regardless of her own desires, her consent and receptive nature are vital to the Qur'an's theological message.'

other women'. They also consider whether these miracles might perhaps have been the decisive factor that encouraged Zechariah to ask God for a child, despite this being a hopeless prospect by all normal standards. And it is indeed the case that this causal link is strongly suggested by the text of the Qur'an (cf. Q 3:37 f.).

However, if this interpretation is true, then these miracles would precisely no longer be evident purely subjectively for Mary, but instead would have a significant public impact, and this would mean that, according to the scholastic theological distinction, they would actually have to be ranked as more than *karāma*. Consequently most exegetes insist that even Zechariah noticed nothing of the supernatural nature of the meals, as evidenced by the question he then asks (Q 3:37). Mary now responds clearly and unequivocally to his enquiry, and Zechariah takes her answer as an opportunity to deliver his prayer of supplication (Q 3:37 f.). As a result, any attempt to square the purely private character of these miracles with the actual wording of the Qur'an seems to us to be extremely contrived.

However, in making this observation our aim is not to suggest that the provision of sustenance to Mary in the Temple amounts to a *muʿǧiza*. In our estimation, this would be a logically perfectly sound conclusion to draw if one followed the logic of classical scholastic theology – and therefore so would be acknowledging Mary as a prophet. But from a modern standpoint, it avails us little to interpret Mary's provisioning by the angels as a breach of the laws of nature. Once again, indeed, the problem of a theodicy raises its head, and we would have to respond by asking why God has not provided all the untold numbers of starving children down the ages with sustenance too, if he did this in the case of little Mary. Yet Mary would also have been supplied with food by Zechariah, so that we misinterpret the general thrust of the Qur'anic text if we see it as presenting God's actions in such a way as to place all the emphasis on direct divine intervention geared solely toward giving Mary sustenance. Clearly it is about much more here than providing for purely material needs.

Even from a purely philological standpoint, the Arabic term *rizq*, which is used here to describe the feeding of Mary, does not simply mean providing a person with a meal, but instead denotes the supply of both material and immaterial sustenance. Classical exegetes talk here about the fruits of winter that Mary receives in the summer and the fruits of summer that Mary receives in the winter, and interpret this as an expression of Mary's exceptional status and of God's boundless creativity.[14] Perhaps it might be apposite here to speak in terms of God's agency becoming apparent in the contingent opening of the laws of nature. Maybe the

14 Cf. aṭ-Ṭabarī, *Tafsīr*, Vol. 5, 353; ar-Rāzī, *Tafsīr*, Vol. 8, 37.

whole episode is not actually about the inexplicability of what takes place, but rather about Mary's special relationship with God, as evidenced by the fact that she is provisioned in this way. The testimony of the Qur'an demonstrates how Mary increasingly comes to realise that everything she receives is a direct gift from God. She also realises that God will never forsake her – a realization that provides here with a psychological lifeline during the crisis of her pregnancy in the desert. Thus as a result of tangible symbolic acts, Mary gains a physical and existential insight which in actual fact is available to each and every one of us: as created beings we are dependent upon God for everything without exception, and God is our sustainer and provider (*rabb*). It is he alone on whom everything depends, and as a consequence our sole purpose is to direct our own lives entirely to the service of God. It is exactly this that Mary achieves with God's help, and this is the end goal of the symbolic acts. And she – like all of us – can rely on the fact that God will not abandon her, provided she places her complete trust in him in all aspects of her life.

All in all, with regard to Mary, this means that God's potency is not some abstract force that operates over the heads of the people concerned or even against their will, but rather one which takes into account the situation as it exists and opens up the potential for new insights and actions. And in the process, it is entirely possible for the laws of logic as defined by humans, or expectations and attitudes based on empirical experience, to be surprisingly broadened – or, to put it in a religious and poetic way, for winter fruits to appear in summer. In using this formulation, it may be that the exegetes were responding to a human experience and reminding us not to try to comprehend God's actions through binary logic. All the same, this does not mean that they were advocating unchecked irrationality. In this sense, in this context too, the efforts of the exegetes may be acknowledged as a rationally responsible handling of a religious and theological insight into something that is ultimately not rationally comprehensible – the majesty of God.

Evidently, the images and the symbolic acts in the story of Mary can be better understood if we see the signs they give, on an objective plane, as permanently ambiguous, while at the same time acknowledging that, on a subjective plane, they impart a definite direction and clarity to Mary thanks to the intensity of her relationship with God. Objectively, the unexpected discovery of food and the unexpected gift of strength to make a fresh start can be interpreted in a different way. They could, for instance, be pure chance or simply luck. Also, Mary's own perception of the food being supplied by an angel might be based on a delusion. As a consequence, there can never be any objective certainty on this matter.

And yet there is a moment where all questioning ceases and trust prevails. From the example of Mary, we can observe how patiently God answers her questions until she reaches this state. In other words, trust is not given in a blind leap of faith, but comes about in a rationally responsible and plausible way as a result of the experience of God's care. At no point is the power of God that Mary finds herself facing defined by sheer coercion.

In view of the angel's visitation, could Mary have possibly acted any differently? Given her life story and her longstanding relationship with God, the answer would have to be 'No'. Her life is already so inextricably interwoven with God that she cannot do anything other than feel her way ever deeper into the mystery of God. But her inability to act otherwise is not a sign of a lack of freedom, but rather a sign of a mature readiness to self-commitment; this also makes itself apparent in the ultimate expression of human freedom – namely the willingness to give oneself over to the incomprehensible mystery that is God, so completely that we grow in our relationship with the creator and this relationship becomes an integral part of our identity.

In this context, it is very exciting to see the way in which the Qur'an describes Mary receiving a sign of encouragement above all through the conception of her child, and how this is a sign that comes to her externally from God as the first step (Q 19:21). Yet in making herself fully receptive to this sign and trustingly allowing it to enter her innermost being, she and her child together themselves become a sign (Q 21:91; 23:50). From a Muslim perspective, this experience too has exemplary significance. Every person and every creature can become a sign of God, in the same way as every verse of the Qur'an is a sign from God (Arabic: *āya*). But if a person, with divine help, manages to say 'Yes' to God as comprehensively as Mary did when he approaches us through signs, then that person, together with the sign that was given to him or her and the 'Yes' of his or her answer, becomes in turn a sign of God.[15] God thus reveals himself to us and invites us to participate in his symbolic acts in order to make his power and majesty tangible reality in this world.

We can see from Mary and her story in the Qur'an that the story of God's relationship with humankind can never objectively escape from a state of ambiguity. But it also shows us how God turns to humanity in a caring and merciful way. Even Mary's mother experiences at first hand how God enters into a relationship

15 Likewise, in an Islamic context there is a corresponding tradition that parallels Muhammad's character with the Qur'an. Cf. Muslim, *Ṣaḥīḥ*, Hadith No. 746, Book No. 6 (*Kitāb ṣalāt al-musāfirīn wa-qaṣruhā*). Vol. II, 257.

of dialogue with her, only then to fulfil and surpass all her human expectations. And it is precisely this aspect of exceeded expectations, evident probably most clearly in Mary's virginity, which time and again confuses people and causes them to struggle with God's plans. But the example of the Qur'anic Mary and her mother clearly shows us that God does not demand blind obedience from us, but instead encourages us to ask questions and aims to lead us towards an ever deeper understanding of his caring power. Thus, rather than trying to identify objective differences between different types of miracles, theology should be emboldened by the story of Mary in the Qur'an to see God's agency as a dialogue and use her example to rethink it entirely.

d) Mary and Muhammad

Following the pioneering work of Annemarie Schimmel, researchers in the fields of Islamic Studies and Comparative Theology have repeatedly drawn attention to the marked similarity between the roles and tasks performed by the biblical Mary and the Prophet Muhammad.[16] Seen from the viewpoint of their respective religions, they are the individuals who receive the word of God, who are bound to it in a mystical way and who implement it in an exemplary fashion in the way they conduct their lives.[17] Both are prepared in a quite special way by God for their extraordinary roles – Mary through her virginity and Muhammad through his illiteracy. Just as, from a Christian standpoint, the miracle of God's being born as man appears all the greater when he is born of a virgin, so is the miracle of the inimitability of the Qur'an highlighted all the more clearly as an act of God by the fact that it is revealed via a man who himself was not some great poet but an illiterate. We do not intend at this juncture to assess whether the Qur'an truly is premised upon Muhammad's illiteracy. Indeed, we do not even want to get involved in examining this well-established comparison of the two figures. Rather, we want to continue to concentrate on the Mary of the Qur'an, and to emphasise how strongly the figure of Mary in the Qur'an adumbrates the Prophet Muhammad and the extent to which her fate is linked to his.

For it is true to say that, like Mary, the Prophet Muhammad struggles with the revelation that is made to him, and has to find his way step by step into his divine mission. And from a Muslim viewpoint Muhammad too is a person who

16 Cf. most recently Takács, 'Mary and Muhammad', 2; Madigan, 'God's word to the world', 166–168.

17 Cf. Takács, 'Mary and Muhammad', 12 f.

takes his cue entirely from God and lives his life wholly in God's service. He is unsurpassed in the way he abandons himself to God's benign will and attempts to fulfil it in the way he lives his own life. From a Muslim perspective, in doing so he attains an even higher degree of perfection than Mary. It is striking to note that his relationship with God is also one of total intensity. And it is profoundly encouraging to see how he too has to struggle with his life history in moments of ambiguity. But like Mary he is so deeply rooted in his relationship with God that he is incapable of doing anything other than acquiesce ever more intensely in God's will and hence – more comprehensively than any other human being – to become the proclaimer of that divine will.

Thus, in stressing the similarities between Mary and Muhammad here, we are not meaning to question the absolute primacy of Muhammad's role within Islam. Rather, our objective is to show how one can gain a deeper and better understanding of Muhammad by examining him in the context of the story of Mary. Let us therefore begin with the quite obvious external parallels: both are the recipients of a revelation imparted by the angel Gabriel, who is also identified as a 'spirit of God'[18] – and in the case of both, this revelation appears in the first instance as dubious, presenting both of them with an extreme challenge.[19] From time to time, the heavenly figure appears to both of them to take on human form.[20] Both are protected from Satan.[21] And both of them also experience God's revelation from behind a veil or curtain.[22]

It is interesting that these parallels can be traced not just back to the Qur'an but are also subject to further embellishment throughout the Islamic tradition. For instance, Muslim tradition is lavish in its praise of the spirituality of both figures, as evidenced in their active prayer regime, which was supposedly so pronounced that their feet swelled up as a result of long periods of standing during their devotions.[23] And just as Muhammad leant against the trunk of a palm tree during his

18 Cf. Robinson, 'Jesus and Mary in the Qur'an', 169.

19 Cf. Kaltner, *Ishmael instructs Isaac*, 215–217. Cf. also footnote 10 on p. 327.

20 Cf. the well-known hadith on the conversation between Muhammad and Gabriel, which concerns the definition of the concepts *islām*, *īmān* and *iḥsān*: Al-Buḫārī, *Ṣaḥīḥ*, Hadith No. 4777, Book No. 65 (*Kitāb at-tafsīr*), 1199 f.

21 Cf. Robinson, 'Jesus and Mary in the Qur'an', 170. Ibn Ishaq, *Das Leben des Propheten*, 30–32, and for Mary see the references in this book to the Qur'anic and Hadith texts on how people can defend themselves against Satan: 155, 167 and 169.

22 Cf. Robinson, 'Jesus and Mary in the Qur'an', 171.

23 Cf. Stowasser, *Women in the Qur'an*, 73; cf. also aṭ-Ṭabarī, *Tafsīr*, Vol. 5, 393, for Mary; and for Muhammad cf. al-Buḫārī, *Ṣaḥīḥ*, Hadith No. 1130, Book No. 19 (*Kitāb tahağğud*), 274.

first sermons, so Mary supported herself against just such a trunk during her labour pains.[24] Mary was known as a pious woman, leaving one with no alternative but to believe her in the matter of Jesus's conception. Likewise, Muhammad was renowned for being an honest merchant and an advocate of social justice, meaning that in his case too we can assume a high degree of authenticity when he began to discover his prophetic calling.

However, the parallels go even deeper. Thus, Ali and Abboud see Mary as being a 'role model' for the Prophet Muhammad, inasmuch as she, like him, initially had to deal with resistance from those around her and was subject to base accusations and only later rehabilitated.[25] They therefore regard Mary as nothing short of a prototype for Muhammad – exerting at least as powerful an influence on him as the male prophets whom the proclaimer of the Qur'an repeatedly invokes. In the same way that people do not believe Mary in the matter of the honourable provenance of her son, Muhammad too is the target of scepticism as to whether the words he imparts really do emanate from God, and he finds himself facing accusations that he is mad, or power-hungry or a confabulator, whose spirit-muse helped him compose the text.[26] Thus, already from within the Qur'an, and not first from a comparative perspective, both are shown as receiving God's word and making space for it in their lives, assisted by gentle pressure from God.[27] Therefore, from a purely Islamic perspective alone, the huge significance of the figure of Mary for the Prophet Muhammad becomes clear and there is much evidence to suggest that she should be viewed as a bridging figure to Christianity. But before we pursue this thought further (see below, 'In Dialogue with Christianity'), we first need to revisit Mary's exceptional status and examine some more recent observations from Islamic feminist theology on this topic.

---

24 Cf. Robinson, 'Jesus and Mary in the Qur'an', 170.

25 Cf. Ali, 'Destabilizing gender, reproducing maternity', 97. Lybarger, 'Gender and prophetic authority in the Qur'anic story of Maryam', 242, even argues in favour of reading the Qur'an's version of Mary's story against the historical background of Judaism's and Christianity's rejection of the Prophet Muhammad and seeing it as an alternative account of their histories of salvation.

26 Cf. Kaltner, *Ishmael instructs Isaac*, 226. This parallel between Mary and Muhammad can also be read in the following way: the accusation levelled at Mary was that the origin of the Word that she was bringing to the world, namely Jesus, was impure – in the sense that he was the product of an act of illegitimate sexual congress. In a similar way, Muhammad faced the accusation that the source of his revelation was not pure, but instead relied upon inspiration from a supernatural spirit-muse (*jinn*) that he had summoned up, as poets were commonly thought at that time to do.

27 Cf. Buisson, 'Subversive Maryam or a Qur'anic view on women's empowerment', 457.

3

Mary as a Figure of Emancipation

Earlier extensive discussions of whether it is legitimate in Islam to regard Mary as a prophet have already brought us into contact with the endeavours of contemporary Islamic feminist theology. We now want to treat this explicitly as a theme by considering the extent to which the figure of Mary in the Qur'an can be employed as a figurehead or role model in the struggle for greater gender equality.

a) The story of Mary in the Qur'an as a stimulus for greater gender equality

One initial major stimulus for greater gender equality can already be found in Mary's genealogy and the way her mother's role is described. In Part II of this book, we presented in some detail the depiction of the special bond of intimacy and the relationship of dialogue that existed between Mary's mother Hannah and God. It is she who dedicates Mary to a life of service in the temple, and whose prayer of supplication is heard by God. And it is she who is the driving force in Mary's genealogy and who on a narrative level manages entirely without the help of a man. Let us now take a closer look at these last two points.

By responding to Mary's mother's prayer of supplication in an unexpected way and giving her a daughter, it seems to us that God was inciting her to call into doubt a central privilege of the patriarchal tradition,[1] which to a large extent still

---

1 Cf. Abboud, 'Is Mary Important for Herself or for Being the Mother of Christ in the Holy Qur'an?', 30, and Buisson, 'Subversive Maryam or a Qur'anic view on women's empowerment', 454: 'When Hanna had initially made her vow to God, she had not meant to break Jewish law; however, through answering Hanna's prayer, God knowingly decided to make the child a girl (Q. 3:36) and thereby set off a dynamic of change that would cause a subversive change of social and religious order.'

preoccupies Judaism and Christianity today. For God's initiative serves to underline the fact that a woman is able to serve in the Temple, and hence naturally also in the synagogue or church, and is permitted to be ordained to perform such a role. Here God himself initiates a rupture of social norms, and it is the young Mary who exemplifies these new possibilities for women to serve in a liturgical capacity. As a result, Johanna Buisson quite correctly sees Mary's time in the Temple as an intervention by God, who wants to instigate social changes in favour of women. According to her, the text on Mary finds its sounding board above all in the change that ensues in the situation for women with the onset of Islam.[2] And nowadays, in all religions, it can only be the spur for energetically pursuing this same course.

However, a second important factor is the key finding that we arrived at in Part II – namely that, in assigning a prominent position to Mary and her mother in Jesus's family tree, the proclaimer of the Qur'an gives women the opportunity to assume a genealogically decisive role. In a sense, it may even be justifiable here to talk in terms of the introduction of a matrilineal genealogy.[3] If we take seriously the fact that the Qur'an as a general rule links prophets with other prophets genealogically, then in Abboud's view the exclusive linking of the prophet Jesus with his mother Mary also constitutes a powerful argument for seeing her role as prophetic.[4] The present authors are not certain that we really want to follow this logic. In any event, though, a convincing case can be made for seeing the proclaimer of the Qur'an's matrilineal logic here as introducing a vital counterpoint to the overwhelmingly patriarchal traditions that prevailed on the Arabian Peninsula,[5] as well as in Judaism and Christianity. Mary's mother thus injects an emancipatory element into the story of Mary. She herself takes on important roles that would otherwise have been reserved for men – in addition to choosing a name for her child – and also introduces her daughter into the male domain of service at the Temple.

But of course the emancipatory impulses of the Qur'an are not confined to the family history of Mary, though they do find a decisive point of reference in the way she is portrayed in the Qur'an. For, as we have already seen in Part II, Mary

2 Cf. Buisson, 'Subversive Maryam or a Qur'anic view on women's empowerment', 453.

3 Cf. Abboud, 'Is Mary important for herself or for being the Mother of Christ in the Holy Qur'anic?', 29 f.; see also the statements we made above when examining the views of Angelika Neuwirth.

4 Cf. Abboud, *Mary in the Qur'an*, 134.

5 It remains a matter of speculation whether the preacher of the Qur'an was intentionally alluding to pagan matrilineal traditions on the Arabian Peninsula dating from the pre-Islamic period.

too is shown here to enjoy a special intimacy with God. Furthermore, she is cared for directly by God and his angels and therefore does not need a male provider in the narrative of the Qur'an.

Nonetheless, we are all to prone to losing sight of what a strong role Mary plays in the Qur'an because, as in the biblical tradition, such a great deal of emphasis is also placed on her passivity. In line with this, we too ascertained above that, in the Qur'an's view, God empties Mary of everything that might distract or impede her,[6] in order that she can focus entirely on her service to God. Put somewhat exaggeratedly, the temptation might be to see this act of emptying as the sum total of God's interaction with Mary and in the process to forget about the independence of her actions.

Yet the logic of the Qur'an, and indeed of the Bible, holds that it is precisely by acquiescing in the will of God with such radical humility and in desiring to make God's benevolent will a reality through her service that Mary gains an unparalleled degree of inner independence and becomes truly free. This state of freedom is expressed programmatically in the word-root *salima*,[7] from which terms such as *islām*, *muslim*, and *salām* derive and can, on the basis of this key role of Islamic terminology, be seen as an important theological guiding category. And the Mary of the Qur'an embodies the spiritual–religious aspect of this category – traces of which can be identified in her every action – in a particularly intense way.[8] Likewise, the narrative details of the story of Mary in the Qur'an show that we should not overlook the active role Mary plays in her (deliberately) chosen state of passivity.

For instance, when Mary is called upon to shake the palm tree in order to try and overcome her despair at the height of her labour pains, Buisson sees this as a piece of divine pedagogy designed to encourage her to be proactive and get to grips with things. She is meant, Buisson claims, to take her share of the responsibility while at the same time remaining focused on her dialogue with God and

6 Cf. our remarks above in Part II.

7 Cf. Lane, *Lexicon*, Vol. 4, 1413–1417.

8 This idea continues to resonate in ethical–legal discussions many centuries later, as the following passage written by Šāṭibī (d. 1388) demonstrates: 'The [ethical] aim of the *Sharīʿa* is to liberate people from their delusional wishful thinking, namely that they can become servants of God of their own volition, whereas in actual fact they are already servants through no act of free will on their part [*al-maqṣadu š-šarʿī min waḍʿi š-šarīʿati iḫrāğu l-mukallafi min daʿīyati hawāhu ḥattā yakūnu ʿabdan li-llāhi iḫtiyāran ka-mā huwa ʿabdan lillāhi iḍṭirāran*]' (aš-Šāṭibī, *al-Muwāfaqāt fī uṣūl aš-šarīʿa*, Vol. 2, 469). Therefore, an ethical code which sees itself as inextricably bound to a concept of freedom, while not being arbitrary, can only ever perform an enabling role, and can never be a truly authoritative and cogent system of ethics.

fully aware that it is he who ultimately sustains and shapes everything and brings it to fruition. Buisson construes God's challenge as a way of helping Mary to help herself, so that she can develop her own strength and use it to shape her life.[9]

John Kaltner asks whether Mary's wish to die during childbirth[10] and to be forgotten cannot simply be explained by the severity of her labour pains and her fear of how her family will react, but might also be an expression of her struggle and her recalcitrance toward the task she has been set. If one follows this interpretation, then at this point Mary would, like Jonah – as we already outlined above – refuse to take on this responsibility. We are not sure whether one can really go so far here as to paint Mary as a rebel. But it should at least be clear that she is certainly not God's puppet, stoically submitting to his will, but rather an active and energetic participant in the task God has asked her to perform. For all Mary's passivity, her attitude remains one of constant questioning, searching and also – as her prayer clearly reveals – wrestling with her destiny. Moreover, Kaltner claims, this prayer to have her existence extinguished remains the only prayer in the whole family history of Mary which God does not grant.[11] This underlines the point at which God's readiness to productively meet our needs definitively stops. At the same time it is evident how far God has accommodated Mary's hopes and wishes and how greatly he has encouraged her on her journey.

b) Mary as a boundary breaker

In our comparison of Mary and Muhammad, we have already speculated that Muhammad's illiteracy might be seen as a functional equivalent of Mary's virginity. This serves to emphasise the fact that not only Mary but also Muhammad remain absolutely passive in the process of revelation. The deeper meaning behind Muhammad's passivity is that, when he preaches, it is really God who is speaking, and that the Prophet does not allow his own ideas and commentaries to permeate the text of the Qur'an. His silent passivity is therefore intended to put the inherent dignity of God's word in the Qur'an into relief. And Mary's passivity should be understood in exactly the same way. She does not stay silent out of a lack of eloquence, but to accentuate the word of God as conveyed through Jesus Christ. Thus, her depiction in the Qur'an is not meant to smooth the path for any

9 Cf. Buisson, 'Subversive Maryam or a Qur'anic view on women's empowerment', 452 f.
10 Furthermore, Mary's death wish has an interesting parallel in Muhammad's experience of revelation, which for him represents such an extreme experience that his first urge is to throw himself off a mountain. Cf. aṭ-Ṭabarī, *Ta'rīḫ*, Vol. 2, 298.
11 Cf. Kaltner, *Ishmael instructs Isaac*, 224 f.

prevailing view of the role of women, but to emphasise that her silent passivity gives the message and the word of God space for expression.

In her feminist comparative theology, Jerusha Tanner Rhodes provides a critical reassessment of the comparison between Mary and Muhammad. She too stresses Muhammad's passivity in the matter of revelation: in behaving completely passively, Muhammad is assuming a role traditionally regarded as female.[12] In addition, the highlighting of his handsomeness, his fine clothes and his sensitivity, but above all the way he is styled as a prophet of compassion display characteristics that are customarily seen as androgynous, Tanner Rhodes claims. Conversely, it is not simply the case that Mary displays the same feminine traits. She is also presented as the patron saint of liberation struggles, while in the Bible she is notable for overturning existing power structures within society, for instance when she topples the wealthy from their thrones and raises up the lowly.

Mary and Muhammad thus combine female and male role models in a way that confounds customary expectations of gender roles.[13] At the same time, they are also boundary breakers as regards the traditional demarcation of transcendence and immanence, inasmuch as both attain a kind of divinity precisely in the great humanity they display. Tanner Rhodes makes striking use of these observations on the transgressive power of both figures in order to analyse them from the standpoint of queer theology and, borrowing a phrase from the Christian feminist theologian Marcella Althaus-Reid, to designate them as the 'Queer of Heaven'[14] – a conclusion which in her book is convincingly argued, though it can easily lead to misunderstandings.[15]

So, following Tanner Rhodes, how is it possible to see Mary the Queen of Heaven not only as queen but also as 'Queer of Heaven'? After all, queer people are by definition those who elude our usual binary gender division. In its divine variant, queerness presents an opportunity to explode restrictive gender clichés and also in more general terms to transcend other boundaries that hem people in and attempt to assign them to hard-and-fast gender roles. Unfortunately, religious

12 On the comparison of Mary and Muhammad, see Tanner Rhodes, *Divine words, female voices*, 121–155.

13 In similar vein, even as early as the eighteenth century Shah Wali Allah praised Mary's masculinity (cf. George-Tvrtković, *Christians, Muslims, and Mary*, 42).

14 Ibid., 139.

15 Of course, we are well aware that neither Tanner Rhodes nor Althaus-Reid means to say that Mary herself is queer, in the sense of a biological disposition. Even so, the formulation 'Queer of Heaven' is open to misinterpretation in this regard, and for this reason we have not adopted it here.

people are not immune to this kind of mental tendency to pigeonhole, and are often quicker to draw boundaries than would seem appropriate from a heavenly perspective. In our reading of the story of Mary, as well as in many other passages in the Qur'an, time and again God confounds our restrictive perceptions and practices and the injustices that arise from them. It gives us pause for thought, for example, when Abboud draws attention to the fact that the historical background to the Surah *Āl ʿImrān* is characterised by negotiations concerning the participation of women in the growing Muslim community in Medina.[16] Against this socio-historical background, the special distinction accorded to Mary can be seen as a transgressive act of partisanship on behalf of women who hoped for and expected greater possibilities for participation to flow from the movement led by the Prophet Muhammad. Precisely the problems regarding the appropriate categorisation of Mary that we have described so extensively above make us aware how dangerous a narrowing of our conceptual distinctions can be when we are trying to expand our thinking to comprehend the infinite breadth of the divine.

In discussing the role of Mary in the Qur'an, which she too defines as 'queer', Kecia Ali uses these reflections as an opportunity to point out the profound inadequacy of feminist theology's customary placement of Mary on a par with the male prophets. Of course, feminist theologians are right to state that the Qur'an contains important references to the equal rights of men and women. However, it does not necessarily follow from this acknowledgement of equal rights that gender equality also exists in the religious and social sphere.[17]

Conversely, Ali claims, we also run the risk of essentialising variations in gender differences. To be sure, in the passages in the Qur'an dealing with Mary, her depiction as a mother, a mother-to-be and as a woman takes up a great deal of space and in doing so lends these typically female life circumstances a dignity of their own,[18] which we will presently examine in greater detail under the next heading. Perhaps one might actually use the sentence in the Qur'an stating that a male is not like a female (Q 3:36) – which God conveys to Mary's mother at the birth of her daughter to apprise her of the life chances of her child seeing that it is a different gender to that which Hannah expected – to reflect the richness in the polarity of the sexes in theology.[19] But all this must not mislead us into reimposing fixed gender roles and denying people opportunities to develop.

16 Cf. Abboud, 'Is Mary important for herself or for being the Mother of Christ in the Holy Qur'an?', 27.

17 Cf. Ali, 'Destabilizing gender, reproducing maternity', 94 f.

18 Cf. ibid., 90.

19 Cf. ibid., 98 f.

Ali therefore argues in favour of looking at the story of Mary in a queer way. She encourages us on the one hand to overcome a dualistic way of thinking involving essentialised categories of male and female, but on the other hand to remain sensitive to gender differences. Yet differences can be identified not just between the sexes but also within their frequently all too stereotypical attribution. In accordance with this, Ali maintains, it is incumbent upon us to spot not only the similarity between Mary and other female figures like the mother of Moses but also her similarities to men like Zechariah or John[20] – as well as the corresponding disparities, which we were at pains to note in detail in Part II.

Similarly, Ali argues, the relationship between religions and that between tradition and modernity should not be narrowed down to binary codes. Even the genuinely clear distinction between virginity and motherhood is undermined by Mary.[21] Rather, we must constantly been on the lookout for possibilities of transgression and fluidity. For Ali, even the differences between the two accounts of Mary given in Q 3 and Q 19 confirm that a queer route is the best way to appropriate the legacy of Mary, since the depictions of Mary in the two surahs are neither totally at variance nor is there any way in which they can be reconciled with one another and combined into one. Ali thus sees a productive and exciting instability in the figure of Mary within the Qur'an too.[22] Instead of identifying only similarities or differences, but also instead of interpreting everything according to a single, neat system, Ali therefore argues the case for cherishing the 'messiness' of the Qur'an, and so proclaiming the virtues of its vagueness, transgressive nature and capacity to confuse as just a different route to God.[23]

Like Ali, Abboud also sees the Qur'an as presenting two sides to Mary that cannot easily be dialectically reconciled with one another.[24] Mary as mother and Mary as prophet are not combined within a single, coherent theory; instead, loose ends of various possibilities of interpretation are joined together to open up new conceptual realms. For example, when Mary is exhorted by God to pray alongside the men in the Holy of Holies, although this was completely out of the question according to a traditional interpretation of the law,[25] this represents one such point

20 Cf. ibid., 103.

21 On the concept of virginity as a 'condition of liminality' cf. Mary F. Foskett, 'Virginity as purity in the Protevangelium of James.' In: *Levine* 67–76, here 70.

22 Cf. Ali, 'Destabilizing gender, reproducing maternity', 92.

23 Cf. ibid., 109.

24 Cf. Abboud, 'Is Mary important for herself or for being the Mother of Christ in the Holy Qur'an?', 30.

25 Cf. Buisson, 'Subversive Maryam or a Qur'anic view on women's empowerment', 454 f.

where new realms are opened up, though these realms are not pinned down in any legal or other systematic framework. In this way, theological and legal thinking begins to shift and cross boundaries, though it is by no means always clear exactly where such a movement might lead. The important thing about the figure of Mary is that her credibility and persuasiveness are not the product of a clearly calculated synthesis but result from her abiding devotion to God.

c) Mary as a stumbling-block and an incitement to subversion

Yet precisely this total commitment to God also repeatedly makes Mary something of a stumbling-block.[26] She frustrates not only the traditional gender-role expectations in a patriarchal society in which women are not trusted to fulfil the function of prophet or priest or to act as a role model for prominent men. She also puts us at sixes and sevens in our theology, for instance when we find ourselves struggling with the concept of her virginity. She confounds our usual expectations when we see a girl being provided with food in the Temple by God's angels. But the extent of her submission to the will of God, which far exceeds anything we normal mortals would be capable of, also acts as a provocation.

Some dimensions of her subversive potential, however, are not so evident and must first be laid bare. Thus, inhabiting as we do a modern world which abounds in stories of heroines, it does not immediately strike us that the Qur'an speaks almost exclusively to men. When men and women are addressed together, this is done using the grammatically inclusive male verb form, meaning that here too women are not explicitly visible. Yet what are we to make of the text of the Qur'an when it suddenly switches to devoting a substantial portion of narrative in such a prominent way to a female voice and women's experiences? Not only does God speak to a woman here, she answers, and a dialogue ensues. In terms of the theology of revelation, this shows that we cannot see the Qur'an as simply a patriarchal text. Assuming God is not speaking with a forked tongue here, the figure of Mary

---

26 In our use of this term, we are referring to the concept of the 'stumbling-blocks' developed from 1995 onwards by the artist Gunter Demnig when designing his memorials to the victims of Nazi persecution. His aim in installing these blocks of stone outside the former homes of Holocaust victims is literally and figuratively to 'stop people in their tracks', causing them to pause and reflect on what happened (cf. http://www.stolpersteine.eu/en/home/). In our view, the Qur'an contains a whole series of such stumbling-blocks, which interrupt our habitual habits of reading and thereby make us receptive to a new, unexpected presence of God. The story of Mary most decidedly constitutes one such stumbling-block. Cf. Tatari, *Gott und Mensch im Spannungsverhältnis von Gerechtigkeit und Barmherzigkeit*, 23.

alone clearly indicates that women's experiences also form part of the overall human experience of God. Women too have a name and a vocation in God's eyes.

Analysing the Surah *Maryam* from a narrative perspective, it is plain to see that Mary – at least in verses 16–33 – is the chief protagonist here, and that she speaks for herself and broaches themes that are of specific concern to women.[27] Mary, not Jesus, is the key figure here – a finding that is all the more striking when one recalls how completely Mary is eclipsed by the figure of Joseph in Mt, for instance, or how in Jn she is not even given a name. In the Qur'an, by contrast, she has a name and her most intimate experiences are recounted, even to the extent of an account of God's spirit touching her private parts. This represents a major stumbling block which deeply unsettled traditional exegeses, as we have seen, and which requires a degree of theological processing.

We would concur with Johanna Buisson in determining that the Mary of the Qur'an is emblematic of profound social, psychological and religious change, which challenged both the Jewish religious community and the patriarchal social structure of her time, as well as the ritual practices of the Temple in Jerusalem, which were focused on men. In this sense, Buisson claims, Mary takes on an emancipatory role, which had a subversive effect on the staying power of the patriarchal social order.[28] Time and again, in standing up for herself and choosing her own path, Mary transgressed against social norms and gender-role expectations.[29]

The subversive, emancipatory force of the Qur'an's accounts of Mary naturally had an effect on the early Islamic community too and undoubtedly also played a

27 Cf. Abboud, *Mary in the Qur'an*, 150.

28 Cf. Buisson, 'Subversive Maryam or a Qur'anic view on women's empowerment', 457: 'Maryam's life was fundamentally subversive insofar as she was the initiator of social, psychological, and religious change: from within her Jewish community, from within the male-dominated religious environment of the Temple of Jerusalem, she stood up, alone and confident in her faith, against discriminatory laws and women's social and religious exclusion. In that sense, she exemplifies women's assertiveness and empowerment.'

29 Cf. Buisson, 'Subversive Maryam or a Qur'anic view on women's empowerment', 455: 'While exceptionally devoted to God, Maryam is far from the patriarchal fable of the meek, obedient, and docile woman. Indeed, from her birth to her preposterous admission in the Temple of Jerusalem as the sole girl child, up to her entry into the sanctuary for prayer, her unexpected pregnancy, single-motherhood, and return to Jerusalem with the child, she stood up in confidence, kept breaking the rules of her community, and being at odds with social norms and expectations. From her youth on, she was educated to have the stamina to face public disgrace, slander, backbiting, stigma, and social exclusion from within a close community, therefore morally exacting and ruthless. She not only broke with the religious rules in the Temple, but she also broke with the social rules of her community; her figure is therefore fundamentally subversive.'

part in encouraging women to question the power structures which prevailed at that time and to participate in shaping Muhammad's movement as community members who enjoyed equal rights. How greatly this perturbed male supporters of Muhammad may be gauged from a grievance voiced by the later caliph ʿUmar, who complained to Muhammad in the following terms:

> God is great! O Prophet, you know us: we, the tribe of the Quraysh, were people who once had their women under their thumbs. Then we came to Medina and found there a people whose wives controlled them instead. And our women began to learn from their women. One day, I was angry with my wife, whereupon she started to argue back at me. I scolded her for contradicting me. Her response was this: 'Why are you criticising me for contradicting you? I swear by God, the wives of the Prophet [...] contradicted him and one of them (even) ostracised him for an entire day.' I replied: 'If any of you do such a thing, it'll be the end of you for sure. How can you be so sure that God won't be prompted by the Prophet's anger to direct his ire at you and ruin you?' At this, the Prophet [by ʿUmar's account] just smiled.[30]

Of course, Mary is not mentioned in this quotation, though one can safely assume that the women in Medina and the wives of the Prophet felt encouraged by the Mary tradition as recounted in the Qurʾan. We need only refer to our statements in Part II above (pages 194–195) concerning Mary's function as a role model for the wives of the Prophet in Surah 66. It is also correct to point out that Muhammad's smile in the quotation is presented without commentary, meaning that the text does not take a clear stance on the question. Does Muhammad share ʿUmar's view in the hadith? In deciding this matter, if we consult Muhammad's attitude toward women as recounted in tradition, there is much to suggest that

30 An-Nasāʾī, *ʿIšrat an-nisāʾ*, 198. The passage quoted here forms part of an exceptionally long hadith, which cannot be reproduced here in its entirety. It can also be found in Buḫārī (al-Buḫārī, *Ṣaḥīḥ*, Hadith No. 5191, Book No. 67 (*Kitāb an-nikāḥ*), 1322); Muḥibb ad-Dīn aṭ-Ṭabarīs, *Riyāḍ naḍrat fī manāqib al-ʿašra*, Bd. 2, 295; and Ǧalāl ad-Dīn as-Suyūṭī, *Durr al-manṯūr*, Vol. 6, 371. In all likelihood, one of the many allusions in the tradition is to the marital conflict between Muhammad, Aisha und Ḥafṣa, which we touched upon briefly in Part II when discussing Surah 66. ʿUmar's intervention, which extends far beyond the passage cited here, seems to be principally motivated by his concern that Muhammad might divorce Ḥafṣa, his daughter, as a result of her disputatious attitude towards the Prophet. His anxiety and solicitude thus prompted ʿUmar to warn Ḥafṣa and reprimand her. Muhammad, however, refrained from commenting on Ḥafṣa's (and Aisha's) behaviour, but merely smiled, as described above, slept alone for 29 nights, returned, and did not divorce Ḥafṣa.

what we are dealing with here is a teacher smiling affectionately and wryly at his pupil, pleased with the fact that the lessons he has imparted have borne some fruit while at the same time indulgently accepting that his student is still a bit slow on the uptake. Or has he in fact capitulated to his wives? In which case his smile would be a sign of his impotence, meaning that 'Umar would have to intervene, with his legendary vigour, to save the Prophet. Incidentally, Muhammad's smile would make a nice companion piece to an oft-cited passage from the Talmud, in which God smiles at the fact that his Jewish children have triumphed over him through their pedantic interpretations of the Torah.[31] In truth, we do not know what Muhammad's smile signified. The text does not expressly advocate more freedoms for women, but either way it does provide impressive documentary evidence that gender roles were renegotiated in Medina. And this subversive effect of the Qur'an's message, which also derives from this same period in Medina, is emancipatory and encouraging from a modern point of view and can with good justification be combined with the narratives concerning Mary.

31 Cf. Baba Metsia 59b.

4

Mary as an Aesthetic Role Model

In the previous chapter we reflected on how the figure of Mary in the Qur'an might have served as a role model within the early Islamic community. In this chapter we will pursue this thought further and spell out some of its wider ramifications. In doing so, it seems essential to us to substantiate Mary's impact as a role model in a Muslim context not on an ethical level but on an aesthetic one. For if one considers, say, Mary's virginity, it makes little sense from an Islamic perspective to see it as an ethical guideline on how to behave. To be sure, we speculated earlier on whether there might somehow also be ways of making the fact that Mary remains unmarried for the sake of the kingdom of heaven – a key tenet of Christianity – at all comprehensible in Islam. Yet Islam is adamant that abstaining from intimate marital relations does not constitute an ethical norm and that consequently a state of perpetual virginity is not an ethical ideal that Muslims should aspire to.[1]

Even so, there is one aspect of Mary's virginity that does invite readers of the Qur'an to imitate it on an aesthetic level. Seen from an aesthetic standpoint, Mary's virginity is emblematic of her complete commitment to the service of God. She can take care of herself and her child without the need for a man's help, and can also become a mother, and thereby fulfil what many women still regard as their primary purpose, without male assistance. As such, therefore, she is a symbol of female autonomy, albeit a form of autonomy that derives from an absolute devotion to God. If one were so inclined, one might even talk in terms of

1 Cf. Smith and Haddad, 'The Virgin Mary in Islamic tradition and commentary', 187: 'Mary was virginal and thus in fact categorically opposed to the ideal of a Muslim woman whose virginity is prized but ultimately sacrificed to allow her to play the role for which she was created, i.e., wife and mother.'

'theonomous autonomy'[2] here. Yet how might Mary, in her state of theonomous autonomy, become a role model for us nowadays from an Islamic perspective?

a) An invitation to visibly reserve something for God alone

In Part II, we saw how the first thing that the Qur'anic Mary does on meeting the angel is to prostrate herself before God. In invoking this image, the narrative of the Qur'an is effectively taking issue with the patristic notion that the angel prostrates himself before Mary as an act of homage to her status as the Mother of God.[3] By contrast, in the Qur'an it is clear that God alone is worthy of veneration and proskynesis. However, we see the fact that Mary's prostration does not follow a bowing of the head as part of a ritual act of prayer, but comes instead at the beginning of her prayer, as a symbolic act which to this day challenges Christians to clarify their attitude to Mary. Above all, though, this symbolic act challenges people in general to resolve their relationship with worldly powers. For we have seen how not just Mary but also, in Byzantine imperial theology, the emperor himself became the object of proskynesis. On this point, the Qur'an's injunction could not be clearer: no earthly power merits people's worship and subjugation.

So, like Mary, we are invited to challenge every bringer of divine messages by posing searching questions and at no stage to confuse the religious sphere with the worldly. And like Mary, we are invited to discover signs which show us that only God deserves our devotion. At the same time, these signs are intended to help us withstand the temptation to ascribe as great a potency – or *de facto* an even greater potency than that which God wields according to our faith – to other entities or ideas. Otherwise, these entities would themselves necessarily become elevated to the status of deities alongside God. Thus, if people strive after wealth and power, it is the purpose of religion to find signs which demonstrate that there is something more important than such worldly matters. We can see an example of just such a

2 On the concept of theonomous autonomy see for example Konrad Hilpert, *Ethik und Rationalität. Untersuchungen zum Autonomieproblem und zu seiner Bedeutung für die theologische Ethik*, Düsseldorf 1980 (Moraltheologische Studien: Systematische Abteilung; 6), 531–551. Cf. also M. R. Hosseini Beheshti, 'Moralisches Handeln als Antwort auf Gottes Ruf. Erläuterung einiger Grundfragen der islamischen Ethik.' In: Klaus von Stosch and Muna Tatari (eds.), *Handeln Gottes, Antwort des Menschen*, Paderborn 2014 (Beiträge zur Komparativen Theologie; 11), 137–149.

3 By contrast, the motif of angels bowing down before all humans is a familiar one in the Qur'an – as epitomised in the figure of Adam (cf. Q 2:34).

sign with Mary in her veil, which separates her from everyday life and expresses her extraordinary devotion to God.

Only in the solitude of the desert and only in the isolation of the veil can Mary encounter the spirit of God.[4] Evidently, by dressing in a particular manner one is able to express an inner attitude of devotion to God. Mary's veil can be seen as a sign that she will not let herself be exposed, but also will not expose others. The veil emphasises that she respects other people's dignity and is attempting to preserve her own. It thereby becomes an aesthetic symbol for the dignity of women who see only God, and not their husband or any other authorities, as their master and sustainer.

Of course, the theonomous autonomy conveyed by the symbol of the veil can also be expressed differently. Indeed, Muslim men and women employ a great deal of diversity in expressing the dedication of their lives to God. This can be manifested in a wide variety of ways in their choice of dress. But it can also be expressed other than through items of clothing. Furthermore, one can show one's veneration of God in other ways than prostrating oneself. It is therefore not necessarily important to exactly imitate the sign that Mary presents, but rather to emulate her example by creating spaces in one's own life where orientation to God alone can become a tangible and visible reality. In our estimation, the purpose of the Qur'anic Mary is precisely to encourage us to apply this same aesthetic stylisation to our own devotion. She demonstrates how much this devotion can also react flexibly to practical challenges and can be altered (for instance by changing the sequence of the ritual prayer). But she insists – as a constant, so to speak – upon a clear corporeality in the act of prayer. And she requires that we set aside an element of our own lives that is devoted solely to God.

In both Islam and Christianity, Mary is the person who exemplifies a devotion to God – the conceptual definition of which is the key concern for Islam – to the fullest extent imaginable.[5] She is the perfect handmaiden of the Lord, or – to translate this concept in a more fitting way from a Muslim viewpoint – servant of the Lord, who is entirely oriented towards God. And it is this orientation that she displays in her dress and her gestures. She also invites us to participate in this symbolic enactment of our innermost attitude to God, though we do not have to emulate her slavishly in this. This symbolic concentration can also be seen as including ritualised forms of religious devotion too (the so-called 'Five Pillars of Islam'), namely as a sign, a conscious decision to give God space to act in one's

4 Cf. Buisson, 'Subversive Maryam or a Qur'anic view on women's empowerment', 452.
5 Cf. Gilis, *Marie en Islam*, 7.

own life. Yet in the case of the Pillars of Islam, this space is formally regulated in a binding way for all Muslims, which means that it is removed from the realm of personal subjective choice and organisation. The figure of Mary indicates that an individual stylisation of a person's relationship with God can also exist on a corporeal and aesthetic level; while such a relationship transcends these ritual principles, it may be construed as an aesthetic reference to God in exactly the same way.

From the point of view of the Qur'an, it remains perfectly clear that Mary lives in a special mystical union with God, which can neither be striven towards in an ethical sense nor would even be an attainable goal for everyone anyway. The fact that she is already marked out as extraordinary even while she is still in the womb distinguishes her from the rest of us and accords her a special role.[6] In the Qur'an, Mary does not appear as an activist whose struggles are focused on external matters – like for example the Pharaoh's wife Āsiya or the Byzantine Mary – nor is she presented as a shrewd political figure like the Queen of Sheba. Generally speaking, she does not operate primarily on the level of human interactions. And although she does face up to the clash with her family, the prime mover in this is her son. In the final analysis, her story is one of inwardness, spirituality and an intimate relationship with God – a story hinting at the challenges and the unsettling situation that can arise when a person consciously makes space for God in his or her life. But at the same time she also shows how important it is to find visible signs and spaces that help keep us grounded when we are exposed to the full reality of God, a redemptive and yet sometimes truly alarming experience. In other words, she gives us the courage to express our own personal vocation in concrete signs.

b) An invitation to a culture of disruption and renunciation

Both Christianity and Islam have the capacity to allow their message to be integrated into cosy bourgeois concepts of the family or ideals of society. The Mary of the Qur'an is something of a recalcitrant figure in this respect, disrupting our traditional conceptions of societal roles and our expectations and forcing us to rethink our position. She freely admits that she is too weak to defend herself against her family's accusations, and as such appears at first to confirm our patriarchally conditioned presuppositions concerning female weakness. But then she does not proceed to seek help from a strong man or a powerful deity, but instead

6 Cf. Kaltner, *Ishmael instructs Isaac*, 209: 'She is someone who, still in the womb, has been set apart and, after birth, will be divinely preserved from harm.'

from a baby. Together, she and this baby become a sign of divine power and majesty. The male figure who still forms part of the Holy Family in Christianity is simply absent in the Qur'an. There could be no more effective way of taking the traditional bourgeois image of the family, with the man as the *pater familias* who protects and provides for his nearest and dearest, *ad absurdum*.

In saying this, however, we should also remember that Zechariah is actually appointed as Mary's guardian in the Qur'anic narrative. But whenever he wants to pursue his typically patriarchal role, it turns out that Mary is already provided for – through divine assistance. In this way, the relationship of the provider and the protégée is turned on its head. For, to all practical intents and purposes, it is Mary who provides for Zechariah – and not vice versa. And what she provides him with through her response and her example is a lesson in trusting in God, which he then wastes no time in putting into practice.[7] To some extent, she can be said to 'become his [spiritual] caretaker'[8] – as Kaltner pithily puts it.

Mary's story in the Qur'an does not therefore simply bring about an inversion of all values, nor does it reveal an alternative societal order. The story of Mary does not present us with any new, stable hierarchies of the sexes and families. What this narrative does achieve, however, is to palpably thwart our traditional expectations and in so doing goes to the heart of what religion is really all about, if one subscribes to the recent political theology expounded by Johann Baptist Metz.[9] Mary's story interrupts us and in so doing helps us to pause and take stock and cast our nets afresh. In Mary, it presents us with a figure who ventures into the wilderness and draws spiritual strength from her experience of pain and hardship. As with Moses, Hagar or Muhammad, so too in the case of Mary the desert becomes a location for renewal and a fresh start.[10]

It is interesting to note the prominent treatment accorded to Mary's woes – which are of such great importance in Christianity – by Islamic mysticism. Whereas in the Christian tradition, they form an element of the sufferings of Jesus Christ, in the Muslim tradition they now take on a new role. They become signs of divine guidance. Rūmi, for instance, writes about her sufferings in this vein:

> It is pain that guides us in every enterprise. Until there is an ache within, a

7 Cf. Kaltner, *Ishmael instructs Isaac*, 211 f.

8 Ibid., 212.

9 Cf. Johann Baptist Metz, *Glaube in Geschichte und Gesellschaft. Studien zu einer praktischen Fundamentaltheologie*, 5th edn., reprint of the 4th edn. (1984) with a new foreword by the author, Mainz 1992, 166. 'The briefest definition of religion is: disruption.'

10 Cf. Buisson, 'Subversive Maryam or a Qur'anic view on women's empowerment', 452.

> passion and a yearning for that thing arising within us, we will never strive to attain it. Without pain it remains beyond our reach, whether it is success in this world or salvation in the next, whether we aim at becoming a merchant or a king, a scientist or an astronomer. It was not until the pains of birth manifested in Mary that she made for the tree. *Those pangs [labour pains] drove her to the [date-palm] tree* [Surah 19:23] and the tree that was withered became fruitful. Our bodies are like Mary. Every one of us has a Jesus within, but until the pangs manifest, our Jesus is not born. If the pangs never come, then our child rejoins its origin by the same secret path through which it came, leaving us empty, without the birth of our true self.[11]

Pain therefore helps Mary to understand her mission and pursue it. In the same way, sufferings can help us discover our own calling in order that we may, in Rūmi's terms, bring our own Jesus into the world. If one wanted to formulate this insight as an ethical principle, this would culminate in an ideologically highly problematic mysticism of suffering that would turn suffering into an end in itself in our relationship with God. From a Muslim point of view, such a development is out of the question. And yet it remains a central tenet of Islam that *one* of the ways in which God can reveal his preferred path to us is through suffering. Not infrequently, it is exactly such painful experiences that we must undergo in order to get closer to God.

This is emphatically not to legitimise any deliberate seeking out of pain on our part. But often it is only through suffering that the scales fall from our eyes and we are brought back on track. And it is also the case that God makes use of pain in his teachings. In this regard, the example of the labour pains is especially eloquent, given that such pains, whose intensity can scarcely be surpassed, nonetheless also have a very clear purpose. This does not make them any easier to bear, but it does make us realise the point of enduring them. It is precisely in this sense that Rūmi invites us to stop constantly avoiding our own woes and to recognise instead that sufferings are sometimes necessary if we are to gain a deeper understanding of our lives.

Of course, this kind of thoroughgoing openness to a deeper meaning of pain is not without its dangers. Even if we construe this idea on an aesthetic plane we run the risk of ideological misuse. But in our reading of the Qur'an the figure of Mary repeatedly makes it clear that we have to relinquish all thought of absolute certainties in our efforts to orient ourselves. We might even go so far as to say

11 *Discourses of Rumi (fīhi mā fīhi)*, trans. A. J. Arberry, London 1961, 37–38.

that the figure of Mary in the Qur'an invites us to do without final guarantees. For example,Ṭabarī recounts a long conversation between Mary and Jesus, in which Jesus exhorts Mary not to be downhearted. She responds bitterly by asking him how that might be achieved, seeing that she is saddled with him and has no husband and does not even have the excuse of being a slave (i.e., she had no right to bear a child out of wedlock). She reminds him that she is exposed to public scrutiny with no excuse or justification for the state she finds herself in. Jesus replies that he alone is argument enough for her – a statement that can actually only be regarded as incomprehensible. And yet, in Ṭabarī's view, Jesus nevertheless succeeds in placating Mary with these words, whereupon she places her fate entirely in God's hands and goes with Jesus to meet her people.[12] In other words, she comes to terms with her mission in life without having received any kind of assurance. She devotes herself entirely to God without being able to make herself understood or protect herself in this world.

This act of renunciation in which Mary invites us to participate is therefore not only characterised by asceticism, it is also an appeal to renounce any form of security that derives exclusively from human society. One can only gauge the full magnitude and dramatic force of this appeal if one calls to mind what radical ruptures the Mary of the Qur'an has experienced in her lifetime. To begin with, she has fears which she overcomes – in the encounter with Gabriel (Q 19:17–21) – but subsequently these fears grow and drive her to a state of complete despair, where she even wishes herself dead; and throughout all this, no one is there to help her (Q 19:23–26). She is weighed down by what has happened to her and experiences it as a total break with everything that she expected from life. She therefore epitomises the courage that it takes to genuinely make room for God in one's life: the consequences of this are not always foreseeable and, as the story of Mary tells us, rarely convenient either. Like Muhammad, she finds revelation a very heavy load to bear.[13] And because she is granted no form of security in the Qur'an, even after giving birth to Jesus, this experience of rupture remains a defining characteristic of her biography. If, despite all this, she still appears as a role model in the Qur'an as well, then this is due to the fact that she has learnt to come to terms with her life without any worldly protection and to discover God within this rupture. Evidently, for her, God is not the saviour who restores order to everything (even

12 Cf. aṭ-Ṭabarī, *Tafsīr*, Vol. 15, 518–519.

13 Ṭabarī relates Muhammad's portrayal of his experiences, in which he recounts how Gabriel pressed him so hard to convey the first words of the revelation that he thought he would die. Cf. aṭ-Ṭabarī, *Ta'rīḫ*, Vol. 2, 301.

though the biblical Mary still dreams of this God in the Magnificat), but rather he accompanies her in her weakness and gives her guidance and direction by means of gentle hints.

In our view, therefore, the Mary of the Qur'an not only invites us to make room for the presence of God in our own lives but also to search tirelessly for signs of God's immanence and guidance – and, what is more, in precisely those places where we least expect to find them. Viewed through and extrapolated from the prism of Mary's life, these signs of God that are meant to guide us in our lives are not only to be found in things that are good, beautiful and bright but also in darkness, ambiguity and ugliness – indeed, even in things that we find repulsive and frightening. From the example of the figure of Mary, theological aesthetics as a doctrine of perception may prompt us to undertake a comprehensive search of our entire lives for signs of God.

We may also be justified in regarding the Qur'an as a reflection of humankind. According to Muslim beliefs, God would be the one holding up a mirror to us here – a mirror that is sometimes magnificent and sometimes banal, just as we humans are. God also shows us the foolish, repellent and abysmal aspects of humanity. But rather than leaving us alone with this revealing mirror image, he embraces all aspects with his wisdom as the creator, preserver and educator who reinforces everything that is good and beautiful in us and shows us the way out of the banal and the abysmal. And this way out does not lie beyond the dichotomy of our earthly everyday existence, but rather runs directly through it.

In the story of Mary as told in the Qur'an, revelation is thus also a revelation about humankind, since here the revelation grows and matures within a human being and has no wish to be there without her. The fact that a person was chosen by God to be the resonating body for God's revelatory power means that God allows his Word to undergo a modelling process which not only enables humans to understand it but also, so to speak, leaves no note unplayed on the human keyboard. The story of Mary can help us see keys that would otherwise remain unplayed.

5

In Dialogue with Christianity

Before we proceed, in Part IV, to incorporate Mary into the ongoing dialogue between Islam and Christianity and to explore comparative opportunities for learning, let us investigate here, however briefly, how Islamic systematic theology portrays the presence of Mary with regard to Christianity. It is striking that, on the one hand, a number of the classic Christian doctrines continue to be perceived as impediments to dialogue (a). On the other hand, though, where popular devotion in the veneration of Mary is concerned, there are clear borrowings from Christian traditions that make it theologically necessary to sensitively enquire how far one can and should legitimately go on the Muslim side (b). Moreover, thus far we have not even taken into account ways in which Muslim reflections on Mary might provide stimuli for Christian theology (c). Our aim here is merely to sketch out a few key terms, and leave a closer investigation of this topic to the final, comparative part of our study.

a) Obstacles to dialogue

For all the esteem that the figure of Mary commands in Islam, there are still a whole host of components of Catholic Mariology which Muslims view at best with perplexity. Thus, at no point in current Islamic systematic theology can we identify an attempt at a productive, positive reception of the Christian belief in the perpetual virginity of Mary. One would also wait in vain for any recognition by Muslims of Mary as the Mother of God. Islamic theology finds the Catholic doctrine of the Immaculate Conception of Mary especially disconcerting. This undoubtedly has to do with Islam's repeated and polemical rejection of the concept of original sin as such, and also with the fact that this doctrine, notably in the Augustinian form it takes in the West, is very difficult to comprehend. It is no coincidence that voices have increasingly been heard in the debate within the Catholic Church in recent years calling for the doctrine of original sin as a whole to be repudiated.[1] Even so, the Catholic doctrine of Mary's lack of sin probably provides the most likely points of contact that can be productively engaged with in the current debate. For this reason, we want to focus in somewhat greater detail solely on this obstacle to dialogue here.

Interestingly, there is a *hadith* that was already the subject of much discussion in classical Qur'anic exegesis which states that, even at their birth, Mary and Jesus, unlike everyone else, were spared from being touched by Satan. Many of the classical commentators on the Qur'an, whose words have guided us throughout this book, question the reliability of this particular *hadith*, because they do not see why God should have protected these two figures alone in such an extraordinary way, and yet not done so in the case of all other prophets.[2] Nonetheless, Ṭabarī is a good example of how even classical exegetes still attempted to process this tradition in a productive manner without accepting into the bargain the problematic Christian doctrine of original sin. Ṭabarī's principal concern here is to establish that God responds to the intercessionary prayer offered up by Mary's mother, which is transmitted by the Qur'an, and how the Qur'an here provides a clear object lesson in the enduring effect that motherly love can have on children – an insight that resonates right up to the present day, say in the story of Harry Potter.

It would actually be quite exciting if were were able to take seriously the idea that prophets too have to try and resist the blandishments of the Arch-Tempter and are therefore in fundamentally the same position as the rest of us. Only the influence of a mother, who stops at nothing in standing up for her child, would be able, with God's help, to bring about a different outcome here. It is a pity that this interpretative route is such a hopeless minefield for Muslim commentators, because for them theoretical components of the doctrine of original sin lurk at every twist and turn, tarnishing this attractive emancipatory vision of Mary's specialness resulting from her mother's intervention.

Perhaps Mary and Jesus are a sign from God for precisely that reason, namely because they have from the outset been free from the influence of all demonic forces – thanks to the intervention by their mother/grandmother. In terms of theological history, one is forced to conclude that the fulfilment of Mary's mother's prayer of intercession and the lack of sin on Mary's part that this reveals in all

1 Cf. for example Pröpper, *Theologische Anthropologie II*, 981–1156.

2 Cf. Abboud, 'Is Mary important for herself or for being the Mother of Christ in the Holy Qur'an?', 31.

probability formed the starting point in the Qur'an for the general doctrine of the sinlessness of all prophets (*ʿiṣma*).[3] The special status of both Mary and Jesus that was engendered by female power is thus swiftly reined in and becomes a constituent part of prophetology. From a modern perspective, this particular component should not necessarily be regarded as helpful.[4] In any event, though, it is interesting to observe that the exclusively male exegetes of the Muslim tradition took a woman's prayer and a woman's example as paradigms for one of the definitions of prophethood – an institution from which they then proceeded to exclude all women. One might note at this point that apologetic endeavours do not always enhance the consistency of trains of thought.

b) Between appropriation and syncretism

The more Islamic theology made sustained efforts to distinguish itself from Christianity, including trying repeatedly to repress Muslim veneration of Mary, the more it seems that Islam continued to appropriate elements of Christian Marian devotion, especially in areas of intensive contact between Islam and Christianity. We will confine ourselves here to merely registering these instances of appropriation in note form, since from the point of view of the sociology of religion, they often constitute examples of syncretism. That is to say, an adequate systematic reflection on these phenomena from an Islamic perspective is for the most part entirely absent, making it difficult for us to see them as legitimate appropriations of the Christian tradition within the context of Islam.

One especially obvious instance is the fusion of classical Christian elements of Marian pilgrimage with popular forms of Muslim religious devotion in Ephesus – or perhaps more accurately, one should say this used to be the case until a few decades ago, when the purging of Islam by the Wahhabist movement also began to make its influence felt on Turkish popular devotion. In the Catholic tradition, particularly since the visions experienced by the mystic Anna Katharina Emmerick (1774–1824) but also on the basis of classical sources,[5] Ephesus is widely

3 Cf. Bayḍāwī's commentary on the Qur'an, Q 3:31: '[…] *inna llāha ʿaṣamahumā bi-barakati hadihi l-istiʿāḏa.*' (al-Bayḍāwī, *Anwār at-tanzīl*, 153). For the corresponding conclusions, see also the entry by Arent Jan Wensinck, 'Maryam.' In: Clifford Edmund Bosworth et al. (eds.), *The Encyclopaedia of Islam*, vol. 6, Leiden 1991, 628–632, here 630.

4 Cf. the questions posed in Klaus von Stosch, 'Replik auf Mustafa Köylu'. In: Tuba Işik (eds.), *Prophetie in Islam und Christentum*, Paderborn and elsewhere 2013 (Beiträge zur Komparativen Theologie; 8), 137–140.

5 Cf. George-Tvrtković, *Christians, Muslims, and Mary*, 134 f.

regarded as the site of Mary's Dormition. In line with this, there is an old tradition of venerating the house there where she supposedly lived, a ritual in which the local Muslim population is (or at least once was) clearly involved. This is indicated by looking at entries in the guest book of the House of the Virgin Mary from as late as the 1960s, which tell of sick people being cured by drinking water from the house and of how other prayers offered up to Mary here were answered.[6] Ali İhsan Yitik has given the following summary: 'All the signs are that, where some of the visitors here are concerned, the Virgin Mary offers the solution to every conceivable problem. For other visitors she appears to be a kind of intermediary who submits people's pleas to God.'[7] According to his analysis, the popular devotion that is in evidence here is also shared to this day by Turkish Muslims. He concludes that 'in the view of many Turkish Muslims, Mary is a noble and righteous woman, as well as being someone who can intercede with God on others' behalf.' Yitik continues: 'When they are assailed by grave concerns, such as incurable diseases, unemployment or the inability to find a life partner, many Muslims go to the House of the Virgin Mary. They present their worries and their hopes to the Virgin Mary and trust that she will intercede with God. In their eyes, the great Creator will surely not turn down any request from a believer who is so beloved to him, and as a result they are firmly convinced that prayers are answered at sites like this, so long as they are offered up sincerely and in a spirit of unwavering faith.'[8]

The peculiarity of Turkish Marian devotion as practised in Ephesus surely resides in the fact that it was heavily promoted by the Catholic Church in the twentieth century, and in the last 150 years alone, no fewer than seven popes have visited the shrine.[9] As a way of fostering Muslim Marian devotion in particular, there is not just a Christian chapel dedicated to Mary in Ephesus but also a Muslim one, which seems to attract hundreds of thousands of Muslims annually.[10] Within Catholicism, the fact that Muslim worship of Mary took place in Ephesus was a prime mover behind the Islam-friendly conciliar declaration of the Second Vatican Council on Catholicism's relations with non-Christian faiths, *Nostra Aetate*.[11]

6 Cf. Sabahattin Türkoğlu, *Efes'te 3000 Yıl*, Istanbul 1986, 131, quoted from Yitik, 'Die Jungfrau Maria und ihr Haus bei Ephesus', 5.

7 Cf. Yitik, 'Die Jungfrau Maria und ihr Haus bei Ephesus', 6.

8 Cf. ibid., 4.

9 Cf. George-Tvrtković, *Christians, Muslims, and Mary*, 122.

10 Cf. ibid., 123.

11 Cf. ibid., 137–141. In view of the prominent position accorded to Muslim veneration of Mary in the re-evaluation of Islam by the Second Vatican Council, it is surprising that the Catholic Church has not, since that council, made more of the figure of Mary as a way of fostering dialogue with Islam (cf. George-Tvrtković, *Christians, Muslims, and Mary*, 153).

In Egypt too – this time, without any Catholic support whatsoever – there are also well-attested reports of places of Marian pilgrimage being frequented by Muslims. In this context, Angie Heo has highlighted the interesting phenomenon that after apparitions of Mary in Egypt, it is repeatedly Muslim witnesses who are cited by the Coptic Church in attestation of their veracity.[12] Whereas Protestants take a polemical and dismissive attitude toward these forms of Marian devotion, more than a few individuals within the Islamic community find themselves infected with this enthusiasm for Mary and fully in sympathy with the traditional rituals involved in her veneration. Nonetheless, at present pilgrimage destinations that actually purport to be mixed shrines are only very thinly populated with Muslims.[13] And the whole phenomenon is viewed somewhat sceptically by official Islamic sources in Egypt, who question its relevance[14] and dispute that Mary also appeared to Muslims. However, in spite of this official scepticism, which doubtless also has to do with the rise of Muslim fundamentalism – increasingly promulgated by Saudi Arabia from the 1970s onwards – there is no denying that traditions of communal Marian worship by Christians and Muslims persist in both Egypt and Turkey. Similar phenomena appear to exist in other places too, for example Macedonia,[15] Lebanon,[16] Iraq, and Pakistan,[17] and they quite clearly continue to gain in strength wherever Islam, at the level of popular belief, encounters a lively Christian cult of Marian devotion.

However strange this form of piety might appear to many Muslims and Protestants, it is wonderful to witness how the veneration of Mary generates a sense of solidarity between Muslims and Christians on the level of popular piety. Thus, we see older Muslim women in Egypt participating in the ritual fasting undertaken by Coptic Christians in the lead-up to the Feast of Mary's Assumption. And in Iraq, Muslims vicariously take prayer requests to the Virgin Mary into church if they think that not enough Christians are present.[18] Finally, there is a sacred site in

12 Cf. Heo, 'The Virgin Between Christianity and Islam', 1123.

13 Cf. ibid., 1120.

14 Cf. ibid., 1131 f.

15 Cf. Glenn Bowman, 'Orthodox–Muslim interactions at "Mixed Shrines" in Macedonia.' In: Chris Hann and Hermann Goltz (eds.), *Eastern Christians in anthropological perspective*, Berkeley, CA 2010, 163–183.

16 Cf. George-Tvrtković, *Christians, Muslims, and Mary*, 45, 144.

17 Cf. ibid., 46 f.

18 Cf. Cuţaru, 'Sittinā Maryam of the Muslims', 73: 'Older women in Egypt use to associate to the Coptic Christians in the fasting days preceding the feast of the Assumption. … More than that, in Iraq there are Muslim women who go to church before the start of the office, when there are not many Christians and they pray the Virgin.'

Jerusalem where according to Muslim tradition Mary is supposed to have bathed on one occasion, and to which in the past Muslim women in particular who were unable to bear children came to seek help, though this tradition has now almost entirely died out.[19]

It is worth mentioning traditions such as this, which are gradually falling into desuetude, because they clearly demonstrate that the idea of Mary as a bridge-builder between Islam and Christianity, broached in Part II of this book, actually bore fruit for quite some time – fruit which unfortunately can no longer be properly savoured and celebrated thanks to the religious puritanism of modern times. For a long while, by virtue of the intercessionary power she wielded, Mary was one of the most important authorities of the Islamic tradition – invoked at healing sessions as well as exorcisms, and of course also by those praying that they might be made fertile.[20]

All the same, we are not seeking to defend all appropriations of Christian Marian devotion by popular Islamic religious piety. Naturally, there are also certain developments here whose demise we can only be thankful for. For instance, Muslims too traditionally invoked Mary as a war heroine when seeking victory in battle[21] – a practice that has since died out and is hopefully lamented by no-one. Where images of Mary are concerned too, there are Muslim traditions which it would be very difficult to plausibly integrate into a modern Islamic systematic theology.

For instance, there is an ancient hadith tradition according to which a picture of Mary and Jesus was still present in the Kaaba when Muhammad adopted it as the central shrine of Islam. In accordance with many hadith collections, Ibn ʿAbbās's account of the iconoclasm in the Kaaba describes Muhammad commanding that the image of Mary and the Christ Child should not be erased.[22] One explanation for this perplexing phenomenon might be that the picture in question was not an icon but a wall painting that would have been difficult to expunge. The iconoclasm was only conducted in the first instance against all movable images and statues, with the result that the mural of Jesus and Mary was still in place

19 Cf. Cuţaru, 'Sittinā Maryam of the Muslims', 73. Within Islam, this tradition always derived legitimacy from the fact that the Caliph ʿUmar supposedly prayed and paid his respects to Mary in this house (cf. George-Tvrtković, *Christians, Muslims, and Mary*, 44).
20 Cf. ibid.
21 Cf. Kaltner, 'The Muslim Mary', 167, with reference to Amy G. Remensnyder, 'The colonization of sacred architecture. The Virgin Mary, mosques, and temples in Medieval Spain and early sixteenth-century Mexico.' In: Sharon Farmer and Barbara Rosenwein (eds.), *Monks and nuns, Saints and outcasts. Religious expression and social meanings in the Middle Ages*, Ithaca 2000, 189–219.
22 Cf. Seppälä, 'Reminiscences of icons in the Qurʾan?', 14.

when Muhammad took possession of the Kaaba. In all likelihood, the image was one of the Virgin and Child enthroned, with Jesus shown seated on Mary's lap.[23] However moving this detail might appear to a Catholic or Orthodox Christian, it is completely baffling in the context of Islamic systematic theology. Nor are we sure whether it is really to be counted as a positive that Mary was also portrayed with a halo in Muslim art.[24] But perhaps it is only logical that a figure whose transcendent, subversive and unsettling power we have described at length should, in the images used to venerate her, also give rise to phenomena that have the capacity to offend and confuse. As a result, we will not make any further attempt to find neat theological pigeonholes for these phenomena, but simply allow them to stand in all their contrariness – as an indication of all that can be achieved theologically if only one is prepared to properly appreciate the figure of Mary in all her unifying power.

c) A warning against projecting

Before we come, in the final part of this book, to take comprehensive stock of the insights each of us has gained for our own theological tradition from this comparative study, we should issue a warning. Precisely the enormous complexity of the Marian tradition can mislead us into projecting our own wants and needs onto the Mary of the Qur'an. If the present book consists in large part of exegetical analysis, then a principal reason for that is that we were intending thereby to fortify the sheer contrariness of the Qur'anic text against any attempt to appropriate it for our own purposes or project our own views onto it. Consequently, with regard to systematic synthesis, we should also warn against precipitate attempts to discover syntheses or overhastily harmonise the inherent dissonance of our source material.

In our view, it would be a prime example of this kind of projecting harmonisation if we were to follow the suggestion made by Christopher Evan Longhurst and apply the Christian way of referring to Mary as 'Our Lady' across the board as a title for Mary in both Islam and Christianity, on the grounds that both religions recognise her personal virtues.[25] Projection also seems to us to be at work when

23 Cf. King, 'The paintings of the Pre-Islamic Kaʿba', 221.

24 Cf. Kaltner, 'The Muslim Mary', 167. However, this phenomenon is not peculiar to Mary in Islamic art. For instance, Adam and Eve are frequently portrayed with halos. The Ottoman, Mughal and Persian empires all had their own traditions for the depiction of Mary, making her a highly prominent figure in art (cf. George-Tvrtković, *Christians, Muslims, and Mary*, 47–49).

25 Cf. Longhurst, 'Maryam bint ʿImran as "Our Lady of Muslims"', 467 f.

Patrick Ali Pahlavi transmits his vision of a prophet for the third millennium onto Mary and professes to find in her the very autonomy, rigour and spirituality that he wants women in the Muslim world to acquire.[26] All this is well-intentioned and does have a grain of truth in it. But as systematic theologians, our business is not to write fiction or air our personal aspirations, but instead to try and bear witness to what our sacred texts transmit.

But since it was the text of the Qur'an itself which drew attention to Mary's nature as a bridge-builder between the religions, it is perfectly legitimate to stress this point when discussing systematic theology and interrogate to productive ends the habits we are prone to slip into while reading. After all, we saw how the Surah *Āl ʿImrān* adopts and intensifies the idea of Mary as a figure of integration and bridge-building already developed in the Surah *Maryam*. As we discovered, in the Surah *Āl ʿImrān* the focus is no longer simply on bringing together Judaism and Christianity, but also on uniting the priestly and prophetic traditions, men and women, and – by means of the traditional literature developed for this purpose in classical exegesis – even Shiite and Sunni Muslims.[27] As regards the intriguing observations above on popular Muslim piety, one might perhaps add that the Mary of the Qur'an may also help to heal the rifts between the Catholic and Protestant traditions of Marian devotion. Certainly, one fascinating finding we believe emerges from the socio-religious observations on the situation in Egypt just outlined above is how eager the Coptic Church is to adduce Muslim witnesses as a way of defending itself against Protestant criticism of the cult of Mary. In the German-speaking world, the battle lines on this question have long since ceased to run between Catholicism and Protestantism. Within the Catholic Church, there are a growing number of people to whom traditional Marian devotion means very little. Perhaps the Qur'anic Mary might provide a way for them to overcome the entrenched positions which in recent times have alarmingly become even more pronounced within Catholicism.

Against the background of Mary's role in the Qur'an, it is extremely interesting to note that at two points in his encyclical *Fratelli Tutti* (3 October 2020), Pope Francis makes prominent reference to Mary in her role as a bridge-builder. Thus, Francis urges us in his encyclical 'to be the sign of unity… to build bridges' and cites Mary as a model in this regard.[28] And from a Christian perspective he

26 Cf. Pahlavi, *La fille d'Imran*.

27 See our justification above for regarding Mary as a bridging figure, in Part II, Chapter 2 (on the first Annunciation scene in the Surah *Āl ʿImrān*).

28 Fratelli Tutti 276. http://www.vatican.va/content/francesco/en/encyclicals/documents/papa-francesco_20201003_enciclica-fratelli-tutti.html

designates her as the mother of the fraternity that exists between all men and women.[29] Clearly, the integrating role that the proclaimer of the Qur'an attributes to Mary is one that can readily be advocated from a Christian standpoint too, and even be extended to embrace the whole of humankind. Pope Francis's sentiments are therefore in complete accord with the pronouncements of the Qur'an, and may even be seen as reiterating its core message.

29 Cf. Fratelli Tutti 278.

IV

IMPLICATIONS FOR COMPARATIVE THEOLOGY

It is now time to take stock. From both a Christian and a Muslim perspective, what instructive conclusions may be drawn from the findings we have reached in the foregoing pages? Or more precisely, what lessons can a Muslim learn from the Christian insights contained within this book's forays into comparative religion, and conversely what lessons can be learned from a Christian standpoint from our efforts in the second and third parts of this study to develop a Qur'anic and systematic Islamic approach to Mary?

To answer these questions, we will have recourse to an extremely helpful suggestion on how to structure methods of learning in comparative theology, which was put forward by the American theologian Catherine Cornille in her recently published introduction to the discipline.[1] Here, Cornille identifies six distinct ways in which one can learn through comparative endeavours in theology, which she designates as: intensification, recovery, reinterpretation, appropriation, rectification and reaffirmation. Taking these categories for our headings, we will present examples of what we have learnt about each other's religion from our analysis of the role of Mary in the Qur'an. In doing so, our aim is not to provide a comprehensive survey of learning gains, but simply to recap certain especially noteworthy points.

Unlike the rest of the book up to this point, we did not write the following two

1 Cf. Catherine Cornille, *Meaning and Method in Comparative Theology*, Hoboken 2020, 115–147.

chapters together, since this part is all about personal testimony to a learning experience from an individual confessional viewpoint. As in the book as a whole, we will begin here with the Christian perspective, since in purely chronological terms this confessional viewpoint is the one that first broached the subject of Mary. Within the Christian section, for each of the six categories above, four points will be named which warrant being called learning experiences. These will then be supplemented by selected learning experiences in the Islamic section, likewise classified according to the six categories.

1

Christian Perspectives

a) Intensification: freedom through devotion

In the course of writing our book, something that particularly moved me was the numerous occasions on which the Muslim tradition responds positively and affirmatively to Mary. Especially considering the many ways in which the veneration of Mary has been contested within the Catholic Church, I see this as an enrichment and a corroboration of my own beliefs. I should like to draw particular attention to the following points.

In the Qur'an, as in the Bible, Mary is intimately connected with Jesus Christ and can almost be seen as a living signpost to him. She is affirmed as the chosen and purified one; indeed, she is even singled out as being the woman who is chosen above all other women in the world. This great esteem in which Mary is held in the Qur'an, which is reaffirmed time and again in moving and poetic words throughout Islamic history, intensifies my own high regard and love for Mary.

And just as in the Bible, Mary comes across in the Qur'an as a woman who, in her search for answers and a greater understanding of her own life, constantly questions and digs deeper. She lives in a relationship of dialogue and intense familiarity with God, as her mother had done before her. All these aspects were perfectly familiar to me from the Christian tradition, but all the same it was wonderful to see them reinforced through being attested in the Qur'an.

Likewise, the relationship between freedom and grace which is made manifest in Mary is established in similar fashion by the biblical and Qur'anic traditions. In both, Mary appears as the most extreme example of human independence, precisely because she devotes herself completely to God. All along, her freedom has been safeguarded, supported and encouraged by God, and yet God does not want to put his benevolent will into effect without first gaining her consent.

Finally, in the Mary of the Qur'an and her relationship with God, I found the very same note of compassion that characterises the Christian image of God, and which could be used to talk in terms of a female, caring and attentive side of God. After all, God is the Compassionate One who attends to us as lovingly as a mother. This too is affirmed by both the Qur'an and the Bible, and also constitutes an important element of my own relationship with Mary and God.

Such experiences of intensification are a typical product of comparative studies, and are clearly in evidence when we look at the figure of Mary in Islamic–Christian dialogue. Consequently, I will not labour this point here, although much more could of course be said on the matter, and notwithstanding that these common features are far from being self-evident.

b) Recovery: Mary as a prophet and as a protagonist of anti-imperial theology

A somewhat less familiar experience was to find how much of my own Christian tradition I rediscovered, and hence could lay bare for my own devotional practice, through comparative dialogue with Muslim testimonies of faith. For example, I had never before encountered the idea of Mary as a prophet, and it made a big impression on my Christian mindset to see the category of the prophetic being strongly associated here with attributes such as approachability, weakness, vulnerability, and tolerance of ambiguity. I now realise how rewarding it would be to rediscover what it means to be a prophet in a Christian context too and to use the figure of Mary as a hermeneutic key in this process. For the prophetology of the Church Fathers often confined itself to merely interpreting the Old Testament prophet figures as typological prefigurations of Christ. However productive and fascinating this interpretative tradition may be, it nonetheless runs a high risk of overlooking the autonomy of the individual prophets and of styling itself as simply attempting to outdo Judaism. The figures of the male and female prophets of the Bible have the capacity to show us a way to a deeper and better understanding of Christ rather than simply reflect what we already know about Christ. Precisely the intensity of the veneration of Mary by the Church Fathers suggested to me that, while such veneration can of course be linked to Christological considerations, it can at the same time take on a highly revelatory life of its own.

I was struck by the wealth of Marian worship, which over the course of history clearly became so expressive and attractive that even Muslims were enthused. Unfortunately, popular belief in Mary has always been a closed book to me, with the result that I have hitherto tended to steer clear of it in my own spirituality. But discovering how greatly the figure of Mary resonates in the Muslim tradition has caused me to reappraise Marian piety within my own Catholic tradition with a fresh eye. The present book is testimony to my reawakened interest in Mary and the history of her veneration, and has opened up new ways for me to engage with this form of spirituality, once so alien to me. Mary herself is therefore a figure whom I have rediscovered through her reflection in Islam and whose central importance for my own faith I now recognise.

This has also come about because the Qur'an has reminded me so effectively and beautifully that Mary is a symbol of God's essential love for humankind only when she is paired with Jesus. In her symbolic function, Mary is so intrinsically bound up with Jesus Christ that I find it easier to reintegrate her into my faith and my relationship with Christ. In this regard, the proclaimer of the Qur'an effectively harks back to a central tenet of the Christian tradition and rebuts a key argument of Protestantism against the cult of Mary in the Catholic Church. Thus, it is through the Qur'an that I have rediscovered that Mary is indissolubly linked with Jesus Christ, and that only through pointing to him as the source of salvation (the *hodegetria*) does she become, with him, an emblem of God's presence for all worlds and peoples.

A fourth and final point that working with the Qur'an has made me rediscover within my own Christian tradition is Mary's role as a protagonist of anti-imperial theology. Prior to researching this book, I was unaware of quite how comprehensively Mary had been exploited by the imperialist theology of Late Antiquity, even to the extent of being co-opted as an emblem of military triumphalism. This makes all the more impressive the clearsightedness with which the proclaimer of the Qur'an disengages Mary from such contexts and presents her in her intensive relationship with God and Christ. Mary thus clearly emerges as a religious figure who does not wage and win wars on behalf of the powerful but who steps in to assist those who have been marginalised. This impressive Qur'anic intervention has caused me to look again at Mary's famous Magnificat, in which she now comes across to me as a prophetic figure who assumes precisely the anti-imperial and emancipatory role that the proclaimer of the Qur'an ascribes to her.

c) Reinterpretation: Mary as a transgressor of boundaries

However, our analysis of Islam's image of Mary does not just represent a strengthening of my own theology and a more profound interrogation of my own tradition. It also indicates new ways in which I can interpret my faith.

Hitherto I was used to viewing Mary through the prism of the Four Marian Dogmas of the Catholic Church. Since time immemorial, the biblical evidence and the great wealth of Marian devotion has been classified and arranged within these parameters. And my relationship with Mary was likewise conditioned by this framework, but was by the same virtue so well-established and settled that it did not pose any new challenges to me in my thinking and my beliefs. As a result of my interaction with Islam, my image of Mary has become more vibrant and diverse. New facets have been revealed, which challenge my theology and bring me personally into contact with Mary.

To begin with, the Qur'an gives us a fascinating indication of Mary's particular sensitivity to God's subtle granting of favours and hence to the gentle and friendly pointers God gives her in her life. Indeed, in the Gospels too, Mary interprets these signs from God and thereby gains new courage. But to see Mary in dogma as a form of support, who precisely by means of her intuitive and tender passion makes God's signs accessible and intelligible to me, strikes me as a wholly new interpretation of her role. Similarly, discovering through her the idea that silence may be seen as a touchstone of the significance of corporeality in the divine–human relationship is, to my knowledge, a line of interpretation of her thoroughgoing spirituality, which is also palpable in the Bible, that has never before been pursued in Catholic theology.

The Islamic perception of Mary and her virginity in terms of queer theology was for me the most strikingly new eye-opener. In actual fact, it turns out that the biblical tradition also has the potential to perceive Mary not just as the Queen of Heaven but also the 'Queer of Heaven'. Muslim feminist theologians are quite correct in identifying this aspect of her. Time and again, Mary breaks down simple dichotomies – and what's more not just the apparent antithesis of mother and virgin but also many other pairs of seeming contradictions. Comparing her with Muhammad, one can see how clearly she puts into question the stereotypical gender attributions and appropriates traditionally male domains. The dispute within Islam over her designation as a prophet is eloquent testimony to how greatly she confounds traditional categories.

At the same time, she impressively demonstrates how important certain dimensions of what we commonly regard as feminine in our typecasting attributions are for our relationship with God. Yet ultimately the re-evaluation of Mary by queer theology and feminism also confounds my categories of 'traditional' and 'modern' theology. Because I would always have assumed that Mary would have been on the side of the traditionalists, I am completely at sixes and sevens to find that she is a pacesetter of modernity in this new interpretation. Indeed, the Mary of the Qur'an whom I have got to know over the course of our work has subversive potential, and has thus helped me to rediscover the stories of Mary in the Bible as dangerous reminders in the sense of the recent political theology of Johann Baptist Metz[1] – in other words as reminders that threaten and subvert the structures of power and oppression within our current society because they present us with a vision of other potential ways of living.

Quite how subversive the effect of a theology inspired by Mary can be is demonstrated nowhere more clearly than in the testimony of Caliph ʿUmar that we quoted above, who complains that gender relations have had to be renegotiated as a result of the subversive message of the Qur'an. He experiences at first hand in his own marriage what it means when religion emboldens a woman to demand sexual equality. And even though Christianity, by means of Mariology, has managed to redeem this sense of insecurity through the imposition of asymmetrical gender relations and patriarchal social orders, the new interpretation that was being aimed at here has nonetheless succeeded, with the result that Mary's role as the Queer of Heaven is effective within Christianity too. For a Queen of Heaven, this should actually be an easy role to adopt.

d) Appropriation: from a Christian mascot to a typological figure binding together religions

Whereas in the categories treated thus far it has always been a question of learning things from the other culture which, at least in principle, are also expressed within one's own tradition, the following form of learning concerns knowledge that is appropriated afresh from the other tradition.

I am thinking first and foremost here of our discovery of Mary in the Qur'an as a bridging figure. Repeatedly, we have seen that, while the proclaimer of the Qur'an certainly considers Mary to be a representative of Christianity, he at the same time assigns to her the role of a typological bridging figure who forms a link between the three great Abrahamic religions. This is an exciting gambit that I am happy to take on board and which seems to me to represent a new element in the Christian tradition. Also, the Bible makes it abundantly clear that Mary was a devout Jew and lived according to the laws of Moses – one need only think of the narrative elements from Lk that we treated above. Yet in theological terms this insight could never be used to bring together Judaism and Christianity, because from a Jewish perspective Mary was simply too firmly associated with Christian apologetics for her to be rediscovered in a new light. In Late Antiquity

1 Cf. Metz, *Glaube in Geschichte und Gesellschaft*, 192–196.

in particular, Mary was an important part of the polemical clashes which took place between Christianity and Judaism, as we have also had cause to note.

Consequently, it is surprising and powerful to see how the proclaimer of the Qur'an uses Mary of all people to reconcile the two religions, by opening up a path of genuine non-Christian Marian devotion while simultaneously attempting to overcome all the anti-Jewish reflexes of the patristic tradition. Through the Qur'an, I have learned for the first time that Mary does not belong to my tradition alone and this has made it easier for me to approach her. Muslims, so to speak, have motivated me to look at Mariology with a fresh eye. As a result, it may even be fair to say that Mary is not just a bridging figure between religions but also, through her re-evaluation in comparative theology, a bridging figure in the ongoing conversation between Christian denominations. At least, in the Qur'an her inclusive understanding of the Word of God is made possible precisely through her intensive relationship with Christ, so that this Christocentric viewpoint might also have the capacity to engender a new enthusiasm for Mary among Protestants. In any event, the Mary of the Qur'an could well be an important figure for realigning the relationship between conservatives and liberals within the Catholic Church, or for emphasising how ultimately unproductive such distinctions are for theology. For despite the fact that, as a general rule, Mariology has a conservative image, an opening for non-Christian appropriations of Mary can be seen as liberal, especially when these come from a queer-theological perspective. But what if this very perspective were to prompt a root-and-branch reappraisal of the whole doctrine of Mary's virginity?

Let us address a second point that I would be happy to learn from the Muslim approaches to Mary that we have examined in this book. In Part II, we saw that the figure of Mary was the catalyst for something of a rehabilitation of the ritualistic aspect of religion within the Qur'an. And in Part III, this line of thought crystallised out into the conclusion that the figure of Mary in the Qur'an invites us to visibly reserve a part of our lives for God alone. What really appeals to me here above all is the aspect of visibility. The Mary of the Qur'an clearly invites us to adopt an all-embracing conception of faith which does not identify belief as residing purely within the realm of private inwardness. The new lesson I have learned here is that faith needs spaces and that Mary is a figure who can open up the whole spectrum of potential for such spaces. At a time when Christianity is becoming ever more invisible, she encourages me to seek out stumbling blocks that will cause us to stop and take stock and reset our relationship with God.

A third point that I found significant about the Mary of the Qur'an and which I would like to adopt in my Christian theology is her impressive independence. She has no need of a male provider, and she alone suffices as a genealogical 'seal of quality' for her son. What she requires is the protection of her mother. In this way, the importance of blessing and intercessionary prayer is made visible through her mother's example, and as a general principle, there is a great deal of feminine autonomy and strength on show here. I would dearly love to see this manifested within the Catholic Church too.

And finally there is the designation of Mary in the Qur'an as a 'friend of God'. Against the horizon of present-day theology there is perhaps no more admirable title than this. As Thomas Pröpper writes so forcefully at the end of the first volume of his theological anthropology, which was published shortly before his death: 'Friendship with God. I cannot conceive of any idea that might sustain a person's faith more reliably or impart greater joy to it. The thought that he who provides everything for us leaves us the dignity of giving our own assent. Our joy that he has chosen us, and his joy at reaching us.'[2] Through the Islamic tradition, I now know that it is just such a view of friendship with God that is paradigmatically realised in the person of Mary. Mary the friend of God – I am happy to adopt this title and promote it within my personal Mariology.

e) Rectification: rehabilitation of a Mariology based on prerogatives

The category of rehabilitation is undoubtedly the most problematic for interfaith dialogue. Purely from a human standpoint, it is hard to confess one's own mistakes and to be corrected by one's interlocutor. But this is especially difficult in the context of religion, since here one generally proceeds from the assumption that one is testifying to a truth that does not emanate from oneself but instead from the infallible truth of the Almighty and Omniscient One. Another factor hampering the dialogue between Islam and Christianity is that traditional Islam explicitly claims to be correcting Christian misconceptions in the exegesis of its own sacred text. In the light of such high-handedness, it is all too tempting for those on the Christian side to adopt an apologetic attitude and become blind to the 'plank in their own eye', which Jesus exhorts us in the Gospels to be mindful of (Mt 7:3). It is always easier to see the speck of dust in another person's eye than to admit to fundamental errors in one's own worldview.

2 Pröpper, *Theologische Anthropologie I*, 655: '*Freundschaft mit Gott. Ich wüsste keinen Gedanken, der den Glauben verlässlicher tragen und ihm größere Freude sein kann. Dass er, der alles uns gibt, uns die Würde eigener Zustimmung lässt. Unsere Freude, dass er uns wählte, und seine Freude, wenn er zu uns gelangt.*'

For Christians, it really ought to be self-evident that they can err in their faith. However perfect God and his self-mediation through Jesus Christ may be, our understanding of his reality is imperfect. And however purely Mary too embodies the perfect figure of the human response to God's commitment, my understanding of her remains imperfect. Consequently, we should not be too perturbed to discover that our endeavours in comparative theology also compel us to acknowledge our own flaws and errors – whether in our own theology or our own tradition. For each aspect I would like to cite two examples, beginning with the flaws in my own theology.

Before I began investigating the Mary of the Qur'an, I assumed that Mary's virginity was a specific token of high Christology within the Christian tradition. At least, this is what I had been taught by my doctoral supervisor Karl-Heinz Menke, who repeatedly dinned it into us students that a belief in Mary's virginity was an indispensable part of all forms of orthodox Christology, and that Christ's divine nature could, by means of transcendental logic, be deduced from Mary's virginity. Even as a student, I did not understand his argument. Nonetheless, the underlying message stayed with me: Mary's virginity is an expression of the Two Natures doctrine and underwrites the Christian belief in the divine-human Jesus Christ.

Now, this notion is demonstrably wrong, as I have come to see. For the proclaimer of the Qur'an affirms the virginity of Mary while at the same time denying the divine nature of Jesus. And he does both with good reason and a well-conceived theology, with the result that to this very day Muslims still proclaim Mary's virginity and the pure humanity of Jesus. On the one hand, this is very challenging and perplexing, but on the other hand it opens up new ways of approaching the mystery of Mary's virginity. It remains a token of the fact that a person can be sent from on high and in the very core of his or her being become the message and the word of God. Yet the virginity of Mary also illustrates how sexual asceticism and devotion to God can belong together. And above all, she breaks apart the binary codes and the dualisms of my theological thinking. I am still only just beginning to understand the consequences of this reorientation. But from a theological viewpoint, it does appear to be a great gift of Islam to Christianity – and moreover precisely at a time when many Christians are finding it difficult to believe in Mary's virginity, and are perhaps in danger of entirely losing touch with her.

Let us come to a second point where my personal theology has been subject to correction through the findings of our comparative theological investigation of Mary. In my theological training, I was taught that Mariology is part of Ecclesiology and that the Second Vatican Council had freed us from the anti-Protestant prerogatives-based Mariology that had traditionally been promulgated by the

Catholic Church. In accordance with this, I also learned that all Marian dogmas are not to be understood as personal distinctions of Mary, but as anthropological and ecclesiological statements. In imbibing all this, I considered myself very modern and a true child of Vatican II.

Correspondingly, I expected from the Qur'an that Mary would be portrayed as a typical believer who shows us what is latent in all of us. Yet the proclaimer of the Qur'an presents us with a Mary who is honoured above all other women and who transcends the boundaries which remain unshakeably firm for the rest of us. She quite clearly has prerogatives and yet precisely through being in her exceptional position she is also accessible, approachable and vulnerable. The proclaimer of the Qur'an therefore clearly represents a form of pre-conciliar prerogatives-based Mariology.

At the same time, through its aesthetic approach to Mary's exceptional position, the Islamic systematic theology outlined in this book showed me a way in which my evaluation of such a theology might be corrected. When Mary, in all her chastity and purity, is loaded with ethical attributes, she becomes a very remote figure to me. The aesthetic approach sketched out above, however, grants me the opportunity to view her through an entirely new cultural prism. It is liberating to not always have to give birth to God and to project Mary's perfection onto the Church and myself. It is also liberating to let Mary's splendour, her magnificence in her very lowliness shine forth and at the same time to marvel at the intensity of her relationship with God and, encouraged by this, to search for one's own very different ways of conveying God's Word to the world. These will of course not achieve anything like what Mary has already achieved for all of us. But they will have the capacity to be every bit as attuned to the signs given by God and to give them visible space in our life.

After these two points, which have more to do with my own personal theology, I want to mention two further points which, while having no bearing on my own theology, do concern the theology of the Catholic Church. I will cite one example relating to a rectification of the Church's beliefs at the time when the Qur'an came into being, and another example of rectification concerning the modern beliefs of the Church.

Let us begin with the beliefs of the Catholic Church today. Even the current Pope stresses repeatedly that he is not free to grant women access to the priesthood. In saying this, he is not just insisting that women cannot become priests but also that they are debarred from every other stage of ordination. In concrete terms, this means that according to the current canon law of the Catholic Church, it is not even permitted for women to be consecrated as deaconesses. Against this background it is extremely fascinating to observe that in the Qur'an Mary was consecrated into service in the Temple even as a child. It is exciting to see how a religion which in actual fact has no priests and no formal act of ordination nevertheless still preserves a memory that, in Mary's case, the consecration of a woman was possible – counter to the traditions of the Temple, what's more – and how the classical exegetes were well aware of this, at total variance with the tradition of the Church. It would be wonderful if the Catholic Church were to allow the proclaimer of the Qur'an to give it pause for thought in this matter and devise a form of ordination in which women would be able to follow in Mary's footsteps in serving the Almighty.

Finally, let us turn to the beliefs held by the Church at the time of the emergence of the Qur'an. We have seen how widespread the view was in the seventh century that Jesus only partook of food and drink because he wanted to. The claim that his body was incorruptible, which often lay behind this assertion, also appears to have rubbed off on Mary and her clothing. This detail, which was once regarded as fanciful, in fact represents a serious threat to the core of Christian belief. For in Christianity, everything depends upon the fact that God himself, in the figure of Jesus Christ, shares our human lot, and knows all of its pitfalls and crises, and in this way transforms us from within. One of the severest hardships known to humans, however, is to suffer from hunger and thirst, a state we do not choose ourselves. Even today, countless children starve to death on a daily basis.

Of course, it does not save these children if we choose to believe that God too is present in their hunger and suffers it alongside them. But it is absolutely key to the Christian message to believe that God is in solidarity with us in our plight and resolves to go hungry alongside us when we find ourselves incapable of overcoming hunger, but more importantly that he instigates us to conquer hunger by bringing about a state of greater fairness in our dealings with our fellow human beings. Quite clearly, Mary ought here to be on the side of a person hungry for fairness, who longs for a situation where there is enough food for everyone, and whose aim is not to be exempted from this hardship by divine magic. How could she otherwise credibly present our plight to God? And, naturally, neither should Jesus be preserved by the character of the hypostatic union from the misery of experiencing hunger. For how otherwise might we be assured that God is in solidarity with us when we are broken by the effects of starvation? Thus, when the proclaimer of the Qur'an maintains that Jesus and Mary needed to eat like the rest of us, he is deliberately touching upon a central tenet of Christian belief at the time and quite rightly rectifying certain theological precepts of contemporary Christianity – not just on the Arabian Peninsula but also in Byzantium, the most important power-political centre of Christianity in the seventh century.

f) Reaffirmation: Mary's lowliness as a pointer to God's kenosis

Comparative theology is confessional theology. It is not primarily committed to reconciliation between religions but to revealing the truth and reality of God. It therefore does not always result in learning from other cultures and adopting the theological tenets of their faith. It is also a completely legitimate outcome of comparative theological endeavours to cleave to one's own position after undertaking a genuine and thorough investigation of the theological intuitions of another religion. Indeed, this reaffirmation can sometimes even lead a person to recognise the true significance of their own tradition for the first time and hence to cling to it all the more tenaciously. At this point, comparative theology can and should flip over into apologetics, and it is particularly challenging to set off on this path of apologetics in a state of lasting vulnerability and without any know-all attitudinising. In any case, there is also a moment in every form of confessional theology when one can, for very genuine reasons, no longer go along with one's interlocutor. Let me cite four examples of this.

Without question, the proclaimer of the Qur'an engages intensively with a number of Christian sources, such as Lk, ProtEvJam and the Syriac Church Fathers, and in this way develops an impressive form of reverence for the figure of Mary. But in my view he leaves those parts of the New Testament account that are critical of Mary too much out of the reckoning. Certainly, there are verses of the Qur'an which quite rightly attack the Byzantine imperial veneration of Mary, but at no point is Mary herself the object of criticism. This is laudable and understandable in the light of the polemical attacks on Mary which abounded in non-Christian circles in Late Antiquity. And yet it means that a key facet of the biblical image Mary is lost. This aspect is important to me in my approach to Mary and I would like to dwell on it at somewhat greater length.

In the chapter on the biblical Mary, we saw that Mk in particular documents a real rift between Mary and Jesus. Mary evidently had a problem dealing with the public ministry of her son, and only found her way to believing in Jesus as the Christ through a great deal of conflict and falling out. And it is precisely this inner struggle of Mary's and her agonising over the path in life he had taken – which demanded the utmost effort from her and which sometimes exceeded her powers of comprehension – which makes Mary's testimony so credible in my opinion. For me, when they are in conflict with one another like this, Mary and Jesus are truly a sign of God. After all, Mary is not constantly a transfigured being who has comprehended every aspect of her faith; instead, she finds herself struggling with things and in this situation arrives at a position of ambiguity which she has to learn to live with, and which I too often find difficult to endure. I would like Muslims to also get to know this conflict-laden, challenging side that characterises Mary and all the other biblical prophets.

A second point may well be one that will forever divide Islam and Christianity. We have seen striking evidence of the dialectical interlinking of grandeur and lowliness in the figure of Mary not just in the Bible but in the Qur'an as well. In the case of both sacred texts, one might perhaps claim that it is precisely Mary's lowliness and devotion which constitute her grandeur and greatness. Her specialness becomes apparent in her very devotion, that is in the very fact that she does not desire to be anything special. Anthropologically the two religions concur on the figure of Mary.

In Christian theological terms, however, the majesty of God is also defined in this dialectical interlinking. God's power itself is exclusively defined in the powerlessness of the Cross. God himself approaches us in a figure characterised by his lowliness and weakness. Of course, in the final analysis this insight is also conveyed through Christology, the theology of the Cross, and the theology of the Trinity. It is not solely evident in the figure of Mary. And yet Mary in her lowliness is an emblematic reflection of a God who approaches us through kenosis.

At this juncture – and this is my third point – the talk of Mary as the Mother of God is also recast in a quite different light. When Mary worries about Jesus, there is something of the motherly care and compassion of God for us humans evident in her purely human action. Indeed, God does not wish to display his caring power to the infant Jesus in any other way than through the love of his mother. Similarly, where my own life is concerned I can attest that the caring love of God first became apparent to me in my mother. God binds himself to us humans through his actions, and in addition honours us by ensuring that his benevolent will is made tangibly real through us. In this way, we bring God into the world, because Mary brought God into the world. Or to quote Felix Körner: 'It is God's wish to bestow his holiness on his creatures through their fellow creatures.'[3] 'In the figure of Mary cradling her child in her arms we can already see what happens when God entrusts himself to us in weakness.'[4]

3 Körner, *Kirche im Angesicht des Islam*, 334: '*Gott will seine eigene Heiligkeit den Geschöpfen durch Geschöpfe schenken.*'

4 Ibid., 336: '*An Maria, die das Kind auf den Armen trägt, lässt sich bereits ablesen, was geschieht, wenn Gott sich uns in Schwäche anvertraut.*'

At this point, we might ask in response how it can be made manifest in a human being that God's power desires to become tangible reality through the signs that we give as humans? Given the inevitable ambiguity of human actions, how can a human being demonstrate the unambiguous power of God that conquers death? Here I can accept Mary as a valid answer to this perfectly legitimate question only if – and this is my fourth and final point – it is the action of God that extricates her from this human ambiguity in her 'Yes' to the birth of Christ. It is only thus that I can declare myself in agreement with a God who uses no other means than those of considerate love to make his power an all-embracing reality. For it is only this which ensures that it is really divine power, power that has dominion over death, which is experienced in the love that we humans show for one another.

In making these final points, I do not in any way mean to disparage the Muslim testimony concerning Mary but merely to indicate why there is still a decisive factor missing here for me. It is no coincidence that this decisive factor is expressed in the dogmas of the Church. Accordingly, at no point did I intend to dispense with these dogmas or to relativise their importance. And yet today we need other, new ways of enabling the Marian devotion of the Church to find its voice again. And I see the joint Islamic and Christian investigation that we have undertaken in this book as a very hopeful example of just such a method.

2

Islamic Perspectives

a) Intensification: on the beauty and the political significance of Mary

An important, but more or less self-evident, learning experience results from a long and concentrated study of Mary on the basis of Islamic sources, which has led to a more intensive understanding of this figure and given me some important theological insights, as revealed in the foregoing chapters. I do not intend to recap these at this point; fully in the spirit of the comparative approach which lies at the heart of this book, I want instead to focus on instances of intensification that have come to light solely as a result of our comparative work on this volume.

One marvellous confirmation of my theology was the discovery that the Church Fathers are concerned to stress Mary's principal qualities such as her humility, purity and beauty. Where Syriac terminology is concerned, I learned that 'beauty' signifies above all inner beauty and hence also alludes to Mary's virtuousness. This idea, which most likely derives from Plato, is also reflected in the language of the Qur'an, especially with regard to Mary: God 'made her grow in goodness', we read in the Surah *Āl ʿImrān* (Q 3:37). The Arabic term that is used here (*ḥasan*) embraces the same dual meanings of 'good' and 'beautiful' as in Syriac. The implication behind this is that anything which is intrinsically good will manifest itself in outward beauty, and conversely that anything which is beautiful is necessarily always good. Yet from a philosophical perspective one might perhaps add that the quality of truthfulness also resonates here. Goodness and truth are evident in beauty and as a result it seems entirely logical to stress Mary's beauty, which, as my next point will demonstrate, can have decidedly tangible effects on human interaction.

A catalyst that helped me to better grasp the multi-faceted nature of the figure of Mary in the Qur'an was my study of the Magnificat and the Christian theological interpretation of this hymn of praise intoned by Mary in the Gospel of Luke. Even before I began studying her from a comparative theological perspective, it was clear to me that Mary, as she is depicted in the Qur'an, confounded customary expectations within sacred texts of what women can amount to in the realm of religion and theology. But before engaging with the Magnificat, I was unaware that, in addition to the extraordinary spirituality and piety she displays in the Qur'an, she not only turns societal norms upside-down but also embodies a decidedly political message and thus in this respect too disrupts all manner of established patterns of reading and thinking. Only by relying on this insight were we able in our project to consciously interrogate Mary's portrayal in the Qur'an for its political implications and to discover them by means of intertextual analysis. Finding that the Qur'an's criticism of an imperial power politics which misused religion for its own ends was exemplified by the figure of Mary immeasurably deepened my appreciation of Mary's sociopolitical relevance. The state of goodness and beauty that manifests itself in her is therefore not something that is remote from the contexts of peoples' lives but that rather has the capacity to take effect precisely there.

b) Recovery: Muhammad's special connection with Mary

In Christian theology, Jesus is the consummate incarnation of the intratrinitarian Logos; he is God's Word of assent to humanity. By contrast, in a subtle distinction that does not categorically negate this theological precept, the Qur'an talks about a Word of God that is Jesus: *kalimatu llāh.*

At no point in the Qur'an is it stated that it was only during the course of his life that Jesus became this one Word of God. On the contrary, when he was still just a baby he was able to eloquently – indeed, possibly without even uttering a word – rehabilitate his mother, solely through his essential being. This idea becomes fascinating when applied even more forcefully to Mary. Since I know of no Muslim theologian who assumes a categorical distinction between an unborn child in the womb and a baby that has been born, the following theological line of thought seems to me perfectly legitimate.[1] Mary received Jesus, this Word of God, she became pregnant with him, brought him into the world and thereby conveyed this Word from God, this message to her people. Muhammad in turn received the Qur'an, words of God, spoke them and brought them to his people. In truth, if one looks for it, the parallel structure is clearly apparent, but it only dawned on

1 On the question of Jesus's distinction as a Word of God while still in the womb cf. above, Part II, Chapter 1, Section c).

me when we were researching and writing this book, and so we included it in our exegetical and systematic sections (Parts II and III).

For all the parallels that may exist, however, we need to reflect theologically that, in contrast to Muhammad, Mary is not called a messenger in the Qur'an and is only indirectly included within the category of prophets (Q 21). Bearing this in mind, therefore, we have not insisted on bestowing this title on Mary. Why the Qur'an, in spite of all the obvious parallels, should have refrained from ascribing this role to her, is open to interpretation. Perhaps the proclaimer of the Qur'an wanted to draw the reader's special attention to the fact that Mary and Jesus are considered signs of God in the context of the story of Mary. In this reading, they would therefore represent the substance of a divine message and not merely be God's messengers.[2]

The traditional historical context of the Surah *Maryam*, in which the story of Mary plays a central part, warrants special attention. According to this, the story is not simply a document of dialogue for Muslims when they asked the Christian king of Abyssinia to grant them asylum from persecution by the Meccans. Instead it is a story that was of vital importance not just to Muhammad's followers but also to Muhammad himself, for his very survival. According to tradition, the depictions of Mary from the Surah *Maryam* were only added to the text of the Qur'an shortly before the first wave of Muslims emigrated to Abyssinia in around 615. At that stage, Muhammad had only been publicly proclaiming the message of the Qur'an for two years (and prior to that for three more years among a close circle of family and friends), and found himself under severe verbal and physical attack. Only now do I begin to wonder what effect the story of Mary might have had on Muhammad – the tale of someone who received a Word from God, found it a heavy burden to bear and also experienced moments of despair, and yet for whom things ultimately worked out well in the Qur'an? It seems obvious to me that we should not simply see Mary as a model for men and women (Q 66) and as a woman especially favoured by God, but also as a comforting and inspiring example, indeed as a role model, for Muhammad. To me, it seems clear that the story of Mary as recounted in the Surah *Maryam* was of huge significance for Muhammad's personal story with God and for his prophetic calling within the society of his time. I have therefore not adopted the Christian theological categorisation of Jesus as the Word of God into my theological understanding, though it has helped me to take more seriously Jesus's designation as *a* word of God. At the

2 On the fact that Muhammad is more than just a messenger of God's revelation, but also epitomises God's message to humankind through his actions, cf. above, p. 250, footnote 15.

same time, thinking about this question has enabled me to appreciate for the first time the connection that exists between Mary and Muhammad.

The category of vulnerability, which I have hinted at in my comments on Mary and Muhammad above and which we elaborated upon in Part III of this book, does not play the same key role in Islamic theology that it occupies in Christian belief and thought. All the same, we were able to show how, once this idea was taken on board, it could uncover further important theological insights for Muslim belief and thought as well. In the context of Mary and Muhammad, the following points clearly emerged: Muhammad was shaken to the core the first time he heard the words of God. Existentially and physically, it had such a profound effect on him that he found himself incapable of dealing with this borderline experience on his own. He turned to his wife for protection and solace. The fact that this episode from Muhammad's life was included in his biography suggests that outward displays of fragility and vulnerability were perfectly acceptable within contemporary conceptions of manliness, including seeking solace and security from a woman, otherwise this episode would have been swept under the carpet out of shame. Mary was alone when the Angel Gabriel visited her and she heard God's voice. She was thus made reliant upon God in a radical manner, the depiction of which in the Qur'an forms yet another bridge to Christianity; I will examine this aspect more closely under f) below, concerning reaffirmation.

c) Reinterpretation: on the dialectical interconnectedness of 'Yes' and 'No' before God – clarity in the process

As a Muslim theologian I am conscious of the possibilities but also of the limitations of my epistemic capabilities. This insight is especially acute where the Qur'an is concerned, a book whose divine origin is an unshakeable article of faith in Islamic theology. And who would presume to completely comprehend God's intentions? At the same time, the Qur'an exhorts us to reflect upon its message and understand what it says. On the one hand, then, I am being challenged not to place my understanding and my interpretation above the text itself and thereby put myself in the awkward position of placing human limitations on the utterances of the divine text. On the other hand, though, I am being asked to bear responsibility for making the text of the Qur'an speak through my interpretation. And yet I can only ever have a limited understanding of the boundless truth of God, as enunciated in the Qur'an and other sacred texts. I will therefore be most likely to do justice to my responsibility for having to take action in this tricky area if I constantly think of theological enquiry as merely provisional, by repeatedly scrutinising its findings and always being ready to learn. In this endeavour, shifts of viewpoint are an important methodological instrument for gaining knowledge, since by incorporating these other perspectives I can add something new to my theological construct. Accordingly, in working on this book, fully in keeping with our comparative approach, I have engaged with Christian statements on Mary in order to determine how they might help me to better understand my Islamic viewpoint. In the following instance, I have discovered two new aspects in my tradition of which I was previously unaware.

My first learning experience came from how Christianity interpreted Mary's assent to God, her *fiat*. In the Latin tradition of Christianity, the biblical phrase 'May your word to me be fulfilled' (Lk 1:38) is taken theologically to be Mary's *fiat*. In a Catholic Christian reading, it signifies that she thereby, thanks to her complete devotion to God, found herself able to give her unqualified assent to her calling and to Jesus Christ. Her clear 'Yes' was in response to the 'Yes' God gave to humankind. In saying this, she bore witness before the whole of humankind to her devotion to God. Thus, according to Catholic doctrine, in Mary humanity is faced with a person who is exactly as God would wish a person to be. And in Karl Rahner's reading of the relationship between God's actions and human freedom, Mary epitomises the faithful believer who is characterised by a 'direct proportionality in the relationship between divine agency and human freedom'. Since God wishes to liberate man to a state of freedom, 'then in this way of thinking, man is more free the more he opens himself to God's liberating grace.'[3]

This relationship between grace and freedom also occurs in the Islamic tradition in astonishingly similar fashion. An Islamic legal scholar from the fourteenth century determined that God's intention in turning towards humankind was to free man from his 'delusional wishful thinking' and thereby enable him to follow his vocation to become a servant of God of his own free will.[4] The common theological element in the Christian and Islamic formulations of this idea is the dialogically determined relationship between God and man. God wishes to be assented to from a position of freedom. It is no coincidence that the Qur'anic term for obedience (*ṭāʿa*) derives from a family of words encompassing insight, voluntary action and capability.

In reading the Qur'an, I had never before noticed any mention there of Mary's *fiat*, although I knew about the general theological substance behind the concept through my religious background. But after having investigated the biblical *fiat*, I

3 Cf. p. 79 f. above.

4 Cf. aš-Šāṭibī, *al-Muwāfaqāt fī uṣūl aš-šarīʿa*, vol. 2, 469.

was able to identify the Qur'anic *fiat* in the Surah *at-Taḥrīm* and interpret Mary's free decision anew as one that was subsumed within a more general transmission of the agency of God.

This brings me on to my second learning experience. In the course of investigating the full scope of God's 'Yes' to humankind, I likewise had occasion to explore the biblical portrayal of Mary's relationship with her son Jesus. Descriptions from sources other than the Qur'an are valuable to me insofar as they can illuminate what lies behind the narratively often very sparse accounts given in the Qur'an. Theological truths are expressed in highly concentrated form in the Qur'an. For instance, the Qur'anic concept of history unfolds from a distinction between the terms *qiṣṣa* and *ʿibra*. *Qaṣṣa* means 'to recount', more specifically to do so on the basis of searching for clues, in other words on the basis of one's ability to read signs. The verses of the Qur'an – that is, the signs from God – must therefore be read in order to be understood, and only then can they become a doctrine (*ʿibra*), a doctrine in the literal sense of 'to emulate something', 'to cross through something' and hence 'appropriate' it.

The Qur'an contains no reports of conflicts between Mary and Jesus. I do find this motif in the Bible, however, and can weigh up the extent to which I want to take account of it in my theological thinking. It becomes theologically interesting for me by virtue of the following observation: In Mk and Jn, there are accounts of serious clashes between Mary and Jesus, where the latter is seen, in accordance with Christian belief, as the embodiment of God's word of assent. Yet while being fully aware of such conflicts, it nevertheless remains possible within Christian theological reflection to hold fast to the idea of Mary giving an unqualified 'Yes' to God through Jesus. We expressed this in the following terms in the third chapter of Part I of this book: 'Clearly Mary's alienation from Jesus, which she has to endure at least for a time, can itself become part of the pure 'Yes' that she speaks in affirmation of Jesus Christ.'[5] Can I use these theological statements to discover anything new in my theology and use them to enrich my theological thinking? I find two aspects particularly striking here: the Qur'an describes humans as ambivalent beings, with great potential but also with an inherent tendency to deny goodness, beauty and truth and therefore ultimately to disavow God (Q 2:30–38 and Q 95:1–8). This denial is not only tantamount to Mary's saying 'No' to Jesus but would, if transferred to the Islamic context, also mean a disavowal of God by every human being. Refusing to own up to this human disposition effectively means preventing oneself from taking an honest look at oneself and one's own

5 Cf. p. 73 ff.

relationship with God. Indeed, refusing to believe the 'No' that is inherent within me actually distances me further from God. Confessing this 'No', on the other hand, makes me honest and in acknowledging this honest 'No', I am paradoxically brought closer to God once more. The Christian interpretation of Mary appears to encourage me to adopt this honest position.

This brings me to the second part of the new insights I gleaned from analysing the Christian image of Mary. The Qur'an itself seizes upon the idea that turning away from God can actually constitute an important part of the cognitive process, so long as one – and this is vital – does not deliberately seek out this 'no' and cleave to it. The formulation *a-fa-lā yataddabarūna l-qur'ān* implicitly contains the injunction to think about the Qur'an from a distance. Alongside other lexical variants that have been adopted, the nineteenth-century British orientalist Edward Lane documents the following intriguing meanings of words within this formulation. He cites not only meanings such as 'to ponder', 'to meditate on something', 'to strive to understand something' and 'to disentangle', but also the meanings 'to turn one's back' and 'to turn away', and finally in the tenth word-stem – as if anticipating a result – 'to recognise'.[6] In my opinion, what is being described here is a gradual process of understanding such as that outlined by Umberto Eco in his book *The Open Work*: in order for the beauty and the suggestive power of a work of art to remain vibrant and to prevent any habituation effect from setting in, which would rob the work of any dynamism, then in Eco's view what is required is distance. One needs, so to speak, to turn one's back on the work.[7] Might it also be possible to repurpose this thought for Islamic theology? Under what circumstances would it be legitimate to turn one's back on God and his Word, in order to re-encounter him later in a new light? As yet, I am still undecided on this question. But at least I can agree with Ibn ʿArabī that I cannot possibly fall from favour with God because God is ubiquitous and so is his saving grace for humankind. Perhaps, therefore, placing the emphasis somewhat differently, I can say from my Muslim theological standpoint that my 'No' to God is enfolded by his 'Yes', inasmuch as God never severs the relationship with man on his own initiative. He always remains *rabb*, in other words not just a creator and sustainer but also an educator. That is to say, right up to the final 'No', he holds open for man the possibility of saying 'Yes' – or to put it in Qur'anic terms, the possibility of performing *tawba*:

6 Cf. Lane, *Lexicon*, vol. 3, 844–848.

7 Cf. Eco, *The Open Work*, 87. This paragraph, with a few minor changes, is taken from my dissertation: Tatari, *Gott und Mensch im Spannungsverhältnis von Gerechtigkeit und Barmherzigkeit*, 31 f.

showing repentance and turning back to God. My inability to say 'Yes' to God at all moments in my life – in other words, to be repeatedly trapped, as a result of my ambivalent human nature, in a state of denial – can precisely for that reason be taken as an integral part of my overall assent to God – especially if the 'No' is seen as a necessary interim step in the integration of all moments of my life in favour of God.

d) Appropriation: Mary and God's unqualified gift of grace

Initially, I found it disconcerting when, in the course of writing this book, we once again had to engage far more intensively with the idea prevalent in Christian theology that God's grace – and what's more a special kind of grace experienced by the individual – can ensue for no reason whatsoever. To quote what we wrote in the first chapter: 'Mary does not earn the encounter with the angel through her grace and virtuousness, but instead is endowed with God's grace for no reason. Even the consoling words "The Lord is with you" in the same verse are offered without Mary having done anything to deserve them.'[8] From my work on the key category of God's mercy in in the Islamic tradition, I was accustomed to distinguishing between different orders of divine intervention, as expressed through the two distinct names given to God, *ar-Raḥmān* and *ar-Raḥīm*. The first name denotes a loving, caring and merciful intervention by God, which applies to all human and other living beings indiscriminately. We are sustained and supported by this loving care. It is a very generalised quality, which finds its echo in the biblical dictum: 'He causes his sun to rise on the evil and the good, and sends rain on the righteous and the unrighteous' (Mt 5:45). By contrast, God's characteristic of caring mercy, which is conveyed by the term *ar-Raḥīm*, comes about through dialogue; God endows it upon those who are receptive and prepared for it. It requires a conscious decision by a person, together with some considerable effort on his or her part, to turn to God. But then the Christian idea of God's grace presented me with a quite different picture: Mary received God's grace for no reason. She did not have to earn it. Of course, as a result of my Muslim upbringing, I am aware that each and every one of my efforts to get closer to God is itself God's work and that I alone can achieve nothing of my own accord. Even so, is it not the case that God waits for me to make an effort – whether it succeeds or not is completely immaterial here – in order that it might act as a sign from me to which God can respond, as the Qur'an so beautifully puts it, 'without measure' (Q 2:212;

8 Cf. p. 17 above.

24:38)? Notwithstanding this, I am still fascinated by the idea of an unconditional consolation from God that has nothing to do with how I think or act. To take on board such an idea as an integral part of practising one's faith surely cannot help but have a liberating effect. This liberating experience of unconditional solicitude from God is paired in Catholic theology with the idea of a demand upon the individual resulting from this experience. Thus, within the experience of God's unconditionally given love there is an imperative. To formulate this in Christian terms, the emphasis should no doubt be placed somewhat differently: it is an inherent property of experienced love to be communicated and shared, it is so to speak intrinsic to its very nature. The human response to this love given by God for no reason calls for nothing other than a 'Yes' to him and – again in Christian terms – should have nothing to do with ethics.

At this point, my appropriation can most probably not be unreserved: consonant with my theological conditioning, my 'Yes' to God ought really to resonate within the core of my being, be this in my actions, words or thoughts – in other words in contexts which do have ethical relevance. But as a stimulus from Christian theology, I certainly take away the following insight: instead of thinking of it chiefly in terms of the assent it requires from me, as I was previously accustomed to doing, I am at liberty to engage with and reconsider God's consolation in its own right and to incorporate it as an important, albeit supplementary, element within my own theological thinking.

e) Rectification: Mary as a warning to exercise care in passing theological judgement on others

Reading the classical works of Islamic exegesis has been of great value to our book and has also given me a number of new insights into Mary. At several points, it became apparent how much the historical–critical method could broaden and deepen an understanding of the text of the Qur'an, to an extent I had not expected, by enquiring after the intertexts that might exist for particular Qur'anic verses. However, I also came across texts in the exegetical tradition whose content, in view of the comparative theological approach I am used to taking, I can only describe as difficult. For example, I had great problems with the classical interpretation of the following verse: *When God says, 'Jesus, son of Mary, did you say to people: "Take me and my mother as two deities beside God"?' He will answer, 'Glory be to You! How could I ever say that to which I have no right? And if I had ever said so, You would surely have known it. You know what is in my mind, while I do not know anything that is within Yours. You alone are the knower of unseen things.'* (Q 5:116).

We have already examined and identified the problems in Rāzī's and Qurṭubī's interpretations of this verse in Part II. I should like to briefly revisit them here and cast a broader eye over their arguments. Both exegetes were clear that there was no official Christian doctrine of Jesus's divinity in the sense of a power that was conceived as being independent of God. Similarly for both exegetes it was self-evident that the Christian designation of Mary as the 'God-bearer' (*Theotokos*) did not mean that it would be commensurate with an official Christian theological understanding to extrapolate from this that Mary should be considered a goddess. The desire to identify truth in the text of the Qur'an, but which intrinsically turned that text into a reproach against Christianity, misled both exegetes into giving their own analysis of Christian ideas. In an almost triumphant tone, they imagine that they have deduced and discovered through their arguments why the rhetorical question that is put to Jesus in the Qur'an might actually be correct.[9] But did the exegetes actually choose the best method of pursuing their perfectly understandable aim of defending the truth of the Qur'an? I do not believe they did. In accordance with the standards of scholarship at the time, it is highly likely that both took the utmost care to interpret the verse diligently with the aim of doing full justice to their sacred scripture and of presenting Christianity in the correct light as they saw it. Apologetic motivations may have also come into play for them, by casting their own religion in a more favourable light than another in the interpretative process. We can only surmise. But what we can say with certainty on the basis of the exegetical work in this book is that our historical–critical research on this question has revealed a way of seeing things that can reconcile both standpoints: namely, confirming the truth of the Qur'an while at the same time doing justice to Christianity's theological self-perception. We found that Jesus and Mary were misused to promote the imperial power politics pursued by the Byzantine emperor Heraclius, and that Mary in particular was interpreted as some kind of warlord, with an icon or a statue of her being deployed in battle. The religious–theological belief in the invulnerability of her body was exaggerated by Heraclius and taken as a guarantee that those who pledged allegiance to Mary would themselves be invincible and victorious in battle. During his reign Mary was virtually turned into a goddess of war. This interpretation of Mary as a quasi-divine figure was therefore a real phenomenon, but was at total variance with the existing theological doctrines of the age! It follows from this that, in this verse, the Qur'an was criticising the imperial exploitation and manipulative skewing of Christian beliefs that had taken place under Heraclius.

As far as I was concerned, the results of this gain in knowledge were threefold:

9 Ar-Rāzī, *Tafsīr*, 12, 132 and al-Qurṭubī, *al-Ǧāmi'*, 8, 301.

firstly, it confirmed my view that, when in dialogue with other religious and theological conceptions, one should always enquire after the particular inner self-perception of one's interlocutor and give a fair account of this when reaching one's own theological judgment. Secondly, it became apparent that the text of the Qur'an responded in a much more subtle and targeted way to contemporary discourses than I had previously thought. And thirdly it became clear that an interpretation of the Qur'an needed to be conducted with the utmost caution and delicacy so as to avoid misusing it for the purpose of making theological misjudgments about other religions.

In a further step, these insights can then be used to pose the self-critical question as to how far religious texts and theoretical points may be altered, distorted and misused for imperialist ends. In all likelihood, the exploitation of one's own religious tradition to serve power-political interests pains any truly religious person, while at the same time inviting us all to make a common effort to confront such tendencies critically yet also constructively.[10]

f) Reaffirmation: radicalism and the Golden Mean

In this book, one of the ideas with which I wrestled especially hard was the concept of the perpetual virginity of Mary. This required that I get my head around the thought patterns of Christian theology and acquaint myself with a terminology that was still very alien to me in many respects in order to divine the meaning behind certain concepts. Despite my best efforts, it remained ultimately alien to me. In the first part of our book we ascertained that the idea of a perpetual virginity of Mary accorded well with the ascetic ideals of the evangelist Luke. Indeed, this idea forms an integral part of the biblical text. As I understood it, the concept of Mary's perpetual virginity was regarded as a symbol of abstinence, purity and sinlessness and was deduced from her physical abstention from any intimacy and her renunciation of a normal married life. It is seen in the Bible as being key to a closeness to God. From an Islamic perspective, this state of 'remaining unmarried for the sake of the kingdom of heaven' (Mt 19:12) is a sacrifice that God does not expect from us. In the view of Islam, for most people this demand represents too great an infringement upon what it means to be human.

10 'The caliphs' predilection for the concept of the "royal Prophet" has parallels in Byzantine political theology' (*Dass die Kalifen den ‚königlichen Propheten' bevorzugten, hat seine Parallelen in der byzantinischen politischen Theologie*). Samuela Pagani, 'König oder Diener'? Die Versuchung des Propheten oder die Wahl eines Modells, Trivium [Online], 29 | 2019, 17 October 2019: http://journals.openedition.org/trivium/6241.

However, I should stress that my dissociation from this concept is not absolute. For as we explained in Part II, looked at through Muslim eyes this notion of Mary – namely her abstinence and autonomy, which are focused entirely on God – can also be seen as a way of paying due respect and tribute within Islam to someone who voluntarily chooses to adopt an ascetic way of life. It helps convey the insight that there are as many different concepts of living as there are people in this world. The ideal of a married life should not become some kind of social diktat to which every individual must submit. The radicalism that characterises Mary in Christian theologies can have a liberating effect for the acknowledgment of lifestyles within Islam which, as the mystic Rabia would put it, are entirely filled with love for God. Certainly, the conviction that physical intimacy is diametrically opposed to the idea of purity and must be seen as an impediment on the way to God has never formed part of the Islamic tradition, nor is there any place for it there.

While reflecting on the results of this book, I became aware of another form of radicalism in a Christian context which was first sparked by the figure of Mary and from which I feel I am somewhat distanced as a result of my theological conditioning. Trying to think of Mary, in radical religious and theological terms, as a counterpart to Eve was almost enough to cause me pain as a theologian. The paralleling of these two figures, resulting from the belief that sin came into the world through Eve's ear and that Mary's ear was the means by which a new path for humanity beyond sin was revealed, means that both of these women are seen as being at the extreme limits of human comprehension. Even some contemporary Christian theologians still insist on this radical antithesis of Eve and Mary – we refer the reader to our comments on the work of Gisbert Greshake.

The difficulty I have with this idea is this: as we established in Part II, as a sign of esteem and her religious–theologically and socially important function, Mary is accorded the Islamic honorific: 'Peace Be Upon Her' (*ʿalayhā s-salām*). However. in Islamic tradition, this honorific formula is also accorded to Eve (Arabic: Ḥawwāʾ). She is considered the grandmother of all people. According to the legend, after their expulsion from paradise she and Adam are said to have journeyed to a number of different geographical locations on earth. One such place was on the coast of the Arabian Peninsula, a site that still bears her name today: Jeddah ('grandmother'). Until 1975 it was even thought to be the site of Eve's supposed burial place, which was regularly visited by pilgrims. For me, it is highly relevant for contemporary theology to note the clear esteem and affection in which the figure of Eve is still held, as reflected in the naming of the city. While the name Ḥawwāʾ is not attested in the Qurʾan for Adam's partner, it quickly established itself as part of Islamic tradition. It literally means 'to live', 'to be alive' – and indeed corresponds to the Hebrew in this regard. It seems to me that it is a fundamental characteristic of Islamic thinking, firmly rooted in the Qur'an, to avoid extremes. Thus, from the way the story of Cain and Abel is interpreted in the Qur'an one can glean the important insight that the proclaimer of the Qur'an is concerned to show that in human interactions there is no such thing as absolute good or absolute evil. Accordingly, the high regard in which Adam and his wife are held in the Qur'an is something that I am very keen to champion against the typecast manner in which they are disparaged in the Christian tradition.

The formulation we examined in the first part of the book, which draws a parallel between Mary's renunciation of her own being in favour of a loving God on the one hand and the brutality of the destructive power of the Cross on the other, also seems radical to me. Against such exaggerations, I am theologically predisposed to believe that Muslims should act as a 'community of the middle way' (Q 2:143). If one takes this exhortation in the Qur'an seriously, then Muslims are charged with the task of shunning radicalism, seeking out a path of conciliation and inviting others to share it.

This imperative in the Qur'an conceals an important theological insight that we should be mindful of, especially nowadays: not only radical emotions and actions but also radical thinking may spell danger if they become too intense, lose all sense of proportion and turn destructive. The Qur'an makes us aware that it takes repeated efforts at mediation, relativisation and conciliation to shape human existence and coexistence in a positive way. In addition, this theological approach on the part of the Qur'an corroborates our finding from Part II that Mary in the Qur'an performs the role of mediator between Judaism and Christianity. Mary thus appears as a bridge joining the two sides in mutual respect. But is there also a downside to striving towards the Qur'anic ideal of being a community of the middle way? I think that there is. Claiming occupancy too precipitately of a supposed middle ground that has not been properly sounded out, and doing so without any hint of trying to provoke or rub another religion up the wrong way, can sometimes lead to a lack of focus, to a mediocrity without any spice or bite which does not do justice to the profundities of human experience.

Even so, against the background of this guiding ideal of the middle way, might it still be possible for me to cast an eye over the language of Christian belief and the corresponding theology in a way that makes sense to me and helps me see the ideal of the middle way not as something static but rather as a dynamic force? In other words, inspired by Christian thinking can I sound out extremes without myself slipping into them?

The terminology of Christian thought resides in large part at the extremities of human epistemic capacities and stretches those extremities almost to breaking point. It is liminal thinking, and this can have a liberating effect. It seems to me that the one thing above all which Christian theology, as I have come to know it, is driving at – through its very style, its choice of vocabulary and its terminology – is the responsiveness of the human heart.

In this sense, I too cannot help but see this key category of love as a radical category, a radical force guiding thinking, feelings and action. It is a particular hallmark of Christian testimonies of faith and Christian theology. We do not find it expressed with the same clarity and openness in the writings of Islamic theology. But perhaps Muslims should not regard this finding as a shortcoming – after all, the motif of love is ubiquitous in Sufism and elsewhere – but rather as a conscious marker of an independent theology which also has the capacity to be an inspiration to a Christian interlocutor. In light of this, the figure of Mary in particular, in both the Bible and the Qur᾽an, seems to me to be a bridging figure who enables me to appreciate the concept of loving devotion to God in all its radicalism while at the same time keeping me grounded in the Golden Mean. This is especially the case if, taking up the Qur᾽anic ideal of the middle way, we interpret Mary as a prophetic figure and thus integrate her into the new theological departure represented by the Qur᾽an, which has both a moderating and an inspiring influence. Her personal fate shows the extent to which, in the final analysis, God's love remains a mystery and how important it is not to use this term too blithely.

It would be wonderful if our book gave Muslims and Christians the impetus to discover Mary afresh in her loving aspect: as a figure who is the focus of divine love and who shows us that love is the way forward.

Bibliography

Abboud, Hosn, *Mary in the Qur'an. A literary reading*, London – New York 2014.

— 'Qur'anic Mary's story and the motif of palm tree and the rivulet.' In: *Parole de l'Orient* 30 (2005) 261–280.

— 'Is Mary important for herself or for being the mother of Christ in the Holy Qur'an?' In: *Al-Raida Journal* 125 (2009) 26–36.

Abou el-Fadl, Khaled, *Speaking in God's name. Islamic law, authority and women*, Oxford 2001.

Abū Dāwūd, *Sulaymān ibn al-Aš'at as-Siğistānī, Sunan Abī Dāwūd*, vols 1–5, ed. by Abū Ṭāhir Zubayr 'Alī Zā'ī, Engl. trans. Yaser Qadhi, Riyadh 2008.

Abramowski, Luise, 'Aus dem Streit um das "Unus ex trinitate passus est". Der Protest des Habib gegen die Epistula dogmatica des Philoxenus an die Mönche.' In: Alois Grillmeier and Theresia Hainthaler (eds.), *Jesus der Christus im Glauben der Kirche*, vol. 2/3, Freiburg and elsewhere 2004, 570–647.

Ackermann, Andrea, '"… und Maria dachte darüber nach". Bekannte und neue exegetische Perspektiven auf Lk 2,19.' In: Weidemann (ed.), *'Der Name der Jungfrau war Maria'*, 243–258.

Ali, Kecia, 'Destabilizing Gender, Reproducing Maternity: Mary in the Qur'ān.' In: *Journal of the International Qur'anic Studies Association* 2 (2017) 89–109.

Alvar, Jaime, *Romanising oriental Gods. Myth, salvation, and ethics in the cults of Cybele, Isis and Mithras*, Leiden – Boston 2008.

Anawati, George C., 'Islam and the immaculate conception.' In: Edward O'Connor (ed.), *The dogma of the immaculate conception. History and significance*, Notre Dame, IN 1958, 447–461.

Appel, Kurt, 'Wen erwarten wir? Was erwartet uns? Eine adventliche Meditation.' In: *IkaZ* 36 (2007) 647–652.

Ashkar, Dominic F., *Mary in the Syriac Christian tradition and Islam. A comparative study*, Ann Arbor 1996 (available on microfilm).

Al-Azmeh, Aziz, *The emergence of Islam in late antiquity. Allāh and his people*, Cambridge 2014.

Barth, Karl, *Credo*, Zollikon – Zurich 1948.

— *Kirchliche Dogmatik I/2: Die Lehre vom Wort Gottes. Prolegomena zur kirchlichen Dogmatik*, Zollikon – Zurich 1960.

Bausenhart, Guido, *'In allem uns gleich außer der Sünde'. Studien zum Beitrag Maximos' des Bekenners zur altkirchlichen Christologie. Zusammen mit einer kommentierten Übersetzung von 'Disputatio cum Pyrrho'*, Mainz 1992.

al-Bayḍāwī, *Nāṣir ad-Dīn Abū Sa'īd 'Abdallāh ibn 'Umar, Anwār attanzīl wa-asrār at-ta'wīl* (no place or date of publication).

Beck, Edmund, 'Die Mariologie der echten Schriften Ephräms.' In: *Oriens Christianus* 40 (1956) 22–39.

Becker, Jürgen, *Maria. Mutter Jesu und erwählte Jungfrau*, Leipzig, 2nd edn., 2013 (BG 4).

Beinert, Wolfgang, 'Die mariologischen Dogmen und ihre Entfaltung.' In: Wolfgang Beinert and Heinrich Petri (eds.), *Handbuch der Marienkunde. Vol. 1: Theologische Grundlegung – Geistliches Leben*, 2nd., fully revised edition, Regensburg 1996, 267–363.

— *Maria. Spiegel der Erwartungen Gottes und der Menschen*, Regensburg 2001.

Bell, Richard, *The origin of Islam in its Christian environment*, The Gunning lectures, Edinburgh University 1925, London 1968.

Benko, Stephen, *The virgin goddess. Studies in the Pagan and Christian roots of Mariology*, Leiden 1993 (Studies in the history of religions; 59).

Berkey, Jonathan P., *The formation of Islam. Religion and society in the Near East, 600–1800*, Cambridge 2003.

Bonfil, Robert, 'Continuity and discontinuity (641–1204).' In: Ibid. et al. (eds.), *Jews in Byzantium. Dialectics of minority and majority cultures*, Leiden 2012 (Jerusalem studies in religion and culture; 14), 65–100.

Booth, Phil, *Crisis of Empire. Doctrine and dissent at the end of late antiquity*, Berkeley and elsewhere 2014.

Bovon, François, *Das Evangelium nach Lukas. 1. Teilband: Lk 1,1–9,50 (EKK III/1)*, Neukirchen-Vluyn 1989.

Bradshaw, Paul, *The search for the origins of Christian worship. Sources and methods for the study of early liturgy*, 2nd edn., Oxford 2002.

Brock, Sebastian, 'St. Ephrem on Christ as light in Mary and in the Jordan: Hymni de Ecclesia 36.' In: *Eastern churches review. A journal of Eastern Christendom* 7 (1976) 137–144.

— 'A letter from the orthodox monasteries of the orient sent to Alexandria, addressed to Severos.' In: John D'Alton and Youhanna Youssef (eds.), *Severos of Antioch, His life and times*, Leiden – Boston 2016, 32–46.

— 'Mary in Syriac tradition.' In: Alberic Stacpoole (ed.), *Mary's place in Christian dialogue. Occasional papers of the ecumenical society of the Blessed Virgin Mary 1970–1980*, St. Paul's publications 1982.

— 'Clothing metaphors as a means of theological expression in Syriac tradition.' In: Sebastian Brock, *Studies in Syriac Christianity. History, literature and theology*, Aldershot 1992, 11–38.

Brown, Peter, *The cult of the saints. Its rise and function in Latin Christianity*, Chicago 1981.

— 'The rise and function of the Holy Man in late antiquity.' In: *The Journal of Roman Studies* 61 (1971) 80–101.

al-Buḫārī, *Abū ʿAbdallāh Muḥammad ibn Ismāʿīl, Ṣaḥīḥ al-Buḫārī*, Beirut – Damascus 2002.

Buisson, Johanna Marie, 'Subversive Maryam or a Qurʾanic view on women's empowerment.' In: *Crosscurrents* 66 (2016) 450–459.

Bumazhnov, Dmitrij, 'Some further observations concerning the early history of the term ΜΟΝΑΧΟΣ (monk).' In: *Studia Patristica* 45 (2010) 21–26.

Cameron, Averil, 'Blaming the Jews. The seventh-century Arab invasion in Palestine in context.' In: *Travaux et mémoires* 14 (2002) 57–78.

— 'The Theotokos in Sixth-Century Constantinople. A city finds its symbol.' In: *Journal of Theological Studies* 24 (1978) 79–108.

Cause of the Commemoration of Mary, MS Catholic University of America syr. 8.

El-Cheikh, Nadia Maria, *Byzantium viewed by the Arabs*, Cambridge, MA – London 2004.

— 'Muhammad and Heraclius. A study in legitimacy.' In: *Studia Islamica* 98 (1999) 5–21.

Cornille, Catherine, *Meaning and Method in Comparative Theology*, Hoboken 2020.

Cuţaru, Caius, 'Sittinā Maryam of the Muslims. Honouring the Virgin Mary in Islam.' In: *Teologia* 66 (2016) 63–76.

Dagron, Gilbert, *Empereur et prêtre. Etude sur le 'césaropapisme' byzantin*, Paris 1996.

aḍ-Ḍaḥḥāk, Aḥmad ibn ʿAmr, *al-Āḥād wa-l-maṯānī*, vols 1–6, ed. by Basīm Fayṣāl Aḥmad al-Ğawābira, Riyadh 1991.

Dassmann, Ernst, *Kirchengeschichte I. Ausbreitung, Leben und Lehre der Kirche in den ersten drei Jahrhunderten*, Stuttgart – Berlin – Cologne 1991.

Debié, Muriel, 'Les controverses miaphysites en Arabie et le Coran.' In: Flavia Ruani (ed.), *Les controverses religieuses en syriaque*, Paris 2016 (*Etudes Syriaques* 13), 137–156.

Devréesse, Robert, 'La fin inédite d'une lettre de saint Maxime. Un baptème forcé de juifs et de samaritains à Carthage en 632.' In: *Revue des sciences religieuses* 17 (1937) 25–36.

Dibelius, Martin, 'Jungfrauensohn und Krippenkind. Untersuchungen zur Geburtsgeschichte Jesu im Lukas-Evangelium.' In: Martin Dibelius, *Botschaft und Geschichte I*, Tübingen 1953, 1–78.

Doerfler, Maria, 'The Holy Man in the courts of Rome. Roman law and clerical justice in fifth-century Syria.' In: *Studies in Late Antiquity* 3 (2019) 192–211.

Donner, Fred, *Muhammad and the believers. At the origins of Islam*, Cambridge – London 2010.

Draguet, René, *Julien d'Harnicasse et sa controverse avec Sévère d'Antioche sur l'incurrupitibilité du corps du Christ. Etude d'histoire littéraire et doctrinale suivie des fragments dogmatiques de Julien (Text syriaque et traduction grecque)*, Louvain 1924.

Eco, Umberto, *The Open Book*, trans. by Anna Cancogni with an introduction by David Robey, Cambridge, MA 1989.

Eggemann, Ina, *Die 'ekklesiologische Wende' in der Mariologie des II. Vatikanums und „Konziliare Perspektiven" als neue Horizonte für das Verständnis der Mittlerschaft Marias*, Altenberge 1993 (Münsteraner theologische Abhandlungen; 22).

Eisele, Wilfried, 'Krieg und Frieden. Maria, Elisabet und die vielgepriesenen Frauen Israels (Lk 1,39–45).' In: Weidemann (ed.), *'Der Name der Jungfrau war Maria'*, 172–203.

Ephraem der Syrer, *Hymnen de nativitate*, ed. by E. Beck, Louvain 1959 (CSCO Syr. 82–83).

— *Hymnen de ecclesia*, ed. by E. Beck, Louvain 1960 (CSCO Syr. 84–85).

— 'Hymns on the Nativity.' In: *Bride of Light. Hymns on Mary from the Syriac churches*, trans. by Sebastian Brock, Baker Hill-Kottayam 1994, 18–32.

Ps-Ephraem der Syrer, *Kommentar zum Diatessaron I.25*, trans. into German by Chr. Lange, Freiburg 2008 (FC 54/1–2).

Ps-Ephraem der Syrer, 'Marienhymnen'. Trans. Sebastian Brock. In: Ps-Ephraem der Syrer, *Bride of Light: Hymn on Mary from the Syriac Churches*, Kottayam 1994.

Evans, Matthew T., 'The Sacred: Differentiating, Clarifying and Extending Concepts.' In: *Review of Religious Research* 45 (2003) 32–47.

Fierro, Maribel, 'Women as prophets in Islam.' In: Marin Manuela (ed.), *Writing the feminine. Women in Arab sources*, London – New York 2002, 183–198.

Fisher, Greg, *Between Empires. Arabs, Romans and Sasanians in Late Antiquity*, Oxford 2011.

Fiores, Stefano de, 'Maria in der Geschichte von Theologie und Frömmigkeit.' In: Wolfgang Beinert and Heinrich Petri (eds.), *Handbuch der Marienkunde. Vol. 1: Theologische Grundlegung – Geistliches Leben*, 2nd, fully revised edition, Regensburg 1996, 99–264.

Frend, W. H. C., *The rise of the monophysite movement. Chapters in the history of the church in the fifth and sixth centuries*, Cambridge 1972.

Frye, Richard N., 'The political history of Iran under the Sasanians.' In: Ehsan Yarshater (ed.), *The Cambridge History of Iran*, vol. 3 (1), Cambridge 1983, 116–180.

al-Ġazālī, Abū Ḥāmid Muḥammad, *Ǧawāhir al-qur'ān*, ed. by Muḥammad Rašīd Riḍā al-Qabbānī, Beirut 1986.

Geagea, Nilo, *Mary of the Koran. A meeting point between Christianity and Islam*, trans. and ed. by Lawrence T. Fares, New York 1984.

George-Tvrtković, Rita, *Christians, Muslims, and Mary. A history*, New York – Mahwah, NJ 2018.

Gerö, Stephen, *Barsauma of Nisibis and Persian Christianity in the fifth century*, Louvain 1981.

Gerwing, Manfred, 'Mariologie.' In: Thomas Marschler and Thomas Schärtl (eds.), *Dogmatik heute: Bestandsaufnahme und Perspektiven*, Regensburg 2014, 399–429.

Ghaffar, Zishan, 'Einordnung in die koranische Prophetologie.' In: Khorchide and von Stosch, *Der andere Prophet*, 176–226.

— *Der Koran in seinem religions- und weltgeschichtlichen Kontext. Eschatologie und Apokalyptik in den mittelmekkanischen Suren*, Paderborn 2020 (Beiträge zur Koranforschung; 1).

— 'Kontrafaktische Intertextualität im Koran und die exegetische Tradition des syrischen Christentums.' In: *Der Islam 98* (2021) issue 2 (in preparation; the page numbers cited correspond to the manuscript copy we consulted).

Gilis, Charles-André, *Marie en Islam*, Paris 1990.

Gillot, Claude, 'Exegesis of the Qur'ān: Classical and Medieval.' In: Jane Dammen McAuliffe (ed.), *Encyclopaedia of the Qur'ān*, vol. 2, Leiden 2002, 99–124.

— 'Kontinuität und Wandel in der „klassischen" islamischen Koranauslegung.' In: *Der Islam* 88 (2010) 1–155.

Gilson, Erinn, 'Vulnerability, ignorance and oppression.' In: *Hypatia* 26 (2011) 308–332.

Gnilka, Joachim, *Johannesevangelium*, Würzburg 1983 (NEB).

Goar, Jacques, *Euchologion sive rituale Graecorum*, reprint Graz 1960.

Goehring, James, *Ascetics, society and the desert. Studies in early Egyptian monasticism*, Harrisburg, PA 1999, 13–35.

Goldschmidt, Lazarus, *Der Babylonische Talmud*, vol. 1, Königstein-im-Taunus, 1980 (reprint of the 2nd edn.).

Grass, Hans, *Traktat über Mariologie*, Marburg 1991 (Marburger theologische Studien; 30).

Greshake, Gisbert, *Maria-Ecclesia. Perspektiven einer marianisch grundierten Theologie und Kirchenpraxis*, Regensburg 2014.

Griffith, Sidney, 'Disclosing the mystery. The hermeneutics of typology in Syriac exegesis.' In: Mordechai Z. Cohen and Adele Berlin (eds.), *Interpreting Scriptures in Judaism, Christianity and Islam. Overlapping Inquiries*, Cambridge 2016, 46–64.

— '*Al-Naṣārā* in the Qur'ān. A hermeneutical reflection.' In: Gabriel Said Reynolds (ed.), *New perspectives on the Qur'ān. The Qur'ān in its historical context 2*, London – New York 2011, 301–322.

— 'The poetics of scriptural reasoning. Syriac mêmrê at work.' In: *Studia patristica* 78 (2017) 5–24.

— 'Syriacisms in the "Arabic Qur'ān". Who were "those who said 'Allāh is the third of three'" according to al-Mā'ida 73?' In: Meir M. Bar-Asher et al. (eds.), *A word fitly spoken. Studies in medieval exegesis of the Hebrew Bible and the Qur'ān*, Jerusalem 2007, 83–110.

Grillmeier, Alois, *Jesus der Christus im Glauben der Kirche. Vol. 2/2: Die Kirche von Konstantinopel im 6. Jahrhundert, unter Mitarbeit v. Theresia Hainthaler*, Freiburg – Basel – Vienna 1989.

Guillaumont, Antoine, *Les ‚Képhalaia Gnostica' d'Évagre le Pontique et l'histoire de l'origénisme chez les Grecs et chez les Syriens*, Paris 1962 (Patristica Sorbonensia; 5).

Hagemann, Ludwig and Pulsfort, Ernst, *Maria, die Mutter Jesu, in Bibel und Koran*, Würzburg 1992 (Religionswissenschaftliche Studien; 19).

Hainthaler, Theresia, *Christliche Araber vor dem Islam. Verbreitung und konfessionelle Zugehörigkeit. Eine Hinführung*, Louvain – Paris – Dudley, MA 2007 (Eastern Christian Studies; 7).

Halleux, André de, 'Le Mamlelā de "Ḥabbīb" contre Aksenāyā. Aspects textuels d'une polémique christologique dans l'Église syriaque de la première génération post-chalcédonienne.' In: Carl Laga, Joseph. A. Munititz and Lucas. van Rompay (eds.), *After Chalcedon. Studies in theology and church history offered to professor Albert Van Roey*, Louvain 1985 (Orientalia Lovaniensia Analecta; 18), 67–82.

Henninger, Joseph, 'Mariä Himmelfahrt im Koran.' In: *Neue Zeitschr. Miss.* 10 (1945) 288–292.

Heo, Angie, 'The Virgin Between Christianity and Islam: Sainthood, Media, and Modernity in Egypt.' In: *Journal of the American Academy of Religion* 81 (2013) 1117–1138.

Himmelfarb, Martha, 'The mother of the Messiah in the Talmud Yerushalmi and Sefer Zerubbabel.' In: Peter Schäfer (ed.), *The Talmud Yerushalmi and Graeco-Roman Culture, III*, Tübingen 2002, 369–390.

— 'Sefer Zerubbabel.' In: David Stern and Mark Jay Mirsky, *Rabbinic fantasies. Imaginative narratives from classical Hebrew literature*, Skokie, IL 2001, 67–90.

Hofrichter, Peter, *Nicht aus Blut, sondern monogen aus Gott geboren. Textkritische, dogmengeschichtliche und exegetische Untersuchung zu Joh 1,13–14*, Würzburg 1978.

Horn, Cornelia, 'Syriac and Arabic perspectives on structural and motif parallels regarding Jesus' childhood in Christian apocrypha and early Islamic literature: the "book of Mary", the Arabic apocryphal gospel of John, and the Qur'ān.' In: *Apocrypha* 19 (2008) 267–291.

— 'Ancient Syriac Sources on Mary's Role as Intercessor.' In: Leena M. Peltomaa, Andreas Külzer and Pauline Allen (eds.), *Presbeia Theotokou. The Intercessory Role of Mary across Times and Places in Byzantium (4th–9th Century)*, Vienna 2015, 153–176.

— 'Intersections: The Reception History of the Protoevangelium of James in Sources from the Christian East and in the Qu'ran.' In: *Apocrypha. Revue internationale des littératures apocryphes* 17 (2006) 113–150.

— 'Mary between Bible and Qur'an: Soundings into the Transmission and Reception History of the Protoevangelium of James on the Basis of Selected Literary Sources in Coptic and Copto-Arabic and of Art-Historical Evidence

Pertaining to Egypt.' In: *Islam and Christian–Muslim Relations* 18 (2007) 509–538.
— 'Tracing the reception of the Protoevangelium of James in late antique Arabia. The case of the poetry of Umayya ibn Abī aṣ-Ṣalt and its intersection with the Quran.' In: Kirill Dmitriev and Isabel Toral- Niehoff (eds.), *Religious culture in late antique Arabia. Selected studies on the late antique religious mind*, Piscataway, NJ 2017, 123–146.
Howard-Johnston, James, 'Heraclius' Persian campaigns and the revival of the East Roman Empire, 622–630.' In: *War in History* 6 (1999) 1–44.
— *Witnesses of a World Crisis. Historians and Histories of the Middle East in the Seventh Century*, Oxford 2010.
Hruby, Kurt, *Juden und Judentum bei den Kirchenvätern*, Zurich 1971.
Hurbanič, Martin, *The Avar Siege of Constantinople in 626. History and Legend*, London 2019.
Ibn Ḥazm, Abū Muḥammad ʿAlī ibn Aḥmad, *al-Iḥkām fī uṣūl alaḥkām*, vols. 1–8, ed. by Aḥmad Muḥammad Šākir, Beirut 1983.
Ibrahim, M. Zakyi, 'Ibn Ḥazm's theory of prophecy of women. Literalism, logic, and perfection.' In: *Intellectual Discourse* 23 (2015) 75–100.
Ioan, Ovidiu, *Muslime und Araber bei Iso'jahb III. (649–659)*, Wiesbaden 2009.
al-Iṣfahānī, Ḥusayn ibn Muḥammad, *al-Mufradāt fī ġarīb al-qurʾān*, ed. by Maktabat naẓar Muṣṭafā al-Bāz, (no place or date of publication).
Jacob of Sarug's homilies on the nativity, trans. with introduction by Thomas Kollamparampil, Piscataway, NJ 2010 (Texts from Christian late antiquity; 23).
— *On the mother of God*, trans. by Mary Hanbury, introduction by Sebastian Brock, New York 1998.
— *Select Festal Homilies*, trans. by Thomas Kollamparampil, Rome – Bangalore 1997.
Jakob von Sarug, 'Gedicht über die selige Jungfrau und Gottesmutter Maria.' In: *Ausgewählte Gedichte der syrischen Kirchenväter*, Kempten 1872, 228–246.
— *Die Kirche und die Forschung*, trans. into German from Syrian and annotated by Severin Grill, Heiligenkreuz 1963.
Kaegi, Walter E., *Heraclius. Emperor of Byzantium*, Cambridge 2003.
Kaltner, John, 'The Muslim Mary.' In: Jeremy Corley (ed.), *New Perspectives on the Nativity*, London – New York 2009, 165–179.
— *Ishmael instructs Isaac. An introduction to the Qurʾan for Bible readers*, Collegeville, MN 1999.

Kampling, Rainer, '"... die Jüdin, aus deren Fleische der geboren wurde..." Zu einem antijudaistischen und antimarianischen Modell der patristischen Auslegung.' In: Rainer Kampling and Johannes Heil (eds.), *Maria –Tochter Sion? Mariologie, Marienfrömmigkeit und Judenfeindschaft*, Paderborn and elsewhere 2001, 13–36.

Kästle, Philipp, 'Die Mutter Jesu im Johannesevangelium. Zeugin des irdischen Wirkens und Garantin der sarkischen Existenz Jesu.' In: Weidemann (ed.), *'Der Name der Jungfrau war Maria'*, 301–334.

Kavvadas, Nestor, 'Das ostsyrische Mönchtum im Spannungsfeld der großen Kirchenspaltung der nachchalkedonischen Zeit. Die antiasketischen Maßnahmen.' In: *ThQ* 194 (2014) 94–104.

— 'Severus of Antioch and changing miaphysite attitudes toward Byzantium.' In: John D'Alton and Youhanna Youssef (eds.), *Severus of Antioch. His Life and Times*, Leiden – Boston 2016 (TSEC 7), 124–137.

Khorchide, Mouhanad and von Stosch, Klaus, *Der andere Prophet. Jesus im Koran*, Freiburg 2018.

King, G. R. D., 'The paintings of the Pre-Islamic Kaʿba.' In: Gülru Necipoglu, Doris Behrens-Abouseif and Anna Contadini, *Muqarnas, An annual on the visual culture of the Islamic world*, vol. 21, essays in honor of J. M. Rogers, Leiden – Boston 2004, 219–229.

Klauck, Hans-Josef, *Apokryphe Evangelien. Eine Einführung*, Stuttgart 2002.

Kolia-Dermitzaki, Athina, '"Holy War" in Byzantium twenty years later. A question of term definition and interpretation.' In: Johannes Koder and Ioannis Stouraitis (eds.), *Byzantine war ideology between Roman imperial concept and Christian religion*, Vienna 2012, 121–132.

Konradt, Matthias, *Das Evangelium nach Matthäus*, Göttingen 2015 (NTD 1).

Kozah, Mario et al. (eds.), *The Syriac writers of Qatar in the seventh century*, Piscataway, NJ 2014.

Kremer, Jacob, *Lukasevangelium*, Würzburg 1992 (NEB).

Kremer, Thomas, 'Bildverständnis, Bilderverbot und Bilderverehrung in den syrischen Kirchen.' In: Dietmar W. Winkler (ed.), *Syrische Studien. Beiträge zum 8. Deutschen Syrologie-Symposium in Salzburg 2014*, Vienna 2016, 271–306.

Krüger, Paul, 'Die Frage der Erbsündigkeit der Gottesmutter im Schrifttume des Jakob von Serugh.' In: *Ostkirchliche Studien* 1 (1952) 187–207.

Kuschel, Karl-Josef, *Juden, Christen, Muslime: Herkunft und Zukunft*, Düsseldorf 2007.

Kyrillos von Skythopolis, 'Vita Cyriaci.' In: Eduard Schwartz (ed.), *Kyrillos von Skythopolis*, Leipzig 1939 (Texte und Untersuchungen; 49.2), 222–235.

Laato, Anni, 'Maria, Eve, Rebecca, and Mary as prophetical images of the church.' In: Pekka Lindqvist and Sven Grebenstein (eds.), *'Take another scroll and write'. Studies in interpretive afterlife of prophets and prophecy in Judaism, Christianity and Islam*, Winona Lake, IN 2016 (Studies in the Reception History of the Bible; 6), 233–254.

Labourt, Jérôme, *Le christianisme dans l'empire perse sous la dynastie Sassanide (224–632)*, Paris 1904.

Lane, Edward William, *Arabic-English Lexicon*, 8 vols., Beirut 1968.

Levine, Amy-Jill (ed.), *A Feminist companion to Mariology*, Cleveland, OH 2005 (Feminist companions to the New Testament and early Christian writings; 10).

Lidova, Maria, *The Earliest Images of Maria Regina in Rome and Byzantine Imperial Iconography, in Niš and Byzantium. The Collection of Scientific Works VIII*, Niš 2010, 231–243.

Longhurst, Christopher Evan, 'Maryam bint 'Imran as "Our Lady of Muslims".' In: *Journal of Ecumenical Studies* 52 (2017) 465–469.

Luz, Ulrich, *Das Evangelium nach Matthäus (Mt 1–7)*, Düsseldorf – Zurich – Neukirchen, Vluyn 2002 (EKK; 1).

Lybarger, Loren D., 'Gender and prophetic authority in the Qur'anic story of Maryam. A literary approach.' In: *The Journal of Religion* 80 (2000) 240–270.

Madey, Johannes, *Marienlob aus dem Orient. Aus Stundengebet und Eucharistiefeier der Syrischen Kirche von Antiochien*, Paderborn 1981.

Madigan, Daniel A., *The Qur'ân's self-image. Writing and authority in Islam's scripture*, Princeton – Oxford 2001.

— 'God's word to the world. Jesus and the Qur'ān, incarnation and recitation.' In: Terrence Merrigan and Frederik Glorieux (eds.), *'Godhead here in hiding'. Incarnation and the history of human suffering*, Louvain – Paris – Walpole, MA 2012, 157–172.

Maraval, Pierre, *Lieux saints et pèlerinages d'Orient. Histoire et géographie des origines à la conquête arabe*, Paris 1985.

Marsman, Hennie J., *Women in Ugarit and Israel. Their social and religious position in the context of the Ancient Near East*, Leiden – Boston 2003.

Marx, Michael, 'Glimpses of a Mariology in the Qur'an: From Hagiography to Theology via Religious-Political Debate.' In: Angelika Neuwirth, Nicolai Sinai and Michael Marx (eds.), *The Qur'ān in Context. Historical and literary investigations into the Qur'ānic milieu*, Leiden 2010 (Texts and Studies of the Qur'ān; 6), 533–564.

McGuckin, John, 'The early cult of Mary and interreligous contexts in the fifth-century church.' In: Chris Maunder (ed.), *The origins of the cult of the virgin*, London 2008, 1–22.

Meier, Mischa, 'Liturgisierung und Hypersakralisierung. Zum Bedeutungsverlust kaiserlicher Frömmigkeit in Konstantinopel zwischen dem 6. und 7. Jahrhundert n. Chr.' In: Nora Schmidt, Nora K. Schmid and Angelika Neuwirth (eds.), *Denkraum Spätantike. Reflexionen von Antiken im Umfeld des Koran*, Wiesbaden 2016, 75–106.

— 'Staurotheis di'hemas. Der Aufstand gegen Anastasios im Jahr 512.' In: *Millennium* 4 (2007) 157–237.

Meister Eckhart, *Deutsche Predigten, mit 18 Illustrationen*, ed. and trans. by Louise Gnädinger, Zurich 1999 (Manesse Bibliothek der Weltliteratur 2000).

Menke, Karl-Heinz, *Fleisch geworden aus Maria. Die Geschichte Israels und der Marienglaube der Kirche*, Regensburg 1999.

Menze, Volker L., *Justinian and the making of the Syrian-Orthodox Church*, Oxford 2008.

Michalak, Aleksander R., 'The Angel Gabriel in the Lukan Infancy Narrative'. In: Weidemann (ed.), *'Der Name der Jungfrau war Maria'*, 204–220.

Moltmann, Jürgen, *Der gekreuzigte Gott. Das Kreuz Christi als Grund und Kritik christlicher Theologie*, Munich 1972.

Moosa, Ebrahim, 'Transitions in the "progress" of civilization. Theorizing history, practice, and tradition.' In: Omid Safi (ed.), *Voices of Change*, Westport – London 2007 (Voices of Islam; 5), 115–130.

Moss, Yonatan, *Incorruptible bodies. Christology, society, and authority in late antiquity*, Oakland, CA 2016.

Mourad, Suleiman A., 'From Hellenism to Christianity and Islam. The origin of the palm tree story concerning Mary and Jesus in the Gospel of Pseudo-Matthew and the Qur'an.' In: *OrChr* 66 (2002) 206–216.

— 'Mary in the Qur'ān. A reexamination of her presentation.' In: Gabriel Said Reynolds (ed.), *The Qur'ān in its historical context*, London – New York 2008, 163–174.

Moyaert, Marianne, *In Response to the religious other. Ricœur and the fragility of interreligious encounters*, London 2014.

— 'On vulnerability. Probing the ethical dimension of Comparative Theology.' In: *Religions* 3 (2012) 1144–1161.

Müller, Alois and Sattler, Dorothea, 'Mariologie.' In: Schneider, Theodor (ed.), *Handbuch der Dogmatik; 2: Gnadenlehre, Ekklesiologie, Mariologie, Sakramentenlehre, Eschatologie, Trinitätslehre*, Düsseldorf 1992, 155–187.

Müller, Christoph Gregor, *Mehr als ein Prophet. Die Charakterzeichnung Johannes des Täufers im lukanischen Erzählwerk*, Freiburg – Basel – Vienna 2001 (Herders Biblische Studien; 31).

Müller, Gerhard Ludwig, *Maria – Die Frau im Heilsplan Gottes*, Regensburg 2002.

Münch-Labacher, Gudrun, 'Cyrill von Alexandrien.' In: *Lexikon der antiken christlichen Literatur, Freiburg and elsewhere*, 3rd edn., 2002, 174–178.

Muqātil ibn Sulaymān, *Tafsīr Muqātil ibn Sulaymān*, vols. 1–5, ed. by ʿAbdallāh Maḥmūd Šaḥāta, Beirut 2002.

Murray, Robert, 'Mary, the second Eve in the early Syriac fathers.' In: *Eastern churches review. A journal of Eastern Christendom* 3 (1971) 372–384.

Muslim ibn al-Ḥaǧǧāǧ, *Ṣaḥīḥ Muslim*, vols. 1–7, ed. by Abū Ṭāhir Zubayr ʿAlī Zāʾī, Engl. trans. Nasiruddin al-Khattab, Riyadh 2008.

Mußner, Franz, *Maria, die Mutter Jesu im Neuen Testament. Mit einem Geleitwort von Joseph Kardinal Ratzinger*, St. Ottilien 1993.

an-Nasāʾī, ʿAbd ar-Raḥmān Aḥmad, *ʿIšrat an-nisāʾ*, ed. by ʿAlī ibn Nāyīf aš-Šaḫūd, Bahāniǧ 2009.

Nellas, Panayotis, *Le vivant divinisé. L'anthropologie des pères de l'Église*, Paris 1989.

Neuwirth, Angelika, 'The house of Abraham and the house of Amram. Genealogy, patriarchal authority, and exegetical professionalism.' In: Nicolai Sinai and Michael Marx (eds.), *The Qurʾān in Context. Historical and literary investigations into the Qurʾānic milieu*, Leiden 2010 (Texts and Studies of the Qur'ān; 6), 499–532.

— *Der Koran. Vol. 2/1: Frühmittelmekkanische Suren. Das neue Gottesvolk: 'Biblisierung' des altarabischen Weltbildes. Handkommentar mit Übersetzung*, Berlin 2017.

— 'Eine "religiöse Mutation der Spätantike": Von tribunaler Genealogie zum Gottesbund. Koranische Refigurationen pagan-arabischer Ideale nach biblischen Modellen.' In: Almut-Barbara Renger and Isabel Toral-Niehoff (eds.), *Genealogie und Migrationshymnen im antiken Mittelmeerraum und auf der Arabischen Halbinsel*, Berlin 2014 (Berlin Studies of the Ancient World; 29), 203–232.

Nöldeke, Theodor, *Geschichte des Qorāns, Zweite Auflage, Erster Teil: Über den Ursprung des Qorāns*, Leipzig 1909.

Pahlavi, Patrick Ali, *La fille d'Imran*, Paris 1991.

Papoutsakis, Manolis, *Vicarious Kingship. A theme in Syriac political theology in late antiquity*, Tübingen 2017 (STAC 100).

Peeters, Paul, 'La légende de saint Jacques de Nisibe.' In: *Analecta Bollandiana* 38 (1920) 285–373.

Pevarello, Daniele, *The sentences of Sextus and the origins of Christian asceticism*, Tübingen 2013 (Studien und Texte zu Antike und Christentum; 78).

Philoxenus of Mabbug, *Tractatus tres de trinitate et incarnatione*, ed. A. Vaschalde (CSCO Syr. 9), Louvain 1907.

Procopius of Caesarea, *De bellis*, 2 vols., ed. by Jakob Haury and Gerhard Wirth, Leipzig 1962–3.

Pröpper, Thomas, *Theologische Anthropologie: 2 Teilbände*, Freiburg – Basel – Vienna 2011.

'Das Protevangelium des Jakobus.' In: *Apokryphen zum Alten und Neuen Testament*, ed. by Alfred Schindler, Zürich 41990, 411–436.

Puthuparampil, James, *Mariological thought of Mar Jacob of Serugh (451–521)*, Baker Hill, AL – Kottayam 2005.

al-Qurṭubī, Abū ʿAbdallāh Muḥammad ibn Aḥmad, *al-Ǧāmiʿ li-aḥkām al-qurʾān wa-l-mubayyin li-mā taḍammana min as-sunna wa-āyāt al-furqān*, vols. 1–24, ed. by ʿAbdallāh ibn ʿAbd al-Muḥsin at-Turkī, Beirut 2006.

Rahner, Karl, *Maria, Mutter des Herrn. Mariologische Studien*, ed. by Regina Pacis Meyer (= Sämtliche Werke; 9), Freiburg – Basel – Vienna 2004.

Ratzinger, Joseph and von Balthasar, Hans Urs, *Maria. Kirche im Ursprung*, Freiburg, 4th edn., 1997.

ar-Rāzī, Muḥammad ibn Abī Bakr ibn ʿAbd al-Qādir, *Muḫtār aṣ-ṣiḥāḥ*, Beirut 1986.

ar-Rāzī, Muḥammad ibn ʿUmar Faḫr ad-Dīn, *at-Tafsīr al-kabīr: Mafātīḥ al-ġayb*, vols. 1–32, Beirut 1981.

Reck, Jonathan M., 'The Annunciation to Mary. A Christian Echo in the Qurʾān.' In: *Vigiliae Christianae* (2014) 355–383.

Regan, Geoffrey, *First crusader. Byzantium's Holy Wars*, Basingstoke 2003.

Reiprich, Torsten, *Das Mariageheimnis. Maria von Nazareth und die Bedeutung familiärer Beziehungen im Markusevangelium*, Göttingen 2008 (Forschungen zur Religion und Literatur des Alten und Neuen Testaments; Vol. 223).

Reynolds, Gabriel Said, *The Qurʾān and its Biblical subtext*, London – New York 2010.

Rezazadeh, Morteza, 'Mary in Early Christianity and Islam.' In: *Religious Inquiries* 6 (2017) 37–49.

Riesenhuber, Klaus, *Maria im theologischen Verständnis von Karl Barth und Karl Rahner*, Freiburg – Basel – Vienna 1973 (QD 60).

Riße, Günter, 'Maria, die Gottesfürchtige: das Marienbild im Koran.' In: *Pastoralblatt für die Diözesen Aachen, Berlin, Essen, Hildesheim, Köln, Osnabrück* 49 (1997) 131–138.

Robin, Christian Julien, 'Ḥimyar, Aksūm, and *Arabia Deserta* in Late Antiquity. The Epigraphic Evidence.' In: Greg Fisher (ed.), *Arabs and Empires before Islam*, Oxford 2015, 127–171.

Robinson, Neal, 'Jesus and Mary in the Qur'an: Some neglected affinities.' In: *Religion* 20 (2016) 161–175.

Rosenberg, Michael, *Signs of virginity. Testing virgins and making men in late antiquity*, New York 2018.

ar-Rūmī, Ǧalāl ad-Dīn Mawlānā, *Table Talk of Maulana Rumi [fīha mā fīha]*, trans. by Bankey Behari, New Delhi 1998.

Saint-Laurent, Jeanne-Nicole Mellon, *Missionary stories and the formation of the Syriac churches*, Oakland, CA 2015.

aš-Šāṭibī, Abū Isḥāq, *al-Muwāfaqāt fī uṣūl aš-šarīʿa*, vols. 1–4, ed. by Ibrāhīm Ramaḍān, Beirut 1994.

Schäfer, Peter, *Weibliche Gottesbilder im Judentum und Christentum*, Frankfurt am Main – Leipzig 2008.

— *Jesus in the Talmud*, Princeton 2007.

Schilling, Alexander, *Die Anbetung der Magier und die Taufe der Sassaniden*, Louvain 2008 (CSCO Subs; 120).

Schleifer, Aliah, *Mary the blessed virgin of Islam*, Cambridge 1998.

Schmaus, Michael, *Mariologie*, München 1961 (Katholische Dogmatik; 5).

Schnackenburg, Rudolf, *Das Johannesevangelium 1. Teil: Einleitung und Kommentar zu Kapiteln 1–4*, Freiburg im Breisgau 1965.

Schreiber, Stefan, *Weihnachtspolitik. Lukas 1–2 und das Goldene Zeitalter*, Göttingen 2009 (Novum Testamentum et Orbis Antiquus/Studien zur Umwelt des Neuen Testaments; Vol. 82).

Schweizer, Eduard, *Das Evangelium nach Markus*, Göttingen 1998 (NTD 1).

Seker, Nimet, 'Raḥma und raḥim. Zur weiblichen Assoziation der Barmherzigkeit Allahs.' In: Mouhanad Khorchide and Klaus von Stosch (eds.), *Theologie der Barmherzigkeit? Zeitgemäße Fragen und Antworten des Kalam*, Münster 2014, 117–131.

Seppälä, Serafim, 'Reminiscences of icons in the Qur'an?' In: *Islam and Christian–Muslim Relations* 22 (2011) 3–21.

— 'Is the Virgin Mary a prophetess? Patristic, Syriac and Islamic views.' In: *Parole de l'Orient* 36 (2011) 367–379.

Shoemaker, Sidney, *Mary in Early Christian Faith and Devotion*, New Haven, CT 2016.

Sinai, Nicolai, 'The Unknown Known.' In: *Mélanges de l'Université Saint-Joseph* 66 (2015–2016) 47–96.

Smith, Jane I. and Haddad, Yvonne Y., 'The Virgin Mary in Islamic tradition and commentary.' In: *Muslim World* 79 (1989) 161–187.

Söll, Georg, *Mariologie* = Michael Schmaus et al. (eds.), *Handbuch der Dogmengeschichte. Vol. 3: Christologie, Soteriologie, Ekklesiologie, Mariologie, Gnadenlehre; Fasz.4*, Freiburg – Basel – Vienna 1978.

Starr, Joshua, 'St. Maximos and the forced baptism at Carthage in 632.' In: *Byzantinisch-neugriechische Jahrbücher* 16 (1940) 192–196.

Stepanova, Elena, 'Victoria-Nike on Early Byzantine Seals.' In: Jean-Claude Cheynet and Claudia Sode (eds.), *Studies in Byzantine Sigillography*, vol. 10, Berlin – New York 2010, 15–23.

Stosch, Klaus von, 'Eine urchristliche Engelchristologie im Koran?' In: Georges Tamer (ed.), *Die Koranhermeneutik von Günter Lüling*, Berlin – Boston 2019 (Judaism, Christianity, and Islam – Tension, Transmission, Transformation; 9), 69–91.

— *Theodizee*, Paderborn 2018 (Grundwissen Theologie).

Stowasser, Barbara Freyer, *Women in the Qur'an, traditions, and interpretations*, New York – Oxford 1994.

Stump, Eleonore, *Wandering in darkness. Narrative and the problem of suffering*, Oxford and elsewhere 2010.

as-Suyūṭī, Ǧalāl ad-Dīn, *Durr al-manṯūr fī tafsīr al-ma'ṯūr*, vols. 1–6, Beirut 2015.

aṭ-Ṭabarī, Abū Ǧa'far Muḥammad b. Ǧarīr, *Tafsir aṭ-Ṭabarī: Ǧāmi' albayān 'an ta'wīl āy al-qur'ān*, vols. 1–25, ed. by 'Abdallāh ibn 'Abd al-Muḥsin at-Turkī, Cairo 2001.

— *Ta'rīḫ ar-rusul wa-l-mulūk*, vols. 1–11, ed. by Muḥammad Abū l-Faḍl Ibrāhīm, Cairo 1968.

aṭ-Ṭabarī, Muḥibb ad-Dīn, *Riyāḍ naḍrat fī manāqib al-'ašra*s, vols. 1–2, Beirut (no publication date).

Ṭabāṭabā'ī, Muḥammad Ḥusayn, *al-Mīzān fī tafsīr al-qur'ān*, vols. 1–20, Beirut 1973.

Taft, Robert, *The Liturgy of the Hours in East and West. The Origins of the Divine Office and its Meaning for Today*, Collegeville, MN, 2nd edn., 1993.

Takács, Axel, 'Mary and Muhammad: bearers of the word – their roles in divine revelation.' In: *Journal of ecumenical studies* 48 (2013) 220–243.

Tanner Rhodes, Jerusha, *Divine words, female voices. Muslima explorations in comparative feminist theology*, Oxford 2018.

Tatari, Muna, *Gott und Mensch im Spannungsverhältnis von Gerechtigkeit und Barmherzigkeit. Versuch einer islamisch begründeten Positionsbestimmung*, Münster 2016 (Graduiertenkolleg Islamische Theologie; 4); (doctoral dissertation, University of Paderborn, 2013).

— 'Eine muslimische Perspektive auf das Handeln Gottes. Eine Replik zu Reinhold Bernhardt.' In: Muna Tatari and Klaus von Stosch (eds.), *Handeln Gottes – Antwort des Menschen*, Paderborn 2014 (Beiträge zur Komparativen Theologie; 11), 35–53.

— 'Ein Plädoyer für die Klage vor Gott.' In: Michael Hofmann and Klaus von Stosch (eds.), *Islam in der deutschen und türkischen Literatur*, Paderborn and elsewhere 2012 (Beiträge zur Komparativen Theologie; 4), 279–285.

— 'Vulnerabilität – ein vernachlässigter Aspekt muslimischer Theologie und Anthropologie.' In: *Religionen unterwegs* 25 (2019) 19–24.

aṯ-Ṯawrī, Sufyān Abū ʿAbdullah ibn Saʿīd, *Tafsīr aṯ-Ṯawrī*, ed. by ʿAlī ʿArš, Beirut 1983.

Tesei, Tommaso, 'Heraclius' war propaganda and the Qurʾān's promise of reward for dying in battle.' In: *Studia Islamica* 114 (2019) 219–247.

Theobald, Michael, *Das Evangelium nach Johannes. Kapitel 1–12*, Regensburg 2009 (RNT).

— '"Siehe, die Jungfrau wird empfangen" (Jes 7,14). Die "Geburtsankündigungen" Mt 1,18–25/Lk 1,26–38 im Licht ihrer schrifthermeneutischen, religionsgeschichtlichen und anthropologischen Voraussetzungen.' In: Weidemann (ed.), *'Der Name der Jungfrau war Maria'*, 20–106.

Thunberg, Lars, *Microcosm and mediator. The theological anthropology of Maximus the Confessor*, Lund 1965.

at-Tirmiḏī, Abū ʿĪsā Muḥammad ibn ʿĪsā, *Ǧāmiʿ at-Tirmiḏī*, vols. 1–6, ed. by Abū Ṭāhir Zubayr ʿAlī Zāʾī, Engl. trans. Abū Khaliyl, Riyadh 2007.

Toepel, Alexander, *Das Protevangelium des Jakobus. Ein Beitrag zur neueren Diskussion um Herkunft, Auslegung und theologische Einordnung*, Münster 2014.

Uthemann, Karl-Heinz, 'Kaiser Justinian als Kirchenpolitiker und Theologe.' In: *Augustinianum* 33 (1999) 5–83.

Vahrenhorst, Martin, *'Ihr sollt überhaupt nicht schwören'. Matthäus im halachischen Diskurs*, Neukirchen-Vluyn 2002 (WMANT 95).

Viezure, Dana, 'Philoxenus of Mabbug and the controversies over the "Theopaschite Trisagion".' In: *Studia Patristica* 47 (2010) 137–146.

Viguera, María J., 'Aṣluḥu li ʾl-Maʿālī. On the Social Status of Andalusī Women.' In: Salma Khadra Jayyusi (ed.), *The legacy of Muslim Spain*, Leiden 1992, 710–724.

al-Wāḥidī, Abū Ḥasan ʿAlī ibn Aḥmad, *Asbāb nuzūl al-qurʾān*, ed. by Māhir Yāsīn al-Fahd, Riyadh 2003.

Weedman, Michelle, *Mary's fertility as the model of the ascetical life in Ephrem the Syrian's Hymns of the Nativity* (Diss.), Milwaukee, WI 2014.

Weidemann, Hans-Ulrich, '"Embedding the Virgin". Die Jungfrau Maria und die anderen jüdischen asketischen Erzählfiguren im lukanischen Doppelwerk.' In: Weidemann (ed.), *'Der Name der Jungfrau war Maria'*, 107–171.

— (ed.), *'Der Name der Jungfrau war Maria' (Lk 1,27). Neue exegetische Perspektiven auf die Mutter Jesu*, Stuttgart 2018 (Stuttgarter Bibelstudien; 238).

Wenger, Antoine, 'L'intercession de Marie en Orient du sixième au dixième siècle.' In: *Etudes Mariales* 23 (1966) 51–75.

— 'Les interventions de Marie dans l'église orthodoxe et l'histoire de Byzance.' In: Ponteficia Academia Mariana Internationalis (ed.), *De primordiis cultus Mariani*, Rome 1970, 423–431.

Wessel, Susan, *Cyril of Alexandria and the Nestorian controversy. The making of a saint and a heretic*, Oxford 2004.

Wielandt, Rotraud, 'Exegesis of the Qurʾān: Early, Modern and Contemporary.' In: Jane Dammen McAuliffe (ed.), *Encyclopaedia of the Qurʾān*, vol. 2, Leiden 2002, 124–141.

Wikenhauser, Alfred, *Das Evangelium nach Johannes*, Regensburg 1957 (Regensburger Neues Testament; 4).

Wilde, Clare, 'Jesus and Mary. Qurʾānic echoes of Syriac homilies.' In: Florian Wilk (ed.), *Scriptural interpretation at the interface between education and religion. In memory of Hans Conzelmann*, Leiden – Boston 2019, 284–302.

Wolter, Michael, *Das Lukasevangelium*, Tübingen 2008 (HNT 5).

— *Theologie und Ethos im frühen Christentum. Studien zu Jesus, Paulus und Lukas*, Tübingen 2009 (Wissenschaftliche Untersuchungen zum Neuen Testament; 236).

Wood, Philip, 'Christianity and the Arabs in the sixth century.' In: Jitse H. F. Dijkstra et al. (eds.), *Inside and out. Interactions between Rome and the peoples on the Arabian and Egyptian frontiers in Late Antiquity*, Louvain 2014, 355–370.

Woyke, Johannes, '"Mit Jesus ist es vor Gott wie mit Adam" (Sure 3,59). Die koranische und die lukanische Jesusdarstellung im Diskurs. Zugleich Überlegungen zum Stellenwert neutestamentlicher Exegese für systematisch-theologische Neuansätze der Christologie.' In: Marco Hofheinz and Kai-Ole Eberhardt (eds., with the assistance of Jan-Philip Tegtmeier), *Gegenwartsbezogene Christologie. Denkformen und Brennpunkte neuer Herausforderungen*, Tübingen 2020.

Yaşar, Hüseyin, 'Maria und die Geburt Jesu im mystischen Korankommentar.' In: *Journal of Religious Culture* 63 (2003) 1–11.

Yitik, Ali İhsan, 'Die Jungfrau Maria und ihr Haus bei Ephesus. Eine religionsvergleichende mariologische Untersuchung.' In: *Journal for Religious Culture* 56 (2002) 1–12.

az-Zamaḫšarī, Maḥmūd ibn ʿUmar, *Tafsīr al-kaššāf ʿan ḥaqāʾiq at-tanzīl wa-ʿuyūn al-aqāwīl fī wuǧūh at-taʾwīl*, ed. by Ḫalīl Maʾmūn Šīḥā, Beirut 2009.

Index

A

Aaron 143, 144–7, 161
  and prophet 151, 154, 231–2, 233
Abboud, Hosn 225, 237, 253, 259, 260
ʿabd (servant) 107–8
Abel 310
Abraha, King 85–7, 89
Abraham 11, 12, 25–6, 161–3
  and prophet 151, 152, 231–2
abstinence *see* celibacy; virginity
Abyssinia *see* Ethiopia
Ackermann, Andrea 17
Acts of Peter 38
Adam 12, 42, 214, 231–2, 309–10
  and genealogy 162, 163
adoration 92
aestheticism 265–72
Aisha 181
Aksūm 85–6
Alexander of Alexandria 74
Ali, Kecia 236–7, 253, 259–60
Allāh (the Lord) 109
allegory 122–5, 126
Althaus-Reid, Marcella 258
ambiguity 160
Ambrose 45–6
Amran 161–2, 163
an-Nisāʾ Surah 192–3
Anastasius, Emperor 207, 208
Āl Anbiyāʾ Surah 151, 153
Ancient Greece 56, 57, 58, 136
al-Andalus 229–31
angels 16, 34, 128, 172–3
  and prophetology 231–2, 235–6
  see also Gabriel, Angel
Anne, St 38–9, 40, 165, 166–7
Annunciation 15–23, 127–32, 176–92
Anointed, the (*msḥ-hw*) 86
Anti-Chalcedonians 89
anti-imperialism 287
anti-Jewish polemics 111
Antichrist 102
Antioch 83
Aphrahat 152
apocalypticism 100–3
Apollo 136
appropriation 283, 289–91, 305–6
Arabian Peninsula 84–90, 96–7
archetype 184–5, 233
Aristotle 56, 57, 58
Ark of the Covenant 47
Armilus 102
asceticism 40, 55, 309
Ashkar, Dominic 152
Āsiya 199

Assumption 6, 41
at-Taḥrīm ('The Prohibition') Surah 194–9
Augustine of Hippo 46, 54, 63, 152
Augustus, Emperor 23–4
Auschwitz 243
autonomy 265–6, 267, 290–1
Avars 83, 84, 93, 97, 98

B

Barth, Karl 62
Basil the Great 152
Bathsheba 13
beauty 48, 298–9
Beinert, Wolfgang 59
Benedictus 23, 112, 118
Benko, Stephen 75
Bible, the 44, 53–4, 286
  and *Maryam* Surah 108, 110–11, 113, 130
  see also John, Gospel of; Luke, Gospel of; Mark, Gospel of; Matthew, Gospel of
birth pains *see* labour pains
Blachernai 96, 98
Boaz 13
Bobzin, Hartmut 197
Book of Mary's Repose 137
boundary breaking 258–61, 287–9
Bovon, François 19
Buisson, Johanna 256–7, 262
Bulgars 83, 93
Byzantine Empire 82–4, 85, 87, 88–9
  and Constantinople 93
  and Heraclius 91–2
  and *al-Mā'ida* ('The Table') Surah 202–5
  and Mary 94–9
  and Qur'an 194

C

Cain 310
Cameron, A. M. 99
Cana, Wedding at 29–31, 148, 210–11
Catholicism 13–14, 80, 273–4
  and Ephesus 276
  and Eve 42
  and Mary 71–3, 286–8
  and miracles 241
  and Protestantism 280
  and virginity 58, 59, 65–6
  and women 293–4
  see also Second Vatican Council
cave births 40
celibacy 52, 55, 63–5, 182–3
Chalcedon, Council of 205, 207
Chalkoprateia 96
Chosroes II, Shah 83, 84, 87, 92, 99
Christ *see* Jesus Christ
Christianity 85–8, 89–90
  and comparative theology 285–97
  and dialogue 273–81
  and Heraclius 90–3
  and *Āl 'Imrān* Surah 161–5
  and *Maryam* Surah 112–13, 118–19
  and patriarchy 254–5
  and women 167–8
  see also Bible, the; Catholicism; Church, the; Mariology; patristics; Syriac Church Fathers
Christmas 23–5
Chronicon paschale 97
Church, the 45–7, 76–7, 78–9, 207–8; *see also* Temple, the
Church Fathers *see* Syriac Church Fathers

Codex Veronensis 27
comparative theology 283
and Christian 285–97
and Islamic 298–311
compassion 119–20, 131–2, 224, 285–6
Constantine the Great, Emperor 92
Constantinople 83, 84, 93, 95–6, 97–9, 204
and Second Council of 63
Coptic Christianity 277, 280
Cornille, Catherine 283
corporeality 224–5
Corpus Paulinum 7–11
Cross, the 32–3, 206–9, 296
Crucifixion 32–3, 206–9
curtain 124–5, 126, 127
Cyril of Alexandria 94, 209

D

David 11, 12, 13, 144–7, 164
and prophet 151, 231–2
Dea Syria 75
desert 33, 39, 133–3, 228, 267, 269; *see also* palm tree
Devil, the 102, 117, 169–70, 274
devotion 285–6
Dhu al-Kifl 151
Dido 75
Diodorus of Tarsus 213
disruption 268–72
divine favours (*laṭāʾif*) 178
divine revelation (*waḥy*) 117
divine scripture (*kitāb*) 112–13
dogmas 74–81, 287–8; *see also* original sin; perpetual virginity
Dormito Mariae 41
Duns Scotus, John 70

E

ear, the 52, 196, 309
East Syriac Christians 87–8
East, the 122–3
Eastern Church 38, 41, 47, 70, 156, 207
eating 210–17
ecclesiology 77, 78
Eckhart, Meister 76
Eco, Umberto: *The Open Work* 304
Egypt 83, 277, 280
Elijah 133, 231–2
Elizabeth 15, 20, 21, 23, 35
and *Maryam* Surah 110–11, 113, 119, 133
emancipation 198–9, 255, 262–3
Emmerick, Anna Katharina 275
Ephesus 275–6
and Council of 6, 41, 74
Ephrem the Syrian 42, 43, 48
and David 145
and eating 213
and Gabriel 128
Hymn on the Nativity of Christ in the Flesh 46–7
and intercessor 94
and Jesus 150
and labour pains 134
and loincloth 214
and Mother of Weakness 93
and prophetology 152
and sin 69–70
and veil 124
and virginity 67
and the Word 191
Epiphanius, Bishop of Salamis 33
Ethiopia 85–6, 300
Evagrius Scholasticus 215

Eve 42–5, 50, 73, 309–10
  and fig-leaf 124
  and loincloth 214
  and the Qur'an 196

F

Fall of Man *see* Adam; Eve
fasting 139–40, 277
Fatima 181, 182
Feast of Mary's Assumption 277
Feast of the Dormition of Mary 41
femininity 109, 288
fiat ('let it be') 21, 25, 35
  and actions 197–8
  and affirmation 72–3
  and Eve 43, 44
  and Islam 302–3
Fierro, Maribel 230, 231
Flavius Josephus 55
food 247–9, 294; *see also* eating
Francis, Pope 280–1, 293
freedom 71–2, 79–80, 285–6
fundamentalism 277

G

Gabriel, Angel 15, 16, 17, 18–20, 34–5
  and childbirth 138–9
  and *Āl 'Imrān* Surah 173–4
  and *Maryam* Surah 127–31
  and Muhammad 252
  and prophetology 231–2
  see also Annunciation
Galatians 7
Galen of Pergamon 57
Al-Ġazālī
  Ǧawāhir al-qur'ān ('Jewels of the Qur'an') 231–2
gender equality 224, 254–7, 258–63
genealogy 144–7, 161–5, 254–5
Georgios Pisides: *Bellum avaricum* 97
Ghaffar, Zishan 102, 103, 123, 144, 183
Ghassanids 88–90
Gilson, Erinn 227–8
God
  and Annunciation 177–80
  and compassion 285–6
  and friendship 291
  and Gabriel 127–8, 130–1
  and grace 305–6
  and Hannah 254–5
  and love 70–2
  and Mary 74–5, 77–9, 165–7, 168–72, 249–51
  and *Maryam* Surah 107–9, 110–11, 113–14, 115–16
  the Merciful (*Raḥmānān*) 86
  and mercy 155
  and miracles 243–7
  and Muhammad 251–2
  and power 202–4
  and prophetology 224, 230, 231–2
  and renunciation 271–2
  and suffering 206–9
  and veil 125, 126, 127
  and virginity 60–1
  and the Word 187–8, 191
  see also Mother of God; Word, the
God-fearing 55, 127, 128, 129
goddesses 75
Golden Mean 310–11
grace 71–2, 79–80, 305–6
Gregory of Nyssa 42, 54, 63, 214
Greshake, Gisbert 42, 46, 59–60

Griffith, Sidney 208–9
guardianship 185

H

hadith 169–70, 222, 274
Hainthaler, Theresia 88
Hannah 21, 254–5
Ḥāriṯ, King 89
Heo, Angie 277
Hephzibah 101–2
Heraclius, Emperor 82, 83–4, 90–3, 100
  and Ghassanids 88, 89
  and icons 148
  and Jews 102
  and Mary 97, 99, 219–20, 307
Herodotus 136
Ḫiḍr 231–2
hijab 126
hijra 134–5
Ḥimyar 84, 85–6
Holy Spirit 8, 20, 55, 56–7, 86
Holy Trinity 208–9
Holy War 90–2, 94–5
Horn, Cornelia 136
Howard-Johnston, James 88–9
hunger 294
hylemorphism 56, 58
hymen 65–6
Hymnus Akathistos 99

I

Ibn ʿAbbās 278
Ibn ʿArabī, Muḥy ad-Dīn 230, 304
Ibn Ḥazm 229–30, 236
Ibn Sīnā (Avicenna) 240
iconography 95–6, 147–8, 156, 219–20, 278–9
Idris 151, 231–2
Ildefonso of Toledo 66
Ilyās *see* Elijah
Immaculate Conception 6, 70, 273–4
imperialism 94–7, 102, 203, 204–10, 287
Āl ʿImrān Surah 159–60, 200, 280
  and beauty 298
  and genealogy 161–5
  and Mary's childhood 165–76
  and women 237, 259
Incarnation *see* virginity
Infancy Gospel of Thomas 41
intensification 283, 285–6, 298–9
intercessor 94–5
Iran *see* Persian Empire
Iraq 277
Irenaeus 27, 42, 77
Isaac 151
Isaiah 16
Ishmael 151, 233
Isis 75
Islam 265, 267–8
  and Catholicism 273–4
  and comparative theology 298–311
  and pilgrimage 275–8
  and suffering 269–70
  see also Muhammad, Prophet; Qur'an
Israel 111, 112, 114; *see also* Jerusalem
Israelites 7, 244

J

Jacob 151
Jacob of Serugh 42, 43, 44–5, 47–9
  and Annunciation 183–4
  and intercessor 94

and labour pains 134
and prophetology 152
and sin 69–70
and veil 124
and virginity 50–2, 66
Jafnids 88, 89
Jeconiah 11
Jeddah 309
Jerome 42, 152
Jerusalem 83, 84, 100–1, 277–8; *see also* Temple, the
Jesus Christ 6
and Adam 42
and Annunciation 15–16, 18–19
and birth 23–5, 50–1, 138–42
and conception 13–14, 48–9, 57–61, 196
and Crucifixion 32–3
and divine scripture 112–13
and eating 210–14, 215–16
and family 7–12
and genealogy 163–4
and God 202–4
and Mary 29–31, 36, 73, 147–9, 150, 287, 303–4
and *Maryam* Surah 114–15, 120–1
and miracles 218–19
and Mother of God 74–5
and name 188–90
and nature 207
and prophetology 231–2
and the serpent 44
and siblings 54
and signs 131–2, 153, 154, 155–6
and virgin birth 28–9
and the Word 187–90, 299–301
see also Messiah
Jews *see* Judaism
Joachim, St 38, 40, 165, 166
Job 152
John Chrysotom 213
John, Gospel of 6, 26–34, 57
John the Baptist 15, 23, 175
and *Maryam* Surah 111, 114–15, 119–21
Jonah 231–2
Joseph 11–12, 13, 14, 16–17, 24
and *Āl 'Imrān* Surah 185–6
and procreation 57, 58
and Protevangelium of James 39, 40
and Qur'an absence 148
and virginity 143
Joseph of Ḥimyar, King 85
Joshua 90
Josiah 11
Judah 146
Judaism 7, 8, 12–13, 14
and apocalypticism 100–3
and Arabians 84–5, 87
and asceticism 55
and Christianity 289–90
and Heraclius 90
and *Āl 'Imrān* Surah 161–5, 192–3
and Luke 15
and *Maryam* Surah 112–13, 118–19
and patriarchy 254–5, 262
and virginity 66
judgement 306–8
Judges 16
Julian of Halicarnassus 211–16
Justin II, Emperor 95
Justin Martyr 42, 164
Justinian, Emperor 94–5, 215
and Scythian monks 206, 207, 208, 209–10

K

kalima (word) 187, 197
Kaltner, John 257
Kampling, Rainer 8
karāma (symbolic acts) 239–40, 242, 246, 247–8
Kuschel, Karl Josef 133, 136, 162

L

labour pains 50–1, 52, 67–8, 133–4, 256–7
Lakhmids 88
Lane, Edward 304
language 225
Last Supper 218
Lateran Synod 65
Lebanon 277
Leontius of Byzantium 213, 215–16
Leto 136
Levi 146
Logos 187
loincloth 214
Longhurst, Christopher Evan 279
Lot 151, 231–2
love 70–2
lowliness 23, 24–5, 35–6, 293, 296
Luke, Gospel of 6, 9, 15–26, 295–6
  and virginity 54–6, 57, 63
Lumen gentium 76–7

M

Macedonia 277
Magi 14
Magnificat 21–3, 133, 287, 298–9
al-Mā'ida ('The Table') Surah 202–20
Al-Manṣūr ibn Abī 'Āmir 230
Mariology 5, 6, 7, 44
  and Catholicism 286–8, 292–3
  and iconography 219–20
  and imperialism 205–10
  and Judaism 102–3
  and *al-Mā'ida* ('The Table') Surah 202–5
  and perpetual virginity 53–69
  and pilgrimage 275–8
  and Protevangelium of James 40, 41–2
  and rehabilitation 291–5
  and Second Vatican Council 76–7
  and war 93–100
Mark, Gospel of 7–11
marriage 182, 185–6, 194–5
martyrdom 91
Marx, Michael 162
Maryam Surah 31–2, 121–3, 158, 199–200
  and Annunciation 127–32
  and genealogy 146–7
  and Mary as prophet 150–1, 152–7
  and Mary's conflicts 142–5
  and Mary's pregnancy 132–42
  and mother–son relationship 147–9
  and Muhammad 300–1
  and prophetology 224–5
  and veil 125–7
  and women 262
  and Zechariah 107–21
masğid (place of kneeling down) 117–18
Matthew, Gospel of 6, 9, 11–14, 16, 163
  and virginity 54, 56, 57
Maurice, Emperor 83, 95
Maximus the Confessor 213, 214

Mecca 83, 84, 85, 86–7
and Kaaba 126, 278–9
Medina 83, 85, 86, 89, 159
and Qur'an 192–9
and women 259, 263–4
men (*rağul*) 235–6
Menahem 101
Menke, Karl-Heinz 60–1, 68, 72–3, 292
mercy (*raḥma*) 107–9, 155
Messiah *see* Jesus Christ
Metz, Johann Baptist 269, 289
miaphysitism 49–50, 51–2, 89–90, 207–8
Michael, Angel 231–2
middle way 310–11
miḥrāb (place of dispute) 117–18, 170
miracles 96, 136–8, 139, 218–19, 247–51
and perception 239–47
Miriam 103, 161, 163, 233
Moltmann, Jürgen 209
monasticism 51–2
monotheism 85
Moses 1, 55, 103, 151, 154
and genealogy 161, 162, 163
and prophetology 231–2, 233
and Red Sea parting 244
Mother of God 6, 74–7, 96, 296–7; see also *Theotokos*
Mourad, Suleiman A. 135–6
Moyaert, Marianne 226–7, 228
mu'ğiza (miracle) 240, 242, 245, 246, 248
Muhammad, Prophet:
and Byzantium 88, 89
and companions 10
and compassion 131
and *Āl 'Imrān* Surah 159
and Mary 251–3, 299–301
and Mecca 83, 84, 278–9
and passivity 257, 258
and prophetology 231–2, 233, 234
and veil 126
and vulnerability 228
and wives 194, 263–4
Muslims *see* Islam
mysticism 269–70

N
Nağrān 136, 205
Negus 85
Nestorius 74
Neuwirth, Angelika 119, 120, 123, 124, 147, 161
and *Āl 'Imrān* Surah 159, 160
new Eve *see* Eve
Nicaea, Council of 58
Nineveh 84, 101
Noah 12, 151, 154, 162, 163, 231–2
numbers 116–17

O
Oecumenicus 33
Old Testament 17
ordination 167–8, 293–4
Origen 64–5, 152, 214
original sin 50, 69–73

P
paganism 58, 75
Pahlavi, Patrick Ali 280
Pakistan 277
Palestine 100
palm tree 135–8, 252–3

passivity 257–8
patriarchy 254–5, 262, 268–9
patristics 6
and the Church 45–7
and Eve 42–5
and Protevangelium of James 37–42
and purity 47–9
and virginity 49–52
Paul, St 7–11
peace 120, 149
Pentecost 26
perfection 80
perpetual virginity 6, 51, 53–69, 182–3, 308–9
Persian Empire 82–4, 85, 87–8, 90
and Constantinople 93
and Jews 100
Peter the Fuller 207–8
Pharaoh 154, 181, 195, 199
Philo of Alexandria 55
Philoxenus of Mabbug 49–50, 207, 208, 209
Phocas, Emperor 83, 99
Pietà 32–3
pilgrimage 275–8
Pillars of Islam 267–8
politics 22, 82–90, 202–5, 298–9
poverty 22–5, 35
power 202–4
prayer 110–12, 113, 115, 117–19
and Annunciation 183–5
and supplication 166–7
Presentation of Mary in the Temple 38–9
procreation 56–7, 61
projection 279–80
Promasius, Bishop 33
propaganda 90–3, 95, 96–7, 99, 203
and Judaism 100, 101, 103
Prophet *see* Muhammad, Prophet
prophetology 223–38
and Christian perspective 286–7
and genealogy 255
and Mary 150–4, 157
and miracles 240
see also Muhammad, Prophet
Pröpper, Thomas 291
proskynesis 92–3, 266
prostration 183–4, 266
Protestantism 13–14, 277, 280
Protevangelium of James 37–42, 66
and Annunciation 130
and *Āl ʿImrān* Surah 165, 185–6
and Mary's pregnancy 133
and Temple veil 123
Pseudo-Matthew, Gospel of 136–7
purity 47–9, 65, 152–3, 179–80

Q

al-Qabrī, Abū Bakr Muḥammad ibn Mawhab at Tuǧībī 230
queerness 258–60, 288–9
Qur'an 5–6
and *al-Fil* ('The Elephant') Surah 86
and gender equality 254–7, 258–63
and Heraclius 91, 92–3
and Judaism 102–3
and Luke 15
and Mariology 41
and Mary 105–6, 285–6
and Medinan period 192–9
and miracles 239–42, 247–51
and prophetology 223–38
and renunciation 270–2

and signs 250
and subversion 268–9
and suffering 245
and virginity 265–6
see also *Āl ʿImrān* Surah; *al-Māʾida* ('The Table') Surah; *Maryam* Surah
Quresh tribe 86
al-Qurṭubī, Abū ʿAbdallāh Muḥammad ibn Aḥmad 141–2, 156
and Annunciation 188
and Christianity 307
and miracles 240–1
and prophetology 157, 230, 232
and purity 179
and women 180–1

R

rabb (the Lord) 108
radicalism 309–11
Rahab 13
Rahner, Karl 59, 60, 62, 67–8
and freedom 79–80
and Mother of God 75
and redemption 78–9
Ratzinger, Joseph 25, 151
al-Rāzi, Fakhr al-Din 128, 129, 135
and Annunciation 177–9, 183
and Christianity 307
and gender 168
and miracles 218, 240
and prophetology 157, 232
and the Temple 170, 171
and virtue 210
reaffirmation 283, 295–7, 308–11
recovery 283, 286–7, 299–301
rectification 283, 291–5, 306–8
redemption 70, 77–9
Reformation 44
reinterpretation 283, 287–9, 301–5
relics 96
remembrance 108
renunciation 270–2
Resurrection 213
Revelation, Book of 33
rhyme 109–10, 149
Ricœur, Paul 226, 227
role model 265–72
Roman Empire 102
Rosenberg, Michael 65–6
Rūmi 269–70
Ruth 13

S

salvation 77–9
Samuel 21
Sanaa 86, 88
Sassanids 82, 87, 90
Satan 169–70
Saudi Arabia 277
Schimmel, Annemarie 251
Schmaus, Michael 43, 61, 64
Scythian monks 206–7, 208
seals 95
Second Vatican Council 76–7, 80, 276, 292–3
Second World War 80
Sefer Zerubbabel ('Apocalypse of Zerubbabel') 100–3
Seppälä, Serafim 148, 156
Sergios, Patriarch 98, 99
Severus of Antioch 152
sexual abstinence *see* celibacy; virginity
Shahrvaraz, General 84

signs 116–17, 131
  and devotion 266–8
  and Mary 250
  and miracles 246
  and prophetology 152–3, 155–6
silence 116–17, 132, 139–40
Silesius, Angelus 76
Simeon 25, 39–40
sin 48–9, 179–80, 274–5; *see also* original sin
Slavs 83, 93
Söll, Georg 59
Solomon 11, 151, 231–2
Song of Zechariah 112
soteriology 77
Spain *see* al-Andalus
Stump, Eleonore 166
Šuʿayb 231–2
subversion 261–4, 288–9
suffering 25, 36, 73, 269–70
  and God 206–8, 243, 245
  and Jesus Christ 211–12
syncretism 275
Synkellos, Theodore 97–8, 203
Syriac Church Fathers 6, 27
  and angels 128
  and beauty 298
  and Byzantium 99–100
  and genealogy 164
  and Judaism 101
  and Mother of God 74
  and prophetology 151, 152
  see also Ephrem the Syrian; Jacob of Serugh; patristics
Syro-Palestine 83

T

aṭ-Ṭabarī, Abū Ǧaʿfar Muḥammad b. Ǧarīr 128, 129, 134–5
  and mother of Mary 167
  and mother–son relationship 149
  and original sin 274
  and renunciation 270
  and signs 156
  and the Temple 170, 171
  and virginity 143
  and women 181
  and the Word 187
Tamar 13
Tanner Rhodes, Jerusha 258
tawba (repentance) 304–5
Temple, the 47, 101
  and Aaron 147
  and Eastern Gate 122–3
  and Mary 170, 171–2
  and *Maryam* Surah 117–18
  and veil 123–4, 126, 127
  and women 254–5
  and Zechariah 174–5
Tertullian 27
Theobald, Michael 14
Theodore of Mopsuestia 213
Theotokos ('birthgiver of God') 74, 96, 98, 109, 183,190, 219, 307
Thomas Aquinas, St 70
Toldeo Lectionary 27
Torah 14, 112, 113, 119, 168
Trisagion ('Thrice Holy') chant 207–8
triumphalism 98
True Cross 83, 84, 92, 100
Turkey 275–6, 277

U

'Umar, Caliph 263–4, 289

V

Van Esbroeck, Michel 137
Vatican *see* Second Vatican Council
veil 123–7, 169–70, 267
virginity 16–17, 26–9, 49–52
  and *at-Taḥrīm* Surah 195–6
  and autonomy 265–6
  and *Āl 'Imrān* Surah 190–1
  and Jesus Christ 292
  and prophetology 152–3
  and Protevangelium of James 39
  and questioning 143
  and veil 124, 125–6
  and verification 242
  see also perpetual virginity
visibility 290
vulnerability 226–9

W

Wahhabism 275
war 96–8; *see also* Holy War
Weidemann, Hans-Ulrich 55
women 12–13, 167–8, 237
  and *an-Nisā'* Surah 192–3
  and *at-Taḥrīm* Surah 194–5
  and equality 261–2
  and Mary 180–2, 198–9, 259
  and Muhammad 263–4
  and ordination 293–4
  and the Temple 254–5
  and veil 267
  see also femininity
Word, the 187–91, 196–8, 203–4, 299–301

Y

Yaḥyā 114–15, 120
Yitik, Ali İhsan 276

Z

Zacharias 39–40
az-Zamaḫšarī, Maḥmūd ibn 'Umar 149, 179, 181, 241
Zechariah 15, 17, 19, 20, 23
  and guardianship 269
  and *Āl 'Imrān* Surah 170, 171, 172–3, 176, 186
  and *Maryam* Surah 107–9, 110–12, 113–14, 115–19, 120, 121, 132, 140
  and miracles 248
  and prophet 151
  and the Temple 174–5
Zerubbabel 100–1